VOLTAIRE'S POLITICS
THE POET AS REALIST

To the memory of

FRANZ NEUMANN

Aufklärer

CONTENTS ·

CONTENTS

PREFACE

THIS new issue of a book I first published nearly thirty years ago gives me extraordinary pleasure, at once exhilarating and a little poignant. Like fathers and mothers, authors are expected to be evenhanded about their offspring, and I must confess to a strong and enduring fondness for all the books I have fathered. It is true that they add up to a *famille nombreuse*, but this has in no way diluted my affection for any of them. Little in an academic's life can match the gratification of seeing most of one's writings in print. But some may be more gratifying than others. Charles Dickens called *David Copperfield* his "favourite child"; if pressed, I should have to confess that I, too, have a favorite child, and it is *Voltaire's Politics*.

I have good reasons for this predilection. While *Voltaire's Politics* has been unavailable for some time—a Vintage paperback edition of 1965 has been out of print for years—I think its central argument has made its way into the scholarly perception of Voltaire and that of the Enlightenment in general. I argued in circumstantial detail, as I followed Voltaire through his career as a political observer and commentator across the Continent and England, that he and his fellow-philosophes were anything but abstract and amateurish coffeehouse politicians. Rather, they were, admittedly with striking exceptions, practical, flexible, realistic thinkers closely engaged with the events of their day—with science, with theology, with politics. And Voltaire, I was to discover, talked politics more intelligently and more intensely perhaps than the rest of the philosophical family for which he was at once leading luminary and father figure. Reviewing this book not long after its appearance in 1959, the brilliant English historian Alfred Cobban optimistically predicted that my "views will doubtless penetrate into general histories in some thirty years' time."[1] That allotted time is almost here, and I have good evidence for the claim that my views have in fact invaded, if not wholly conquered, the textbooks somewhat earlier than Cobban thought likely. Not all of this invasion has been fully acknowledged, but I choose to take that as a backhanded tribute to my reading of Voltaire: what seemed revisionist, even eccentric, at the end of the 1950s has come to appear quite obvious at the end of the 1980s. I trust that this revival of *Voltaire's Politics* may consolidate whatever hold my once unconventional ideas about the true style of Enlightenment thinking may have.

I have a second reason for taking special pleasure in the reappearance of *Voltaire's Politics*. It was a peculiarly personal creation, a book I had not planned to write at all. Looking back, it seems plain to me that most of my writings have had a way of imposing themselves on me, growing in bulk, changing in shape and in conclusions, as my material forced me to rethink my starting assumptions and to cast aside my first outlines. When I began to think about Voltaire in 1955, the argument of *Voltaire's Politics* was only remotely implicit in my ideas about eighteenth-century thought. The book I eventually wrote came quite literally as a surprise to me.

This account requires a retrospective glance. About 1950, I started to teach a year-long undergraduate course in the history of political theory at Columbia University, more precisely Columbia College. Offering the course year after year gave me an opportunity to rethink one theorist, or one century, and then another. After the second or third time around, when it was the Enlightenment's turn for a new look, a colleague strongly recommended Carl Becker's *The Heavenly City of the Eighteenth Century Philosophers*, first published in 1932. It

---

[1] *The American History Review*, LXV (October 1959), 118.

had been hailed as a classic virtually upon its first appearance and had retained its grip on the scholarly community with virtually no dissenters for two decades. Indeed, this small, delightfully presented set of lectures was still in print when I first read it (and it is still in print today). Urbane and mischievous, Becker suavely denigrated the philosophes for presenting themselves as modern, revolutionary thinkers when they had merely dressed up medieval rationalism in fashionable language. The men of the Enlightenment were, in Becker's account, unworldly and wholly innocent of a sense of history. I knew about the political ideas of the philosophes what others knew, which was not very much, and found no quick way of testing Becker's provocative propositions. There were, to be sure, respectable monographs on seminal thinkers like John Locke and Jean-Jacques Rousseau, but the secondary literature on eighteenth-century political theory was in general thin, impressionistic. But even on first reading, Becker's book wholly failed to persuade me. I thought *The Heavenly City* extremely clever, but as far as I could judge, it was no better than an amusing and wrongheaded jeu d'esprit which the historical profession—disregarding Becker's own earnest warnings—had taken far too seriously and accepted all too uncritically. When, in the fall of 1954, I published a programmatic article on the political theory of the Enlightenment, I called *The Heavenly City* "witty and perverse" and observed that it had "probably prevented more students from thinking about the Enlightenment than any other."[2] From the work I had done up to that point, it appeared to me that the philosophes were not the cold rationalists, naive optimists, or shallow journalists that Becker and his many admirers thought them to be.

[2] "The Enlightenment in the History of Political Theory," *Political Science Quarterly*, LXIX (September 1954), 374–89; quotation at 376.

But I thought it obvious that much further research needed to be done on eighteenth-century political thought, especially among those writers who were not principally political theorists.

I came to think that I would be the man to do that research, and my opportunity came in 1955, when I spent a year of delicious freedom as the Alfred Hodder fellow in the Council of the Humanities at Princeton University. The program I had assigned to myself was nothing if not ambitious: I intended to write three volumes that would gather substantial essays on such playwrights, essayists, historians, and psychologists as Lessing and Holbach, Gibbon and Lichtenberg and Helvétius. In the summer preceding my stay at Princeton, while traveling in Europe, I began to prepare for one of these essays, and chose to start with Voltaire. Of his enormous output I mainly knew *Candide*—like everyone else. Reading him proved a revelation. I still remember the excitement of my weeks at Oxford, where I went through the first ten volumes of Theodore Besterman's scholarly edition of Voltaire's correspondence, which had just appeared. Later that summer, I studied Voltaire's other tales and his historical writings and tackled his *Dictionnaire philosophique*. By the time I arrived in Princeton, my three-volume project was in shambles—or, to put it less portentously, had been wholly redefined. I had become convinced that Voltaire's political ideas badly needed, and richly deserved, a book of their own. The scanty and superficial monographic literature on those ideas, a literature which for the most part solemnly took all his abstract pronouncements literally, was a further stimulus. The subtitle of the book I eventually published in 1959, "The Poet as Realist," sums up what I had learned about Voltaire, and to a lesser extent about the other philosophes, in the previous years. The tentative diagnosis of Enlightenment thought I had ventured in my article of 1954 was proving more satisfactory than I had been able to recognize earlier.[3]

The book I wrote on Voltaire was far more than a confirmation of ideas I already held. It was, as I have said, a surprise. In the course of my years' study of Voltaire's writings, I had come to two distinct but related conclusions: first, Voltaire was so deeply engaged in the political culture of his age and his world that he talked about politics most of the time, even in his poems (like his interminable Vergilian epic, the *Henriade*), his histories, his plays and stories, to say nothing of his humanitarian pamphlets. Second, he was in mortal, not wholly unjustified fear of the authorities, what with his impious, highly subversive opinions which challenged cherished and ferociously held views. Hence he was self-protective— which is to say, elliptical, deliberately allusive or deceptively banal, evasive, often mendacious about his authorship. This meant that in his openly political texts, he would speak in vague, allusive generalities that required deciphering.

The first of these conclusions offered no intellectual difficulties. It meant that I must read as much of Voltaire as I possibly could. The second was more problematic, for if there was one central intention behind his stylistic polemical devices, it was to disguise his active, continuous meddling in the politics of his time. One day in that year 1955–56, I got dazzling confirmation of Voltaire's self-protective ways. I was studying his years in Geneva and stumbled upon an anonymous memorandum relating to the political struggles of the

---

[3] Later I generalized what I had learned about Voltaire. See my *The Party of Humanity: Essays in the French Enlightenment* (1964), in which I continued my studies on Voltaire and moved on to Rousseau and other figures in the French-speaking Enlightenment; and my two-volume study, *The Enlightenment: An Interpretation*, volume I, *The Rise of Modern Paganism* (1966), and volume II, *The Science of Freedom* (1969), in which I cast my net more widely still, including American thought in my purview.

early 1760s that were tearing the little republic apart. Though almost certainly in large part, perhaps wholly, by Voltaire, this memorandum had never been included in Voltaire's collected works and was first published in 1908. Yet it read to me like a rehearsal for Voltaire's best-known political pamphlet, the *Idées républicaines*. This little essay is an exercise in studied generalities and had usually been taken to be a response to Rousseau's *Contrat social*. But, that startling memorandum in mind, I could see in an instant that in *Idées républicaines* Voltaire was in fact commenting in the most precise detail on, and indeed helping to shape, the political events swirling around him. I had the rhetoric of Voltaire's *Idées républicaines* almost by heart, and to come upon this long-forgotten document that linked him firmly to reality, to read this dramatic product of a historic Genevan moment, was an unforgettable experience.[4] It was—to borrow James Joyce's famous formulation—an epiphany that came over me in the bowels of the Princeton University library. Here was my thesis exemplified. Going over *Voltaire's Politics* after all these years has revived that excitement for me.

There is yet a third reason why the reprinting of *Voltaire's Politics* is so welcome to me. In it I launched what I soon came to call the social history of ideas. I do not want to claim too much: surely other historians of ideas, including their dean, Arthur O. Lovejoy, had long before advocated this type of intellectual history. And for Marxists, persuaded that ideas are the product of the social base from which they rise and which they mirror, my way with ideas was hardly news. The

---

[4] See below, Appendix II, where I briefly compare Voltaire's *Idées républicaines* with that memorandum, *Propositions à examiner pour apaiser les divisions de Genève* (first printed by Fernand Caussy in the *Revue bleue*, Vth series, IX [January 4, 1908], 13–15). For a fuller analysis of my discovery and its implications, see my "Voltaire's *Idées républicaines*: From Detection to Interpretation," in *The Party of Humanity*, 55–96.

essential point of the social history of ideas was after all simple, even trite-sounding. Yet I found that there was something daring, even rebellious, about its application. Intellectual history had long been principally concerned with displaying famous thinkers in converse with one another or with mapping the route of seminal ideas traveling down through the centuries from great mind to great mind; indeed, most intellectual historians only enjoyed strolling, as the German historian Friedrich Meinecke once put it, along the summits. In sharp contrast, I took the view, as obvious in formulation as it was rare in practice, that historians must treat ideas emerging from an intricate social texture—cultural, religious, political—that gives them their vocabulary and dictates their contemporary importance. What is more, and here I departed from the Marxists: I insisted that ideas powerfully act upon, often decisively shape, the very culture from which they have emerged. Certainly reading Voltaire that way gave me a richer, more complex and credible figure than had been available to those who had merely catalogued his pronouncements and mechanically fitted them into the grand history of political theory.

Much has happened since the days when I first ventured into that kind of historical inquiry. Social historians concerned with writing intellectual history from the bottom up have added a new dimension by investigating literacy, or the residue that popular notions leave on the culture of the elite, or the traffic in ideas facilitated by booksellers, itinerant pamphleteers, or the spread of rumor by word of mouth. As for myself, for almost two decades now I have been exploring with the aid of psychoanalysis yet another dimension of ideas: their hidden roots in the mind, including the unconscious mind. What I see as the next assignment for intellectual history, which remains open to new departures, is to combine the social history of ideas with the psychological history of ideas to reach for that ultimate ideal of historical inquiry: cultural history, total history.

No doubt, if I were writing *Voltaire's Politics* now, I should pay more attention to some of the internal pressures that informed Voltaire's nimble and delightfully witty mind.[5] But a book has its time, and it is unreasonable to demand that I should have written thirty years ago the book I might have written now. At the same time, my pleasure in seeing *Voltaire's Politics* in print once again is more than nostalgic indulgence. The book strikes me upon rereading as not just of "mere" historical interest. It sees Voltaire as I think he should be seen: as a political animal.

[5] There is one minor amendment that I should also mention here: in Appendix III, I offer a brief discussion of Voltaire's anti-Semitism, and I think that the essential point I make there still holds true. But returning to the issue in 1964, in an essay in *The Party of Humanity* (pp. 97–108), I looked upon Voltaire's selective bigotry—that from him, the principled nemesis of bigots!—with a more jaundiced eye. It is not anachronistic to find Voltaire's anti-Jewishness disturbing and (if a historian may express such feelings) disappointing. After all, such contemporaries as Montesquieu and Lessing found it possible to surmount age-old prejudices, and Voltaire did not. At the same time, I remain committed to the view, expressed in this appendix, that Voltaire's dislike of Jews was rooted in his hatred for Christianity, and that his anti-Christianism was far stronger, far more vehement, and far more consequential than his anti-Semitism.

PROLOGUE
VOLTAIRE'S REPUTATION

Au fait! est ma devise.—VOLTAIRE to d'Argenson, 1 August 1739
Jean-Jacques n'écrit que pour écrire, et moi j'écris pour agir.
—VOLTAIRE to Vernes, 25 April 1767

1. "ABSTRACT, LITERARY POLITICS"

VOLTAIRE has had many reputations, most of them unjustified. He has been portrayed as a cynic or humanitarian; servile courtier or blunt critic; Catholic, deist, atheist, or mystic; noble builder or corrupt destroyer. His character has been dissected, his religious and metaphysical opinions have been debated in hundreds of books and articles, and still there is little agreement. As for his politics, the bewildered reader is offered a wide choice: we have been given Voltaire the radical, the conservative, the liberal, the authoritarian, the constitutionalist, and the admirer of "enlightened despotism."

Yet, while there is no consensus about his philosophy or his character, there has emerged a composite portrait of Voltaire, a figure that is the property of educated men everywhere: the toothless, shrunken poet in an ill-fitting wig, greedily accumulating riches, vilely maligning his adversaries, bravely sustaining the victims of injustice, wittily challenging the evils of his day, basely flattering royalty, cynically inventing a God for the masses.

This Voltaire is not the true Voltaire; certainly he is not the whole Voltaire. Nor is he the Voltaire of the scholars, who know most of the innumerable anecdotes about him to be the inventions of fatuous admirers or malicious detractors. He is an ill-drawn caricature (containing a pinch of truth, no more) pithily dismissed almost a century ago in Flaubert's *Diction-*

3

naire des idées reçues: "VOLTAIRE. Famous for his frightful grin or *rictus*. His learning superficial."

This laconic entry caricatures the caricature to perfection, but Flaubert's wit and the labors of Voltaire scholars have persuaded only a small public. The flighty and irresponsible poet, the undignified courtier and the lascivious story teller, the butterfly, the electric spark—in a word, the popular Voltaire, with his frightful grin and superficial learning, marches on. The legend, although not unresisted, is irresistible.

It was created in Voltaire's own lifetime, partly by himself—his constant and public quarrels, his intrigues at Versailles or in the theatre, his unsavory lawsuits, his attacks of temper and his seizures of panic—partly by the malice of others. In 1735, when he was forty, there appeared an anonymous "portrait de M. de Voltaire," which set the tone and supplied the information for many subsequent denigrations of Voltaire. With its facile antitheses, so beloved of eighteenth-century classicists, it mingled truth and falsehood, suggested plausible and malevolent interpretations of Voltaire's conduct, and offered a keen-eyed and spiteful account of his appearance: "His eyes are sparkling and mischievous, all the fire you find in his works he has in his actions; lively to giddiness, he is an ardent man who comes and goes, who dazzles you and who sparkles. . . . Open without frankness, politic without finesse, sociable without friends, he knows the world and forgets it. . . . He loves greatness and despises the great, he is at ease with them and constrained with his equals. . . . He loves the court and is bored there; susceptible without attachment, voluptuous without passion, he holds to nothing by choice, and holds to everything by inconstancy." His views—and that includes his political views—are without value, for they are not built on sincere feeling: he "argues without principles, his reason has fits as does the madness of others . . . he thinks everything and mocks everything"; while he moralizes he has no morals himself, and his literary endeavours are "less for reputation than for money, for which

4

he hungers and thirsts." He is little more than a "facile, ingenious, elegant writer," whose opinions are simply reflections of his temper; he is "always discontented with his country, and praises to excess that which is a thousand miles away."[1]

Even some of Voltaire's associates, who should have known better, accepted this caricature.[2] Montesquieu and Frederick the Great derisively spoke of him as a superficial wit; David Hume, who admired him, called him "that sprightly, agreeable, libertine Wit" whose arguments were brilliant rather than sound;[3] Théodore Tronchin, the fashionable Genevan physician who was his doctor, called him an "old child" in a letter to Grimm, and Grimm, for whose *Correspondance littéraire* Voltaire often furnished excellent copy, promptly conveyed the phrase to some of his princely customers.[4]

These epithets quickly became commonplaces in the Voltaire legend. German Augustans like Herder harshly denounced Voltaire as a "vain and impudent" man who "thinks he is distinguishing himself when he is only being witty,"[5] while Schiller claimed that Voltaire was too frivolous to be a true satirist: "Everywhere his sarcasm is founded on too little gravity."[6] Chateaubriand, extolling Voltaire's abilities as a historian, agreed that "he lacked nothing but gravity";[7] and Carlyle, praising

[1] R. A. Leigh, "An anonymous eighteenth-century character-sketch of Voltaire," *Studies on Voltaire and the Eighteenth Century*, II, 242-243.

[2] Berger, a close friend, called the *Lettres philosophiques* a *"chef d'oeuvre* of vanity"; Formont, another intimate, dismissed Voltaire as facile and shallow. *ibid.*, 245, 245n.

[3] Hume to the abbé Le Blanc, 24 October 1754, *The Letters of David Hume*, ed. J. Y. T. Greig, 2 vols. (1932), I, 207-208. See also Hume to Lord Minto, 1 May 1760: "That Author cannot be depended on with regard to Facts; but his general Views are sometimes sound, & always entertaining." *ibid.*, I, 326.

[4] See Desnoiresterres, *Voltaire et J.-J. Rousseau*, 295; Grimm to the duchesse and duc-héritier of Saxe-Gotha, 30 June 1765, *Correspondance littéraire*, XVI, 435.

[5] R. Haym, *Herder*, 2 vols. (1880), I, 340.

[6] "Über naive und sentimentalische Dichtung," *Werke*, ed. Ludwig Bellermann, 8 vols. (n.d.), VIII, 348.

[7] *Génie du Christianisme*, 2 vols. (ed. 1948), II, 13.

Voltaire's capacity for loyalty, his wide-ranging charity, and an adroitness that made him a "lion-fox which cannot be captured," yet discovered "one deficiency in Voltaire's original structure . . . his inborn levity of nature, his entire want of Earnestness."[8] In 1820, de Maistre compiled quotations from the *Essai sur les moeurs* to prove that Voltaire could not be taken seriously as a historian;[9] and over half a century later Emile Faguet compiled quotations almost at random to prove that Voltaire could not be taken seriously as a political thinker.[10] Even Byron, usually a shrewd judge of character, echoed and contributed to the legend in *Childe Harold's Pilgrimage*:

> fire and fickleness, a child
> Most mutable in wishes, but in mind
> A wit as various,—gay, grave, sage, or wild,—
> Historian, bard, philosopher, combined;
> He multiplied himself among mankind,
> The Proteus of their talents: But his own
> Breathed most in ridicule,—which, as the wind,
> Blew where it listed, laying all things prone,—
> Now to o'erthrow a fool, and now to shake a throne.[11]

A wind, a Proteus, an old child, a lion-fox—to this impressive collection of metaphors Taine added a collection of his own in *L'Ancien régime*: Voltaire is like a gushing fountain, the founder of a sect, an apostle and a prophet. "Such a spirit is incapable of reserve; it is by nature militant and fiery; it apostrophizes, insults, improvises, writes under the dictates of its impression, permits itself all words—if necessary the crudest. It thinks by explosions; its emotions are jumps, its images are sparks; it lets itself go completely, surrenders to the reader, and that is why it masters him. Impossible to resist it; the contagion

---

[8] "Voltaire," *Critical and Miscellaneous Essays*, 5 vols. (1899), I, 409-411.

[9] J. de Maistre, *Du pape* (ed. 1928), II.

[10] Emile Faguet, *La politique comparée de Montesquieu, Rousseau et Voltaire; Dix-huitième siècle*, 199-288.

[11] Canto III, verse cvi.

is too strong. Creature of air and flame, the most excitable that ever lived, composed of atoms more ethereal and more vibrant than those of other men. . . ." and so forth, for eight more ethereal and vibrant pages.[12]

Such a volatile creature does not think—he has prejudices. In the electric nervous process that serves him as a substitute for reflection, he generates convictions that are as strongly held as they are feebly grounded. He is alive, more intensely alive than other men, but in the peculiarly dreamlike manner of the poet: alive to feelings and remote from practical realities. Such politics as he has—and this is the inevitable conclusion to be drawn from such a portrayal—need not be taken seriously; they are bound to be abstract, Utopian, unrealistic, literary.

Perhaps the boldest and certainly the most influential attempt to deny Voltaire the quality of political realism was undertaken by Tocqueville in the middle of the nineteenth century. In *L'Ancien régime et la révolution française*, Tocqueville depicted French writers as keenly interested and wholly unschooled in practical questions: they dealt with politics "casually, even, one might say, toyed with them. But all took notice of them in one way or another. This kind of abstract, literary politics found its way, in varying proportions, into all the writings of the day." As abstract, literary political thinkers, whatever their divergences of opinion, the philosophes unanimously extolled a society based on "simple, elementary rules deriving from the exercise of the human reason and natural law." All they adored were reason and intellect—their own. Such a political philosophy was the height of Utopianism and impiety, but it was the only philosophy available to them: "Their very way of living led these writers to indulge in abstract theories and generalizations regarding the nature of government, and to place a blind confidence in these. For living as they did, quite out of touch with practical politics, they lacked the experience which might have tempered their enthusiasms . . .

[12] H. Taine, *L'Ancien régime*, ii, 92-93.

they had little acquaintance with the realities of public life, which, indeed, was *terra incognita* to them."[13]

Thus Tocqueville; Jacob Burckhardt went further, suggesting that the philosophes did not even take an interest in politics: "In the Age of Reason, when the state seemed unchanged, it was actually cast into the shade by people who did not care to discuss the events of the day, but ruled the world as philosophes—a Voltaire, a Rousseau, etc. . . . The State was subjected to the most powerful action of thought, of philosophical abstraction. . . ."[14]

This estimate, a notable contribution to the Voltaire legend, lends authority to the widespread notion that Voltaire supported, perfected, or perhaps even invented "enlightened despotism."[15] This abstract, literary conception of the omnipotent ruler, who governs an obedient people by the sole light of reason and under the guidance of his court philosophe, is precisely the Utopian political philosophy—contemptuous of tradition and existing institutions, oblivious to the power of irrationality—to be expected from an old child, a man "quite out of touch with practical politics."

But the Voltaire legend, which inevitably leads to such unjust oversimplifications, is wholly untenable. That Voltaire

---

[13] *The Old Regime and the French Revolution*, 138-140. Despite the power of Tocqueville's book, despite its suggestiveness, it is unjust in many details and unsatisfactory in its general thesis. Tocqueville uncritically adopted the interpretation of the French constitution offered by the aristocratic party; he greatly exaggerated the power of the central government against competing institutions such as the church and the parlements. He therefore misunderstood the real issue that led to the Revolution—the aristocratic counteroffensive. As for his analysis of political ideas, he took the pronouncements of the physiocrats and generalized from them to thinkers who rejected most if not all physiocratic doctrines. That his book remains interesting and valuable is a tribute to his style and to his penetration in areas in which he was not blinded by his preconceptions.

[14] *Force and Freedom* (ed. 1955), 199-200.

[15] I shall try to show in some of the following chapters that the very term "enlightened despotism" collects a wide variety of ideas and practices current in eighteenth-century politics, and that, even if it could be used without obscuring political realities—which I doubt—Voltaire can be counted as at most an occasional and uncertain supporter.

was excitable, that he changed his mind, that he contradicted himself—all this no student of his writings and his correspondence will deny. He lived too long, wrote too much, expressed opinions too casually, participated in affairs too vividly not to be on opposite sides of various questions at different times. But it does not follow that his political philosophy was a "chaos of clear ideas," as Emile Faguet characterized it in an epigram that has become only too familiar; it does not follow that he was incapable of practical thought, addicted to abstract ideas, fundamentally unserious. These charges are all the more grave for being repeated so often and for being so untrue. The variety of his interests and the shifts in his political opinions sprang not from flightiness but from an empiricist's temper, not from detachment but from a deep engagement with reality. When he talked nonsense about politics, he did so because he was remote from the events on which he was commenting so rashly. When he knew what he was talking about, when he observed events, talked to politicians, studied documents, as he did in England, France, and Geneva, his political judgments were cool and penetrating, hardheaded and practical.

In fact, Voltaire and his fellow philosophes were closer to affairs than Tocqueville asserts: d'Argenson was intendant, ambassador, and foreign minister; Turgot was intendant and finance minister; Quesnay was the king's physician and close to the makers of policy; Montesquieu and Hénault were prominent magistrates, Helvétius held a position at court and was a tax farmer; Rousseau, who was on the edges of politics in France, was at the center of politics in Geneva, and while it can be argued that his *Discours sur l'inégalité* and the *Contrat social* are abstract, theoretical works, his political writings on Geneva, Poland, and Corsica display the tough-minded common sense of a man in touch with reality. And Voltaire spent much of his life with diplomats, ministers, intendants, politicians, magistrates, and courtiers; he wrote dispatches for d'Argenson, went to Prussia on a diplomatic mission, corresponded with min-

isters like Choiseul and Turgot and powerful judges like Hénault, was intimate with Bolingbroke in England and with the
political leaders of Geneva, and kept in touch with the controversies of his day.[16]

But Voltaire was the symbol of his age, and it is the fate of
symbols to be exploited rather than to be understood. Writers
seeking to strike at the Enlightenment through him saw only
what they wanted to see. The German *Stürmer und Dränger*
repudiated Voltaire as a son repudiates his father to gain maturity.[17] German Augustans—earnestly in search of their German past, energetically dedicated to the creation of a German
literature, humorlessly insistent upon the superiority of the
German character—found it necessary to depict Voltaire as
the incarnation of French irreverence, superficiality, and fri-
volity.[18] The antirevolutionary tradition in France, from Cha-

---

[16] Tocqueville mixes shrewd observation with erroneous deduction when
he writes: "Taking no personal part in [public life] and unable to see what
was being done by others in that field, they lacked even the superficial
acquaintance with such matters which comes to those who live under a
free regime. . . . As a result, our literary men became much bolder in their
speculations, more addicted to general ideas and systems, more contemptuous of the wisdom of the ages, and even more inclined to trust their individual reason than most of those who have written books on politics from
a philosophical angle." *The Old Regime*, 140-141. It is surely true that
there are less "politics," less open debate and public adjustment of interests, in absolutism than in constitutionalism, but to the extent that politics
was possible at all in France, the philosophes were involved in it.

[17] On 3 January 1830, Goethe told Eckermann: "You have no idea of
the significance of Voltaire and his great contemporaries in my youth, and
how they dominated the whole civilized world. My biography does not
make it clear enough what influence these men had on my youth, and
how much it cost me to defend myself against them, and to stand on my
own feet in a truer relation to nature." J. P. Eckermann, *Gespräche mit
Goethe in den letzten Jahren seines Lebens*, in Goethe, *Gedenkausgabe*,
24 vols. (1949-1954), XXIV, 383. This little-known passage corrects the far
better-known passage from *Dichtung und Wahrheit* in which Goethe describes the chill he felt in reading Holbach's *Système de la nature*. In the
study of the German repudiation of France, too, much has been made of
substantive, philosophical disagreements, too little of the struggle between
generations.

[18] For one example see Schiller's outraged poem "Das Mädchen von
Orleans" (1801), which scolds Voltaire for degrading Jeanne d'Arc in his
Pucelle. La pucelle was no more than a private entertainment, a joke. It

teaubriand to Taine, from de Maistre to Faguet, evolved an image of Voltaire the brilliant, impious conspirator, subverting the Old Regime which had deserved to survive for all its flaws. Tocqueville and Taine conceded that its taxes had been inequitable, its privileges infuriating, and its critics often right, but they implied that men of practical sense would have tried to preserve and reform it. Instead, the philosophes, addicted to the geometric, classical spirit, feverishly and irresponsibly destroyed it. Such lighthearted *littérateurs* do not understand the meaning of politics.[19]

Herder's low opinion of Enlightenment historians is no longer unchallenged; Taine's account of the philosophes has been refuted by recent research, but the legend of Voltaire the abstract, literary thinker has surprising vitality. German historians developed it in a highly sophisticated form: the Enlightenment, led by Voltaire, was mechanistic, universalistic, unhistorical; it had to be "overcome" toward the end of the eighteenth century by the organic, individualistic, historicist philosophy of the German Augustans.

It may be admitted that while Enlightenment historians often wrote good, and sometimes great history, all too often they used history as propaganda, generalized too freely, and allowed their anticlericalism to distort their judgments.[20] These

---

was perhaps a poor joke, but scarcely the work by which to judge Voltaire. It is a sign of Goethe's maturity and independence of spirit that once he had gone through his *Sturm und Drang* period he found it possible to admire Voltaire.

[19] During the nineteenth century, Voltaire was the victim not only of his enemies but also of his friends. John Morley's influential biography, first published in 1872, underlines Voltaire's humanitarianism, dwells on his generous emotions (such as his hatred of cruelty and war), and neglects his participation in controversies, except the famous legal cases. This portrait may be more accurate than, say, Faguet's, but it fails to come to grips with Voltaire's practicality, and thus involuntarily lends support to the Voltaire legend.

[20] That Ranke's conception of history was more objective, more "historical," than Voltaire's needs no demonstration. But the celebrated remarks made by Hume and Voltaire about unchanging human nature do not do justice to their own work—their sense of history, of change, of the

limitations deserved to be overcome, and were indeed overcome, by nineteenth-century historians. But German historians were more didactic and less historical than they knew. Tocqueville struck at the philosophes to defend the Old Regime, Ranke and his followers struck at them to create an ideology for Prussian and German expansionism. They posited a dichotomy between the irrational, amoral character of politics, and the rational, moral character of private life; they criticized the philosophes for failing to do justice to the "demonic," the "impenetrable," the "irrational" nature of power; and they dismissed the philosophes' political judgments as Utopian, unrealistic, in a word, unpolitical.[21]

In a profound passage, Nietzsche warned his readers against this self-satisfied historicism in the 1880's. He castigated German "hostility to the Enlightenment" as a regression to the "first and oldest stage of speculation," a "prescientific kind of philosophy"; accused "German historians and romantics" of seeking a "place of honor for older, primitive feelings," like Christianity, the national soul, folk tales, medievalism; and criticized German scientists for opposing "the spirit of Newton and Voltaire" and for rehabilitating a "deified or satanized nature." To Nietzsche the German intellectuals of his time were reactionaries: "Piety toward everything then in existence sought to translate itself into piety toward everything that had existed," but he hoped that the very spirit of the Enlightenment they had tried to destroy would be victorious over this "obscurantist, enthusiastic, atavistic spirit."[22]

His hopes have not been fulfilled; Voltaire continues to be thought of as the shallow poet with an unrealistic faith in

---

evolution of unique events was far superior to their methodological pronouncements.

[21] Of course I am not accusing Ranke of being a mere ideologist or a precursor of the Nazis. He was obviously one of the greatest of historians. But he did not "banish himself from his books," as has often been suggested.

[22] *Morgenröte, Werke,* 11 vols. (1906), v, 189-190.

reason. Friedrich Meinecke speaks of Voltaire's appeal to "unfettered, sovereign human reason";[23] Franz Schnabel uses Voltaire as an example of the modern "deification of science and technology," the final consequence of an "intellectualism" which cannot understand the power of the irrational; Heinrich Ritter von Srbik calls Voltaire a "fanatic of the Enlightenment, of a faith in reason hostile to theology, of a dogmatism of man's sovereign reason," who lacked all sense of development, irrationality, individuality, and the "historically conditioned nature of man"; Martin Göhring likens Voltaire to Frederick the Great with his "belief in the omnipotence of reason."[24] A classicist with such a naïve faith in reason cannot be expected to comprehend concrete reality: the philosophes, Meinecke tells us with decision, were guided by "abstract universalism," and their ethics were "in their deepest nature unpolitical."[25]

There are two ways of being unpolitical: to think that politics can do everything, and to think that politics can do nothing. The first leads to Utopianism and fanaticism, the second to Epicureanism and apathy; yet, despite their opposite effects, both are symptoms of the same disease, a failure of realistic

[23] *Entstehung des Historismus*, 82. Like his master Ranke, Meinecke was of course far more than an ideologist, and his powers of observation continually break through his schematic presentation of the Enlightenment. Thus in the same book, he points to Voltaire's "realistic sobriety," his lack of illusions concerning human nature, his realistic appraisal of the ugliness of international affairs. But, he concludes, Voltaire never integrated his realism with his philosophy. We may say with greater justice that Meinecke never integrated his observations with his scheme.

[24] Schnabel, *Deutsche Geschichte im neunzehnten Jahrhundert*, 4 vols. (1929-1937), I, 60-61; Srbik, *Geist und Geschichte vom deutschen Humanismus bis zur Gegenwart*, 2 vols. (1950-1951), I, 112; Göhring, *Weg und Sieg der modernen Staatsidee in Frankreich* (ed. 1947), 152. This notion of the "unpolitical Enlightenment" even found its way into Heinz Holldack's brilliant "Der Physiokratismus und die absolute Monarchie," *Historische Zeitschrift*, cxxxxv (1932), 532n. A caricature of it was naturally popular during the Nazi period; see Gerhard Ritter on optimistic and irresponsible philosophes, *Friedrich der Grosse* (1936), 71-72; and Adalbert Wahl, *Über die Nachwirkungen der französischen Revolution vornehmlich in Deutschland* (1939), on the "overcoming" of "alien and Jewish influences."

[25] *Idee der Staatsräson* (1924), 368, 385.

vision. The makers of the legend have freely attributed both symptoms to Voltaire—cannot a flighty poet easily move from fanaticism to apathy? He has been charged with overestimating the efficacy of politics, believing that all unhappiness can be cured and all social problems solved, and at the same time wanting to dissolve politics into ethics, wishing to achieve impossible goals by the mere application of reason without the use of force.

This legend does violence to the truth. Voltaire accepted limitations on political action; he agreed with the Machiavellians that private and public spheres are separate and that political power has imperatives of its own. But he rejected a philosophy that frees political actions from criticism and permits statesmen to act ruthlessly, faithlessly, brutally, with the excuse that power is demonic and that necessity knows no law. Far from seeking to make politics a panacea or from dissolving it in ethics, Voltaire sought to humanize it.[26]

This position on power has close affinities to the liberal and the democratic traditions. The liberal, Franz Neumann has written, is deeply concerned with "the erection of fences around political power . . . the dissolution of power into legal relationships, the elimination of the element of personal rule, and the substitution of the rule of law in which all relationships are to become purposive-rational, that is, predictable and calculable." The democrat, on the other hand, has "a positive attitude to-

[26] Paul Tillich has some wise words on the relation of politics to power which may be useful here: "Politics and power politics are one and the same thing. There are no politics without power, neither in a democracy nor in a dictatorship. Politics and power politics point to the same reality. It does not matter which term you are using. Unfortunately, however, the term 'power politics' is used for a special type of politics, namely, that in which power is separated from justice and love, and is identified with compulsion. This confusion is possible because there is indeed a compulsory element in the actuality of power. But this is only one element, and if power is reduced to it and loses the form of justice and the substance of love, it destroys itself and the politics based on it." *Love, Power, and Justice* (1954), 8. Voltaire's politics loses neither the element of compulsion, nor the form of justice and the substance of love.

ward political power which appears essentially as a rational instrument to be used for desired and desirable ends."[27] In Voltaire's political thought both elements, the control of power and the rational uses of power, are constantly at play; there is a continual tension between the need for effective action and the desirability of freedom.

This tension appears most sharply in Voltaire's treatment of the rule of law. Like most proponents of the rule of law since the Greeks, Voltaire was deeply devoted to it as an ideal: he alludes to it early and late, in his correspondence as in his political writings.[28] Countries that possess it are to be envied and to be imitated: "Liberty consists of depending on the laws alone. On this basis, every man is free today in Sweden, England, Holland, Switzerland, Geneva, Hamburg. . . . A citizen of Amsterdam is a man; a citizen several degrees of longitude from there is a beast of burden."[29] Freedom, and indeed civilization itself, depend upon the rule of law: "The only civilized country (*bien policé*) is the one in which vengeance is in the hands of the laws alone."[30]

Voltaire fully grasped the psychological significance of the rule of law: it is a rational guide in an irrational world; it helps men to be certain in the midst of uncertainty by permitting

[27] "Approaches to the Study of Political Power," *The Democratic and the Authoritarian State*, 6-7. It must be remembered that these oversimplified definitions are Weberian ideal types, designed to bring out an essential quality. They are also a reaction against the prevalent tendency to make the democratic and liberal traditions identical.

[28] "The finest right of humanity is to depend on the laws alone and not on the caprice of men." Voltaire to d'Argental (ca. 8 May 1734), *Correspondence*, III, 246. While it is a violation of the principle that underlies this book, I have thought it useful just this once to collect quotations at random without considering their specific environment. Indeed, Voltaire repeated this injunction against arbitrariness throughout his life; it is one guiding line that runs through his entire political thought, and the only development we can discover is the growing frequency with which he emphasizes that "the magistrates are not the masters of the people; it is the laws which are the masters." *Idées républicaines*, XXIV, 421. Or: "Let law govern, and not caprice." *L'A,B,C*, XXVII, 382.

[29] *Pensées sur le gouvernement*, XXIII, 526.

[30] *Notebooks*, 111.

them to predict the consequences of their actions. In England, under the rule of law, "Everyone knows what he has, what his duty is, and what he can do. Everything is subject to the law, starting from the crown and the church."[31] Yet in absolute states, such as France, the chief executive also claimed to be the chief legislator with no effective restrictions on his powers. Here the rule of law either did not apply at all, or applied only through the self-restraint of the ruler. In this vexing situation—vexing, because Voltaire was anything but an opponent of absolutism—Voltaire had recourse to the traditional distinction between absolutism and arbitrariness,[32] and to the traditional but rather unsatisfactory French theory of constitutional absolutism,[33] a theory that solved the conflict between power and law largely on the level of rhetoric. Yet rhetoric or reality, Voltaire treated the rule of law as a standard that judged all existing governments. In the *Dictionnaire philosophique* he invented a little fable, a dialogue between a European official and a Brahmin:

[31] *L'A,B,C*, xxvii, 330. See his description of the English judicial system, *ibid.*, xxvii, 385-388; and, "Everyone wants to be sure that he can sleep at home without another man arrogating the power to send him to sleep elsewhere; everyone wants to be sure of his fortune and his life." *Dictionnaire philosophique*, article "Patrie," 335. Voltaire always extolled the English as models for their neighbors, although not always with a straight face: "To be free is to depend on the laws alone. Thus the English love their laws as fathers love their children: because they have made them, or because they think they have made them." *Questions sur l'Encyclopédie*, article "Gouvernement," Part vi, 224-225.

[32] See: "A prince who imprisons or executes his subjects without justice or due process of law is nothing but a highway robber who is called 'Your Majesty.'" *Pensées sur le gouvernement*, xxiii, 530. In his late play, *Les lois de Minos*, he had spoken of *suprême pouvoir*, and explained his meaning in a long footnote: "By 'supreme power' I do not understand . . . arbitrary authority." Rather, "I understand by 'supreme power' . . . reasonable authority, founded on the laws themselves, and tempered by them; that just and moderate authority, which cannot sacrifice the liberty and the life of a citizen to the malice of a flatterer, which submits itself to justice. . . . Whoever gives a different idea of monarchy would be guilty toward mankind." Act v, scene 4; vii, 232n. See also Voltaire's objection to the French formula for royal assent, *Car tel est notre plaisir*, as a flaunting of arbitrary power. *Dictionnaire philosophique*, article "Dogmes," 174.

[33] See below, chapter vii.

16

" 'But, once more,' said the European, 'which state would you choose?'

The Brahmin replied: 'That in which one obeys the laws alone.'

'That is an old reply,' said the official.

'That doesn't make it any worse,' said the Brahmin.

'Where is that country?' asked the official.

The Brahmin replied, 'We must look for it.' "[34]

We must look for it and fight for it; the rule of law can be won or preserved only through political action. It is true that Voltaire said more than once that he was not interested in politics, but we need only to read him—his letters and his *Dictionnaire philosophique,* his plays and his tales, his occasional works and his histories—to know that this is a typical Voltairian disclaimer, designed to protect himself rather than to communicate to others, to lull authorities into believing that he is not active, and to warn his friends that he does not wish it known that he *is* active. His empiricism made him hostile to political theorizing, but throughout his life he intervened in political controversies; he meddled whether he was asked to or not, and even, as sometimes happened, when he was earnestly begged to mind his own business. He always said demurely that he was only cultivating his garden, but privately he defined his garden as Europe.

His constant involvement with practical politics, obvious to Voltaire's contemporaries, has been obscured for his later commentators by the general and abstract tone of his writings. But this tone does not reflect his true attitude; it is a mask for the censors. The only way to penetrate this mask is to read Voltaire's writings in the light of the circumstances that called them forth. Ideas have meaning, logic, significance of their own, apart from time and place. But a political pamphleteer like Voltaire, unwilling and perhaps unable to compose a

[34] *Dictionnaire philosophique,* article "Etats, Gouvernements," 188.

17

theoretical treatise on politics, called into action by public controversy and private aspiration, diverted from a candid statement of his position by his attempts to persuade a large audience and to evade a suspicious censorship—such a writer demands the examination of the environment that created and nourished his political ideas. A single example may suffice: in late May or early June 1750, Voltaire published *La voix du sage et du peuple,* a political pamphlet that has been much quoted since. It is filled with generalizations in favor of absolutism, undivided sovereignty, and a politically feeble clergy. *La voix du sage* is a concrete controversial work, supporting the tax program of Controller General Machault, and opposing the resistance to this program by the Assembly of the Clergy. But Voltaire does not once mention Machault, the tax program, the Assembly; still these are the reasons for the pamphlet and they lurk behind every paragraph.[35] It is only when we read *La voix du sage* in this way that we understand Voltaire's politics. It is only when we grasp Voltaire's passion for polemics, his deep sense of reality, his distrust of deductive schemes, that we grasp the extent of Tocqueville's misconception and the injustice of the Voltaire legend. Voltaire's politics was not "abstract, literary politics." It was literary, but only in the sense that his pamphlets are well written; it was abstract, but only to those who do not catch his allusions. Voltaire was indeed a *littérateur,* but he was a *littérateur engagé.*

2. "OVERWEENING CONFIDENCE, INFALLIBLE RATIONALITY"

As a *littérateur engagé*—d'Alembert aptly called him a *philosophe du théâtre*—Voltaire was the poet in politics, the social

---

[35] See below, chapter II, section 3. The most specific single statement in the pamphlet is, "In France, where reason is perfecting itself every day, that reason teaches us that the church should contribute to the expenditures of the state in proportion to its revenues, and that the corps especially designed to teach justice, should begin by giving an example of it." XXIII, 467.

reformer with great literary gifts. His neoclassical plays, which made him the most famous writer in Europe, sometimes labor heavily under the burden of their message; his brilliant philosophical tales, at once propaganda and literature, instruct while they entertain. Amusing as they are, the tales carry a serious meaning; being serious, they provide valuable clues to Voltaire's philosophy of politics. And that philosophy is wholly at variance with the Voltaire legend—the legend of the "fanatic of faith in reason," the naïve believer in the "omnipotence of reason," the abstract system-builder, the propagandist for an "overweening confidence in a human rationality which, although insolently disavowing supernatural direction, asserts its own infallibility."[36]

Consider *Micromégas*, one of Voltaire's most delightful tales. Micromégas is a giant from the planet Sirius who takes an interest in men, these "infinitely insignificant atoms," and promises that he will reveal to them the secrets of nature in a large book of philosophy. When the secretary of the Academy of Sciences opens the book, he finds nothing but blank pages. "Aha!" says the secretary, "just what I expected."[37] *Micro-*

[36] Russell Kirk, *The Conservative Mind* (1953), 27. Kirk is indicting the "Age of Reason" in general, but Voltaire evidently plays a leading part in that Age. I think it worth repeating that this legend is not universally accepted. As I have said before, this is the popular Voltaire, not the Voltaire of the scholars, and there are other writers, not specialists in Voltaire, who reject it. Even Emile Faguet, whose writings on Voltaire are a mass of prejudiced *bon mots*, said that "Voltaire is a business man of genius, and the sense of reality is his most developed and his surest sense. . . . I almost thank him for having been a very mediocre political theorist, since, after all, to neglect higher sociology and to apply himself to reforms of detail in administration, police, and justice, was to give an excellent example. . . . This is good sense itself, aided by a very good, very extensive, very vigilant information." Unfortunately, Faguet neglects this insight when it comes to Voltaire's politics: "Voltaire did not apply himself to politics. He had little to do with it, and did not like it." *Dix-huitième siècle*, 200, 224, 237. See also the shrewd observations on Voltaire in W. E. H. Lecky, *A History of England in the Eighteenth Century*, v, 310: "His political writings display most eminently the admirable good sense and moderation of opinion, and the no less admirable good nature and humanity, which amid all his caprices, petulances, and meannesses, never wholly abandoned him. . . ."

[37] XXI, 122.

mégas' point is an exaggeration, adorning a tale and pointing a moral: Voltaire did not believe that the pages of science are empty. He did believe that knowledge begins with the admission of ignorance.

Pride, on the other hand, brings misery. In *Memnon*, one of his most biting stories, Voltaire invented a hero who conceives the foolish notion of being wholly wise and of establishing the supremacy of reason over passion. This fatuous, self-satisfied rationalist is made to suffer for his *hubris*: in his short career as a wholly wise man he loses an eye, his money, all his property, and his ridiculous presumption. Memnon is the anti-Voltaire, the opposite of his creator in trait after trait.[38] Yet all too often, critics have given us Memnon and told us that they are giving us Voltaire.

Memnon is not an isolated or uncharacteristic outburst. In *Songe de Platon*, Voltaire tells us in Stoic fashion that while God himself is perfect, he left the creation of the world to a minor angel who was too incompetent to do a good job of it.[39] Such an imperfect world must naturally make life a series of grotesque misadventures, a scene of wars, carnage, fanaticism, injustice, and victorious stupidity. The good man must become the victim of the bad;[40] reason and merit must give way to love, ambition, money, and a good digestion;[41] the pilgrimage of Candide is the pilgrimage of man, made tolerable only by humor and self-abnegation, made intolerable by complacent optimism. In one of those laconic witticisms that were the delight

[38] XXI, 95-100.

[39] XXI, 133-136. "But what says Zeus? 'Epictetus, if it were possible I would have made your body and your possessions (those trifles that you prize) free and untrammelled. But as things are—never forget this—this body is not yours, it is but a clever mixture of clay. But since I could not make it free, I gave you a portion in our divinity. . . .'" *The Discourses of Epictetus*, trans. P. E. Matheson, in *The Stoic and Epicurean Philosophers*, ed. Whitney J. Oates (1940), 224-225.

[40] *Aventure indienne*, XXI, 243-244.

[41] *Les oreilles du comte de Chesterfield*, XXI, 577-594. Digestion may seem a trivial companion in this weighty list, but its presence reflects the importance that Voltaire, a perpetual sufferer, attributed to it.

of his friends and the despair of his enemies, Voltaire summed it all up in *Candide*: "If this is the best of all possible worlds, what are the others like?"[42]

Man's goal is happiness, but all too often the goal is a mirage. Man is the prey of his passions, the victim of his stupidity, the plaything of fate; the human condition is beset with ills that no amount of rationality can cure. "Man is the only animal who knows that it must die," Voltaire wrote into his notebook. "Sad knowledge, but necessary, since he has ideas. There are thus misfortunes necessarily attached to the condition of man."[43] This world then is a shipwreck, and man's motto is *sauve qui peut!*[44] Even this great age, this "age of philosophy" is also an "age of fanaticism."[45] Every advance against brutality and stupidity is immediately endangered; philosophes must avoid the cheap complacency of optimism: "Profit from these moments; perhaps they will be short."[46]

[42] XXI, 149.

[43] *Notebooks*, 352. "There are few pure pleasures in this life." Voltaire to madame Denis, 11 August (1753), *Correspondence*, XXIII, 134.

[44] *Aventure indienne*, XXI, 244. He liked this phrase well enough to use it repeatedly in his correspondence. See Voltaire to Cideville, 28 (January 1754), *Correspondence*, XXIV, 34; Voltaire to La Harpe, 1 March (1776), XLIX, 538.

[45] Voltaire to d'Argental, 3 October (1752), *Correspondence*, XXI, 84.

[46] *Prix de la justice et de l'humanité*, XXX, 586. That Voltaire was not an optimist needs no extended discussion here—the despair of his poem on the Lisbon earthquake and the pessimistic Epicureanism of *Candide* are too familiar. Still, the fact is worth recalling; only too often a critic will admit that Voltaire was not an optimist, and then attribute to him opinions and expectations that only an optimist could have.

Voltaire's attack on optimism has been widely thought to be a result of his shock over the Lisbon earthquake of 1755. I do not accept this view. As early as 18 March 1736, Voltaire expressed doubts concerning the philosophy of "whatever is, is right" in a letter to madame du Deffand, *Correspondence*, V, 87-89, and about March 1744, Voltaire wrote to Martin Kahle, a Göttingen professor who had published a polemic against him: "When you will have demonstrated, in verse or otherwise, why so many men slaughter one another in the best of possible worlds, I shall be much obliged to you." *ibid.*, XII, 198.

Voltaire's objection to "whatever is, is right" was not to its complacent optimism but to its half-complacent, half-despairing pessimism—it struck him as a philosophy which made action impossible and preached sub-

Voltaire repeats these despairing injunctions with such gusto that it is clear they are not signs of despair but of realism. As with Oliver Edwards, Samuel Johnson's acquaintance, cheerfulness was always breaking in. This world is a shipwreck, but we can try to save ourselves; it is a jungle, but we can try to build ourselves a garden. We still have philosophy and, as long as life lasts, life itself. Voltaire took Pascal seriously, but he objected that the "sublime misanthrope"

enseigne aux humains à se haïr eux-mêmes;
Je voudrais, malgré lui, leur apprendre à s'aimer.[47]

To the Augustinian philosophy of man, which Voltaire rejected as dismal and self-abasing, he opposed a Stoic philosophy of autonomy, responsibility, and dignity. "Dare to think for yourself," he wrote; and "We should say to every individual: 'Remember your dignity as a man.' "[48]

Despite their sufferings, men can hold up their heads because they are capable of reasonable activity. "Man is born for action," wrote Voltaire in his first polemic against Pascal. ". . . Not to be occupied and not to exist are the same thing for man."[49] He preached the gospel of work early and late: "Let us work without arguing," he wrote in *Candide*, "that is the only way to make life endurable."[50] And near the end of his long life, when he was eighty-three, he told d'Argental: "We must battle nature and fortune until the last moment, and never despair of anything until we are good and dead."[51] His writings—thou-

---

mission, an invitation to passivity that was deeply uncongenial to his temperament. Voltaire's attack on "optimism" was an attack on pessimism in the name of a philosophy of activity. See *Dictionnaire philosophique*, article "Bien (tout est)," 59, and *Homélies prononcées à Londre en 1765*, XXVI, 319.

[47] *Épitre à Mlle de Malcrais*, x, 276.

[48] *Dictionnaire philosophique*, article "Liberté de penser," 280; *ibid.*, article "Méchant," 301. Compare Epictetus: "Consider who you are. First, a man. . . . Such will I show myself to you—faithful, self-respecting, noble, free from tumult." *Discourses*, 296, 298.

[49] *Lettres philosophiques* (ed. Lanson), 2 vols., "xxve Lettre," II, 205-206.

[50] XXI, 217.

[51] Voltaire to d'Argental, 31 August (1777), L., 263.

sands of letters, scores of plays, voluminous histories, innumerable occasional pieces—show that he practiced what he preached; he worked even harder than the other philosophes, who were notorious for their indefatigable activity. Robert Burton wrote the *Anatomy of Melancholy* to keep off melancholy; Voltaire, in addition to the sheer joy of laboring, worked—at court, on his travels, in retirement—to console himself against misfortune: "Study and work are sure remedies" for sufferings caused by injustice.[52] But while he was feverishly active, Voltaire was not an unhappy man. *Le monde comme il va,* less ferociously pessimistic than his other tales, expresses his philosophy most accurately: the world is a mixture of beauty and ugliness, refinement and grossness, loyalty and treachery, success and failure, and "if all is not good, all is passable."[53] As a practical man, at home in his world, Voltaire possessed a sober confidence that the spread of philosophy would reduce the sufferings of some men, and console others.

Such a moderate philosophy is the philosophy of a political man. Indeed, Voltaire's political program, radical as it is, does not seek perfection. Voltaire explicitly separated himself from the Utopianism of a Saint-Pierre or a Fénelon; he deplored poverty, hated war, campaigned against torture, but he admitted that poverty was necessary, war inevitable, and torture, in exceptional circumstances, useful.[54] His expectations were more modest than his wishes.

[52] Voltaire to madame Denis, 25 (July 1753), *Correspondence,* XXIII, 105. He wrote these lines after his disgrace at Potsdam and his detention in Frankfurt, but he expressed similar feelings at other times. "My situation is extremely distressing, and when illness is joined to misfortune, that is the peak of human misery. I console myself with work and *belles lettres.* . . ." Voltaire to Roques, 18 May 1753, *ibid.,* XXII, 165. Later, when he had settled at Ferney, he was happier, but he still worked, almost as if to justify his existence through good works. But work was also pleasure and a professional requirement. In *Emile,* Rousseau asks how Racine and Boileau achieved superiority over inferior writers. Voltaire made this laconic marginal note: "They worked, consulted, corrected." George R. Havens, *Voltaire's Marginalia on the Pages of Rousseau,* 90.
[53] XXI, 16.
[54] On poverty, see *Dictionnaire philosophique,* article "Egalité," 177, and

Voltaire's conviction that ours is not the best of all possible worlds reflects a mood and a temperament. It also reflects a philosophy: Voltaire was the faithful disciple of the French skeptical tradition of Montaigne, Saint-Evremond, and Bayle, and the energetic propagandist of British empiricism. With the triumph of the sciences in the seventeenth century, natural philosophy was liberating itself from theology and turning its attention from metaphysics to epistemology. As the natural sciences departed ever further from common sense, the question of what knowledge is reliable became more acute than before. Starting with Bacon, the British empiricists addressed themselves to this question.[55]

Voltaire extolled this enterprise, somewhat misleadingly, as "philosophic modesty." It was philosophic, but it was not modest; in deflating what they called the pretensions of metaphysicians and the useless verbal games of the Schoolmen, the empiricists were seeking to substitute dependable for chimerical knowledge. They were trading the dream of a neat, universal system for the reality of solid information. Bacon succinctly expressed their expectations: submission to nature meant mastery of nature.[56]

---

below, chapter VII; on war, see *ibid.*, article "Guerre," 232, and below, chapter III, section 1; on torture, see below, chapter VI, section 3. In *l'A,B,C,* an important late political pamphlet, Voltaire argues that there is no such thing as an ideal government in reality: "The height of human perfection is to be powerful and happy with enormous abuses." XXVII, 349.

[55] The philosophes were indebted not only to the British empiricists, but to Descartes as well, for Descartes, too, made epistemological investigations central. Partly for strategic reasons (Cartesianism had been assimilated to Christian philosophy by Malebranche) the philosophes minimized their debt to Descartes.

[56] Arthur O. Lovejoy, discussing this position as it derives from Locke, shrewdly refers to it as a "tone of becoming diffidence," an "ostentatious modesty," which is accompanied by an extreme confidence that the truths that man needs are attainable and indeed relatively easy to attain. However, he notes that Voltaire was almost alone in the eighteenth century (with his incongruous ally Samuel Johnson) to oppose the complacent acceptance of the great chain of being. *The Great Chain of Being*, 8-9, 252-253. The notion that men should concern themselves with immediate problems is also familiar to the Christian thought of the seventeenth cen-

Whitehead was right to call the seventeenth century a "century of genius." Its great natural philosophers accumulated the capital that was expended by their eighteenth-century disciples. But the seventeenth century was also a century of preparation; it was large with a sense of fruitful enterprises to come. At its beginning, Francis Bacon called himself a "bell-ringer which is first up to call others to church"; at its end, John Locke called himself an "under-labourer in clearing the ground a little, and removing some of the rubbish that lies in the way of knowledge."

It was this unpretentious concentration on attainable goals that awakened Voltaire's enthusiasm. This was the world view appropriate to his crusade for practicality, his passion for reform, his conviction that theory and practice must be intimately related.[57] Francis Bacon, the patron saint of Diderot's *Encyclopédie*, was for Voltaire the "father of experimental philosophy," the builder of the "scaffold with which we have built the new philosophy," the thinker who did not know nature but "knew and showed all the paths that lead to it," the supreme enemy of the pseudo philosophy of the scholastics.[58] John Locke, wise, practical, logical, was Voltaire's favorite philosopher. Others had written "the romance of the soul," but Locke was the sage who "modestly wrote its history" and modestly disclaimed any knowledge of its nature. "As for me," Voltaire said proudly, "I boast of the honor of being as stupid on this point as Locke."[59] And Sir Isaac Newton was unquestionably the greatest man who ever lived—the sublime natural philosopher who "made no hypotheses," eschewed loose talk of "essences," and avoided the dangerous *esprit de système*: "Mon-

---

tury. See *Paradise Lost*: "That not to know at large of things remote/ From use, obscure and subtle, but to know/ That which before us lies in daily life,/ Is the prime wisdom. . . ." Book viii, 191-194.

[57] Voltaire could have said, as Marx said a hundred years later: "The philosophers have only interpreted the world in different ways; the point is to change it."

[58] *Lettres philosophiques*, "xiie Lettre," i, 154-155.

[59] *ibid.*, "xiiie Lettre," i, 168-169. Voltaire refers to Locke in the same vein many times throughout his work.

sieur," Voltaire advised a young man in 1741, "if you wish to apply yourself seriously to the study of nature, permit me to tell you that you must begin by making no system. You must conduct yourself like Boyle, Galileo, Newton: examine, weigh, calculate, and measure, but never conjecture. M. Newton never made a system: he saw, and he made people see; but he did not put his fancies in place of truth. That which our eyes and mathematics demonstrate to us, we must hold to be true. In all the rest we must say only: I do not know."[60]

Say "I do not know," make no system, admit that the mysteries of nature are forever impenetrable—here is no naïve rationalist. Voltaire was a rationalist only in the sense that he considered the scientific method the most reliable method of gaining knowledge—superior to revelation, authoritative pronouncements by the pope, church tradition, the Bible—but he never thought of reason as infallible, unfettered, or omnipotent.[61]

Nor was he alone in his healthy skepticism; most of the philosophes were indefatigable opponents of rationalism, metaphysics, and system-building. Locke said that philosophy begins only after philosophers had determined the limits of reason. Hume argued that reason was the slave of the passions, and demonstrated that perfect induction was impossible. Diderot and Vauvenargues gave the passions a central place in their world view. Montesquieu and Gibbon had a firm grasp of the irrational in politics—of terror, mass manipulation, the use of ideology. Kant's profound and subtle critical philosophy hard-

[60] Voltaire to Le Cati, 15 April 1741, *Correspondence*, xi, 85; see also his earlier reproof to his friend Formont: "I find it very bad that you speak of Newton as a maker of systems. He did not make any." 13 (?December 1735), *ibid.*, iv, 208. Incidentally, Voltaire's three heroes, Bacon, Locke, and Newton, were also Jefferson's three immortals. See Dumas Malone, *Jefferson the Virginian* (1948), 101.

[61] "Reason is now looked upon rather as an acquisition than as a heritage . . . not as a sound body of knowledge, principles and truths, but as a kind of energy, a force which is fully comprehensible only in its agency and effects." Ernst Cassirer, *The Philosophy of the Enlightenment*, 13.

ly testifies to a naïve faith in rationality. The Enlightenment was not an Age of Reason but a Revolt against Rationalism.

The most systematic refutation of the systematic spirit was undertaken by the abbé Condillac, the sensationalist psychologist, whose *Traité des systèmes* was deeply influenced by Voltaire's popularization of English philosophy.[62] In his treatise, Condillac dissected the great seventeenth-century system-makers—Descartes, Malebranche, Leibnitz, Spinoza—and inquired into the psychological sources of their urge to construct impressive metaphysical structures. He concluded that system-making is the child of impatience: faced with unsolved problems, troubled by mysteries, philosophers are tempted to make conjectures based on fancy rather than fact, and to consult their imaginations instead of interrogating nature. The real philosopher must rise above such temptations; true science is possible only after men have rejected the deductive method of Descartes, "which has bred nothing but errors," and adopted the inductive method of Newton. Descartes had boasted that he could construct the world with matter and movement; Newton had contented himself with observing the world, "a project less beautiful than Descartes', or rather less daring, but wiser."[63] In an important chapter on politics which would have pleased and surprised Burke if he had troubled to read it, Condillac decried the *esprit de système*, but defended systematic inquiry into the central fact of social existence: social change. Only inquiry oriented toward the facts can make rational reform possible; after a sequence of bad governments, when reform is as essential as it is delicate, men "must not seek in their imagination for the most perfect government; they will only create a romance. They must study the character of the people, do

---

[62] The *Traité des systèmes* was first published in 1759, after he had already published his major psychological and epistemological works, *Essai sur l'origine des connaissances humaines* in 1746 and *Traité des sensations* in 1754. Voltaire praised him to La Harpe as "one of the first men in Europe." 31 October (1768), XLVI, 152.

[63] *Traité des systèmes, Oeuvres*, 23 vols. (1798), II, 343, 345.

research into its usages and customs, unravel abuses."[64] The *esprit de système* in politics creates romance, not reality; it is Utopianism in action.

As propagandists, the philosophes carried on their campaign against Utopianism with witticisms and parables. In his pornographic novel, *Les bijoux indiscrets*, Diderot recounts a most instructive dream: the dreamer feels himself transported to a huge building suspended in space, inhabited by feeble, aged, deformed men. Then a small, healthy child walks toward the building, grows into a colossus, enters the building and destroys it. The building is the land of hypotheses, the cripples are the makers of systems, and the colossus is Experiment.[65] Voltaire said that metaphysics is for philosophy what bad novels are for women; he likened it to the minuet, in which the dancer displays much agility and grace but ends where he started; he compared all metaphysicians from Plato to Leibnitz with travelers who have entered the anterooms of the Grand Turk's seraglio, observe a eunuch from afar, and conjecture from this evidence how many times His Highness had made love to his odalisque that night. "One traveler said three times, another four times, etc. The truth is that the grand sultan had slept the night through."[66]

This is hardly fair, but propagandists are rarely fair. The philosophes were in rebellion against theory, and as rebels they

[64] *ibid.*, 382. This reasonable empiricism had a conservative tinge. Condillac holds that in a good government all men are to be made as happy as possible, but he lists the orders in France as "[nobility of] the sword, [nobility of] the robe, the church, commerce, finance, men of letters, and artisans of all kinds" (*ibid.*, 377)—in other words, he accepts the social structure of the old regime without questioning it, and he urges that reforms be made slowly and only after all the facts are known. As Ernst Cassirer points out, even "such a fanatical theorizer" as Holbach advocates extreme caution in social reform: it should be pacific and gradual. *Philosophy of the Enlightenment*, 267.

[65] *Oeuvres complètes*, IV, 255-258.

[66] Voltaire to des Alleurs, 26 November (1738), *Correspondence*, VII, 462-463. His last word on the *esprit de système* is probably his satiric poem *Les systèmes* (1772), X, 167-176.

28

were more concerned with being persuasive than with being precise. Voltaire was an intelligent reader and a thorough scholar, but his comments on metaphysicians are often unfair and embarrassing: he called Plato an eloquent moralist and bad metaphysician, "more poet than philosopher."[67] He said that Descartes had destroyed the errors of the ancients, but had introduced his own: the man who had taught men to reason was himself a victim of the *esprit de système*.[68] Voltaire treated his contemporaries little better. He had political reasons for criticizing Montesquieu, and he was right to uncover Montesquieu's gullibility, errors, and false inferences, but he never understood Montesquieu's search for universal laws of sociology. "Hardly has he established a principle, when history opens before him and shows him a hundred exceptions."[69] Again, Voltaire had excellent personal reasons for disliking Rousseau, but his criticisms of Rousseau's *Emile* and *Contrat social* are petty and intellectually vulgar.[70] Empiricism had its dangers as well as its advantages.

It would be unjust to conclude that in his pragmatic, reformist fervor Voltaire became hostile to speculation and to theoretical science. Other philosophes, notably Diderot and Rousseau, took the Stoic view that scientific inquiry was also ethical inquiry, that the study of nature revealed the moral character and moral duties of man. Hence they denounced mathematics, criticized Newton for introducing "occult qualities" into natural

[67] *Dieu et les hommes*, xxviii, 221-222; see *Dictionnaire philosophique*, article "Chaine des êtres crées," 101-102.

[68] *Lettres philosophiques*, "xive Lettre," ii, 6. Leibnitz, he told Condorcet, was a great man, but also "a bit of a charlatan." 1 September (1772), xlviii, 162.

[69] *Commentaire sur l'Esprit des lois*, xxx, 411. Voltaire's view of Montesquieu is complicated. He rejected his conservatism, his acceptance of venality of office in monarchies, and his praise of aristocracies, but he accepted his opposition to slavery, his humanity, and he called Montesquieu "le plus modéré et le plus fin des philosophes." *Lettres à S.A. Mgr. le prince de ****, xxvi, 509.

[70] See below, chapter iv; Voltaire's correspondence after 1762, his *Idées républicaines*, *La guerre civile de Genève*, and his marginalia on Rousseau's writings.

science, preferred chemistry (the science of the ordinary man) to physics (the science of a remote elite), and extolled technology at the expense of theoretical research. Voltaire was too good a disciple of Newton to accept the anti-intellectual position that the value of science must be judged solely by its practical consequences: "I am far from implying that we must hold only to a blind practice, but it would be fortunate if natural philosophers and geometricians would join practice to speculation as much as possible."[71] Like the other philosophes, he was first and foremost a reformer; like the Encyclopedists, he was impatient with knowledge that did not leave men happier than it found them. But he understood, as Charles C. Gillispie has said, that "Newton's world offered virtue no purchase,"[72] that mathematics, unpalatable though it was, was the appropriate language of science, and that it had been Newton's supreme contribution to free science from involvement in ethics. Diderot and Rousseau told men to live according to nature, to use science as the method to distinguish conventional behavior that was beneficial from artificial behavior that was pernicious.[73] Voltaire told men to live as civilized human beings, to understand their nature not through science but through history. Nietzsche's complaint against German scientists, that they were rehabilitating a "deified or satanized nature," may be applied to Diderot, but not to Voltaire.

Yet while Voltaire rejected the humanist, moralizing science of the Stoics, he was far from untouched by the Stoic revival of the seventeenth and eighteenth centuries. Epictetus was one of his favorite philosophers; the "divine Marcus Aurelius" was

[71] *Lettres philosophiques,* "xxıve Lettre," ıı, 175.

[72] Charles C. Gillispie, "The *Encyclopédie* and the Jacobin Philosophy of Science," *Critical Problems in the History of Science,* ed. Marshall Clagett (1959).

[73] As recent writers have emphasized over and over again, the injunction "live according to nature" is not an invitation to primitivism. To be natural, for Diderot and for Rousseau, is to live appropriately; it does not mean the rejection of all civilization but of some civilizations; it is not a praise of the noble savage but a criticism of an artificial society in which genuine emotions are replaced by empty forms.

his favorite king, the very model of royal greatness;[74] and the social philosophy of the Stoics—their cosmopolitanism, their stress on equality and the rule of law, their demand that the prince serve society, their emphasis on merit rather than status, their praise of duty—is also the social philosophy of Voltaire.[75] It is beside the point to object that these are well-meaning platitudes, piously uttered and callously disregarded by men in all ages. Their prominence in Voltaire's political writings constitutes a radical criticism of the Old Regime.

The same critical function is performed by another survival of Stoic thought in Voltaire's political philosophy: natural law. His many pronouncements on natural law should be read as a political program: "What is tolerance? It is the endowment of humanity. We are all steeped in weakness and error; let us forgive each other our stupidities, that is the first law of nature."[76] And again: "KOU: 'What must one do to dare look upon oneself without repugnance and without shame before the Supreme Being?' CU-SU: 'Be just.' KOU: 'And what else?' CU-SU: 'Be just.' "[77] And more specifically: "Entire freedom of the person and his goods; to speak to the nation by means of one's pen; to be judged in criminal matters only by a jury formed of independent men; to be judged in any case only in accord with the precise terms of the law; to profess in peace whatever religion one wishes. . . ."[78] Voltaire's great trinity—

[74] "You are quite right in believing that monarchical government is the best of all, but that is provided Marcus Aurelius is the monarch." Voltaire to M. Gin, who had sent Voltaire his treatise on politics, 20 June (1777), L, 236.

[75] Voltaire admitted to Frederick the Great that he was an Epicurean rather than a Stoic, but this is a playful allusion to his zest for life, his love of civilization, his pleasure in pleasure, rather than a serious acceptance of the Epicurean world view. It is of course true that Voltaire was not simply a Stoic: he thought the Stoics too proud and too prim to be wholeheartedly a disciple of their teachings. But the affinity of his thought with that of the Stoics (always with the important exception of the Stoic view of science) deserves to be explored further.

[76] *Dictionnaire philosophique*, article "Tolérance," 401. See Appendix 1: "Voltaire and Natural Law."

[77] *ibid.*, article "Philosophie," 342.

[78] *Questions sur l'Encyclopédie*, article "Gouvernement" in a section

31

toleration, the rule of law, freedom of opinion—defines the conditions that make it possible for men to realize their purpose on this earth: to live in dignity and in happiness; in a word, it defines Voltaire's platform for social reform.[79]

Yet Voltaire was enough of a historical relativist to know that these ends must be realized in different countries in different ways;[80] he was enough of a realist to know that there was a long, often tragic, distance between stating goals and achieving them. Voltaire was not complacent enough to believe that the evils besetting humanity would disappear at the bidding of a few philosophes; he was not foolish enough to believe that all men can be happy. He did not think that ours is the best of all possible worlds. Nor did he think that men have it in their power to make this the best of all possible worlds. But as an indefatigable reformer, who found more and more abuses that needed attention the older he grew, he never ceased to preach that men had the obligation to make this the best world it was possible for them to make.

---

added in 1774, xix, 296. Many other examples can be given: the discovery that all men really worship the same being—that the moral law is the same in the whole world despite the variety of ritual and doctrine—converts a violent argument into fraternal harmony in *Zadig*, xxi, 61-64. Again, that free speech is a natural right is a recurrent theme in Voltaire's writings. See: "In a republic worthy of that name, the liberty to publish one's thoughts is the natural right of the citizen." *Idées républicaines*, xxiv, 418.

[79] These various political demands occur throughout Voltaire's work: they only grow more insistent and rather more radical with the years. In certain areas, such as the administration of justice, Voltaire did not discover the need for reforms until he was in his late sixties; in other areas, such as the free expression of opinion, he was radically critical of contemporary practices while he was in his twenties. But again and again, he admitted himself what I have been suggesting here: that his statements on natural law are a kind of shorthand statement of his political program. See, as an excellent example, his comment to Frederick the Great on his poem *La loi naturelle*: "The true goal of this work is tolerance." (ca. 25 August 1752), *Correspondence*, xxi, 45.

[80] Voltaire's relativism on forms of government must not be understood, however, as complete indifference. Other philosophes, like Holbach, d'Alembert, and Helvétius, sometimes talk as though they feel "whate'er is best administered is best," but as I shall show in the sequel, Voltaire had distinct preferences.

32

ENGLAND:
A NATION OF PHILOSOPHERS

Reason is free here and walks her own way, hippokondriaks especially are well come. No manner of living appears strange; we
have men who walk six miles a day for their health, feed upon
roots, never taste flesh, wear a coat thinner than yr. ladies do in
the hottest days.
—VOLTAIRE to des Alleurs (in English), 11 April 1728

1. AROUET INTO VOLTAIRE

THE EIGHTEENTH CENTURY has often been called the Age of
Voltaire. The phrase is a deserved tribute to one of the wittiest
writers who ever lived, but it is more than that: it is a tribute,
too, to a spectacular career which produced a social revolution
in France. Voltaire was the first literary man to enter polite
society after an arduous and often humiliating struggle to attain prestige and dignity; others followed him, their path to
social acceptance smoothed by Voltaire's success.[1] In 1750,
Charles Pinot-Duclos, historian, novelist, member of the *Académie française*, observed that "the taste for literature, science,

---

[1] Louis XIV made Racine historiographer of France, but Racine was a
skillful careerist, and his success at court was a startling exception. The poet
J.-B. Rousseau became a popular figure in the Paris of the last years of
Louis XIV despite his low middle-class origins, but he "was tolerated by
gentlemen of quality, and admitted to their society as an entertainer. . . ."
Henry A. Grubbs, *Jean-Baptiste Rousseau* (1941), 40. Cleveland B. Chase
therefore is wrong to say that Rousseau's "attention was coveted by the
whole of the Parisian society." *The Young Voltaire*, 24.

and the arts has grown gradually, and has reached such a point that people affect it when they do not have it. . . . Of all empires, that of the intellectuals is the most extensive."[2] In his opening address to the Academy in 1762, the abbé Voisenon suggested that men of the world and men of letters had learned much from each other: "Courtiers learned to reason, men of letters learned to converse. The former ceased to be bored, the latter ceased to be bores."[3] And even Voltaire, who liked to exaggerate his sufferings, wrote to d'Alembert in 1765: "People clamor against the philosophes. They are right; for if opinion is the queen of the world, the philosophes govern that queen."[4]

But that was in the middle of the eighteenth century, when Voltaire was the most famous playwright in Europe, after a slow and painful social ascent. In Voltaire's early years—during the last decades of the age of Louis XIV, the Regency which amiably misgoverned France from 1715 to 1723, and the first years of Louis XV—writers were little more than hired entertainers. It was still fashionable for aristocrats to adore poetry and to condescend to poets, to applaud plays and to snub playwrights. In a few salons, shepherded by ambitious ladies of exquisite sensibilities or by libertines who relished the democracy of conversation, a poet might trade *bon mots* with a count, but neither the ladies nor the libertines ever mistook the poets for their equals. "Are we all princes or poets here?" the young Voltaire impudently asked the Prince de Conti at an elegant party.[5] It proved easier to distinguish princes from poets than Voltaire liked to believe. The regent joked with Voltaire, and condescended to hear him recite, but when the poet complained to the prince in 1722 that a police spy had beaten him in public, the regent put Voltaire in his place: "You are a poet and you have got a cudgelling. . . . That is in order and I have nothing

---

[2] *Considérations sur les moeurs*, 135.
[3] Roger Picard, *Les salons littéraires et la société française*, 150.
[4] 8 July (1765), XLIV, 21.
[5] Gustave Lanson, *Voltaire*, 18.

to say to you."[6] France was a caste society, and the only force that could breach it was money.

Spoiled by his aristocratic companions, confident of his wit, the young Voltaire irrepressibly defied these realities again and again, but each defiance brought a rude reminder of his uncertain social position. That first beating had taught him nothing; a second beating, administered early in 1726, greatly advanced his political education. Late in 1725, Voltaire had become embroiled in an absurd but instructive quarrel. The chevalier de Rohan, whose ancestors figure prominently in the pages of French history, made some offensive remarks which Voltaire, far from intimidated by the crude nobleman, countered with equal if not greater insolence. Beaten by words, Rohan retaliated with blows. Early in February 1726 he lured Voltaire from a fashionable supper and watched while his lackeys gave the poet a thrashing.[7]

It was a degrading experience for Voltaire, but its denouement was even more degrading. Mathieu Marais, Parisian lawyer and diarist, reported shortly after the affair that men in society had little sympathy with Voltaire: "The bishop of Blois said, 'We would be pretty unfortunate if poets didn't have shoulders.' . . . Nobody pities him, and those he believed his friends have turned their back on him."[8] But the most painful and the most illuminating part of the business was still to come:

---

[6] Maurice Pellisson, *Les hommes de lettres au* xviiie siècle, 237.

[7] The story was too good not to be immediately embroidered by Paris gossips. It is therefore hard to know precisely what happened. It is almost certain that Rohan was the aggressor, and that he passed some reflections on Voltaire's recently adopted name. Some accounts report that the men met twice, once at the *Comédie Française*, once at the Opera; others, that while the chevalier de Rohan was watching the beating from a nearby cab, he warned his men to spare the poet's head, since something valuable might come out of it. Since this remark is probably apocryphal, I have reluctantly omitted it from my account in the text.

[8] Marais to Jean Bouhier, quoted in *Correspondence*, ii, 3. In those years aristocrats with literary talents either hid them in embarrassment, or, when they displayed them, found them an obstacle to their careers: "Montesquieu found access to a diplomatic career closed because of his writings." Henri Carré, *La noblesse de France et l'opinion publique au* xviiie siècle, 208.

the duc de Sully and the other aristocrats whom Voltaire had entertained with his charming impudences found him even more amusing as a victim than as a dinner companion and did not come to his defense. Voltaire demanded redress and ostentatiously prepared for a duel; to prevent bloodshed the government imprisoned him in the Bastille. A poet had tried to break class barriers by talking back to a nobleman; he soon discovered that in a conflict between rank and justice, it was justice, not rank, that gave way.

The writer whom Rohan had bullied so disdainfully was not an obscure hack but a respectable bourgeois and France's leading young poet. Voltaire had been born François-Marie Arouet on 21 November 1694 into a prosperous middle-class family. His mother's ancestors had recently reached the lower rungs of the *noblesse de robe*; his father first bought the post of *notaire* at the *Châtelet de Paris*, one of the most powerful courts in France, and later was prosperous enough to buy the position of *receveur des épices* at the *Chambre des comptes* in Paris.[9] As a distinguished official with close ties to the parlement of Paris, François Arouet had noblemen among his friends as well as among his clients. The duchesse de Saint-Simon and the duc de Richelieu stood godfather to his eldest son, Armand, while a suave worldling of the best society, the abbé de Châteauneuf, was godfather to the future Voltaire.[10] Thus it was reasonable for the elder Arouet to plan a legal career for François-Marie,

---

[9] A *notaire* is a notary, but a *notaire* at the *Châtelet* authenticated documents of considerable importance, and from all parts of France; he was like a solicitor, with distinct and desirable privileges; a *notaire*, especially in Paris, was therefore a far more eminent official than a notary is in the United States. Arouet's second post, *receveur des épices*, was more expensive and more eminent than his first. Arouet's wife's brother was entitled to call himself "esquire," while her sister married an "esquire"—in a word the Arouets were a step or two below nobility.

[10] The duchess was the mother of the famous diarist; the latter has confused many a biographer with his contemptuous reference to Voltaire, "the son of my father's notary."

and to expect his son to rise into the judicial or administrative aristocracy.

For the sake of these paternal ambitions, Arouet swallowed his rigid Jansenism and sent his son to a Jesuit school, the *collège* Louis-le-Grand, one of the best and most fashionable schools in Paris. There François-Marie met the sons of leading families—the brothers d'Argenson, who later became ministers under Louis XV; the comte d'Argental, who remained his lifelong friend; the young duc de Richelieu; de Cideville, who became a magistrate in Rouen. As his father had wished, young Arouet made profitable connections with his fellow students, but as friends, not clients; despite cajolery, bribery, and threats, Voltaire did not want to be a lawyer. He wanted to be a poet.

Voltaire's unshakeable determination to make a career in literature suggests the seriousness of his purpose and the rebelliousness of his spirit. Lawyers with good connections could rise high in eighteenth-century France, but Voltaire threw away the advantages of the career his father was so anxious to obtain for him; to Voltaire, literature was not a caprice or a trade but a profession and a vocation. Gustave Lanson has suggested that Voltaire adhered to the middle-class maxim, "in the bourgeoisie only the fool remains a bourgeois."[11] Perhaps, but literature was a far more uncertain and laborious road to social

[11] *Voltaire*, 9. It seems beyond question that one element in his stubborn refusal to follow the career marked out by his father was his rejection of his family. I agree with René Pomeau that we do not have sufficient evidence to give a psychoanalytic account of Voltaire's development, but certain facts are patent: Voltaire greatly disliked his family, except for his elder sister; he rarely spoke of it, and when he did, he made critical remarks or tasteless witticisms. He detested his elder brother Armand, who was a good Jansenist; in his notebook he made this revealing entry (in English): "Seldom brothers agrée together. T'is for this reason sovereigns of Europe are stiled brothers to each other. They pursue, they deceive, they betray, the hate one another like true brothers, and after having fight with the utmost fury and having lay wast respectively their kingdoms, they take a solemn mourning upon the death of one another." *Notebooks*, 39. It is further worth noting that Voltaire's mother died when he was only seven and that he spent his life seeking affection. Had his search for a benevolent authority in religion and politics its roots in this need for affection?

ascent than the law. To be a poet, his father told him, was to be useless to society, to be a burden to his parents, and to die of starvation. Voltaire did not agree; he intended to be useful, independent, and rich.

He did not take long to realize his intentions. At Louis-le-Grand he had scribbled schoolboy verses that had impressed the Reverend Fathers. After he left school in 1710, he moved easily in the aristocratic society he had known since his childhood. Pathetically and futilely the elder Arouet tried to divert his son into diplomacy or law, but young François-Marie was too witty, too sociable, too facile a poet, to engage in professions that bored him.

These were heady days for a clever young man. With the death of Louis XIV, an oppressive paternal authority disappeared, and sentiments that had been whispered before were now said out loud.[12] Young Arouet was ready for the libertinism of the Regency. The abbé de Châteauneuf had early introduced his godson to clandestine deist and epicurean writings; only a few years out of school, François-Marie became a regular member of the Temple, a society of aging worldlings from the most brilliant circles, who delighted in their witty recruit and encouraged his irreverence with their scandalous reminiscences, their deist poems, their earnest devotion to pleasure.

But in the midst of these frivolities, between elegant suppers in Paris and during week ends in country châteaux, the young poet worked. Since 1715 he had been writing a tragedy; an eleven-month stay in the Bastille for some impolitic verses (only some of which he had written) gave him the leisure to complete it. In 1718, when he was only twenty-four, he scored an impressive hit with Oedipe. Men of taste, parched for a good play, hailed "M. de Voltaire" as the worthy successor to

[12] The king's authority gradually declined in the last years of his reign. "The Regency began before the Regency," as Philippe Sagnac remarks in La formation de la société française moderne, II, 1. But it was necessary for the Regency itself to begin before a book like Montesquieu's brilliant Lettres persanes (1721) could be published.

Corneille and Racine. Young Arouet, a familiar figure at court, a playwright with a reputation, had felt it necessary to adopt a new, aristocratic name. Since Voltaire did not exist, it was necessary for François-Marie Arouet to invent him.

It was one thing to make a literary reputation, quite another to sustain it. Restless, ambitious, Voltaire now explored a genre neglected in French letters, the epic. He composed a long poem, the *Henriade*, celebrating Henri IV, read it to his aristocratic hosts, adroitly demanded and gracefully accepted criticisms. His poem made a great impression. Lord Stair, the English ambassador to France, to whom Voltaire recited portions in 1719, reported home that "he's ye best poet maybe ever was in France."[13] The French public agreed. The first version, *La ligue*, published clandestinely at Rouen because the government would not grant permission to print it, was greeted with unanimous approval. Mathieu Marais noted in his journal with more enthusiasm than judgment that *La ligue* was a marvelous masterpiece, "as beautiful as Virgil."[14] At thirty, Voltaire was the successor of Virgil as well as Racine—truly an eminent citizen in the Republic of Letters.

Yet all his friendships with the great, all his brilliant successes, had availed nothing before the insults of the cowardly and brutal nonentity, Rohan, whose sole merit was to have a cardinal for a cousin. The aggressor was at liberty, while the victim was in the Bastille; the barriers of class had appeared so fragile, but had proved so firm!

During his imprisonment, Voltaire's thoughts turned to England, which he had long wanted to see.[15] For several years he

[13] Fernand Baldensperger, "Voltaire Anglophile avant son séjour d'Angleterre," *Revue de littérature comparée*, IX, 30n.

[14] February 1724, *Journal et mémoires*, III, 89.

[15] All too often, critics of Voltaire assume that he is lying even when they do not have evidence. Thus it has repeatedly been suggested that Voltaire was lying when he claimed that he had wanted to visit England even before the Rohan affair. His claim is confirmed by a letter of 6 October (1725) to King George I, asking him to sponsor the *Henriade* and offering to come to England. See *Correspondence*, I, 329.

had been the friend of distinguished English diplomats like Lord Stair, celebrated English exiles like Lord Bolingbroke, and prosperous English merchants like Everard Fawkener. Bolingbroke had taught him to read Locke, to admire Pope, to investigate English deism and empiricism; even more important, Fawkener had invited him to his house at Wandsworth near London. Voltaire now requested permission to go to England, a request that the French authorities granted with an evident sigh of relief.[16] When he landed in England in May 1726, he was as little disposed to find fault with his new home as to be charitable to the old. England would be different.

2. A NATION OF PHILOSOPHERS

England *was* different. Voltaire has given us a charming if rather fanciful account of his first English impressions: the people were gay, their bearing was free and equal—except when the wind was in the East, for then Englishmen turned morose and even suicidal.[17] For several months the wind was in the East for Voltaire. He was too lonely, too depressed by recent events, to share English gaiety, enjoy English freedom, or practice English equality. "You have seen me pretty unhappy in Paris," he wrote to Thieriot in August 1726. "The same fate pursues me everywhere."[18] After a secret and futile visit to France in July to seek out Rohan, whom he could not find, he retired to Wandsworth to revise the *Henriade* and to study English.

Voltaire was too volatile and active to be depressed long. In January 1727, he was presented to George I; in the same year Bolingbroke, who had been permitted to return to England,

[16] Strictly speaking, Voltaire's trip to England was not an "exile." The government only banished Voltaire "50 lieues" from Paris. See *Correspondence*, ii, 12, 16, 21, 23-24.

[17] See *Lettres philosophiques*, ii, 261-263. Lanson has shown that this letter, which was not included in the book Voltaire published on England, was not written at the time of his arrival, but probably as late as 1728. *ibid.*, ii, 266-267.

[18] *Correspondence*, ii, 31.

introduced him to literary and fashionable society. He came to know all the prominent Augustans—Chesterfield, Pope, Swift, Gay, Congreve, Young, Berkeley, Lord Hervey—some of them well. He attended the theatre, where he followed the plays with a copy furnished him by the prompter; argued religion with Andrew Pitt, a prominent Quaker; steeped himself in English philosophy and literature; read the English deists on whose writings he was to draw so liberally in later years; familiarized himself with Shakespeare, of whom he never approved but whom he did not scruple to pillage; attended Newton's funeral at Westminster Abbey, and sought out his family, who told him the story of Newton and the apple. He was intensely curious, intensely busy, and intensely sociable.

The England that Voltaire was studying with such insatiable curiosity was Walpole's England, yet his closest associates were Walpole's most implacable opponents: Bolingbroke, who conspired against the ministry as soon as Walpole had let him return; Swift, who contemptuously called Walpole "Bob, the poet's foe"; Pope, who claimed to stand above politics, but whose sympathies and friendships allied him with the Opposition.[19] Voltaire's lifelong admiration for England is thus not without irony: Bolingbroke was supplying him with political reading matter and gossip hostile to the very ministry that was creating a government stable enough to permit wide latitude

[19] Since Voltaire came to England highly recommended by Robert Walpole's uncle, Horatio Walpole, then the English ambassador to France, Voltaire naturally came to know Robert Walpole as well as Lord Hervey, Walpole's faithful supporter and Pope's celebrated victim "Sporus" in the *Epistle to Arbuthnot*. It was inevitable that such diversified acquaintances would create some misunderstandings. These misunderstandings are reflected in some famous, but untrue, stories, two of which are repeated by Samuel Johnson in his *Life of Pope*. The first reports that Voltaire greatly shocked Pope's mother with his coarse wit; the second, far more serious, reports that Pope withdrew his confidence from Voltaire when he discovered that Voltaire was a spy for the Court and the Ministry. Lucien Foulet has decisively refuted this latter anecdote. *Correspondance de Voltaire*, Appendix VI, 258-269.

to the expression of opinion. It was Walpole, not Bolingbroke, who gave Voltaire so much to admire.

Voltaire's social, intellectual, and financial success in England enabled him to appreciate the work of the minister his friends hated. Bolingbroke might say what he liked, but Voltaire knew that England, even an England built by Bob, the poet's foe, was superior to France. In France, Voltaire had been compelled to bring out his *Henriade* clandestinely; in England, he could openly publish a revised version, elegantly printed and sponsored by eminent personages, and the revision brought him gratifying financial rewards and critical acclaim. England was a revelation that he was eager to impart to his French public. When he returned to France late in 1728, his notebooks contained the draft of a history of Charles XII of Sweden, a tragedy on Brutus, and, most important, notes for a book on England.

England was a revelation to Voltaire, but he had come knowing what to look for. Lord Morley, in understandable if excessive pride, has written that "Voltaire left France a poet, he returned to it a sage."[20] That is inaccurate: Voltaire had developed a social philosophy—rudimentary and rhetorical, but serious enough for a worldly young poet—in the years before his visit to England. In his first two tragedies, *Oedipe* and *Mariamne*, he had criticized despotic power and superstitious religiosity; the *Henriade* was a cautionary tale exposing fanaticism, extolling toleration and secular supremacy. Voltaire was a humanitarian, anticlerical, secular writer before he went to England. What England did for him was to prove that his ideal of a humane, tolerant, open society was not a poet's Utopia but a politician's reality.

Voltaire's discovery of England has sometimes been attributed to his "bourgeois consciousness." His values were, indeed, middle class—hostility to the aristocracy, advocacy of careers open to talents, respect for merchants, preference of pacific over military heroes—but his admiration of England had its

[20] *Voltaire*, 58.

roots in craft consciousness, not class consciousness. He appraised England as a man of letters, convinced that what was good for literary men must be good for the country. A civilization that treated its artists and writers well—rewarded them, honored them, allowed them free range—must be sound in all respects: prosperous, progressive, happy.

England was such a civilization; France was not. "This is a country where all the arts are honored and rewarded," Voltaire wrote to his friend Thieriot in August 1726, in the flush of his discovery, "where there are differences in rank, but only those based on merit. This is a country where one thinks freely and nobly without being held back by any servile fear. If I were to follow my inclination, I would stay right here, for the sole purpose of learning to think."[21] He invited Thieriot to visit a "nation fond of their liberty, learned, witty, despising life and death, a nation of philosophers."[22]

The nation of philosophers nourished its literary men with freedom of thought and rewarded them with lucrative posts, social prestige, and sumptuous funerals. In his notebook, Voltaire reminded himself: "Adisson secretary of state"; and "Wit better rewarded in England"; and rather cryptically: "Eschilus, Tirtaeus, Sophocles great men in their republicks, Adisson, Ofelds etc."[23] In his book on England, Voltaire reminded his French readers that Addison, Congreve, Prior, Newton, and Swift had all held important public posts: "Such is the respect that this nation has for talents, that a man of merit here always makes his fortune." In life as in death, Newton had been honored as he deserved: "He was buried like a king who had done good to his subjects. . . . The magnates of the nation disputed

---

[21] 12 August 1726, *Correspondence*, II, 31.

[22] (26 October 1726), *ibid.*, II, 37, in English. Several years after his return to France, he told Thieriot (also in English): "An author at London may give a full career to his thoughts, here he must stint them. We have here but the tenth part of our soul." (? November 1734), *ibid.*, III, 325.

[23] *Notebooks*, 72, 82 (in English), 84 (also in English). "Ofelds" refers to Mlle Oldfield, a celebrated English actress, who was buried in Westminster Abbey. See below, pp. 62-63.

the honor of being his pall bearers."[24] England was the intellectuals' paradise.

Infatuated with England and resentful against France, Voltaire was not an objective observer, and his account of English society is too uncritical to be wholly accurate. Yet it is not without merit: at home with the *littérateurs* of the two countries, Voltaire was in an unequalled position to appreciate the difference between England and France. In his infatuation and resentment, Voltaire rather overestimated the freedom of English writers, and neglected to report that freedom of expression was far from complete.[25] The Restoration Licensing Act, the English counterpart of French restrictive legislation, had been allowed to lapse in 1695, but both houses of parliament could call authors before the bar for breach of privilege; severe laws of libel restrained the expression of extreme opinions; and the Lord Chamberlain could refuse to license plays. Only a few years before Voltaire's visit, Steele had been expelled from the House of Commons for some Whig essays; Defoe had been pilloried for a sarcastic pamphlet; and in 1721, the House of Commons had imprisoned a printer for publishing a Jacobite broadside. Writers exercised a policy of self-restraint, a kind of voluntary self-censorship, which greatly reduced the danger of free speech to the constituted authorities.[26]

Still, Englishmen had some justification to boast of their freedom. For all of Walpole's disdain of literature and patronage of hacks, he could truly say that "no government has prose-

[24] *Lettres philosophiques*, "xxiiie Lettre," ii, 158; "xive Lettre," ii, 2, 5.

[25] His notebooks reveal that he was privately aware of what he did not publicly avow: "Mr. Shipping [i.e. Shippen] sent to the Tower for having said that the Kings speech was calculated for the meridian of Germany, rather than that of London." *Notebooks*, 45 (in English).

[26] Fielding wrote in 1747: "In a free country the people have a right to complain of any grievance which affects them, and this is the privilege of an Englishman; but surely to canvass those high and nice points, which move the finest wheels of state, matters merely belonging to the royal prerogative, in print, is in the highest degree indecent, and a gross abuse of the liberty of the press." Laurence Hanson, *Government and the Press, 1695-1763*, 2.

cuted so few pamphleteers and no government had every provocation to prosecute so many."[27] Most writers were dependent on patrons and the handouts of politicians; too much of their attention was diverted from poetry to preferment. But the greatest literary men lived on a footing of relative equality with the eminent. Swift wrote nagging and even insulting letters to Mrs. Howard, the mistress of the Prince of Wales; no French writer would have been so impolite and so imprudent. His virulent attacks on English foreign policy only made Walpole court him and George II curse him: "God damn Dr. Swift," the king said, and that was all. In France, Swift would have been bought off, imprisoned, or exiled; in England, he was permitted to rage in freedom.[28] John Gay, who showed his *Beggar's Opera* to Voltaire before it was produced in January 1728, had risen from a silk mercer's apprentice to a duchess' secretary, lived his last years with the Duke and Duchess of Queensberry, and was buried in Westminster Abbey in 1732. The *Beggar's Opera*, despite its daring allusions to persons in power, had an unprecedented run; his even more impudent sequel, *Polly*, was refused a license, but this did not prevent it from being printed and from netting Gay over £1,200.[29] "Adisson," as Voltaire noted, became secretary of state; he retired with a lucrative pension and married a countess.

Even more impressive was the career of Alexander Pope, who was not unlike Voltaire in his craving for independence and pride in his calling. In these years, Voltaire admired Pope extravagantly: he was "the most elegant, the most correct, and what is still more, the most harmonious poet England has ever had."[30] He was also the wealthiest: Pope was the first English

[27] Alexandre Beljame, *Men of Letters and the English Public in the Eighteenth Century*, 343n.

[28] John Middleton Murry, *Jonathan Swift* (1955), 414-415n. Swift did complain of his Irish years from 1714 to 1723 as a kind of exile. *ibid.*, 312-328.

[29] A. S. Collins, *Authorship in the Days of Johnson*, 148.

[30] *Lettres philosophiques*, "xxiie Lettre," ii, 136.

writer to establish his financial independence. His translations of the *Iliad* and the *Odyssey* had brought him over £9,000, and this income permitted him to refuse several pensions. In an age when most writers were party hacks, he tried to hold himself aloof from politics; when literary works were prefaced by fulsome dedications to persons of power and wealth, Pope dedicated his translation of the *Iliad* to Congreve; when poets flattered the great, the great flattered him; when writers sought to excuse their profession, he was proud to be a man of letters,

> Above a Patron, though I condescend
> Sometimes to call a Minister my friend.[31]

Voltaire, who took his craft seriously, noted with amazement that English writers were achieving a position and obtaining a recognition that were still denied to French writers. In the *Lettres philosophiques* he reported an encounter with Congreve which shows that Voltaire did not understand levity in this matter: Congreve "had one fault, he did not have enough esteem for his main profession, that of author, which had made his reputation and his fortune. He spoke to me of his works as bagatelles beneath him, and asked me at our first conversation to see in him only a gentleman who was living very simply. I replied to him that if he had had the bad luck of being merely a gentleman like any other, I would never have come to see him, and I was deeply shocked at this misplaced vanity."[32]

Congreve's "misplaced vanity" was an exception; other Eng-

[31] *Epistle to Arbuthnot*, lines 265-266. Pope's remark, that he liked "liberty without a coach," is famous. Beljame, *Men of Letters*, 378; Collins, *Authorship*, 114-212. The translation of the *Odyssey* was completed in 1726, the year that Voltaire landed in England.

[32] *Lettres philosophiques*, "xixe Lettre," ii, 108-109. Samuel Johnson, as humorless as Voltaire in this matter, accepted Voltaire's account and shared Voltaire's condemnation of Congreve: it was "despicable foppery," he wrote in his *Life of Congreve*. But as Bonamy Dobrée observes, too much has been made of this anecdote: Congreve was either joshing his visitor, or was striking a pose that Voltaire took for the real thing. *Variety of Ways* (1932), 58-63. Still, the story reveals much about Voltaire's attitude toward literature.

lish writers were properly proud of their calling, and Voltaire was proud of them. "I am confident," he wrote to an English friend over thirty years after he had left England, never to see it again, "no body in the world looks with a greater veneration on yr good philosophers, on the crowd of yr good authors; and I am these thirty years the disciple of yr way of thinking."[33] His affection for Englishmen, English institutions, English philosophy, never wavered. When Boswell came to plague him in 1764, Voltaire had much fun at the expense of his importunate visitor, but when the conversation turned to England, Voltaire became serious. "You have the better government," he said. "If it gets bad, heave it into the ocean; that's why you have the ocean all about you. You are the slaves of laws. The French are slaves of men."[34] In 1776, when Voltaire was eighty-two, he told another English visitor that Frenchmen were jealous of the English for their government: "Ah! Sir, you are happy, you may do anything; we are born in slavery, and we die in slavery; we cannot even die as we will, we must have a priest. . . . The English sell themselves, which is a proof that they are worth something: we French do not sell ourselves, probably because we are worth nothing."[35]

This feeling that England was something special—free, dignified, in a word enviable—came to Voltaire during his stay there; it was not the fruit of old age, of the sentimental glow that distance in time and space casts over early experiences. "I think and write like a free Englishman," he told his friend, the chevalier des Alleurs, in 1728. "I heartily wish to see you and my friends, but I had rather to see them in England than in France. You, who are a perfect Briton, you should cross the

[33] Voltaire to George Keate, 16 January 1760. XL., 284. This letter is in adequate English.

[34] Frederick A. Pottle, ed., *Boswell on the Grand Tour, Germany and Switzerland* (n.d.), 301.

[35] Rev. Martin Sherlock, *Letters from an English Traveler* (translated from the French original in 1780), quoted in Archibald Ballantyne, *Voltaire's Visit to England*, 323.

Channel and come to us. I assure you again that a man of your temper would not dislike a country where one obeys to the laws only and to one's whims."[36]

A country where one "obeys to the laws only and to one's whims"—this is the England that emerges from Voltaire's *Lettres philosophiques*. The book is a mature political essay, informed by his new awareness that political freedom is closely related to intellectual liberty and commercial prosperity. *Oedipe* and the *Henriade*, for all their humanitarian propaganda, had been the productions of a facile and ambitious worldling in search of a literary reputation. The *Lettres philosophiques* is a more serious work; it is the first radical critique of the Old Regime.

3. THE FIRST BOMB

Ever since Gustave Lanson, half a century ago, called the *Lettres philosophiques* "the first bomb thrown at the Old Regime,"[37] it has become almost obligatory to compare the book to a declaration of war. The military metaphor may be worn, but it has remained popular because it is apt. When the reader compares the rational society which the book delineates with such verve to the society to which it was addressed, he discovers the true nature of the *Lettres philosophiques*. It is a revolutionary tract.

The government censors, too lenient or too unperceptive, did not object to its politics, but other readers were deeply scandalized. When the *Lettres philosophiques* was published in France in April 1734, the abbé Le Blanc, journalist, traveler, translator, by no means hostile to the philosophes, was "shocked by a tone of contempt which prevails throughout. This contempt applies equally to his nation, to our government, to our ministers, to everything that is most respectable—in a word to religion. . . . It is horribly indecent."[38] And a Jesuit journal de-

[36] 11 April 1728, *Correspondence*, ii, 67, in English.
[37] *Voltaire*, 52.
[38] 15 April 1734, *Correspondence*, iii, 225-226.

nounced the book for attacking "religion, good morals, the government, and all good principles."[39]

These outraged Christians had some justification for their alarm. Earlier critics of the Old Regime had preserved their respect for "all good principles"; they had confined themselves to sighing for medieval France and to lodging humanitarian appeals with their king. The reign of Louis XIV had opened with a burst of hope and public acclamation, but the king's search for glory had proved expensive, and in the second half of his reign there was only expense and no glory. By 1685, the year that Louis's revocation of the Edict of Nantes drove many thousands of Huguenots into exile, French expansion had been checked. The brutal devastation of the Palatinate in the winter of 1688 and the Wars of the League of Augsburg and of the Spanish Succession brought France no diplomatic or military advantage, dissipated the economic gains made under Colbert, and pushed large masses of Frenchmen to the verge of starvation. A select coterie of tax-exempt courtiers wasted millions, while the costs of the king's adventures were borne by the poor. In 1694, Fénelon pleaded with Louis XIV to attend to his people who were dying of hunger: "France is nothing but a great desolate poorhouse. . . ."[40] Four years later marshal Vauban, who knew all regions of France, wrote compassionately: "The highways of the country and the streets of towns and villages are full of beggars, whom hunger and nudity have chased from their homes. . . . Nearly a tenth of the people is reduced to beggary . . . of the other nine-tenths, five cannot give it charity, since they themselves are almost reduced to this miserable condition; of the four-tenths that remain, three are badly off, and

---

[39] *Journal de Trévoux*, January 1735, p. 96; quoted in Pomeau, *La religion de Voltaire*, 246. It is interesting that the myth of Voltaire, the abstract literary politician, has pursued him even here. R. L. Graeme Ritchie writes in *France, A Companion to French Studies* (1951), 166: "Voltaire's book on England . . . was abstract and general."

[40] *Remontrances à Louis XIV sur divers points de son administration*, quoted in Henri Sée, *Les idées politiques au xvııe siècle*, 212.

embarrassed by debts and lawsuits."[41] Other critics, like the duc de Saint-Simon and the comte de Boulainvilliers, waited until the death of Louis XIV to publish similar indictments of the Great Reign.

These reformers were not revolutionaries. They placed responsibility for the misery of France upon excessive, "despotic" royal power, and looked to the restoration of a strong nobility as the salvation of their country. Their social program was humanitarian and, in the eighteenth century, profoundly conservative. But stringent censorship under Louis XIV discouraged radical and relevant criticism; the essayist La Bruyère complained that "all great subjects" were closed to Frenchmen.[42]

While in the Regency great subjects were no longer closed, the only notable book of social criticism to appear was Montesquieu's *Lettres persanes*, a witty, comprehensive indictment of French life and politics, of corrupt officials, lax judges, immoral society. But Montesquieu disguised his critics as orientals and infidels, beset with their own problems in a very imperfect Persia; he offered no program of social reform, and overlaid his opinions with an elegiac despair that invited philosophic acquiescence in the evils of this world.

The predecessors of the *Lettres philosophiques*, then, were either conservative or playful; they breathed the spirit of *noblesse oblige*, an aristocratic concern for the lot of the poor. Voltaire, on the other hand, showed little concern for the poor and no sympathy for the restoration of aristocratic power. In taking for his model neither the France of the Middle Ages, nor a Utopia, nor a Persia, but a neighboring country which many educated Frenchmen knew and admired, Voltaire was able to

---

[41] *Projet d'une Dixme royale*, 7. This book, which proposed a drastic reorganization of the tax system, was first written in 1698, then rewritten and published in 1707, the year of Vauban's death, and immediately suppressed. Vauban was not as ideologically conservative as the other critics of Louis XIV, but he was neither a social nor a political innovator. Voltaire rejected the *Dixme royale* as "chimerical." Voltaire to madame Denis, 19 August (1752), *Correspondence*, XXI, 31-32.

[42] *Les caractères* (ed. 1948), 88.

offer an aggressive program of reform to any French reader acute enough to read between the lines.

Voltaire could make his *Lettres philosophiques* a pioneering radical tract precisely because he was not the first of the Anglomaniacs.[43] In the seventeenth century, and after the Peace of Utrecht in 1713, several continental visitors published accounts of English life, praised English freedom, analyzed the English government, and puzzled over English manners. These loquacious travelers enabled Voltaire to concentrate on essentials: to preach to Frenchmen the gospel of English liberty. "I have been your apostle and your martyr," he told Horace Walpole in 1768.[44]

[43] Anglomania was the derisive term coined by Frenchmen hostile to England for those Frenchmen who admired England. Voltaire was the most distinguished and most faithful of Anglomaniacs—he never ceased to use England as a good example. In November 1752, he wrote to madame du Deffand from Prussia, "It is very unfortunate that there are so few people in France who imitate the example of the English, your neighbors. You have been obliged to adopt their physics, to imitate their system of finance, to build vessels according to their methods; when will you imitate them in the noble liberty of giving the mind all the scope of which it is capable . . . ?" *Correspondence*, xxi, 133. And on 14 November 1764, he told the *Gazette littéraire* that he was proud of his Anglomania: "A thousand people, messieurs, arise and declaim against 'Anglomania.' I don't know what they mean by that word. . . . If, by chance, these orators want to make it a crime that we wish to study, to observe, to philosophize like the English, they would certainly be very much in the wrong." xxv, 219-220.

[44] 15 July (1768), xlvi, 80. "I was the first who made Frenchmen acquainted with Shakespeare," he told Walpole in affectionate and exaggerated recollection. "I translated passages from him forty years ago, as well as from Milton, Waller, Rochester, Dryden, and Pope. I can assure you that before me nobody in France knew English poetry; hardly anyone had heard of Locke. . . . My destiny also decreed that I should be the first to explain the discoveries of the great Newton to my fellow-citizens." The many omissions in his account, particularly concerning manners and politics, were deliberate. "Let others give an exact description of St. Paul, Westminster, etc.; I consider England from a different perspective; I look at it as the country that has produced a Newton, a Locke, a Tillotson, a Milton, a Boyle . . . whose glory in the profession of arms, politics, and literature deserves to extend beyond the borders of that island." *Avertissement, Essai sur la poésie épique*, viii, 303. And in the Preface to the English edition of the *Lettres philosophiques* we read: "Some of his English Readers may perhaps be dissatisfied at his not expatiating farther on their Constitution and their Laws, which most of them revere almost to Idolatry; but, this

Apostles are proselytizers, martyrs dedicate themselves to a cause; neither can be a trustworthy reporter. The *Lettres philosophiques* does, indeed, contain much shrewd reporting; it brilliantly popularizes English philosophy and literature. But Voltaire deliberately foreshortens, omits, overemphasizes; his apparently informal collection of essays is actually a cunningly arranged series of arguments in favor of English institutions.

Consider his celebrated description of the stock exchange, perhaps the best known passage in the book: "Enter the London stock exchange, that place more respectable than many a court. You will see the deputies of all nations gathered there for the service of mankind. There the Jew, the Mohammedan, and the Christian deal with each other as if they were of the same religion, and give the name of infidel only to those who go bankrupt; there, the Presbyterian trusts the Anabaptist, and the Anglican accepts the Quaker's promise. On leaving these peaceful and free assemblies, some go to the synagogue, others go to drink; this one goes to have himself baptized in the name of the Father, through the Son, to the Holy Ghost; that one has his son's foreskin cut off and Hebrew words mumbled over the child which he does not understand; others go to their church to await the inspiration of God, their hats on their heads, and all are content."[45]

This is not reporting designed to give the reader facts, but propaganda designed to make him accept a political philosophy. The paragraph conveys almost no information about the stock exchange or the religious practices of its members; it ridicules ritual and slyly suggests that the world of business is more rational than the world of religion. But that marvelous last swift phrase, *et tous sont contents*, raises the passage above sarcasm to a positive vision of a civilization that assimilates, protects, and

---

Reservedness is an effect of M. de Voltaire's Judgment." Quoted by Lytton Strachey, "Voltaire and England," *Books and Characters,* 126.
[45] *Lettres philosophiques,* "vie Lettre," I, 74.

profits from a variety of citizens. A sound civilization, Voltaire tells his readers in one vivid image, is unity in multiplicity; since its virtues and vices constantly act upon each other, the strength of one institution is the strength of all. The rule of law, commercial prosperity, religious toleration, the flourishing of arts and sciences, civil liberties—all are necessary, all sustain each other.[46] This is Voltaire's thesis, and he ruthlessly excises or revises inconvenient facts that contradict it.

The thesis was not invented by Voltaire; he assimilated it from his English experience. After a century of revolutions and the clash of extremes, the Augustans were extravagantly praising the absence of extravagance and enthusiastically proclaiming the end of enthusiasm. The middle way, the way of common sense—all the safe, sane bourgeois qualities—were the refuge of an age that had seen enough of discord. Commerce at once caused and symbolized newly-won stability. "Great Britain," proclaimed the 1708 edition of Edward Chamberlayne's popular book on the state of the kingdom, "is of all countries the most proper for trade, as well from its situation as an island as from the freedom and excellency of its constitution."[47]

Despite all his flirtations with the aristocracy, Voltaire always remained a good bourgeois, and he found the Augustan values profoundly congenial. He observed that "in a republic, toleration is the fruit of liberty, and the origin of happiness and

[46] This understanding of the relevance of institutions to each other gives Voltaire's book its power. Tocqueville, who respected the *Lettres philosophiques*, said that Voltaire had come to know political freedom in England without learning to like it, that he had been impressed with England's skeptical philosophy but not with its political institutions: ". . . he envied the English above all for their freedom to write as they liked, while their political freedom left him indifferent and he quite failed to realize that the former could not have survived for long without the latter." *The Old Regime*, 158. Of course, Voltaire's enthusiasm for England was first awakened by the lot of its writers, but it is a serious misreading of his book to say that he did not understand the relation of political to intellectual liberty.

[47] *Magnae Britanniae Notitia*, quoted by A. R. Humphreys, *From Dryden to Johnson*, ed. Boris Ford (1957), 29.

abundance."[48] England was such a republic: "Where there is not liberty of conscience, there is seldom liberty of trade, the same tyranny encroaching upon the commerce as upon Relligion. In the Commonwealths and other free contrys one may see in a see port, as many relligions as shipps(.) The same god is there differently whorship'd by jews, mahometans, heathens, catholiques, quackers, anabaptistes, which write strenuously one against another, but deal together freely and with trust and peace; like good players who after having humour'd their parts and fought one against another upon the stage, spend the rest of their time in drinking together."[49]

These observations, so significant for Voltaire's estimate of the English character, naturally found their way into the *Lettres philosophiques*: "The commerce which has enriched the citizens of England, has contributed to making them free, and that freedom, in turn, has extended commerce; from this has come the greatness of the state."[50] And as a man of letters he did not forget to remind his readers that in England, "literature is more highly honored than in France. This advantage is a necessary consequence of their form of government."[51]

[48] *Notebooks*, 126. Voltaire included England among republics—he called it a "republic under a king."

[49] *ibid.*, 43. As Theodore Besterman, the editor of Voltaire's notebooks, points out, this is an early version of the stock-exchange paragraph in the *Lettres philosophiques*. What is probably the first version occurs somewhat earlier: "England is the meeting of all religions, as the Royal exchange is the rendez vous of all foreigners." *Notebooks*, 31. (Both entries are in English.) Now that we have Besterman's edition, it should be easier to understand the process of creation in Voltaire. It is obvious that he worked and reworked his ideas and his prose, and that the effects he achieves in the published book are deliberate.

[50] *Lettres philosophiques*, "xe Lettre," I, 120.

[51] *ibid.*, "xxe Lettre," II, 119. In 1733, the year that the first English version of the *Lettres philosophiques* was published in London, Voltaire wrote: "An honest liberty elevates the spirit, slavery makes it crawl. If there had been a literary inquisition in Rome, we should have today neither Horace, nor Juvenal, nor the philosophical works of Cicero. If Milton, Dryden, Pope, and Locke had not been free, England would have had neither poets nor philosophers." *A un premier commis*, xxxiii, 353. A year later he told a friend that if Locke had lived in France, he might never

Voltaire's repeated use of commercial metaphors—the stock exchange, the "see port"—is thus not accidental. The *Lettres philosophiques* is the defense of an open, middle-class England and an attack on a caste-ridden, aristocratic France. In England, but not in France, all are subject to the same laws: "Nobody here speaks of high, middle, or low justice." In England, but not in France, there are no privileged groups freed from contributing to the treasury: "Here a man is not exempt from paying certain taxes because he is a nobleman or a priest," and taxes are proportionate and rational. "Everyone gives, not according to his quality (which would be absurd) but according to his income; there are no *tailles* or arbitrary *capitations*. . . ."[52] In England a merchant can point to the dignity of his calling; in France "Whoever wants to is a marquis; and whoever arrives in Paris from the provinces with money to spend and a name that ends in *ac* or *ille* can say, 'A man like me, a man of my quality,' and disdain a businessman in sovereign fashion. The businessman hears himself speak of his profession with contempt so frequently that he is fool enough to blush for it. Still I do not know who is more useful to a state, a well-powdered seigneur who knows precisely at what hour the king arises, at what hour he goes to bed, and who gives himself airs of greatness in playing the role of slave in the antechamber of a minister, or a merchant who enriches his country, and gives from his office orders to Surat and Cairo, and contributes to the well-being of the world."[53] In England, but not in France, men of peace are popular heroes. Aristocratic idols, like generals and

---

have written his *Essay Concerning Human Understanding*. Voltaire to Formont (June 1734), *Correspondence*, III, 278.

[52] *Lettres philosophiques*, "IXe Lettre," I, 106-107. The *taille* was the basic tax in the French Old Regime; it was borne chiefly by the poor, especially by the peasants; the two privileged estates, and numerous members of the third estate were exempt. The *capitation* was a kind of income tax, in theory to be paid by all, in practice easily escaped by the privileged. Still, Voltaire's comparison is too simple. As R. R. Palmer notes, much comparative research is still needed before we can say definitely how much more inequitable French taxes were than English.

[53] *ibid.*, "Xe Lettre," I, 122.

kings (only too often "illustrious villains" and "highway robbers" with impressive titles), take second place to great men like Newton, who have used their genius to enlighten themselves and others. It is "to the man who governs minds by the force of the truth, not to those who make slaves by violence; it is to him who knows the universe, not to those who disfigure it, that we owe our respects"—and England pays such men the respect they deserve.[54]

In English politics, respect for bourgeois virtues is causing a decline of aristocratic power—this is the point of Voltaire's political letters. The English middle class is politically mature; it is fully equipped to govern the country. A member of the House of Commons can properly speak of "the majesty of the English people,"[55] for in that country the people is "the most numerous, even the most virtuous, and consequently the most

---

[54] *ibid.*, "xiie Lettre," 1, 152. Voltaire was delighted when the English government confirmed his diagnosis in 1736 by knighting his good friend and host Everard Fawkener and sending him to Constantinople as the English ambassador. "Now the honest, the good and simple Philosopher of Wandsworth represents his king, and his country and is equal to the grand signior. Certainly England is the only country where commerce and virtue are to be rewarded with such an honor." Voltaire to Fawkener, 22 February 1736, *Correspondence*, v, 66, in English. Three years before, Voltaire had pointedly dedicated his successful tragedy *Zaïre* to M. *Falkener, marchand anglais.* In his dedicatory epistle, Voltaire called Fawkener his fellow citizen in the republic of letters and added: "At the same time I enjoy the pleasure of being able to tell my nation how businessmen are looked upon in your country; what high esteem people have in England for a profession which makes the greatness of the state, and with what superiority some of you represent your country in the Parliament and are among the ranks of the legislators. I know well how that profession is despised by our *petits-maîtres*, but you know too that our *petits-maîtres* and yours are the most ridiculous species crawling proudly upon the surface of the earth. Another reason that has engaged me to talk literature with an Englishman rather than with another, is your happy freedom of thought; it communicates itself to my spirit: my ideas find themselves more daring with you." 11, 537-538. In the *Lettres philosophiques*, Voltaire pointed out that the younger sons of peers did not disdain going into trade. "xe Lettre," 1, 121-122. His claim is rather exaggerated: younger sons of peers usually went into the army, the church, or the diplomatic service, and Voltaire's examples are by no means representative.

[55] *ibid.*, "viiie Lettre," 1, 88.

respectable class of men, consisting of those who study the law and the sciences, of businessmen, of artisans." It had not always been so. There is now a "happy balance" in the English government, but in the Middle Ages the English people, like all other people, had been exploited by "ecclesiastical tyrants and plunderers called barons." These "birds of prey" had finally been subdued—the same happy antiaristocratic process that had enfeebled the French nobility had enfeebled the English nobility.[56]

Voltaire noted that the "legitimate authority" of the English people, gathered in the House of Commons, was growing "from day to day."[57] The monarch's power is circumscribed by the laws—he is "all powerful to do good, but he has his hands tied to prevent him from doing evil";[58] the nobility has lost its economic basis for independent action—its vassals—and must depend upon the king's creation of peers to prevent the extinction of the order.[59] Unlike Montesquieu, Voltaire did not fear this development. A rational system of laws, an open society, a prosperous commerce, a sensible middle class—all these made Voltaire anticipate the predominance of the House of Commons with pleasure rather than with pain.

His observations do not deserve to be called an objective analysis. They are too episodic, too rhetorical, too one-sided; they celebrate freedom, common sense, and sturdy self-reliance. Voltaire pointedly reminded his readers that Englishmen had

---

[56] *ibid.*, "ixe Lettre," I, 101-104. Voltaire's reading of English history is antiaristocratic throughout. Magna Carta, far from being a liberal document, shows only "how little liberty was known" in the age of a strong nobility. English liberty resulted from "the quarrels of tyrants"—that is, the disunity of the nobility, and the wars of the nobility with the crown. *ibid.*, I, 104. See this notebook entry, historically inaccurate, but revealing of Voltaire's politics: "It was under king John that the three estates assembled for the first time, and that the people had a deliberative voice. There was then open warfare between the towns and the tyrants called nobles." *Notebooks*, 71.

[57] *ibid.*, "ixe Lettre," I, 105.

[58] *ibid.*, "viiie Lettre," I, 89. As Lanson points out (*ibid.*, I, 95), this sentence is a direct quotation from Fénelon's *Télémaque.*

[59] *ibid.*, "viiie Lettre," I, 89; "ixe Lettre," I, 105-106.

won their precious freedom by resistance to despotism: "The idol of arbitrary power was drowned in seas of blood. . . . The English nation is the only nation in the world that has succeeded in moderating the power of its kings by resisting them."[60] Frenchmen all too often thought of Englishmen as cruel and unstable, but Voltaire urged them to compare the deliberate legal process by which Charles I had been sentenced to death with the vile murders that had deprived France of Henri IV and other kings: "Weigh these *attentats* and judge."[61]

Weigh and judge—this could be the motto of the *Lettres philosophiques*. But it would be doing Voltaire an injustice to treat his letters on English politics simply as propaganda. In foreseeing the eventual supremacy of the House of Commons, Voltaire was making a shrewd prediction as well as a thrust at the French aristocracy. In describing the existing constitutional arrangements as a happy mixture, a "concert between the Commons, the Lords, and the king,"[62] a balance of three powers,

> Les députés du peuple, et les grands, et le roi,
> Divisés d'intérêt, réunis par la loi,[63]

[60] *ibid.*, "VIIIᵉ Lettre," I, 89. In view of Voltaire's reputation as a slavish admirer of absolutism, this pronouncement is important. In the *Siècle de Louis XIV*, first published in full in 1751, Voltaire confirms his pro-British views in numerous allusions. Of William III he remarks that he "reigned peacefully in England simply because he did not try to be absolute." XIV, 342.

[61] *Lettres philosophiques*, "VIIIᵉ Lettre," I, 92.

[62] *ibid.*, "IXᵉ Lettre," I, 101.

[63] These lines occur in the 1728 version of the *Henriade* for the first time. The whole passage is worth quoting, since Voltaire thought enough of it to use it again later in a defense of the English constitution. See *l'A,B,C*, XXVII, 349.

> Aux murs de Westminster on voit paraître ensemble
> Trois pouvoirs étonnés du noeud qui les rassemble,
> Les députés du peuple, et les grands, et le roi,
> Divisés d'intérêt, réunis par la loi;
> Tous trois membres sacrés de ce corps invincible,
> Dangereux à lui-même, à ses voisins terrible.
> Heureux lorsque le peuple, instruit dans son devoir,

Voltaire was transmitting to the French public what amounted to the official version of the English constitution. It omitted some inconvenient facts—facts of which Voltaire, with his ties to Walpole's opposition, was aware.[64] It failed to disclose that the ministry made majorities, not majorities the ministry; it said nothing of the disfranchisement of the poor, the manipulation of the electorate, and the oligarchic character of English politics.

Yet this official version of the English constitution was not wholly fanciful. Augustan balance was not a Utopia; the Age of Walpole, as Sir David Lindsay Keir has said, was the "classical age of the English constitution." In the seventeenth century, Englishmen had passed with bewildering rapidity from government to government, executing one king and exiling another. By the time of Voltaire's visit, Walpole's calculated policy of inaction was settling the Hanoverian dynasty ever more firmly on the throne, his management of parliament was securing public peace by giving most influential groups in the country some

---

Respecte, autant qu'il doit, le souverain pouvoir!
Plus heureux lorsqu'un roi, doux, juste, et politique,
Respecte, autant qu'il doit, la liberté publique!
VIII, 55.
In *Montesquieu et la tradition politique anglaise en France*, 120n, Joseph Dedieu argues that Voltaire is mocking England in these lines. That is a misreading.

[64] There was much bitter talk among Bolingbroke and his friends of "corruption," and it was a commonplace to denounce English politics as corrupt. We know today, thanks to Sir Lewis Namier, that the term "corruption" is much too simple a word for a process that mixed much charity with shrewdness, and that contributed to the stability of the political system. It is however significant that Voltaire hinted at parliamentary corruption in the *Lettres philosophiques* only to suggest that it probably did not exist. To the best of my knowledge, he never published the little story he recorded in one of his notebooks: "An English member of parliament said: 'If Mr. Robert Walpole doesn't send me money, I shall vote according to my conscience.'" *Notebooks*, 377. In his hymn to liberty, *L'Auteur arrivant dans sa terre, près du Lac de Genève* (1755), he categorically denied corruption in England:

Mais on prétend qu'on te vend quelquefois.
Non, je ne le crois point. . . .
x, 365.

share in the government, freedom of speech (by no means complete, but unusually generous for the early eighteenth century) permitted criticism to vent itself in harmless diatribes. Even such strong rulers as Henry VIII, Charles I, and Cromwell had tried to govern with parliament, and had used the rhetoric of mixed government; when Voltaire was in England, the rhetoric had some relation to political reality.[65]

For Voltaire, the "happy mixture" of the English constitution was more than a fortunate political arrangement: it symbolized the spiritual consensus of the English people. England, like France, was a country of religious sects and disputes, but in Voltaire's opinion Englishmen had solved the task of establishing religious concord while Frenchmen had bungled it. His letters on religion reflect his admiration; they are a cautionary tale against intolerance rather than a report on the religious situation in England. Voltaire knew enough dissenters and Catholics to know the disabilities under which they labored; he either did not know or did not care to report that ministry after ministry had refused to repeal these disabilities and held to a narrow policy of "toleration."[66] But his distortions and oversimplifications greatly enhanced the effectiveness of his sermon for French readers, some of whom remembered with dismay the emigration of the Huguenots; most of whom witnessed with dismay the unpleasant and continuous wrangles between Jansenists and Jesuits.

[65] Except for a divine right theorist like James I, the most autocratic of English kings insisted that they were exercising their power through and with parliament. Charles I, for example, rejected the constitutional demands of the Long Parliament in 1642 on the grounds that these demands tended to destroy a wisely balanced government, a mixture of monarchy, aristocracy, and democracy. Sir David Lindsay Keir suggests that the complacent eighteenth-century theory did not correspond to eighteenth-century practice, but he admits that at least to some extent the panegyrists' "praise for the rule of law and the separation of powers which preserved it was justified." *Constitutional History of Modern Britain, 1485-1951*, 295.

[66] In his letter on English men of letters, Voltaire does report, casually and without comment, that Pope's religion had prevented him from getting a "place," a remark that suggests Voltaire's familiarity with the effects of the Test Acts.

Voltaire's sermon was on a simple text: tolerate one another. The Quakers, to whom he devotes four letters of rather wry praise, are only the most picturesque of the many religious groups living at peace in the nation of philosophers: "If there were only one religion in England, one would have to fear despotism; if there were two, they would cut each other's throats; but they have thirty, and they live happy and in peace."[67] Anticipating Frederick's *mot* that in Prussia everyone is saved after his own fashion, Voltaire observes that "an Englishman, as a free man, goes to heaven by the road that pleases him."[68] This is a strong hint that it is more important to be free to choose one's road to heaven than to get there.

Voltaire's letters on religion, which occupy almost a third of the *Lettres philosophiques,* are more important for what they imply than for what they say directly. They imply that religious concord, like political self-reliance, intellectual freedom, and commercial prosperity, springs from the English spirit of common sense, which in turn is the fruit of English philosophy. In the letters that stand, as it were, geographically and strategically in the center of the book, Voltaire offers a splendid popular exposition of the "philosophical modesty" of Bacon, Newton, and Locke—their empiricism, their devotion to peace, their immersion in true science. Like the letters on religion, the letters on natural philosophy are not directly political, but they

[67] *Lettres philosophiques,* "vie Lettre," 1, 74. In a pamphlet of the 1760's when Voltaire's religious opinions had become more radical, he made the same point in more outspoken fashion. He wrote (in the guise of an Englishman): "I believe that since our revolution England is the country in which Christianity does the least harm. The reason for this is that this torrent is divided with us into ten or twelve brooks, be it Presbyterian, be it other dissenters. Without this it might have submerged us." *Lettre de Milord Cornsbury à Milord Bolingbroke,* xxvi, 305.

Voltaire's letters on the Quakers are eminently worth reading. He praises them for their simplicity, fraternity, honesty, and pacifism, and gently twits them with their odd customs. His description of William Penn's colony is a Utopia: "A government without priests, a people without arms, citizens who are all equal almost including the magistrates, and neighbors without jealousy." *Lettres philosophiques,* "ive Lettre," 1, 48.

[68] *ibid.,* "ve Lettre," 1, 61.

make a political point: a society like France, with its useless aristocracy, its privileged clergy, its irrational tax structure, its medieval system of social status, is fated to engender social discord, economic waste, feeble philosophy. The very existence of a Newton and a Locke is a reproach to France—these men are representative of a reasonable, open society where merit is the passport to advancement, where the arts are honored and commerce is encouraged, where diversity has led to unity, where unity has not stifled creativity, and where, not surprisingly, "all are content."

In England people "obey to the laws only," but in France, as Voltaire discovered upon his return late in 1728, caprice and injustice still ruled. To his friends he seemed the same Voltaire: gay, irresponsible, flippant, attached to aristocratic society, turning out fashionable plays and witty poems, making money.[69] But amidst all these pleasures, harsh reality would not leave him alone. In March 1730 his intimate friend, the celebrated actress Adrienne Lecouvreur died suddenly. She was buried, as actresses were in the Old Regime, at night and in unhallowed ground. In pain and rage, Voltaire wrote a moving and inflammatory tribute, perhaps the most personal of all his poems:

> Ah! verrai-je toujours ma faible nation,
> Incertaine en ses voeux, flétrir ce qu'elle admire;
> Nos moeurs avec nos lois toujours se contredire;
> Et le Français volage endormi sous l'empire
> De la superstition?
> Quoi! n'est-ce donc qu'en Angleterre
> Que les mortels osent penser?

[69] Voltaire was never exactly poor. His father left him some money in 1722; the regent and later the young king and queen gave him generous pensions; and he started to speculate not long after he entered the polite Parisian world. In 1730, he made a killing speculating on Parisian municipal bonds, and after that he was a wealthy man.

O rivale d'Athène, ô Londre! heureuse terre!
Ainsi que les tyrans vous avez su chasser
Les préjugés honteux qui vous livraient la guerre.
C'est là qu'on sait tout dire, et tout récompenser;
Nul art n'est méprisé, tout succès a sa gloire.

- - - -

Et Lecouvreur à Londre aurait eu des tombeaux
Parmi le beaux-esprits, les rois, et les héros.
Quiconque a des talents à Londre est un grand homme.
    L'abondance et la liberté
Ont, après deux mille ans, chez vous ressuscité
    L'esprit de la Grèce et de Rome.[70]

Here was another shameful contrast between England and France, a contrast he did not fail to exploit when he wrote the *Lettres philosophiques*. French barbarians had thrown "Mlle Lecouvreur's body into the sewer," while Englishmen, rewarding merit with gratitude, buried "the famous actress Mlle Oldfield in Westminster with almost the same honors accorded Newton."[71] He could not forget the incident. "I join my feeble voice to all the voices of England," he wrote to Thieriot in 1731, "to make us feel a little the difference between their liberty and our slavery, between their sage daring and our crazy superstition, between the encouragement which the arts receive in London and the shameful oppression in which they languish in Paris."[72]

"Shameful oppression" was Voltairian overstatement. He produced play after play with no interference other than the usual hostile claques—*Brutus* in 1730, *Eriphyle* in 1732, and, in the same year, *Zaïre*, a distinguished dramatic triumph. "It is sweet not to be despised in one's country," said the cosmo-

[70] *La mort de Mlle Lecouvreur, célèbre actrice,* IX, 370.
[71] *Lettres philosophiques,* "XXIIIe Lettre," II, 159.
[72] 1 May 1731, *Correspondence,* II, 174.

politan Voltaire who loved his France.[73] He was not despised, but he was not as free as an Englishman; in 1730 the government hastily withdrew its permission to print Voltaire's brilliant *Histoire de Charles XII*. He replied not by silence—silence was never possible to him—but by a clandestine edition. His cries of outrage, mingling bravado, bitterness, and self-pity, were by now familiar to his correspondents. "It is pretty sad for literature to be in such a fright and in its last throes over almost every book that is written with a little freedom," he complained to Cideville in January 1731.[74] And as always he was sick, although not as sick as he thought. He told Thieriot that he had one foot in the grave and was gambolling with the other. "I suffer and make rhymes," he summed up his existence to Cideville in December 1731.[75]

Still, he found the energy to revise his *Lettres philosophiques*, rewriting, negotiating with the authorities, adding a letter on Pascal at the last minute, arguing with his friends over controversial passages. An English translation, *Letters concerning the English Nation*, appeared in London in 1733, and a year later the book was published in France. It was immediately suppressed and immensely successful. The reception of the book alternately amused and appalled Voltaire. "To tell you, madame," he wrote to the marquise du Deffand, "who is the most insane—the Jansenists, the Molinists, the Anglicans, the Quakers—that is pretty difficult. But it is certain that I am much more insane than they are for having told them truths which will do them no good and which will do me great harm."[76]

Voltaire was being melodramatic; the truth did Voltaire no harm and the French public much good. French bourgeois were not noted for their political awareness or social aggressiveness; few among them demanded social equality with the no-

[73] Voltaire to Cideville and Formont, (25 August 1732), *ibid.*, II, 343.
[74] *ibid.*, II, 161.
[75] *ibid.*, II, 261.
[76] 23 May (1734), *ibid.*, III, 255.

bility, the abolition of the privileged estates, the initiation of drastic reforms. There was discontent, but it was inarticulate. Voltaire gave that discontent a voice and a program; the *Lettres philosophiques* was the first warning that there were at least a few Arouets in France who were losing patience with its Rohans.

FRANCE:
THE KING'S PARTY

Les petits contretemps que j'ai essuyés en France ne diminuent rien assurément de mon zèle pour le roi et pour ma patrie.
—VOLTAIRE to comte d'Argenson, 5 July 1743

1. VOLTAIRE AGAINST THE CENSORS

VOLTAIRE flourished when he was in danger, but he flourished better when he was safe. He was too indiscreet to keep subversive views to himself, too discreet to acknowledge them openly—censorship that he could circumvent was a goad; risks were an incitement to him. "Misfortune never dejected me," he boasted to Thieriot shortly after the *Lettres philosophiques* had been published, "and my genius grew always bolder when they indeavour'd at submitting it."[1]

While Voltaire was preparing what he called his "burnable" letters on England for publication in France, his genius grew bolder than ever. "The philosophical, political, critical, poetical, heretical, and diabolical letters are selling in English in London with great success," he informed Formont, a friend from Rouen, and he saw no reason why they should not sell in French in Paris with even greater success.[2] The censor who read the manuscript did see a reason: the letter on Pascal, un-

[1] (? January 1735), in English. *Correspondence*, IV, 12-13.
[2] (ca. 15 August 1733), *ibid.*, III, 128.

related to the letters on England, was too impious to be approved; and the letter on Locke seemed to contain a guarded attack on the Christian doctrine of immortality.[3] Voltaire sought the support of his old teachers, the Jesuits, and refused to retract a line: "If I displease those madmen, the Jansenists," he wrote to Cideville in 1733, "I'll have on my side those buggers, the Reverend Fathers."[4] Voltaire's friends were more afraid for him than he was for himself. "If the English letters appear at this time," Formont worriedly told Cideville in April 1733, "there won't be enough water in the river to drown him, but he laughs at all that."[5]

Voltaire laughed, but when the clandestine printers had the book ready he grew cautious; he pleaded with them not to release any copies. It was too late—by April 1734 the "cursed English letters" were in the hands of the delighted French public. Early in May, the government issued a *lettre de cachet* for Voltaire's arrest, searched his and Formont's house, arrested the printer, and confiscated copies of the book. And on 10 June 1734, on orders of the parlement of Paris, the common hangman solemnly lacerated and burned the *Lettres philosophiques* in the courtyard of the *Palais de justice* as "scandalous, contrary to religion, good morals, and the respect due to authority."

What the *Lettres philosophiques* lacked in *respect dû aux puissances*, their author made up in respect for the police: he had prudently left Paris two months before. While the hangman was reciting the censor's litany over his book, Voltaire was on his way to the marquise du Châtelet, the bluestocking who had been his mistress since 1733. Her château, Cirey, was in Champagne, a reassuringly short ride from the border of Lor-

---

[3] In the "xiiie Lettre" (Lanson ed., i, 170), Voltaire quoted a passage from Locke's *Essay Concerning Human Understanding*, book iv, chapter iii, paragraph 6: ". . . possibly [we] shall never be able to know whether any mere material being thinks or no. . . ." For once, Voltaire did not mean more than he said: he agreed with Locke that the question must be left open.

[4] (14 July 1733), *Correspondence*, iii, 104.

[5] *ibid.*, iii, 47.

raine and a reassuringly long distance from the Paris authorities. In safety, Voltaire made *bon mots* on the burning of his book: "If this zeal continues," he wrote Cideville wryly in July 1734, "it will make the tour of the kingdom and I shall be burned twelve times. *Entre nous*, that's honorable enough, but we must be modest."[6] To everyone else he wrote indignant and unconvincing disclaimers. Nobody believed him, and Voltaire, shrewd and vain, neither expected nor desired anybody to believe him. His denials were part of a ritual required by the conventions of the Old Regime: as long as the authorities did not have a writer's direct acknowledgement of authorship, he was relatively safe.

Cirey became far more than a temporary refuge, far more than an amorous interlude. For fifteen years it was Voltaire's home, a place of intense intellectual and tepid erotic activity. Madame du Châtelet's passion for science equalled, if it did not exceed, her passion for passion. Voltaire complained humorously that his "lady Newton" preferred scientific experiments to love-making:

> Il faut pour lui faire sa cour
> Lui parler de métaphysique
> Quand on voudrait parler d'amour.[7]

Other educated ladies could not forgive her the virility of her intellect; they dwelt maliciously on her awkward hands and large feet, and accused her of seeking in the realm of mathematics the glory that had escaped her in the realm of love. But restless as he was, Voltaire was content with his "belle Emilie." He left Cirey only on occasion—to visit Frederick II, to prosecute an interminable lawsuit in madame du Châtelet's behalf, and, in the middle-1740's, to play courtier to Louis XV. For

[6] 24 July (1734), *ibid.*, III, 291. In the early eighteenth century there were twelve parlements; a thirteenth was added later in the century.

[7] Voltaire to abbé de Sade, 29 August 1733, *ibid.*, III, 133.

Voltaire these were splendid and creative years. With his mistress he studied theology and Biblical exegesis, performed experiments in physics, wrote papers on mathematics and metaphysics, and entertained a steady succession of scientists, statesmen, and men of letters. Under her loving and critical eyes, he began his major historical works, wrote essays in natural philosophy, short stories, and plays. The Cirey years were indeed splendid years, and they bore splendid fruit, despite Voltaire's intermittent difficulties with the authorities.

Voltaire's embroilments with the French government were as complicated as his character: he was in turn daring and circumspect, generous and petty, proud and servile. His inconsistencies have created two traditions in interpretation, each fastening on one aspect of Voltaire's actions and ignoring the other. His defenders have exalted Voltaire as a knight of truth who combatted despotism for the sake of humanity; his detractors have deprecated him as a professional liar who spread heresies for the sake of notoriety. Voltaire's friends knew that his character was not so simple. "Above all I am afraid of his follies," Formont wrote to Cideville in 1735. "He will retract, and then he will be angry and ashamed of himself, and his bad mood will make him break out in a violent outburst against the very prejudices in whose behalf he had made the retraction."[8] It is a perceptive remark, for nothing made Voltaire braver than the fear that he was being a coward.

But Voltaire's inconsistencies were not merely a personal idiosyncrasy; with much justice Condorcet said in his *Vie de Voltaire* that the Old Regime compelled men of letters to be liars.[9] The writer in France was harassed by a bewildering maze of ordinances and by the capricious actions of officials. When Voltaire came to live at Cirey, he had already had abundant experience of finding his way through this maze. The *Henriade*,

[8] *ibid.*, IV, 15.
[9] Condorcet's biography is printed in the Moland edition of Voltaire's works; see I, 209-210.

the *Lettres philosophiques*, the *Histoire de Charles XII* had all been published clandestinely. In 1736, a traumatic year that he never forgot, Voltaire felt compelled to deny his paternity of the comedy *L'enfant prodigue*, because the censor objected to some verses containing the words "exorcise" and "patriarch." In the same year, Voltaire thought it prudent to flee to Holland before the wrath of the *dévots*, who had been aroused by *Le Mondain*, a gaily impious poem that extolled worldliness, praised luxury, and expressed doubts that Adam had had clean fingernails in Paradise. In the following year, Voltaire conscientiously submitted his epoch-making popularization of Newtonian physics, the *Eléments de la philosophie de Newton*, to the censor, got no decision for over half a year and then was informed that his remarks on the age of the world had dangerous irreligious implications.[10] As Ira Wade reminds us, "with the exception of his dramas, every major work from *Oedipe* of 1719 to *Zadig* of 1748 is a clandestine work."[11]

Voltaire often expressed disdain at the efforts to prevent the spread of new ideas. "Foreign journals are prohibited here," he wrote from Brussels in 1741, "but despite this, people don't subscribe to them."[12] And in 1756 he told a correspondent that the parlements' burning of a book only increased its sale.[13] Voltaire is boasting and exaggerating; Diderot's appraisal is more accurate. Proscribed books were read more avidly than others, but proscription also made them hard to find and expensive to buy. Censorship was effective only for the poor—whoever could

[10] Voltaire to Jeanne François Quinault, 26 (November 1736), *Correspondence*, v, 328. For the objectionable verses in *L'enfant prodigue* and Voltaire's changes, see III, 485n, 486n. In January 1741, Voltaire wrote to La Noue that the authorities had also objected to his satirical portrayal of a judge in the comedy. *Correspondence*, xi, 12-13. For *Le Mondain*, see Voltaire to Cideville, 8 (December 1736), *ibid.*, v, 347-348; and Voltaire to Thieriot, 24 November 1736, *ibid.*, v, 325. For *Eléments*, see Voltaire to Maupertuis (ca. 10 January 1738), *ibid.*, VII, 14-15; Voltaire to Thieriot, 10 April 1738, *ibid.*, VII, 131.

[11] *Voltaire's "Micromégas,"* viii.

[12] Voltaire to de Missy, *Correspondence*, xi, 157.

[13] Voltaire to abbé de Voisenon, 24 July (1756), xxxix, 75.

afford to buy a prohibited book usually could manage to find a copy. When Toussaint's secularist *Les moeurs* was prohibited in 1748, the Parisian lawyer Barbier wrote in his journal: "I have finally managed to get the book *Les moeurs*, which the condemnation of 6 May has made very expensive and very scarce. It must be said that few people would have paid any attention to this book, but in certain circles that take pride in having some wit there isn't a man or woman who wants to miss it now. Everybody asks, 'Have you read *Les moeurs?*' A single copy rapidly circulates through fifty hands. Forbidden things always multiply desire and curiosity."[14] Voltaire's books, too, were sometimes driven off the market. In 1728 the lawyer Marais noted in his journal that he had been unable to buy the *Henriade* anywhere, "for gold or silver."[15]

Even to the most adroit of writers censorship could be a nuisance, if not a serious danger. In the 1740's, when he was already Europe's leading dramatist, Voltaire had to withdraw *Mahomet* because its philosophy offended the devout as "the triumph of Deism, or rather of Fatalism" over true religion;[16] and in 1748 the playwright Crébillon the elder, who censored *Sémiramis* before its first performance, harassed Voltaire over some unorthodox verses. "It is easier for me to write books," Voltaire said in disgust, "than to get them published."[17]

Such conflicts between author and authorities were not mere-

[14] E. J. F. Barbier, *Journal historique et anecdotique du règne de Louis XV*, III, 34-35.

[15] Mathieu Marais, *Journal et mémoires sur la régence et le règne de Louis XV*, III, 569. ". . . publishers were quick to recognize and exploit the fact that suppression was a powerful form of advertising that usually resulted in greater sales and higher prices," writes David T. Pottinger. "Authors like Voltaire aided and abetted them in securing the condemnation of books with just this object in view." "Censorship in France during the Ancien Regime," *Boston Public Library Quarterly*, VI, 28. Whatever the practice of other writers, I have found no evidence that Voltaire courted condemnations for the sake of sales.

[16] See the letters printed in *Correspondence*, XII, 79-89.

[17] Voltaire to chevalier d'Espinasse (ca. 1 May 1744), *ibid.*, XIII, 221; on *Sémiramis* see Voltaire to Nicholas Berryer de Ravenoville, 30 August (1748), *ibid.*, XVI, 59-60, and editor's notes, *ibid.*, XVI, 60-62.

ly the work of unintelligent, hostile, or overzealous censors; they were built into the very character of the Old Regime. French subjects could not legally claim freedom of expression; the state was empowered to control all publications, down to the most insignificant broadside and the most fugitive placard. Censorship had begun in the Middle Ages, when copyists and booksellers had to submit their wares to the theological faculty of the University of Paris, which tested them for correctness of expression and unimpeachable orthodoxy of opinion. With the invention of printing, the control over books became at once harsher and harder to enforce; with the emergence of the Protestant heresy, it became more significant. Strengthened by a series of edicts of Francis I, the Sorbonne condemned Lutheran and, in the 1540's, Calvinist writings. In 1543, it published its first index of forbidden books, which included such distinguished works as Rabelais' *Gargantua* and *Pantagruel*.

The threat of Protestantism, the disorders of the French religious wars, the growth of royal authority—all these gave the state a stake in the policing of opinion. In 1624, over the lively resistance of the Faculty of Theology, Louis XIII appointed four members of that faculty as royal censors. His Letters Patent tentatively established the principle of secular control over publication. This principle was confirmed by the ordinance of 1629 which provided that publishers must submit two copies of each manuscript to the Chancellor or the Keeper of the Seals for approval; it was further confirmed in 1658 by Séguier, Chancellor of the young Louis XIV, who appointed royal censors independently of the Faculty of Theology and paid them salaries.

The need for repression increased with the growth of the reading public. By 1741, the year of Voltaire's *Mahomet*, the government was employing seventy-six censors—ten for theology, ten for jurisprudence, ten for medicine, two for surgery, eight for mathematics, thirty-five for *belles lettres*, history and related subjects, and one for prints. In 1789, the last year of the Old Regime, the number of royal censors had grown to 178. Never have so many officials prohibited so much with so little effect.

The old ordinances, dating back to Francis I, remained in force until the French Revolution and were strengthened by new enactments. "No publishers or others," proclaimed the edict of 1723, "may print or reprint, anywhere in the kingdom, any books, without having obtained permission in advance by letters sealed with the great seal." In approving the book, the censor testified that it contained nothing—not a word—contrary to religion, public order, or sound morality. Legally, a book could circulate in France only with the imprint of orthodoxy, which all too often meant the imprint of innocuousness: *Avec permission et privilège du Roi.*

This system invited timidity and caprice. Many censors were ill-educated or lazy;[18] an author with influential enemies found it impossible to secure the *privilège*, but an author with influential friends could safely publish novel opinions. The censor worked under vague directives and found it safer to err on the side of strictness than on the side of liberality; it was less inconvenient to incur the ill will of a few men of letters than of the leaders of church and state. Delays were common and irritating; censors were slow to approve and quick to condemn. In the first half of the eighteenth century alone, they prohibited over a thousand books.

To make matters worse, French authors also faced other repressive authorities. Neither the parlements nor the clergy had ever fully accepted the supremacy of royal censors, and the censor's approval of a manuscript was no guarantee that it would remain unmolested. Time and again, the magistrates or the clergy drove the government into repressive action. It was the parlement of Paris that goaded the censors into withdraw-

---

[18] One censor approved a translation as follows: "I have read, by order of the Chancellor, a work called *The Koran*, by Mahomet, and I find nothing in it contrary to religion and morals." Pottinger, "Censorship in France," 89.

ing the royal *privilège* accorded to the *Encyclopédie*; the Sorbonne, the Archbishop of Paris, and the parlement of Paris together compelled the government to renege on a tacit agreement with Rousseau's publisher to let *Emile* appear.[19] Sometimes when the parlements had a particular grievance—and they often did—they condemned books before the censors acted.

This profusion of authorities, rarely in harmony, greatly reduced the value of an official permit, and made it almost impossible for a writer to predict the fate of his work. Censors and parlements, parlements and clergy, clergy and police frequently quarreled over what constituted a "dangerous" book. The censors, favorably inclined to the Jesuits, refused to grant the *privilège* to Jansenist writings that the magistrates liked; the parlements, favorably inclined to the Jansenists, condemned Jesuit writings approved by the censors; police officials, venal and easily swayed, harassed authors who could not afford to pacify them. Sometimes the police exceeded the orders of higher authorities, but sometimes they failed to carry them out. "When pedants battle, the philosophes triumph," Voltaire remarked to d'Alembert in 1756, after observing these conflicts for forty years.[20]

The philosophes triumphed, too, because many powerful aristocrats rejected the divine-right philosophy on which the Old Regime was based, and were inclined to be indulgent with anticlerical or even anti-Christian views which they shared or, at least, did not fear. Ministers like Choiseul and the marquis d'Argenson, administrators like Malesherbes and Turgot, courtiers like Richelieu and madame de Pompadour subsidized, protected, and often agreed with the philosophes. La Tour ap-

---

[19] The history of Helvétius' notorious *De l'esprit* is illuminating. This utilitarian treatise was approved by a lax censor and published with the *privilège* in July 1758. It was censured by the Sorbonne, and the royal council withdrew the *privilège* on 10 August 1758. Subsequently, the book was condemned by the Archbishop of Sens (22 November 1758), burned on order of the parlement of Paris (6 February 1759), and condemned once again by the Assembly of the Clergy in 1765.

[20] 13 November (1756), XXXIX, 131.

propriately painted madame de Pompadour, the king's intelligent
mistress, friend, and adviser, with *L'esprit des lois* and the *Encyclopédie* at her side; when she died, Voltaire truly called her
"one of us"—an observation that illustrates not the conservatism
of the philosophes but the extent to which new ideas were infil-
trating the heart of the Old Regime, the court.[21] Philosophes
who had violated the stringent edicts on publishing could count
on support in high places. Voltaire never hesitated to use his
aristocratic friends; and even Rousseau, the bearish, independent
democrat, obtained the protection of the Prince de Conti and
the maréchal de Luxembourg in the crisis over *Emile*. What
was more, the most urbane and literate defenders of the Old
Regime were hesitant to persecute the philosophes; the editors
of the Jesuit *Journal de Trévoux*, civilized, well-informed,
worldly, were sensible and sympathetic critics of Diderot's *Encyclopédie* and were reluctant to call upon the censors to suppress it.

While men of power helped subversive authors to escape the
rigors of the law, sympathetic public officials established a
routine for breaking it. From 1750 to 1763 Malesherbes was in
charge of censorship as *Directeur de la librairie*. He was an honorable administrator with a deep sense of fairness and love for
literature. It was this love that led him to violate his duty:
called upon to enforce laws in which he did not believe, he
broke them systematically by helping writers to evade them.
Malesherbes perfected a technique developed by earlier censors,
the *permission tacite*, an informal and illegal assurance by the
Keeper of the Seals that a publisher could bring out a book
without fear of prosecution. The state could not officially approve the new doctrines, but it could promise not to interfere
with them. The procedure of procuring these assurances, illegal
as it was, was perfectly regular—publishers applied for them
by the thousands, and officials granted them by the thousands.
As Malesherbes said, most of the significant works of the

[21] Voltaire to d'Alembert, 8 May (1764), XLIII, 205.

eighteenth century—Montesquieu's *Esprit des lois*, Voltaire's *Henriade* and *Siècle de Louis XIV*—had appeared without a *privilège* and under the protection of a *permission tacite*.[22]

All this—conflicts among authorities, protection of authors by influential personages, connivance of law-enforcement agencies —facilitated the spread of subversive ideas under Louis XV. The system of rigorous repression of protest and debate that had silenced writers under Louis XIV steadily decayed under his successor. Half a century after La Bruyère had lamented that important subjects could not be discussed, Voltaire, himself a prominent victim of the censors, admitted that the persecution of authors had become less vigorous. The clandestine printing industry flourished, the most subversive of books circulated widely in manuscript, foreign publishers smuggled thousands of books into France.[23] The church thundered against materialism, the parlements burned books, the police harassed writers, the royal council renewed old ordinances and published new, ferocious edicts against the expression of heterodox ideas, but the philosophes were finding allies and acquiring a sense of confidence and solidarity. As the eighteenth century progressed, their enemies paid the philosophes the tribute of denouncing them as a conspiracy.[24] But in reality they were not conspirators; rather, shared grievances, shared confidence, shared dangers had welded them into an open interest group.

Defenders of the Old Regime have exaggerated the power and the impunity of this literary interest group. True, the law was far more rigorous than its application, and there is some

[22] "A man who has never read any books but those that originally appeared with the express approval of the government . . . would be behind his contemporaries by nearly a century." Malesherbes, *Mémoire sur la liberté de la presse* (1809), 300.

[23] "No law can be enforced," wrote Malesherbes about the press laws, "when an entire nation seeks to advance its evasion, and when the government itself recognizes that it must often close its eyes." *ibid.*, 299.

[24] D'Alembert thought it necessary to refute the charge. See "Réflexions sur l'état présent de la république des lettres," written in 1760, published for the first time by Lucien Brunel, *Les philosophes et l'académie française au dix-huitième siècle*, 361-366.

justice in Tocqueville's remark that in the reign of Louis XV "authors were harried to an extent that won them sympathy, but not enough to inspire them with any real fear. They were, in fact, subjected to the petty persecutions that spur men to revolt, but not to the steady pressure that breaks their spirit."[25] But the petty persecutions did inspire authors with real fear. Under Louis XIV and Louis XV over a thousand booksellers and authors were incarcerated in the Bastille alone. Among the prisoners were not only many a clandestine printer who had stolen and disfigured the writings of reputable authors, but also a sizable number of the reputable authors themselves.[26] The very restrictions on printing created and nourished a race of rascally publishers, shady businessmen who were not averse to using against authors the criminal skills they had perfected in their skirmishes with the authorities. In the absence of a free press and enforceable copyright law some control over publishing was doubtless necessary—Voltaire was only one among many writers who demanded the imprisonment of printers who had pirated his works.[27] But the government constantly interfered with authors as much as with publishers, and imprisonment, however comfortable it could be made, was a depressing experience.

It was not wholly disagreeable to be lodged in the Bastille: more than one unknown writer got there the notoriety he

[25] Alexis de Tocqueville, *The Old Regime and the Revolution*, 152-153.

[26] Paul Dupont, *Histoire de l'imprimérie*, I, 214, reports that between 1660 and 1756 the number of incarcerations was 869. Pellisson estimates (*Les hommes de lettres*, 24) that at least one-tenth of that number were authors.

[27] Voltaire's critics—Funck-Brentano, F. C. Green and others—have confused the question of Voltaire's "persecution" of his enemies by lumping together his literary quarrels with his requests to the authorities to imprison pirates. For characteristic samples of the latter, see *Correspondence*, XIV, 45-47, 48-49, 67-68. His methods may have been harsh, but before we condemn Voltaire, we must recall the conditions of the eighteenth-century book trade: a writer had little protection from pirates who stole manuscripts and printed them (often very inaccurately) without rewarding him.

craved, or the leisure he needed to complete a book. The young Voltaire, as I have said, was imprisoned in the Bastille for eleven months, which gave him time to finish *Oedipe*, the play that made him famous. Still, he retained, as he told d'Argental, "a mortal aversion to prisons," and this aversion affected his attitude toward money and toward friendships with the influential.[28]

Other prisons were worse than the Bastille. One Dubourg, the editor of a satirical gazette, was put in a tiny cage at Mont Saint-Michel in 1745 and died there in a fit of madness a year later.[29] Diderot was more fortunate. In 1749 he spent almost four weeks in solitary confinement in the fortress of Vincennes. His room was large and airy and the food was good, but he suffered from solitude and from wondering how long he would remain alone. It is impossible to know how long he might have remained in solitary confinement, if he had not abjectly confessed to the authorship of books he had hitherto disavowed, if the publishers of the *Encyclopédie*, aided by madame du Châtelet, had not used all their influence to secure his release, and if he had not degraded himself by promising to put the name of the comte d'Argenson, then director of publications, at the head of the first volume of the *Encyclopédie*. It is impossible to know because in French law the *lettre de cachet* was valid indefinitely. Who can judge of the effects of Vincennes on Diderot? Is it not enough to say that his most delightful works, the *Neveu de Rameau*, the *Entretien entre*

[28] Morellet was put in the Bastille for two months (six weeks of which were in solitary confinement) in 1760 for an attack on Palissot's *Les philosophes*. It is true that he later wrote of his experiences gaily and without apparent resentment, but his sufferings were greater than he admitted, and in any case, he was treated better than most prisoners, since he had good connections.

[29] Pellisson, *Les hommes de lettres*, 26-27. Voltaire reports on this case very briefly and mistakenly puts it in 1748. *Des mensonges imprimés et du testament politique du cardinal de Richelieu*, XXIII, 434. In 1757 the poet La Martellière was sentenced to nine years on the galleys, and as late as 1768 several *colporteurs* were sentenced to the galleys for hawking obscene books. Pottinger, "Censorship in France," 97.

d'Alembert et Diderot, the *Supplément au Voyage de Bougainville*, were all published after his death?

Imprisonment was the strongest, but not the only weapon against the philosophes. The government banished writers to the country, exiled them from France, used *agents provocateurs* to secure unguarded admissions of authorship, confiscated books, and violated privacy by intercepting letters. "One can no longer think by mail," Voltaire wrote angrily.[30] The travail of the *Encyclopédie*, that monument to Aesopianism, suggests how hard it was for writers to publish their ideas freely. The editors of the *Encyclopédie* masked their views so drastically that even Voltaire, who did not dislike caution, was dismayed;[31] d'Alembert, Diderot's valued associate, withdrew from the venture after the furore over his article on Geneva; in 1764, Diderot discovered that Le Breton, his printer, had taken it upon himself to tamper with the proofs of numerous articles, weakening or omitting statements that he feared would annoy the authorities. Tocqueville's judgment is too sweeping; the French government did more than irritate its intellectuals—only too often it intimidated them.

Face to face with caprice and intimidation, Voltaire made his adjustment in accord with his conscience, his ambitions, and his image of himself. He knew that orthodoxy was no guarantee of immunity: Elie Fréron, by far the most competent journalist on the side of the Old Regime, was imprisoned and exiled in 1746 for a moderate satire against madame de Pom-

---

[30] Voltaire to madame du Deffand, 12 January (1759), XL, 14. Later he slyly summed up the case against censorship of the mails: "In France . . . the minister who had the department of the mails has never opened the letters of any individual, except when he needed to know what was in them." *Questions sur l'Encyclopédie*, article "Poste," Part VIII, 151.

[31] Voltaire's constant complaints on this score brought d'Alembert's much-quoted reply: "Doubtless we have poor articles in theology and metaphysics, but with theologians as censors and with a *privilège*, I defy you to make them better. There are other articles, less conspicuous, where everything is repaired. In time it will be possible to distinguish what we thought from what we said." 21 July (1757), XXXIX, 235.

padour. He was reluctant to follow Diderot's practice of suppressing his writings; madame du Châtelet could persuade him not to circulate *La Pucelle*, his burlesque epic, but his vitality and his vanity did not permit him to file his writings in his desk. He was even more reluctant to follow Rousseau in acknowledging his writings—in the Old Regime candor could result only in compelling the writer to spend more time seeking asylum than writing his books.[32]

What remained to him was a compromise. Voltaire secured his freedom of action and his effectiveness as a propagandist by cultivating those who could protect him against harassment, by lying about his writings, by libeling his critics, and by accumulating wealth. Voltaire liked money, but contrary to his reputation his acquisitiveness was not simple greed. "I have always preferred liberty to everything else . . ." he wrote candidly in his *Mémoires* of 1759. "Most [men of letters] are poor; poverty

[32] On 27 October (1766) Voltaire wrote to Helvétius: "At present I don't have a single *Philosophe ignorant*. . . . As you know, that little book is by the abbé Tilladet; but people attribute to me everything printed by the Cramers and everything that appears in Geneva, in Switzerland, and in Holland. This is a misfortune attached to that fatal celebrity of which you have had to complain as much as I. Doubtless it is better to be unknown and tranquil than to be famous and persecuted. What you went through for a book that would have been cherished by La Rochefoucauld must make all men of letters shudder for a long time to come. That barbarity is always in my mind, and I love you all the more for it.

"I sent you a little brochure by an advocate of Besançon [the *Commentaire sur le livre des Délits et des Peines*, which, like the *Philosophe ignorant*, was of course by Voltaire] in which you will see matters relating to a much more horrible barbarity. I am still afraid that people will attribute that little brochure to me. Men of letters, and even our best friends, do each other a grave disservice with the passion they have of always wanting to guess the authors of certain books. Who actually wrote this work attributed to Bolingbroke, to Boulanger, to Fréret? Eh! my friends, what difference does the author make? Don't you see that the vain pleasure of guessing becomes a formal accusation which villains abuse? You expose the author whom you suspect; you deliver him over to the full rage of fanatics; you ruin the man you would like to save. Far from taking pride in guessing so cruelly, make on the contrary all possible efforts to divert suspicions. . . . The abominable conduct of Jean-Jacques does greater wrong to philosophy than a bishop's charge; but this Judas of the troupe should not discourage the other apostles." XLIV, 472-473.

weakens courage; and every philosophe at court becomes as much a slave as the first official of the crown. . . . I have seen so many men of letters who were poor and despised, that I decided a long time ago not to increase their number."[33] Diderot, whose style of life was very different, nevertheless agreed with Voltaire. "The first step," he wrote in Le neveu de Rameau, "is to secure the means of life apart from servitude."

But Voltaire used such crude methods to escape servitude that even his admirers were appalled. Few people, said Goethe mildly, have made themselves so dependent in order to be independent;[34] Voltaire is a man, said David Hume more severely, "who never forgives, & never thinks any Enemy below his Notice."[35] Voltaire mischievously admitted that he liked a good fight: "When I'm attacked, I defend myself like a devil. I don't yield to anybody, but I am a good devil, and I end up by laughing."[36] More seriously, he argued that he must defend himself from calumny, not only for his own sake, but for the sake of his cause.[37] He thought of himself and his friends as the vanguard of his civilization; philosophes rise above all faction and "have no particular interest whatever." Hence "They can only speak in behalf of reason and the public interest."[38]

[33] I, 39, 44.
[34] See Franz Mehring, Die Lessing-Legende (ed. 1953), 308.
[35] Hume to Hugh Blair, 26 April 1764, The Letters of David Hume, I, 436.
[36] Voltaire to Formey (23 January 1753), Correspondence, XXII, 44.
[37] See his detailed justification in a long letter to König (ca. 5 June 1753), ibid., XXII, 192-196.
[38] La voix du sage et du peuple, XXIII, 470. "I know very well that people say the philosophes demand tolerance for themselves, but it is quite mad and quite foolish to say that when they have attained it they will no longer tolerate any religion but their own; as if the philosophes could ever persecute. . . ." Voltaire to d'Alembert, 13 February (1764), XLIII, 127. As I shall show on the next two pages, there were indeed times when the philosophes persecuted their enemies.
Paradoxically, Voltaire's friendships with the prominent sometimes reduced his independence. In writing recent history, he often had occasion to allude to forebears of his friends, and if his allusion was critical he was faced with protests by personages whose good will he needed. His old friend, the powerful magistrate Hénault, for instance, complained that

Like all ideologists, Voltaire exaggerated his disinterestedness; unlike many ideologists, Voltaire was sincere. He pointed to his cause to explain why he exploited his friendships with ministers like the d'Argensons, why he libeled those men of letters whom he considered enemies of the common cause, like Fréron, or traitors, like Rousseau. On occasion, his tactics were so merciless that they made him feel guilty, but he never felt guilty enough to give them up. "Good Prussian that I am," he wrote about the hated Fréron from Potsdam, "I'll find . . . the secret of making this bulldog shut up."[39] But in old age this swagger gave way to resignation: "I have mocked friend Fréron so much," he wrote to d'Alembert in 1775, "that it is quite just that he should pay me back."[40] Voltaire was the great advocate of toleration, but he never said, "I disagree with everything you say, but I shall fight to the death for your right to say it."[41] Nor would he have been entitled to say it—this immortal defender of free speech all too freely denounced criticism of himself as criminal libel.

It is easy to make too much of these limitations.[42] Other

Voltaire had not said one "obliging word" for Hardouin Mansard in the *Siècle de Louis XIV*, an omission particularly startling after the praise heaped on François Mansard, Hardouin's uncle, the famous architect. Hardouin Mansard, wrote Hénault, was a great architect, as Louis XIV himself recognized. "Besides, he was my wife's grandfather." Hénault to Voltaire, 1 August (1752), *Correspondence*, xxi, 1. Voltaire added some "obliging words" in the next edition. See xiv, 152.

[39] Voltaire to Thieriot (ca. 15 November 1750), *Correspondence*, xviii, 207.

[40] 24 August (1775), ii, 364.

[41] E. Beatrice Hall, better known under her pseudonym S. G. Tallentyre, said it for him. Burdette Kinne, "Voltaire Never Said It!" *Modern Language Notes*, lviii (November, 1943), 534-535.

[42] Voltaire was often generous, even to personal enemies, even to Fréron, and Diderot's sensible observation should be kept in mind: "If you make Voltaire less restive under criticism, he will not delve into the soul of Mérope and will no longer move you."

Nevertheless, there were occasions when even his brethren objected to Voltaire's tactics. On 9 April (1761), d'Alembert wrote to Voltaire, after the latter had publicly denounced Rousseau: "I admit that he wrote you an impertinent letter, I admit that you and your friends have something to

philosophes were equally insecure and equally humorless. D'Alembert requested Malesherbes to prosecute several critics of the *Encyclopédie*; in 1758, he asked him to proceed against Fréron; and madame Helvétius urged him to silence the editors of the *Journal chrétien*, who had vilified her husband's *De l'esprit*. With dignity, Malesherbes rejected these importunities, and gave the philosophes a needed lecture on the obligations of liberalism.[43]

Such touchiness displays the impact of insecurity upon men of letters. By mid-century the philosophes were no longer powerless and isolated, but their embattled mood, appropriate in the first half of the century, did not leave them in the second. As late as 1765, when Voltaire was far more dangerous to others than others were to him, he gave way to self-pity in the *Dictionnaire philosophique*: "The man of letters," he wrote pathetically, "is without assistance. He resembles the flying fish; if he raises himself a little, the birds devour him; if he dives, the fish eat him."[44] It is sometimes easier to achieve success than to believe in it. By continuing to harass the philosophes into the waning years of Louis XV, the French government kept up their delusion that they were a persecuted and ineffectual minority.

While Voltaire was not as helpless as he liked to think, it was realistic of him to provide for his safety and to keep his radical opinions before the public without making himself responsible for them. To criticize the Old Regime was not to

---

complain about; despite all that I don't approve of your publicly declaring yourself against him as you have done, and I only need to repeat your own words to you: 'What will become of the little band if it is disunited and dispersed?' " xli, 262.

[43] Wilson, *Diderot*, 286-287; Pellisson, *Les hommes de lettres*, 71: "You are too fair, Madame," Malesherbes told Madame Helvétius, "not to agree that my personal sentiments must not influence my administration, and that I cannot shut the mouth of authors who believe that they must avenge religion and good morals."

[44] Article "Lettres, gens de lettres, ou lettrés," 273. For a repetition of the image, see below, p. 230n.

conduct a debate, but to carry on a war, and much is fair in
hate and war. Voltaire invented none of the strategies that he
used in his campaigns, but no one ever employed Aesopianism
more skillfully. He published books anonymously, disavowed
works that bore the stamp of his wit, attributed his most daring
productions to authors who were safely abroad or even more
safely dead, used printers who forged title pages and places of
origin, misdated his writings to confuse the censors, had books
printed abroad and smuggled into France.

These were familiar strategies. Less familiar and more ingenious were his internal strategies—like a good poker player he
used a variety of bluffs. Sometimes he said more than he meant.
In the virulent anti-Christian writings of his last years he omitted
those qualifications and favorable judgments that characterized
his treatment of Christianity in his serious histories. Sometimes
he said less than he meant—he diluted the dangerous opinions
he held with innocuous opinions he did not hold. In writing
his celebrated *Traité sur la tolérance* (1763), he sought the
advice of ministers, carefully muted his anti-Christian views,
called Protestantism a "heresy," praised the Jansenists and extolled the virtues of the Catholic church.[45] Sometimes he said
precisely what he meant but disavowed responsibility for it by attributing his own opinion to a heretic or to an oriental heathen.
In some of his transparent dialogues he put criticisms of France
in the mouth of an Asiatic and criticisms of Catholicism in the

[45] The *Traité* was designed for a Catholic audience, and its object was
to persuade it to agree to a series of legal reforms which Voltaire considered
essential as a result of the Calas case (see below, pp. 273ff). On the other
hand, his anti-Protestant remarks did him no harm with his Genevan
readers, since they urbanely understood him to be a Catholic, and since
they were told by Voltaire that their own preachers had assisted him.
See Voltaire to Gabriel Cramer, 4 January (1763): ". . . I have consulted
ministers of the Holy Scriptures on it, and consequently it will be approved
by God and men." *Lettres inédites à son imprimeur Gabriel Cramer*, 97.
See the interesting comment on the *Traité* by the Kehl editors: "This
work must be regarded as a species of pleading in which M. de Voltaire
believed himself obliged to conform sometimes to public opinion."

mouth of a Protestant.[46] Sometimes he said precisely what he meant but professed to deplore his own opinion. In the *Lettres philosophiques* he quoted a long anticlerical poem by Lord Hervey and added piously: "You know very well that a translator need not be responsible for the sentiments of his author. All that he can do is to pray to God for his conversion, and that I have not failed to do for my lord."[47] Sometimes he wrote in such a manner that his meaning was clear to some readers but not to others, a method that was particularly useful to him in correspondence.[48]

With his propagandist's flair for the striking phrase, the memorable illustration, the convenient oversimplification, with his moral fervor and his unsurpassed wit, Voltaire made these stratagems so subtle that they appear perfectly natural. He wrote so much and so quickly that they appear, too, to be almost unconscious, but Voltaire never lost control over his ma-

[46] An early example occurs in the *Henriade*, where Henri IV makes some remarkably heterodox observations.

[47] *Lettres philosophiques*, "xxe Lettre," II, 120-122. To give but one other example: in the *Dictionnaire philosophique* he offers lengthy analyses of Unitarian doctrine and then weakly "disproves" it as contrary to church councils.

[48] Voltaire's correspondence with his intimates is filled with disclaimers of great precision—they are designed to give Voltaire credit for a work with his friends, disavow responsibility for it with the authorities, and give his friends precise instructions as to how to make the disclaimers. See Voltaire to Damilaville, 19 September (1764): "I never want it said that I wrote this book [the *Dictionnaire philosophique*]; I have written to M. Marin in this vein, since he spoke to me about it in his last letter. I flatter myself that the true brethren will back me up. This work must be regarded as a collection from several authors put together by a Dutch editor. It is very cruel to name me: it is to deprive me henceforth of the freedom to render services. The philosophes must make the truth public and hide their persons." XXXIX, 318. Evidently the word was spread among the brethren, for on 4 October (1764) d'Alembert wrote to Voltaire in a half-joking vein: "My dear master, so you absolutely refuse to be the author of this alphabetical abomination which is circulating to the great dismay of the Garasses of our century! You are surely right not to wish to be suspected of this hellish production; nor do I see on what grounds one could impute it to you. As you say it is evident that the work is from different hands; as for myself, I have recognized at least four: Beelzebub, Ashtaroth, Lucifer, and Ashmodai." XXXIX, 335.

terial and always knew precisely what he was doing.[49] In December 1732 he wrote to Formont about his unacceptable letter on Locke: "The only philosophical matter I treat is the little bagatelle of the immateriality of the soul, but the thing is too consequential to be treated seriously. I had to liven it up so as not to shock our seigneurs the theologians, folk who see the spirituality of the soul so clearly that they would burn, if they could, the bodies of those who doubt it."[50] A quarter century later he told Diderot: "It is a real pity that in everything that concerns metaphysics and even history, one cannot tell the truth. . . . One is obliged to lie, and then one is still persecuted for not having lied enough."[51]

Voltaire's justification for his stratagems was that he had to use them; it illustrates the paradox that there are times and conditions when the intellectual serves the truth best by lying.[52] It has been said, mistakenly, that Voltaire always lied, for the sheer pleasure of lying. In fact, he used the lie as a strategy, but not without misgivings. "I always tremble lest I say too much or too little," he wrote to d'Argental after he had completed *Le siècle de Louis XIV*. "One must show the truth to posterity with boldness and to one's contemporaries with circumspection. It is very hard to reconcile these two duties."[53]

[49] On occasion other people knew what he was doing too. The Genevan pastors condemned Voltaire's *Questions sur l'Encyclopédie* for containing "practically the same pieces against revealed religion that the author has strewn through other books . . . although these things are said a little less openly in this latest work, they are not less dangerous just because they are mixed with other interesting matters or because of the ironic or joking tone that accompanies them." *Lettres à Gabriel Cramer*, XXII.

[50] (ca. 15 December 1732), *Correspondence*, II, 398-399.

[51] 26 June (1758), XXXIX, 462.

[52] ". . . in certain periods of history, it is the liar who becomes the hero. The lie (in its many forms) becomes the protection of the individual against a universalized system of propaganda." Franz Neumann, "Approaches to the Study of Political Power," *The Democratic and the Authoritarian State*, 18.

[53] 28 August (1751), *Correspondence*, XX, 31. Voltaire sympathized with Molière as a fellow-craftsman who, too, had been unable to tell the whole truth: "We admire the plan of the piece [*Tartuffe*] down to the

But when his safety was at stake, Voltaire had no hesitation. Unlike Rousseau he had no taste for martyrdom. "A lie is a vice only when it does harm," he wrote to Thieriot from Cirey in 1736, when the secret of his authorship of *L'enfant prodigue* was in danger. "It is a very great virtue when it does good. So be more virtuous than ever. You must lie like a devil, not timidly, not for a while, but boldly, and all the time. . . . Lie, my friends, lie, I shall repay you when I get the chance."[54]

It is an illuminating plea; it reveals the conduct which Louis XV was imposing on French intellectuals and the futility of his attempt to silence them. The censorship was too weak to be wholly effective, too active not to alienate writers from the government. It deprived the state of the natural spokesmen for its reforms and needlessly enlarged the circle of its critics. In its caprice, vacillation, uncertainty, the censorship was less a policy than a symptom—a symptom of the declining authority of the Old Regime.

2. VOLTAIRE AGAINST THE NOBILITY

When Voltaire fled to Cirey in 1734, France seemed as formidable as ever. The damages inflicted upon its economy by the wars of Louis XIV and the financial adventures of the Regency had been repaired. But when Voltaire left Cirey fifteen years later, he deplored the decadence of France, and there were many who agreed with him. One might discount the marquis d'Argenson's gloomy forecasts as the spiteful musings of an ex-minister who thought himself more indispensable than he

---

denouement; we feel how unnatural that is, and how the praises of the king, however beside the point, were necessary to sustain Molière against his enemies." *Vie de Molière*, XXIII, 118.

[54] 28 October (1736), *Correspondence*, v, 286-287. The matter was evidently much on his mind. A little earlier he wrote to another friend, Berger: "To lie for your friend is the first duty of friendship." *ibid.*, v, 280. This is a little different from John Adams' laconic marginal note on a printed letter of Frederick the Great's to Voltaire: "Voltaire was too much addicted to lying." Zoltan Haraszti, *John Adams and the Prophets of Progress* (1952), 102.

was; but it is harder to ignore the apprehensions of Vauven-argues, Diderot, Turgot, all of whom shared d'Argenson's ex-pectation that "everything points to a great revolution in re-ligion as well as in the government."[55] The old families—the nobility of the sword—were regaining power without learning responsibility; the ennobled magistrates—the nobility of the robe—were doggedly defending their class interests with gran-diloquent rhetoric; the bourgeoisie was acquiring wealth, con-fidence, and influence but had no political institutions that permitted it to express its interests rationally; the king and his ministers claimed prerogatives which they could not sustain. In the midst of national prosperity and immense accumulations of private wealth the state was approaching bankruptcy, skilled workers conducted futile strikes which the authorities brutally repressed, the poor staged desperate bread riots all over France, and peasants starved to death. "The highways are inundated with unhappy citizens who have become mendicants or rob-bers," wrote Rousseau in the early 1750's.[56] But the French state and French society rigidly held to traditional values and institutions; in the midst of a social and economic revolution, the government changed only its finance ministers. "To call in new doctors constantly," Voltaire commented, "was to show the sickness of the state."[57]

There was nothing new in deploring the selfishness, stupidity, cruelty of the governors and the sufferings of the governed. What was new in French politics was the conviction that the sickness of the state could be cured. As philosophes, freemasons, and worldly aristocrats spread the secular spirit among the edu-

[55] 5 March 1754, marquis d'Argenson, *Journal et mémoires*, VIII, 241-242. Voltaire principally lamented France's cultural decline. With obsessive regularity he returned to this theme: the great age of Louis XIV had come to an end. See chapter XXXII of *Le siècle de Louis XIV*, written during his Cirey years. XIV, 539-555.

[56] *Discours sur l'inégalité*, *Oeuvres complètes*, Hachette ed., 13 vols. (1887), I, 137, note i.

[57] Voltaire wrote this sentence in 1769 and was referring to the 1750's, but he had similar views earlier. *Histoire du parlement de Paris*, XVI, 99.

cated, they awakened confidence in human will, hope for man's mastery of his environment, desire for political action. More and more people saw a great gap between the performance of the French government and the needs of the French public; and they believed that they had the means of closing this gap. Voltaire never tired of exhorting the public to action, of berating it for being too modest in its expectations, too timid in its demands, too conservative in its hopes: "I repeat . . . we do not want enough," he wrote at the end of his stay at Cirey.[58]

Men who believe that their wishes can be translated into reality look for a party that will realize their hopes. Voltaire did not hesitate; in France the only possible agent of reform, the only party that the philosophes could support, was the crown: "The cause of the king is the cause of the philosophes."[59] And, if Louis XV could only be made to see it, the cause of the philosophes was the cause of the king: ". . . the philosophic spirit that has penetrated practically all classes of society except the masses has done much to enhance the rights of sovereigns."[60]

This unequivocal support of the French monarchy has often been taken as evidence of Voltaire's supposed doctrinaire predilection for enlightened despotism. In fact, Voltaire's royalism was a modern version of the *thèse royale*, a political position that dates from the fifteenth century, and was popular among administrators and practical politicians in Voltaire's own time. Voltaire's royalism was the result not of detachment from practical affairs and addiction to geometrical speculation, but of involvement in French politics and an intimate knowledge of French history.

For three centuries the kings of France had struggled to subdue a firmly entrenched feudal nobility and an influential clergy.

[58] *Anecdotes sur le czar Pierre le Grand*, xxiii, 288. See also: "Once again, we must want things." *Des embellissements de Paris*, xxiii, 303.

[59] This is the most succinct statement of a lifelong conviction; it is from a letter to d'Alembert, 16 October 1765, xliv, 88.

[60] *Siècle de Louis XIV*, xiv, 538.

Louis XI, "the first absolute king in Europe,"[61] overpowered the Duke of Burgundy, his greatest competitor, in the 1470's; for all his infamous vices he was the first to humiliate the nobility, a policy that "about fifty families deplored and more than five hundred thousand had cause to celebrate."[62] In the first half of the sixteenth century, Francis I created a court of dependent nobles, took over the domains of several feudal houses, and concluded a concordat with Pope Leo X that strengthened the king's hold on the French clergy by giving him the right to nominate the dignitaries of the church—"an essential service to the nation."[63] However, the religious wars of the second half of the century proved that the French monarchy was still far from possessing absolute authority. The allegiance of the nobles to their king was the personal allegiance of a feudal vassal to his lord rather than the political allegiance of a subject to his sovereign. When Henri IV, Voltaire's hero and one of France's most impressive monarchs, liquidated the religious wars in the 1590's, he negotiated with the rebellious aristocrats as if they were his equals.

When Richelieu became chief minister of Louis XIII in 1624, he told his king that "the magnates conduct themselves as if they were not your subjects, and the most powerful provincial governors as if they were sovereign in their offices." He promised that he would do everything in his power to "lower the pride of the magnates, and to reduce all . . . subjects to their duty. . . ."[64] Richelieu kept his promise: he executed seditious nobles without pity and without regard for their high station, severely restricted the parlements' right to remonstrate

[61] *Essai sur les moeurs*, XII, 116.
[62] *ibid.*, XII, 121.
[63] *ibid.*, XII, 327-328. See *Histoire du parlement de Paris*: in this concordat of 1516 "The king and the pope took what did not belong to them, and gave what they could not give; but it remains true that the king, in taking back with this treaty the right to name the bishops and abbots of his kingdom, took back no more than the prerogative of the first kings of France." xv, 486.
[64] Richelieu, *Testament politique*, 93, 95.

against royal edicts, curtailed the autonomy of the provincial estates, increased the power of the intendants. The great noble houses did not dare to challenge Richelieu's work until after his death, and even then the *frondes* failed to restore aristocratic power.

The humiliation of the nobility and the centralization of authority in royal hands seemed complete in the long personal reign of Louis XIV, beginning in 1661 with the death of Mazarin and ending with his own death in 1715. Louis XIV claimed absolute executive, legislative, and judicial authority and demanded unqualified obedience. He justified his claims and his demands by his dedication to public business and by the overriding importance he assigned to *raison d'état*—he was no longer a feudal lord, sharing power with fellow aristocrats, but a modern sovereign, at once the master and the servant of the state.

His pretensions were more than words. Louis XIV enlarged the power and the functions of the intendants, continued Richelieu's attack on the provincial estates, and deprived the parlements of their limited right to remonstrate. To strengthen his hand against the nobles, Louis XIV perfected the dual hierarchy of prestige and power created by Richelieu: he compelled nobles to live at court, where they performed useless if ornamental tasks and lived ruinously expensive lives; he taught them to associate their country homes with "exile"—nothing was more disgraceful than to be deprived of the Sun King's rays, although nothing was more futile than to be basking in their warmth. Toward the end of the century La Bruyère observed that "a nobleman, if he lives at home in his province, lives free but without substance; if he lives at court, he is taken care of, but enslaved."[65] The king first tamed the nobles and then fed them.

From the end of the fifteenth century onward, royalist ideologists justified these actions with the *thèse royale*; they argued

[65] Quoted in Franklin L. Ford, *Robe and Sword*, vii.

that only the undisputed sovereignty of the crown could make France formidable to her enemies, establish internal peace, secure prosperity, lighten the tax burden, and insure justice to all. In his celebrated *Mémoires*, Philippe de Commines defended the ruthless policies of his master, Louis XI, on the ground that the stability essential to France's survival could have been achieved only at the expense of her nobility. Under Francis I, constitutional lawyers turned to Roman law to find principles that denied feudal notions of contract, mutual obligations between lord and vassal, and universal subjection to the law. They argued that the king is the sole source of law, created a new formula of royal assent to legislation designed to underscore his supreme power—*"Car tel est notre bon plaisir"*—and asserted flatly that the King of France is emperor in his kingdom. With the outbreak of the Religious Wars in the 1560's, there emerged a new royalist party, the *politiques*, who pleaded guilty to their opponents' charge that they placed public tranquility above the salvation of their souls. Michel de l'Hôpital, Catherine de Medici's chancellor, whom Voltaire "idolized" as a "true philosopher" and "excellent citizen,"[66] held that the king is free from the law since he is the source of law and that the subject's first duty is obedience. The principle that civic duty is even more important than religious conviction received authoritative statement in the *Six livres de la république* (1576) by Jean Bodin, the greatest of the *politiques*. Public peace, said Bodin, can be guaranteed only by universal obedience to the sovereign prince who is *legibus solutus*.

These royalist rationalizations were freely restated in the seventeenth century, the high point of French absolutism. Shortly before the assassination of Henri IV, the jurist Charles Loyseau set the tone for the royalists in *Des seigneuries* (1608) by criticizing medieval French thinkers for confusing two kinds

---

[66] Voltaire to Hénault, 1 June 1744, *Correspondence*, xiv, 1. See *Essai sur les moeurs*, xii, 501: "that great legislator in a time that lacked laws. . . ."

of power, public and private. Private power is power over property, and belongs to the territorial nobles; public power extends to persons and property, and belongs to the sovereign state. The sovereign makes the laws, appoints officials, declares war, coins money, and acts as the highest court of appeal; his prerogatives carry with them the grave duty of governing in behalf of the people. Servants of the crown like Richelieu, Gallican divines like Bossuet, did little more than elaborate Loyseau's position, and lend it the authority of administrative or theological arguments.[67]

This was the *thèse royale*, which Voltaire adopted early in his career, and for which he found justification upon justification in his historical studies at Cirey. It had never gone unchallenged; indeed, under Louis XIV the opposing *thèse nobiliaire* recruited some of France's most persuasive writers— Fénelon, Saint-Simon, Boulainvilliers—who attacked the *thèse royale* as an elegant version of despotism. They argued that absolutism must result in inefficient and dictatorial government by upstart intendants and ministers, the violation of the traditional rights of the nobility, clergy, towns, and provinces, and an ugly social revolution attractive only to parvenus.

The proponents of the *thèse nobiliaire* relied heavily on history or, rather, pseudohistory: they dramatically pictured a French kingdom founded by the Frankish invaders of Gaul, who had brought with them the practices of constitutional monarchy. In Montesquieu's celebrated phrase, French liberties had come from the German forests.[68] Every spring, the Frankish kings had assembled their noble associates on the *champs de mars* to consult them on legislation, and this salutary practice had developed into the institutions of feudal France. The seigneur's right to administer justice to his vassals was not a

[67] For the limitations the advocates of the *thèse royale* imposed upon absolutism, see chapter VII.
[68] *L'Esprit des lois*, book XI, ch. 6; book XXX, ch. 18; Franz Neumann, "Montesquieu," *The Democratic and the Authoritarian State*, 109.

delegation of royal power but inherent in the noble's position as a landed proprietor: "Fief and jurisdiction are one."[69] In undermining such feudal institutions, hallowed by centuries of practice, Louis XI and his successors were no better than usurpers.

The aristocratic party thus saw its task as a task of restoration. But it was divided. The split between the old nobility of the sword and the new nobility of the robe was reflected in a split in the aristocratic position: true feudal conservatives like Fénelon and Boulainvilliers advocated a return to a powerful estates general; aristocrats in the parlementary camp, like the anonymous author of *Judicium Francorum* (1732), claimed that the parlement of Paris was the true successor of the *champs de mars*.

These divisions in the aristocratic party lost their sharpness in the eighteenth century as robe and sword nobles intermarried and coalesced to fight the common enemy, bureaucratic centralization. But it was the parlements that carried the hopes of the nobility after the Regency. The parlements were high courts of law, divided into several chambers,[70] with trial and appellate jurisdiction over civil and criminal cases, a share in the police power, and a significant, if ill-defined, duty of registering royal edicts. The oldest and politically the most powerful among them was the parlement of Paris, which had been in continuous existence since 1302; eleven other parlements, with smaller areas of jurisdiction, had been created in the fifteenth, sixteenth, and seventeenth centuries.[71] Their political importance arose

[69] Ford, *Robe and Sword*, 241.

[70] The highest court within the parlement was the *grand' chambre*, which was staffed by the highest dignitaries of the parlement and sat as a court of appeals; other courts were *chambres des requêtes*, which were trial courts; *chambres des enquêtes*, which conducted investigations; the *tournelle*, which dealt with certain appeals in criminal cases; and the *chambres des vacations*, which sat during the annual court vacations of September and October. *ibid.*, 46-47.

[71] *ibid.*, 38. The complexity of this system was further complicated by the existence of other courts, like the *chambres des comptes*, the *cours*

from their right of remonstrance and their duty to register laws. Proponents of the *thèse royale* held that this duty was an administrative function and that the right to remonstrate was no more than the right to ask the sovereign, dutifully and obediently, to change his mind on an edict. Edicts had force of law even without parlementary registration. Proponents of the *thèse nobiliaire*, on the other hand, claimed a share in the legislative power for the parlements as the spokesmen and the representatives of the French people. "It is a fundamental law," wrote the author of *Judicium Francorum*, "that nothing can be imposed upon the subjects of the king, and that no officer can be created, no new title can be granted, without the consent of parlement, which represents the general consent of the people. That is the essential form of the French government."[72]

That the *thèse nobiliaire* accurately represented the "essential form of the French government" was more than doubtful; the aristocrats' legal claims were as pretentious as their history was fanciful. But that did not matter—the nobility were seeking to regain political power, and the truth of their argument was less important than its persuasiveness. And in the lengthy reign of Louis XV the nobility, which had lost battle after battle under his predecessors, suddenly threatened to win the war. "It is customary," writes Georges Lefebvre, "to characterize the eighteenth century as the age of the rise of the bourgeoisie and the triumph of 'philosophy,' but the century also witnessed the last offensive of the aristocracy, of which the beginnings of the Revolution were merely the crowning effort."[73]

This last offensive began, with purposeful if undignified haste, on 2 September 1715, the day after Louis XIV died. Louis XIV had slighted the peers and silenced the parlements; the regent induced the parlement of Paris to break the late king's will,

---

des aides, and others, which constantly quarreled with the parlements for precedence and about jurisdiction.

[72] *ibid.,* 93.
[73] *The Coming of the French Revolution,* 15.

and to consent to government by councils in which the representatives of the great families were to wield a power that their ancestors had not wielded for over a century. In return, the regent restored to the parlements their right to remonstrate; the nobility of the sword allied itself with the nobility of the robe in a determined assault on royal absolutism. The alliance was convenient but unstable; the parlements soon rebelled against the regent, and only a few years after this bargain had been concluded, the incompetent peers allowed the leadership of the aristocratic cause to pass into the capable hands of the magistrates.

This restoration, a triumph of class interest over public need, was possible because France's absolute monarchs had only neutralized the power of the nobility, not destroyed it. Nor had they wished to destroy it: Saint-Simon's lamentation that Louis XIV hated the aristocracy is a characteristic overstatement. Like his predecessors, Louis XIV was too fond of pomp, too enamored of rank, too conscious of precedence to deprive the nobility of its privileged status. He confined himself to reducing its usefulness; he rendered it unemployed and, as the reign of Louis XV was to show, largely unemployable, but he was unwilling to tamper with its prerogatives. The aristocracy retained its tax exemptions, its privilege to be tried by its peers, its right to certain offices and to precedence.

The new nobility, the nobility of the robe, was as invulnerable as the old. Again, Louis XIV could muzzle, but not destroy it. Secure in their posts through the venality of offices, the ennobled magistrates could have been removed only by an administrative or financial revolution too drastic even for a ruler with the Sun King's energy.

The French monarchy had introduced a primitive form of venality in the thirteenth and fourteenth centuries as a device for raising money; the practice was decried and expanded by every French king. Indeed, it was the great Henri IV who, in an edict of 1604, confirmed the principle that offices could be inherited. In French law, a venal office—a judgeship, administrative post, army commission—was the property of its holder. He could trade it, sell it, borrow money on it, dispose of it in his will. A venal office was like a chattel, but superior to it in one respect: certain offices, such as all higher parlementary posts, conferred noble status, and this status was handed down from father to son. Even the kings and ministers who exploited venality admitted that it had a deleterious effect on public administration. Ineffectual functionaries could not be fired, officials who resisted royal orders could be dismissed only with difficulty, kings in need of money multiplied useless offices, thus increasing confusion, delays, and squabbles over precedence.

Venality constantly furnished new recruits to the nobility, an unwelcome blessing for the old families. The magnates relished the restrictions imposed on the monarchy by an irremovable magistracy, but they deplored the accession of newcomers to noble status as a dilution of aristocracy and a subversion of the social order. *Des gens de fort peu*, as Saint-Simon called them, associated themselves with the old aristocracy by purchasing the right to bear a title, to carry a sword, to flaunt a coat of arms, to enjoy legal and fiscal privileges. Venality, said Saint-Simon, speaking for all the aristocratic critics of Louis XIV, was a "gangrene that has been corroding all orders and classes in the state for a long time."[74]

Saint-Simon was both right and wrong. Venality made good administration impossible and undermined the exclusive status of the old families. But social circulation did not result in a social revolution: the new nobility took over not only the power but also the style of life of the old nobility. The ennobled magistrates offered implacable resistance to social change, and energetically defended feudal habits and institutions. Many of the robe nobles were able and tenacious; having recently ascended to new dignities, they were anxious to forget—and to make others forget—their undistinguished middle-class past, the

---

[74] Quoted in Sée, *Les idées politiques en France au* xviie *siècle*, 260.

ancestor "in trade," the unpretentious family home in the bourgeois neighborhood. Social anxieties made the robe nobility more conservative, more stubbornly caste-conscious, more punctilious than many an aristocrat who could trace his ancestry to Saint Louis.

Venality and the privileges associated with it thus represented an immense investment in feudalism and a gigantic obstacle to reform. That it was an abuse was recognized by all but the most partisan advocates of the *thèse nobiliaire*, but that it must be abolished was admitted by few. Venality had created such powerful vested interests that to attack it seemed to attack the heart of the French constitution.[75] Only subversive philosophes could be so disrespectful.

During the Regency, when Voltaire first became interested in French politics and French history, the debate between the royal and aristocratic parties was raging with full force, although the decisive battles between king and parlements did not break out until the 1750's, after Voltaire had left Cirey.[76] But these political squabbles, or the continuous squabbles between king and clergy, barely penetrated into the worldly circles in which Voltaire moved during these years. There was less talk of parlements than of pleasure, and Voltaire was making epigrams and a reputation. But his first play, *Oedipe*, displays rudimentary ideas about politics, and *La ligue* of 1723 and later versions of the *Henriade*, mark an important step in Voltaire's political development: his epic poem has a distinctly royalist orienta-

---

[75] "The vested interests created by venality were enormous. They naturally sought protection for their investments. A strong monarchy must, of necessity, appear to them the greatest danger. Support for this investment could come only from groups and theories that made the king subject to effective controls by the privileged. A new theory of feudalism corresponded to the growing process of infeudation." Franz Neumann, "Montesquieu," *The Democratic and the Authoritarian State*, 107-108.

[76] For these battles, and for Voltaire's royalist position in the 1760's and his position on venality, see below, chapter VII.

tion.[77] In Voltaire's version of Henri IV's career an undivided and unchallenged sovereignty is sketched in glowing colors. Horatio Walpole recommended the *Henriade* to Bubb Dodington for its "bold strokes . . . against persecution and the priests,"[78] while others denounced it for spreading sedition and impiety. But the *Henriade* is more than the expression of impious spleen: it warns against the danger of a powerful corps within a state, especially a powerful church, rather than the danger of religion itself. Voltaire's choice of Henri IV as the hero for his epic is not an accident; he tells the reader that Henri's victory over the Catholic League strengthened the monarchy in France and restored public order.[79] Voltaire's analysis of the Religious Wars is far too mechanical and tendentious to do justice to the complexities of French politics in the sixteenth century, but Voltaire was less interested in political complexities than in presenting a spotless hero, an idealized Henri of Navarre, at war with melodramatic villains, a priest-ridden League.[80] As Voltaire described it, the Papacy drove the League into action, brought war, sedition, and regicide; Henri strove for order, stability, and mercy. Voltaire has Henri exclaim:

> Et périsse à jamais l'affreuse politique
> Qui prétend sur les coeurs un pouvoir despotique,
> Qui veut, le fer en main, convertir les mortels,
> Qui du sang hérétique arrose les autels,

[77] We know from Voltaire himself that he conceived the poem in 1716, as a result of conversations with the marquis de Caumartin, a high official under Louis XIV, "the one man in France who knew the most anecdotes about the life of Henri IV," and whose royalist views doubtless helped to shape Voltaire's. See Besterman's note, *Correspondence*, I, 77-78; Voltaire to *Journal des savants* (ca. 15 February 1742), *ibid.*, XII, 15-16.

[78] 29 May 1726, *ibid.*, II, 28. For a virulent anti-*Henriade* diatribe, see the long anonymous letter (ca. May 1731), *ibid.*, II, 179-196.

[79] There were of course other reasons. In *Siècle de Louis XIV* Voltaire reports that the abbé Dubos believed that Henri IV was the only subject worthy of an epic in the whole of French history; Dubos' observation was published ca. 1714. See XIV, 553.

[80] In *Essai sur les moeurs* he attributed the Religious Wars to "religion, ambition, lack of good laws, bad government." XII, 498.

Et, suivant un faux zèle, ou l'intérêt, pour guides,
Ne sert un Dieu de paix que par des homicides![81]

Such a policy of violence is the bitter fruit of sectarianism; a
strong monarch like Henri looks beyond sects to the welfare of
all his people. Henri, in fact, is a *politique*, and acts in the poem
as the chancellor de l'Hôpital might have acted:

Il sait dans toute secte honorer les vertus,
Respecter votre culte, et même vos abus.

. . . . . .

Comme un roi, comme un père, il vient vous gouverner;
Et, plus chrétien que vous, il vient vous pardonner.[82]

There is little in the *Henriade* that deserves the name of political theory; it is humanitarian propaganda in the guise of a
historical poem. But it shows Voltaire taking sides among con-
tending parties in French politics, dramatizing the royal cause
and belittling its opponents.

In the *Histoire de Charles XII*, which appeared eight years
after *La ligue*, Voltaire dramatized a similar cause and belittled
similar opponents. Much has been written about Voltaire's
histories, but little has been said about their part in his political education. As Voltaire collected material—reading memoirs, biographies, documents, chronicles, listening to reminiscences, consulting experts[83]—he became aware of a contest for
power in every country in Europe: the struggle of the state,
whatever its form, to subdue potent domestic rivals. And in this
struggle, which was a struggle for public order, the nobility, seeking to retain its feudal privileges, was the enemy of progress
and stability. Sweden had been dominated by the bishops, "who
owned almost all the wealth" of the country, "and used it to

[81] VIII, 67.   [82] VIII, 154.

[83] Like the *Henriade*, the *Histoire de Charles XII* resulted from numerous
interviews and correspondence with statesmen. Much of the immediacy of
Voltaire's portrayals in his historical works can be traced back to his indefatigable search for reliable eye-witness reports.

oppress the subjects and to war on the kings." Their tyranny was overthrown by Gustavus Vasa (1523-1560), who governed "happy and absolute," but his absolutism was distorted into a despotic caricature by Charles XI, who abolished the authority of the Senate, and "reduced his subjects' feelings for him to fear."[84] Thus in his very first historical work, Voltaire took care to differentiate absolutism from despotism; he used Peter the Great of Russia as the example of a ruler who combined the virtues of the first with the vices of the second. Still, while despotism was a calamity, the anarchy created by a powerful nobility was an even greater calamity. Witness Poland: the "proud and lazy" Polish nobility elects its kings and plots against them; it "often sells its votes and rarely its affections." Its predominance has made orderly government impossible and has reduced the Polish people to dismal servitude: "The nobility and the clergy defend their liberty against their king, and take it away from the rest of the nation. The people there are all slaves."[85]

It was not without significance that Voltaire wrote his biography of a Swedish king while he was among Englishmen, observing the institutions of a people who "obeys to the laws only." It taught him that the task of establishing public order out of "feudal anarchy" was the same all over the civilized world, but that different traditions, cultures, and historical circumstances imposed different solutions for the same problem. The Swedes had needed to liberate themselves from their ecclesiastical nobility, just as the English and French had needed to liberate themselves from their military nobility, and each nation had solved the problem in a manner suitable to its condition. "The authority of these small brigands," Voltaire wrote in the *Lettres philosophiques*, "was extinguished in France by the legitimate power of our kings, and in England by the legitimate power of kings and people."[86] This is not what Emile

---

[84] *Histoire de Charles XII*, xvi, 148, 150.
[85] *ibid.*, xvi, 181.   [86] "ixe Lettre," i, 104.

Faguet has called Voltaire's "chaos of clear ideas"—Voltaire's shifting support of monarchies and republics, absolutism and constitutionalism reflects, rather, his historical understanding of the variety of political traditions.

But in France, Voltaire was an unswerving royalist, and in the 1730's and early 1740's, this position had wide support. The king and the king's cause were genuinely popular. France was prosperous and at peace, the government imposed no new taxes, Louis XV was still young and had not yet had time to disappoint his partisans. The king was *le bien-aimé*; the public expected great things from him. When he fell dangerously ill at Metz in 1744, public alarm was profound; when he recovered, public relief was immense. Madame de Châteauroux, his mistress, reports that the enthusiasm of the Parisians upon his return was beyond description.[87]

The prosperity of the royal cause in this decade and a half was reflected by two authoritative restatements of the *thèse royale*; Voltaire studied them with intense interest in his Cirey retreat, and liberally borrowed from them for the histories he was then composing. In 1734, the abbé Dubos, whose writings Voltaire greatly admired, published an exhaustive refutation of the aristocratic version of the French past, the *Histoire critique de l'établissement de la monarchie française*. Dubos showed that the history upon which the parlements based their claims to a share in the legislative power was largely imaginary: the Frankish kings had not conquered the Gauls but had served with them in the Roman empire—they were the heirs, not the enemies, of the Roman emperors; the *champs de mars* had not been a legislative assembly to which the parlements succeeded, but a spring rally of troops; if any part of French history de-

[87] In his journal, Barbier is somewhat more restrained but he does report that upon the news of the king's illness, "Paris was put into an alarm and consternation that can't be expressed, and that holds true of all classes: upper, lower, and the masses (*grands, petits et peuple*)." August 1744, *Journal*, II, 402.

served to be stigmatized as a usurpation, it was feudalism and not absolutism. Voltaire was delighted with this interpretation and echoed it in his *Essai sur les moeurs* and his other excursions into medieval French history. He characterized feudalism as a form of anarchy, destructive of urban life, commerce, the arts and sciences; Boulainvilliers' claim that the French nobles are the descendants of Frankish conquerors is unprovable and, in any event, irrelevant to contemporary politics. In the age of Saint Louis, "Kings were the chiefs of vassals who were disunited among themselves and frequently united against the throne." These vassals' "usurpations became respectable rights."[88] There was no reason why eighteenth-century Frenchmen should obey such usurpers.

Dubos's book was authoritative and successful, and it impressed Voltaire.[89] The marquis d'Argenson's *Considérations sur le gouvernement ancien et présent de la France*, which Voltaire read in manuscript in 1739, impressed him even more. His instincts were sound: the *Considérations* is the most powerful, the most economical, and the most radical statement of the *thèse royale* in the eighteenth century. It was received at Cirey with effusive joy.[90]

Voltaire was never a severe critic of his friends' work, and

[88] *Panégyrique de Saint Louis*, XXIII, 316; see *Essai sur les moeurs*, XII, 115-141; and: "In France the kings of the first race gave out all the benefices [i.e., fiefs]"—a royalist statement denying the aristocratic contention that jurisdiction came with the land. *Notebooks*, 124.

[89] Voltaire to Dubos, 30 October 1738, in which he thanks Dubos for having "ably disentangled the chaos of the origins of the French," and pays him the subtle compliment of asking him for help with the *Siècle de Louis XIV*. *Correspondence*, VII, 424-427. That Voltaire consulted Dubos's work on French history is revealed in a notebook entry, *Notebooks*, 332. Ford reports (*Robe and Sword*, 232), that Dubos's book went into five editions in eight years.

[90] In view of their irreconcilable divergences of temperament and opinions, it is remarkable that Voltaire and Rousseau agreed on one thing: the virtues of d'Argenson. In his *Contrat social*, published two years before the *Considérations* was printed, Rousseau quotes the manuscript several times and praises d'Argenson as a "good and illustrious man . . . a good citizen." Book IV, chapter 8.

when his friend was influential he was even more inclined to praise than to censure. The marquis d'Argenson, like many another of Voltaire's schoolmates at Louis-le-Grand, was of an ancient family with a long tradition of public service. His father had held a number of distinguished posts; he had been *lieutenant de police* under Louis XIV and *garde des sceaux* in the Regency. It was as *garde des sceaux* that the elder d'Argenson had faced the defiant parlement of Paris in 1718 with an emphatic definition of the *thèse royale*: the king's sole authority to establish new laws as well as to maintain the old.[91] The marquis' younger brother, the comte d'Argenson, had a brilliant career under Louis XV, rising to minister of war in 1743; the marquis himself, ambitious, jealous, sarcastic, and as brusque as his younger brother was charming, advanced more slowly. When he completed the *Considérations*, his reach for office still exceeded his grasp; he did not become foreign minister until late in 1744, and was curtly dismissed two years later. But even in the 1730's, bitterly impatient for office, the marquis d'Argenson was not a man to neglect, and Voltaire did not neglect him.

On 8 May 1739 Voltaire acknowledged d'Argenson's manuscript with an ecstatic but sincere letter from Cirey: "I find all my ideas in your work."[92] In the following month he complimented d'Argenson for being a realist whose political program compared most favorably with the woolly-minded Utopianism of the abbé de Saint-Pierre and of Fénelon. This praise was not mere Voltairian politeness—Voltaire's remarks are much too detailed to be routine flattery. Moreover, d'Argenson's manuscript strengthened opinions Voltaire had already formed. Like d'Argenson, Voltaire deplored venality: "I thank you for the fine things you say about the venality of charges, unhappy invention that has relieved citizens of [the spur of] emulation, and deprived kings of the finest prerogative of the throne." Like d'Argenson, Voltaire refused to sentimentalize medieval history:

[91] Ford, *Robe and Sword*, 229.
[92] *Correspondence*, IX, 128.

"I can congratulate myself for always having thought that feudal government is a government of barbarians and savages in comfortable circumstances." Like d'Argenson, Voltaire rejected Boulainvilliers' Germanic interpretation of French history: "How can you have the courage, you who belong to as ancient a house as M. de Boulainvilliers, to declare yourself so generously against him and his fiefs?"[93]

Voltaire found d'Argenson's political stance—hardheaded, utilitarian, reformist—profoundly congenial. As a true philosophe and a firm secularist, d'Argenson was convinced that man can know his social environment and has the power to control it. There is a science of politics, an empirical discipline that the statesman can use to transform institutions, bringing them "to the highest degree of perfection of which they are capable."[94] D'Argenson admitted that "other sciences have been deeply investigated; political science is in its infancy," but this lag must be blamed not on the discipline itself but on the conservative reluctance of savants and statesmen to reflect upon and to use the laws of politics.[95]

Such resistance to political science, which is really resistance to reform, can be overcome only by political power. In d'Argenson's thought the good state is a machine for the manufacturing of social justice, and that machine can function only if royal

[93] 21 June (1739), *ibid.*, IX, 171-173. Voltaire paid d'Argenson the sincere compliment of lifting some of his statements for the political pamphlets of the 1750's, especially *La voix du sage et du peuple* and *Pensées sur le gouvernement*. For Boulainvilliers, see Voltaire's *Siècle de Louis XIV*: Boulainvilliers was a learned historian, but "too systematic." His praise of feudalism is misguided—it was not a "masterpiece of human intelligence" but a "masterpiece of anarchy." His "profound and useful" works must thus be read with caution. XIV, 45.

[94] *Considérations*, 11-12. I am citing from the edition of 1765, which appears to be very similar to, if not identical with, the manuscript that Voltaire read.

[95] *ibid.*, 13. This idea of a conspiracy of the learned—not just priests but lawyers and philosophers as well—to prevent the spreading of knowledge is a pervasive theme in Enlightenment polemics that deserves further study. It appears prominently in Condorcet's *Tableau des progrès de l'esprit humain*.

authority is undisputed, if the pretensions of "intermediate powers," whether of great nobles or of parlements, are decisively rejected. D'Argenson attacked these pretensions on historical and practical grounds: "Feudal law is in all respects merely a usurpation upon royalty"; the "bizarre system," so extravagantly praised by Boulainvilliers, rested not on ancient right but simply on the right of the strongest. "Is that a good claim?"[96] It was not, partly because the French nobility had proved time and again its incapacity to govern. Feudal France had tended toward political disorder, contempt of hard-working commoners, and disregard of the public interest. If strong French kings had not gradually destroyed the aristocracy, France would probably have fallen into irreparable anarchy.[97]

Like most advocates of strong monarchy, d'Argenson was at pains to show that absolutism was not identical with despotism. The purpose of the *Considérations*, he said in the preface, was to overcome the common prejudice that "the glory and power of royal authority reside in the servile dependence of the subjects."[98] The contrary is true: "Liberty is the support of the throne, order renders liberty legitimate."[99] Paradoxical as it might sound, democracy is as much the ally of monarchy as aristocracy is its enemy,[100] and it is only long-standing prejudices that have prevented Frenchmen from recognizing the truth in Racine's couplet:

> Que dans le cours d'un règne florissant,
> Rome soit toujours libre, et César tout-puissant.[101]

In despotism, a single ruler confounds his passions with the public good; in a true monarchy, royal authority is "balanced, but not shared."[102] The despot admits no higher law; the legiti-

---

[96] *ibid.*, 78-80.   [97] *ibid.*, 4, 36, 74.
[98] *ibid.*, 1.   [99] *ibid.*, 199.   [100] See *ibid.*, 119.
[101] This couplet headed the manuscript of the *Considérations*, but is not included in the edition I am citing here. It is from *Britannicus*. See Rathéry's "Introduction," *Journal et mémoires du marquis d'Argenson*, i, xl.
[102] *Considérations*, 79.

mate sovereign recognizes that his power comes from "a contract between king and people" which demands the observance of "fundamental laws." A despot rewards and punishes arbitrarily; in a legitimate monarchy, the rule of law prevails, and subjects "obey only the laws and not men."[103]

D'Argenson admitted that even legitimate monarchies are subject to the vice of excessive centralization; it was to prevent this vice, to establish "a true democracy . . . in the midst of a monarchy,"[104] that d'Argenson proposed a bold program of a decentralized popular absolutism. His projected political organization gave no part to the aristocracy, excluded the parlements from all administrative, fiscal, and legislative matters, simplified and redistributed taxes, and extirpated venality, the strongest prop of the robe nobility.[105] D'Argenson suggested that powerful local magistrates represent their semiautonomous communities in the central government, levy taxes, supervise public works, establish local industry; and that superior officials, with longer terms and larger areas of jurisdiction, hold the aristocrats in check by telling them, "The magistrates are acting in everything in the name of the king, from whom all public power emanates."[106]

Utopian as it sounded, d'Argenson considered his plan feasible and indeed essential. He knew that he was proposing a social revolution, that the nobility and the magistrates would fight to the death a program that reduced their social and eliminated their political power. "People will say that the principles of the present treatise, favorable to democracy, tend to the

---

[103] *ibid.*, 78, 191.

[104] *ibid.*, 17.

[105] Venality, wrote d'Argenson, is a "miserable invention which has produced all the evils that must be redressed today . . . it has prevented the happy progress of democracy . . . it has destroyed in France all idea of popular government. . . . With it the king has alienated forever the finest of his prerogatives, which is the choice of his officials . . . the venality of charges has the lowest of all motives, which are avarice, money, and cupidity." *ibid.*, 98-100.

[106] *ibid.*, 158.

destruction of the nobility, and they will not be mistaken. But that is not an objection: it is a confirmation of our conclusions."[107] The state of France was desperate, and the survivals of feudal government made it more desperate year after year. Revolution was painful, but chaos was yet more painful. "France demands," he noted passionately and privately in 1739, "that we pull it out, not from under its kings, God forbid! but from under an odious aristocracy. . . ."[108] No wonder Voltaire marveled at this aristocrat's self-denial! No wonder the *Considérations* could circulate only clandestinely in d'Argenson's lifetime!

It is not possible to say how much of this revolutionary program Voltaire was prepared to accept. Evidently he did not fully understand d'Argenson's administrative proposals for decentralizing the French government.[109] But on the major political issue—the imperative need to curb the political power of aristocracy and clergy for the sake of good government—d'Argenson and Voltaire were at one.[110]

[107] *ibid.*, 193. Nobility would not be abolished, and an "absolute and Platonic equality" was impossible; still, the good society would strive toward equality. *ibid.*, 196.

[108] Rathéry, "Introduction," xxxix.

[109] Voltaire paid d'Argenson's plan the highest compliment he had: "Is England not living testimony to the wisdom of your ideas?"—a compliment that d'Argenson, no Anglomaniac, must have received rather wryly. In England, wrote Voltaire, "The king with his parliament is legislator, as he is here with his *conseil*. All the rest of the nation governs itself according to municipal laws, as sacred as those of parliament itself. The love of the law has become a passion with the people, for everyone is interested in the observance of the law. All highways are repaired, poorhouses are founded and maintained, commerce flourishes, and no order from the *conseil* is necessary." 8 May 1739, *Correspondence*, IX, 128-129. Voltaire was right: the English parliament took only scant interest in local government, but he overlooked d'Argenson's explicit rejection of the English system for its division of public power. See *Considérations*, 15.

It is hard to categorize d'Argenson's political thought; Jean Lamson's attempt to make it "enlightened despotism" (*Les idées politiques du Marquis d'Argenson*, 72ff) and to liken it to the regimes of Catherine II, Frederick the Great, Joseph II, is unsuccessful. We need only consider the divergent attitudes of d'Argenson and Frederick on the nobility to see that their ideals of government were far from identical.

[110] In the later part of his Cirey period, Voltaire also read Charles Hé-

Voltaire showed his agreement with Dubos and d'Argenson most strikingly in *Le siècle de Louis XIV*, which he began before he had completed his book on England, and on which he continued to work through the years at Cirey. In that great history, Voltaire emphasized that "if a state is to be powerful, either the people must enjoy a liberty based on its laws, or the sovereign power must be affirmed without contradiction."[111] The institutions of Englishmen could serve as standards to other states, but not as models; what was appropriate to one country might not be appropriate to another. Frenchmen had good reason to admire the English constitution, but they need not imitate it.[112] Men's loyalties, and the direction of politi-

---

nault's *Nouvel abrégé chronologique de l'histoire de France*, published in May 1744. Hénault was a *président à mortier* in the parlement of Paris, whose high position, great wealth, and celebrated wit made him one of the most distinguished robe nobles in France. He was an old friend of Voltaire's and, for a long time, the lover of madame du Deffand. Although a parlementarian, he was a moderate, full of admiration for powerful kings, critical of the *thèse nobiliaire*, fearful of parlementary intransigeance. He urged his colleagues to use their right of remonstrance with caution, and to obey the king once he had made his decision. Voltaire professed to esteem Hénault's book as a "masterpiece of wit and reason." He cannot have been sincere: the *Nouvel abrégé* is a tedious work of reference, filled with charts, dates, names, anecdotes, easy to consult and hard to read. But Voltaire certainly used it, and took of its opinions those he agreed with. "What you say of Louis XII, Henri IV, Louis XIII, Louis XIV, should be learned by heart." Voltaire to Hénault, 1 June 1744, *Correspondence*, XIV, 1. For all their differences, both men were antifeudal. In denouncing the multiplicity and contradictions of French laws, Voltaire wrote to Hénault on 26 August (1752): "These contradictions are the consequences of the feudal government, which you don't like any better than I do." *ibid.*, XXI, 47.

[111] *Siècle de Louis XIV*, XIV, 157.

[112] See Voltaire's letter to the Jacobite journalist Richard Rolt of 1 August 1750 (in English): "You are certainly in the right, when you assert the privileges of mankind. T'is yr duty to love and to praise the form of the british governement but do not believe we blame it in France. The situation of our country, the genius of our nation, and many other reasons have submitted us to monarchik power mitigated by the amiable mildness of our manners rather than by our laws. All wise men amongst us live happy under such a government, and admire that of great Britain." *Correspondence*, XVIII, 108. And this notebook entry: "Politics. The poor folks who maintain that we should govern ourselves in Paris as at Lacedaemonia and that the same laws are equally good for us voluptuous Parisians and for the Dutch." *Notebooks*, 132.

cal reform, are relative to unique historical situations.[113]

In France, a subject's first loyalty is to the crown. This commitment, not as servile as it sounds, was Voltaire's conclusion on French history and politics. In his youth, his royalism was little more than an emotional rejection of the nobility's and clergy's pretensions to political power; with the *Henriade* and the accompanying *Essay upon the Civil Wars in France* (1727), Voltaire tested his opinion on the late sixteenth century; in the researches at Cirey that grew into his two historical masterpieces, he generalized his royalist position to apply to French history as a whole. The *Siècle de Louis XIV* and the *Essai sur les moeurs* are pioneering ventures. For all their faults of perspective, their tendentious anticlericalism, their neglect of economics, these two histories are among the first to break away from the sectarian preoccupations of Christian historians and to treat civilizations as units of study, understanding, and appraisal. And they are something more: they are detailed statements of the *thèse royale*.

The *Siècle de Louis XIV* is generally considered a panegyric to a despot, uncritical, adulatory, courtier-like.[114] But Voltaire is no more indulgent to Louis XIV than is, say, Lord Acton; his praise is often hedged by serious reservations. Moreover, Voltaire's admiration of Louis XIV should be read as a political preference for the king over his opponents, a reasoned and reasonable judgment that with all its dangers a strong monarchy

---

[113] See his poem, *Stances à M. van Haren* (1743):

Notre esprit est conforme aux lieux qui l'ont vu naître.
A Rome, on est esclave, à Londres, citoyen.
La grandeur d'un Batave est de vivre sans maître;
Et mon premier devoir est de servir le mien.

VIII, 514.

[114] A representative view is that of Alfred Cobban in *Rousseau and the Modern State*, who speaks (p. 49) of Voltaire's "hero worship of Louis XIV." Ironically, Hénault, Voltaire's friend and himself a French historian, complained that the *Siècle* was too harsh, too ironical with Louis XIV. See Voltaire to Hénault, 28 January (1752), *Correspondence*, xx, 190-191.

is preferable to a strong nobility.[115] In Voltaire's reading of French history, church and aristocracy had again and again thrown France into turmoil. In the Fronde "An archbishop and a parlement of Paris, two authorities established among men with the sole object of maintaining peace, began the disturbances. . . ."[116] Under Louis XIV the court and the ministers looked upon the parlements as judicial bodies, dependent for their authority upon the crown; the lawyers and citizens of Paris looked upon the parlements as defenders of popular rights, with legal authority akin to that of the English parliament. Voltaire accepted the royalist and rejected the parlementary interpretation of the French constitution, but he was willing to concede that the legal position was not clear: "After all, there was no recognized law other than that of opportunity and time. Parlement was nothing under a vigorous government; it was everything under a feeble king. . . ."[117] All the more reason for kings not to be feeble with their rebellious magistrates. "Supreme authority, which may be abused, is dangerous; but a divided authority is even more so."[118]

Voltaire conceded that public opinion inclined to the parlements, and that the parlements could have contributed to good government. But the magistrates, proud and stubborn, had wasted their opportunity to make their right of remonstrance a part of the French constitution: "Nearly all citizens were con-

[115] See this notebook entry: "France a poor thing up to Louis XIV. Kings without power before Louis XI. Charles VIII and Louis XII unlucky conquerors. Francis I beaten, civil wars up to Henri IV, under Louis XIII feebleness and factions." *Notebooks*, 110.

[116] *Siècle de Louis XIV*, xiv, 188.

[117] *loc. cit.* In the notebook jotting that served as the basis for this passage, Voltaire's partisanship is more explicit: "The people regarded the parlement of Paris as a corps as old as the monarchy, made to serve as a screen between the king and his subjects, tutor of kings, father of the people etc. (The court?) regarded it as a tribunal of justice, and nothing more. The truth is that the authority and the functions of this corps have never been well regulated, that it was powerful only under feeble ministers. It is ridiculous to say that it represents the nation. The very word 'parlement' makes up part of its power. . . ." *Notebooks*, 94.

[118] *Siècle de Louis XIV*, xiv, 481.

vinced that if parlement, knowing the causes of the misfortunes and the needs of the people, had confined itself to bringing to the sovereign's attention the dangers of taxation and the even greater danger of such taxes being sold to tax farmers who deceived the king and oppressed the people, this practice of making remonstrances would have become a sacred resource of the state, a check on the rapacity of financiers, and a continuous lesson to the ministers. But the strange abuses of such a salutary remedy had so irritated Louis XIV that he saw only the abuses and outlawed the remedy."[119]

The French clergy was as irritating as the magistracy. With its dependence on Rome, its position as a separate estate, its wealth in land and rents, and its spiritual influence, the church was a corporation whose power often became dangerous to public order; Louis XIV needed all his tact and all his impressive authority to keep it within proper bounds. Voltaire described the anti-Papal Gallican declaration of 1682 and the revocation of the Edict of Nantes in 1685 as the two extremes of Louis's religious policies—absolutism at its best and at its worst.

The absolute rule of Louis XIV had its dark side. Since Voltaire's justification of French absolutism was pragmatic rather than doctrinaire, he had no hesitation in criticizing le roi soleil for his excesses and his crimes. Voltaire argued that at his best Louis XIV had used his unprecedented power wisely, humanely, and (what was perhaps even more important to Voltaire) with good taste. His program of public works had created employment and beautified cities; his sponsorship of arts and letters had contributed to a renaissance in literature and encouraged rational thinking; his administrative regulations had improved public administration, reformed the law code, disciplined the army, built a navy, and ended the spirit of faction: "The state became a perfect whole with all lines leading to the center."[120]

Such unremitting and zealous activity in behalf of his people deserved the gratitude of posterity, but Voltaire admitted that his own gratitude was dimmed by Louis's numberless failures. The king's achievements "fell far short of what he might have done"; measured against his opportunities, his accomplishments became less impressive.[121] In his later years, in the 1680's, the king became more haughty, more intolerant, and more arbitrary. It was in these years that Louis XIV abandoned his half-completed administrative reforms, revoked the Edict of Nantes —"one of the greatest calamities" in French history[122]—and conducted a series of imperialistic and fruitless wars that impoverished the French countryside and ruined prosperous, pacific neighbors. Voltaire sarcastically described Louis's first invasion of the Palatinate in 1675 as a "glorious campaign" that anyone with "more humanity than reverence for warlike acts" must deplore.[123] The second invasion of 1689, which devastated this lovely country, "struck Europe with horror." Voltaire made Louis himself responsible for the atrocities: "If the king had witnessed this spectacle, he would have put out the flames himself. He signed the destruction of an entire country in his palace at Versailles, in the midst of pleasures, because he saw in that order nothing but his power and the unfortunate law of war; but had he been there, he would have seen nothing but its horror."[124] In the 1690's there was famine in France as a result of the king's search for glory: "People were dying of starvation with *Te Deums* ringing in their ears."[125] The greatest good any monarch can do, wrote Voltaire, was to bring peace; Louis XIV had signally failed to do this greatest good.[126]

[121] *ibid.*, xiv, 513. See the criticism that Voltaire puts in the mouth of a Roman citizen addressing his country's officials: "O you, who take pride in being good, why do you not do all the good you can do?" *Ce qu'on ne fait pas et ce qu'on pourrait faire* (1742), xxiii, 184. For similar criticisms of Louis XIV, see *Notebooks*, 98, 108.

[122] *Siècle de Louis XIV*, xv, 28.

[123] *ibid.*, xiv, 268.   [124] *ibid.*, xiv, 309.   [125] *ibid.*, xiv, 317.

[126] Voltaire's elaborate comparison of Louis XIV and William III is too little known: "Those who esteem more highly the merit of defending his country, and the success of acquiring a kingdom without any natural right,

Voltaire's judgment of Louis XIV is thus anything but simple. "The age of Louis XIV"—one of the world's four great ages—was larger than the man for whom it was named, and larger indeed than France. It included Christian Europe, now one "great republic"; it included the achievements of princes whom Louis XIV fought, of artists whom he did not subsidize, and of philosophers to whom he was indifferent. Voltaire's history of this age was, of course, far more than a political document; it was, above all, history, and brilliant history. But behind that history stood a political position and, implicitly, a political program.

Voltaire was unfortunate: in 1751, the year of its publication, the position of the *Siècle de Louis XIV* was unpopular and its program unattainable. Voltaire was in Prussia, discredited, even among some of his admirers, for his "desertion" of France. Louis XV was embroiled with his rebellious clergy, demonstrating to his most uncritical supporters that he was ill-prepared to sustain the royal eminence so painfully built up by his predecessors. In 1751, Voltaire's approval of an energetic Louis XIV

---

of maintaining himself there without being loved, of governing Holland in sovereign fashion without subjugating it, of being the soul and the leader of half of Europe, of having the resources of a general and the courage of a soldier, of never persecuting anyone for his religion, of despising all of men's superstitions, of being simple and modest in his manners—such persons will doubtless give the name 'great' to William rather than to Louis. But those who are more impressed by the pleasures and the *éclat* of a brilliant court, by magnificence, by patronage of the arts, zeal for public welfare, passion for glory, and a gift for ruling; those who are more struck by that haughtiness with which ministers and generals annexed provinces to France, on orders of their king; who are more astonished at seeing a single state resist so many powers; those who esteem a king of France who can give Spain to his grandson rather than a son-in-law who dethrones his father-in-law; in a word, those who admire the protector rather than the persecutor of king James, will give the preference to Louis XIV." *ibid.,* XIV, 343.
And this notebook entry: "The idolatry for Louis was at such a point that a man who would have spoken of liberty would have seemed more ridiculous than all the personages in Molière." *Notebooks,* 96. Still, Voltaire conceded that "with all his faults he was a great king." Voltaire to madame du Deffand, 23 September 1752, *Correspondence,* XXI, 74.

sounded suspiciously like criticism of his inadequate successor; the bourgeois poet was more royalist than his king.

Louis XV did much to make the *thèse royale* unpopular; Montesquieu's *Esprit des lois,* published while Voltaire was finishing the *Siècle de Louis XIV,* did more: it gave the *thèse nobiliaire* its most brilliant restatement. Montesquieu's long, ill-organized masterpiece has been many things to many scholars: a pioneering work in political sociology, a penetrating analysis of the relation of liberty to authority, a reasoned plea for a humane legal system. But to its contemporary readers, *L'Esprit des lois* was also, or perhaps mainly, a powerful defense of the aristocratic interpretation of French politics. Despite his assertion that he was seeking a true balance between the royalist and aristocratic positions, Montesquieu, himself a member of a robe family and former *président à mortier* of a provincial *parlement,* adopted the aristocracy's historical and political views with few modifications. France's constitution, he wrote, was of Germanic origin; the holders of fiefs had jurisdiction over their vassals; in monarchies, venality of office and laws penalizing nobles for entering bourgeois trades are reasonable; judges are the proper depositaries of the laws; intermediate powers are essential to prevent despotism; of all intermediate groups, the nobility is the most useful: "No monarch, no nobility; no nobility, no monarch."[127]

One reason for the immense success of Montesquieu's book was that it was more than a partisan document. This conservative jurist was also a philosophe; perhaps, as Voltaire acknowledged, one of the most brilliant of philosophes. His defense of liberty rose above an ideological defense of the nobility's prerogatives; he was detached enough to criticize the selfishness and ignorance of his peers; in book XII he laid down rules for the treatment of accused persons that earned it the title "The Magna

---

[127] For the *thèse nobiliaire* in *L'Esprit des lois,* see above all, book II, chapter 4; book V, chapters 9, 19; book VIII, chapter 9; book XI, chapter 6; book XIII, chapter 20; book XXX, passim.

Carta of the criminals"; he excoriated imperialism, exploitation, religious intolerance. To embattled nobles and magistrates no defender could have been more welcome.

But it was not the resurgence of the aristocratic party that kept Voltaire from participating actively in politics on the side of the crown; it was, ironically enough, his friend d'Argenson's promotion to foreign minister in November 1744. Not long before Voltaire went to Cirey, he had airily dismissed the conflict of Louis XV with the parlements: "I don't meddle with those farces."[128] At Cirey those farces became important to him, and Voltaire appeared ready to join in political controversy. But the time had not yet come. In favor at court, he became too busy being a courtier to waste his time on serious matters: for several years, his only political program was the advancement of Voltaire.

3. VOLTAIRE AGAINST TRAJAN

Courtly pleasure was hard work, and Voltaire labored at it mightily. But as he said in *Zadig*, that disenchanted tale of life among the great, "constant pleasure is not pleasure."[129] He was reduced to writing slight comedies, slighter poems, and inconsequential fetes. His *Temple de la gloire*, first performed at Versailles in November 1745 with delightful music by Rameau, was crassly addressed to its exalted audience; it contained a part for the Emperor Trajan, a thinly disguised Louis XV. It is said that after the performance Voltaire asked fatuously in the king's hearing: "Is Trajan content?" and that Louis XV, too proud or too embarrassed to reply, turned away without a word.

This is one of those improbable stories that deserves to be credited whether it is authentic or not. Voltaire at court was not a pleasant spectacle. Here was Europe's leading playwright, who had preached, time and again, on the dignity of literary men, putting aside that dignity himself as he importuned the

---

[128] Voltaire to Cideville (15 November 1732), *Correspondence*, II, 387.
[129] *Zadig* came out in 1748; a first version, entitled *Memnon*, in 1747.

mighty for favors. Not long after his friend, the marquis d'Argenson, had been appointed foreign minister, another friend, madame d'Etioles, soon to be created marquise de Pompadour, became the king's mistress. Voltaire made sure that these friends did not forget him. Early in 1745 he hinted that nothing would be more agreeable to him than to have Louis XV appoint him historiographer of France and *gentilhomme ordinaire de la chambre*.[130] Trajan, evidently content, granted Voltaire the first wish in April 1745 and the second in November 1746. Now the *bourgeois* was at last a *gentilhomme*.

While he was thus engaged in securing his position at court, he launched a shameless campaign for a place in the *Académie française*, anticipating by a century Flaubert's cynical advice: "Run it down but try to belong to it if you can." Voltaire tried as only Voltaire could try. He richly deserved to be a member of the Academy; writers of far lesser stature but superior connections had been elected at a much younger age. But in the flush of his vogue at court he was determined to leave nothing to chance—that is, to merit. He wrote pious and disingenuous letters to his old Jesuit teachers, corresponded with Pope Benedict XIV, and in May 1746 finally became one of the Forty Immortals.

In the midst of these triumphs, Gustave Lanson has asked, why should Voltaire persecute the poet Roy for writing a few libels, and the violist Travenol and his aged father for hawking some sarcastic pamphlets? The answer is that it was precisely in the midst of these triumphs that Voltaire was unbearable. He had some reason for his vindictiveness; his enemies were undermining his reputation for orthodoxy which was already shaky enough. But as his letters from court show, his unmeasured fury against insignificant slanderers was less the result of rational policy than of uneasiness at his new life. He was a suc-

[130] See Voltaire to d'Argenson, 8 February (1745); to the same, (20 March 1745); to madame Denis (3 April 1745), *Correspondence*, XIV, 104, 115-116, 118-119.

cess, but with trivia; his comedy-ballet *La princesse de Navarre* was greeted with applause, but he found no evidence that his major works had made an impression at court:

> Mon *Henri Quatre* et ma *Zaïre*,
> Et mon Américaine *Alzire*,
> Ne m'ont valu jamais un seul regard du roi;
> J'avais mille ennemis avec très-peu de gloire:
> Les honneurs et les biens pleuvent enfin sur moi
> Pour un farce de la foire.[131]

He confided to his friends that he felt out of place. "I see nobody here, I work a great deal . . ." he told Thieriot early in 1745, "and I cut at Versailles the same figure as an atheist in a church."[132] He was wryly aware of his ambiguous position. "Like Aretino, I am in commerce with all crowned heads," he told d'Argenson, "but he made them pay him so he could bite them, and I ask nothing from them so I can flatter them."[133] This was inaccurate; as a court official Voltaire was drawing comfortable salaries, but he had to work hard for his money. In a charming apology to Cideville he explained that he had little time to write to his friends: "Don't complain of a poor devil who is the buffoon of the king at fifty, and who is more embarrassed with musicians, decorators, actors, actresses, singers, dancers, than are the eight or nine German electors to make themselves a German Caesar. I run from Paris to Versailles, I write verses in post chaises. I must praise the king loudly, madame the dauphine discreetly, the royal family very delicately; I must content the court and not displease the town."[134]

Some of these comical plaints are high spirits or Voltaire's thoughtfulness: what could be better designed to give pleasure to a Cideville, whose duties kept him in the provinces, or a

---

[131] I, 89.   [132] (? February 1745), *Correspondence*, XIV, 105.
[133] 25 June (1745), *ibid.*, XIV, 180.
[134] 31 January 1745, *ibid.*, XIV, 103.

Thieriot, who would never be invited to Versailles, than to know that Voltaire was not happy at court? But there was more than politeness to Voltaire's laments. His devotion to his calling, his pride in serious literature, his need to work, all made him uncomfortably aware that he was wasting precious time. He liked applause, glitter, proximity to the center of affairs; he enjoyed being on familiar footing with ministers and in the same château with a king. Voltaire would have been less—or more—than human if he had been indifferent to these trivia which philosophers tell us mean so little.[135] Yet he knew that comedy-ballets and verses written in post chaises were no substitute for the major writings he had laid aside.

He did not lay them aside for long. He soon discovered that he could not please the court and work hard at the same time; his urge to work won out over his desire to please, probably against his conscious intention. His behavior was so maladroit as to suggest that the artist in him was sabotaging the courtier; some of his indiscreet remarks were overheard and it was hinted that he might be happier away from the court. Also, madame de Pompadour was cooling toward him, and the marquis d'Argenson had been dismissed from the foreign office in January 1747, so it was easy for Voltaire to accept the hints. By 1748, he was working again—at Cirey and sometimes a few miles away at Lunéville in Lorraine, where Stanislas, the ex-king of Poland, was holding court.[136] Reminiscing late in life, Voltaire confessed that these had been far from glorious years: "In 1744 and 1745 I was a courtier. . . . I reformed in 1746 and repented in 1747. . . ."[137] He was ill and depressed: *Sémiramis* (1748) is

---

[135] Even Rousseau, the Spartan republican, the unbending democrat, confessed that his contempt of high society was not really disdain but fear. In his *Confessions*, Book VIII, he admits that he decided to adopt manners of his own since he was unable to learn the manners of the polite world. "Awkwardness made me cynical and sarcastic, and I affected to despise the manners I did not know how to practice."

[136] In 1749, Voltaire sold his charge as *gentilhomme ordinaire* for 30,000 livres but retained the right to use his title.

[137] Voltaire to the abbé du Vernet, February (1776), IL, 537.

one of his gloomiest tragedies; in *Zadig* he expressed all his spleen against courtly life, his painful conviction that Zadig, the rational and humane minister in an irrational society, will be misunderstood and despised and miserable: "Zadig said, 'At last, then, I am happy!' But he was deceived."[138]

Voltaire reformed and repented, but his reform was less thorough and his repentance came more slowly than he remembered later. Even in 1748 he could write a servile panegyric to Louis XV that was more successful than it deserved to be.[139] Evidently, Voltaire found the disease of flattery easier to catch than to cure.

For the student of Voltaire's political ideas, this courtly interlude has chiefly negative value. It has been suggested that Voltaire went to Versailles hoping to enlighten, or at least influence, the king of France.[140] But this estimate of his intentions finds no support in his published writings, his notebooks, or his correspondence. He liked to play at diplomacy—in 1743 he went to Prussia on a rather absurd secret mission for France— but there is no evidence that he became the courtier to influence policy or to promote reform.[141] Nor is there good evidence that he sought to mold the king's character. "The Voltairian

---

[138] xxi, 45. V. L. Saulnier has called this tale an "anti-Versailles." See his introduction to *Zadig* (1946), xii.

[139] *Panégyrique de Louis XV*, xxiii, 263-280. It went quickly into several editions.

[140] "Deluded by his own weakness for the glamor and pageantry of court life, he persuaded himself that he could win over personally those individuals who officially or unofficially governed the affairs of the kingdom. Secure in the confidence of his king, he would soon be granted admission to the secret meetings of the royal council. Thus, he, a philosopher, might at last have his chance to influence the policies of the State." Constance Rowe, *Voltaire and the State*, 48; see also 44. Rowe's authority is Desnoiresterres' biography of Voltaire (iii, 424-425), but Desnoiresterres' only evidence is a statement by Marmontel, which is as good as no evidence at all.

[141] Like other literary men of the Old Regime, he lent his literary talents to friendly statesmen—while d'Argenson was foreign minister, Voltaire did some writing for him. See xxiii, 197-204.

message is present in all his court trifles," writes Constance Rowe. "The Poem on Fontenoy and the Temple of Glory breathe the same hatred of war, the same impartial fairness toward other nations, and the same appreciation of the arts that the author expressed throughout his writings."[142] It is true that Voltaire did not become a chauvinist or a militarist at Versailles—although he did celebrate France's victory at Fontenoy (1745) with a popular and mediocre poem—but the preachments of his courtly productions are so commonplace, so larded with flattery, so remote from specific political issues, that they scarcely deserve to be classified as philosophic propaganda.

This is not to suggest that Voltaire underestimated the influence that a thinker might have on a ruler. In a short essay of 1742 he imagined a private Roman citizen presenting a memorandum to the rulers of the state who ignore it; and yet, "The pamphlet of the obscure citizen was a seed that sprouted little by little in the heads of great men."[143] The obscure citizen is Voltaire, and he could think of some great men in whom he would like to cause the seeds of good ideas to sprout. But Louis XV was not among them. "There is always hope for a prince who likes poetry," Voltaire wrote in *Zadig*—a confession that he had no expectation of guiding the King of France, who cared little for poetry and less for France's greatest living poet.

Voltaire's years at Versailles, then, were devoted to the advancement of his career, not to the advancement of some fanciful conception of "enlightened despotism." They taught him only one thing: the need for complete independence. In 1750 he told his niece from Potsdam: "To write the history of one's country, one must be far from one's country."[144] Even before he went to Prussia, he discovered that to defend the king's cause one must be far from one's king.

[142] *Voltaire and the State*, 50.
[143] *Ce qu'on ne fait pas et ce qu'on pourrait faire*, XXIII, 186.
[144] Voltaire to madame Denis, 28 October (1750), *Correspondence*, XVIII, 192.

The king's cause needed defense. In 1748 France had concluded the expensive and fruitless War of the Austrian Succession with Great Britain and Austria. There had been a generous outpouring of public affection during the king's illness at Metz and after his victory at Fontenoy, but in 1746 the war had required an increase in taxes and the popularity of the king waned as rapidly as the popularity of the war. The peace of Aix-la-Chapelle, concluded in the spring of 1748, satisfied the public even less than the war: "stupid as the peace" became a byword in the Parisian markets.[145] The public was in an ugly mood. Starvation and despair in the countryside, bread riots and coffeehouse grumbling in the towns, corruption and profiteering in the government—there was nothing new in that. What was new was the vehemence and openness of the criticisms. D'Argenson reports that when the king showed himself in public, there were none of the customary shouts, Vive le roi! On 19 February 1749, he noted in his journal that there was great ferment among the lower classes and discontent with the government everywhere. The king's personal popularity was suffering from the hatred that enveloped his associates. "Taxes are too high for the people, life is expensive . . . people spend without earning; the odious reign of the financiers afflicts the public and degrades the government. . . . People read gazettes."[146] Beggars, fleeing from rural misery, thronged the streets of Paris. Deist propaganda, libels on madame de Pompadour, sarcastic verses on the ministers circulated openly through the city. A bitter story about the king was making the rounds. In a dream, Louis XV had seen four cats fighting, one skinny, one fat, one one-eyed, and one blind; asking what the dream meant, the king was told: "The skinny cat is your people, the fat cat is the

[145] D'Argenson, 19 January 1749, *Journal et mémoires*, v, 362; confirmed by Barbier, 12 February 1749, *Journal*, iii, 63.

[146] *Journal et mémoires*, v, 393. These remarks are strengthened by later entries throughout 1749, and confirmed by Barbier.

corps of financiers, the one-eyed cat is your ministry, and the blind cat is Your Majesty, who wants to see nothing."[147]

The government struck back by attempting to stifle its critics and to reform its tax system. It failed in both. In July 1749, Barbier noted that a "great quantity of persons, ecclesiastics, men of letters, and others" were being arrested daily.[148] D'Argenson confirms the report and specifies that the arrested persons were accused of "making verses against the king, reciting them, distributing them, jeering at the ministry, writing and printing in favor of deism and against good morals. . . ."[149] The best known among the "great quantity of persons" was Denis Diderot, who was sent to Vincennes apparently because the prisons in Paris were full.[150]

More far-reaching, and much more constructive, was the tax reform proposed by Machault d'Arnouville, *contrôleur général des finances*, who persuaded Louis XV to decree a 5% income tax, the *vingtième*, on all French subjects. Machault, born into the robe nobility, a former intendant, finance minister since 1745, was the kind of official whom absolute kings need so much and find so rarely. Hard-working, impatient with social graces, opinionated, cruel and courageous, contemptuous of the incrustations of tradition and the obstacles of privilege, Machault single-mindedly dedicated himself to the restoration of the public finances.[151] In May 1749, Louis XV proclaimed two edicts drafted by Machault, establishing a fund to amortize the national debt, suppressing the wartime *dixième* and substituting a *vingtième*, to be levied after 1 January 1750.

---

[147] Henri Carré, *Louis XV*, 166.
[148] *Journal*, III, 88.
[149] 25 July 1749, *Journal et mémoires*, VI, 11.
[150] *loc.cit.*, and 2 August 1749, *ibid.*, VI, 15; Wilson, *Diderot*, 96.
[151] When Damiens, who had tried to assassinate Louis XV in 1757, was tortured, Machault participated in person. Voltaire suppressed this fact (which appears in a letter of Damiens to the king) in his *Précis du siècle de Louis XV*; more daringly, he included it in the later *Histoire du parlement de Paris*.

Frenchmen had borne income taxes before this, but they had been imposed as wartime expedients, and had never been truly equitable: nobles who resisted payment on the ground that the tax was incompatible with their status were not compelled to pay; towns and other corporations transformed the onerous tax into light and intermittent burdens by arranging lump sum payments; wealthy tax payers falsified their returns without fear of prosecution.[152] As the royal edicts made clear, Machault's *vingtième* would be different: there would be no exemptions, no lump sums, no special favors, no profiteering; there would be strict enforcement, thorough control, efficient levies. "We have preferred this impost to all the other methods we could have used," the king told his people, "because there is no juster and no more equitable one, because it is raised from all our subjects in proportion to their wealth and their capacities. . . ."[153] Two decades before, Voltaire had praised England for just such a tax system—there was no question what his position would be now.

French tax farmers were far more honest than their reputation, but the prevailing method of collecting taxes invited fraud, made millionaires, and cheated the state of needed revenue; the exemptions enjoyed by clergy and nobility, towns, and provinces placed the burden of taxation on those least able to bear it. Machault's proposed *vingtième* boldly attacked the privileged orders. To cancel privileges in a society founded on privilege, to refuse exemptions in a society where everybody hunted for exemptions, was to challenge all that was powerful in the Old Regime. But the king, appalled at the desperate state of his finances, supported his minister. Machault, he said, "is the man after my own heart."

Machault was also the man after Voltaire's heart: about

---

[152] Carré cites an example: "In 1734, 'the king of wines' of Bordeaux, the *président* de Segur, whose revenue reached 160,000 livres, declared . . . an income of 6,000." *Louis XV*, 230.

[153] Marcel Marion, *Les impôts directs sous l'ancien régime*, 288-289.

two weeks after Machault's edicts on the *vingtième* had been issued, while the parlement of Paris was awaiting the king's reply to its courteous remonstrance, Voltaire sent a detailed letter to Machault in support of the tax. Here is the "obscure citizen" helping to shape policy, or at least providing ammunition for the defense of policy. Voltaire's letter is a set of justifications, a kind of memorandum that a finance minister would write if he were called upon to explain his program: since the conclusion of the peace of 1748, France has been prosperous, and can afford to tax itself; Louis XIV raised immense revenues without ruining the country; the British were taxing themselves at a rate of 10% to pay off the national debt—surely the French, twice as rich as the English, could absorb half their burden. To pay for the costs of war in times of peace, to provide for invalids and war widows was both just and convenient. Arguing like a modern economist, Voltaire suggested that taxes do not weaken a country if they are fairly levied and rationally spent. On the contrary, taxes are payments that a nation makes to itself, precisely as a farmer sows that he may reap. In this severe array of reasons for the *vingtième*, general principle appears only once, and then briefly: Machault's tax "rests with equality upon all ranks which all, without distinction, should contribute to the common good."[154]

[154] Voltaire to Machault, 16 May 1749, *Correspondence*, xvii, 75-81. Voltaire sent this letter to the finance minister through the marquis de Coudray, and it is possible that Machault never received it, since it was found among Coudray's papers after his death. Moland treats it as an essay rather than a letter and reprints it among Voltaire's miscellanies.

Voltaire restated these ideas in a *Dialogue entre un philosophe et un contrôleur général des finances*, first published in 1751: Taxes should fall on all those capable of paying them; the aim of the state is to improve the standard of living so that more taxes can appropriately be collected: "It is not on the poor, on the laborer, that a tax should be imposed; in making him work, he must be given the hope to be one day lucky enough to pay taxes." xxiii, 505. In the dialogue, Voltaire revives his middle-class scale of public heroes, which he first enunciated twenty years before in the *Lettres philosophiques*: "Do you know that a minister of finance can do much good, and be consequently a greater man than twenty marshals of France?" xxiii, 501. And he concludes the piece with his image of the "obscure

Voltaire's letter, cogently reasoned and moderately argued, singled out no group for attack. In his studies of French history, Voltaire had come to the conclusion that both church and nobility were obstructionist, but in May 1749 he could not know which of these estates would defend its privileges more vigorously. In fact, resistance to the *vingtième* varied greatly in intensity. The parlement of Paris and the provincial parlements registered the decrees after remonstrances of surprising mildness; the *pays d'élection*, the provinces governed directly by the crown, accepted the tax with only minor difficulties. On the other hand, as *pays d'état* Languedoc and Brittany had retained a degree of fiscal autonomy which was threatened by the *vingtième*; having much to lose by compliance, they sabotaged the decrees.

But the most stubborn and the best publicized opposition to the *vingtième* came from the clergy. While estates general, provincial estates, and local corporations had receded before royal intendants, France had never been administratively unified, despite its absolute kings and centralizing ministers. The clergy had remained wealthy, influential, and tightly organized. The parish priests were poor, dissatisfied, and hostile to privileges in which they did not share, but their bishops were rich, proud, aristocratic, well-connected, and it was the bishops, not the parish priests, who made policy for the French clergy. The French church was a political force that a minister defied at his own peril.

It was no secret that the church was prosperous, but its many sources of income, its reluctance to divulge the state of its finances, and the elegance displayed by its princes led the public to fanciful notions concerning its wealth. It was widely believed, and not only by philosophes, that the church owned a third of France, a figure easier to use in an argument than to

citizen" influencing public policy: the minister read some papers written by the philosopher, "liked them, secured a copy for himself; and that is the first manuscript of a philosopher that has ever been seen in the portfolio of a minister." xxiii, 506.

substantiate; a tenth would have been more accurate.[155] Machault estimated the church's income at an impressive 250 million livres a year, of which about half was taxable.[156] In its voluntary contribution to the state—the so-called *don gratuit*—the church paid about 3 millions a year, less than 3% of its taxable income. The *vingtième* would have doubled this contribution. That was bad enough, but the threat of depriving the first estate of immunity from taxation was worse.

Machault was stubborn, but he was also politic; he attempted to conquer the clergy by dividing it. The *clergé étranger*, located in the provinces acquired by France since the sixteenth century, was less well organized and hence easier to intimidate than the *clergé de France*. Machault addressed himself to the former late in June 1749, hoping to create a precedent that the latter would find hard to evade. A few bishops complied, but most of them, emboldened by their self-interest and their colleagues among the *clergé de France*, refused to surrender their privileges. On 11 September 1749, the Bishop of Verdun pleaded with Machault "not to put into opposition the obedience we owe to the king with the obedience we owe our conscience: the king himself has too much religion not to feel which of these two duties must have the preference if they should be incompatible."[157]

The bishop's confident tone carried an implicit slur against the king: few highly-placed clergymen expected Louis XV to stand by his minister. For the moment at least, they were disappointed. In August Machault issued an edict strictly regulat-

---

[155] Lefebvre, *The Coming of the French Revolution*, 8. Barbier says flatly that the clergy owns more than a third of the kingdom. June 1740, *Journal*, II, 258. In his anticlerical propaganda writings, Voltaire accepted this figure, but in his serious histories, as in the *Siècle de Louis XIV*, he is more cautious and merely writes that the clergy is "reported to own a third of the country." XV, 3.

[156] Voltaire privately estimated the clergy's taxable income more modestly at 80 millions. *Notebooks*, 377.

[157] Marion, *Machault*, 233; Voltaire misquotes this plea and makes it sound more subversive, in *Précis du siècle de Louis XV*, XV, 376.

ing the church's feudal right to *mainmorte*: legacies to the church, which were withdrawn from taxation, as well as new religious foundations, had to be authorized by royal letters patent. The decree bore heavily upon pious establishments—monasteries, nunneries, schools, orphanages—which had hitherto acquired property from devout citizens without public supervision; it suggested that Machault still had the king's confidence.

Voltaire had intended to whip up public support for the *vingtième*,[158] but in 1749 his domestic troubles took precedence over his political interests. In May 1749, at the time the royal edicts were being issued, madame du Châtelet was evidently pregnant, but neither by her famous lover nor by her husband.[159] Voltaire and his *belle Emilie* had long ceased to be lovers; and friendship, even with Voltaire, was not enough for the irrepressible marquise: in 1748 she fell in love with Saint-Lambert, a young poet of modest literary and impressive amorous accomplishments, a disciple and now the successful rival of Voltaire. In bitter jest, Voltaire called him "my terrible pupil";[160] in tasteless jest, Frederick of Prussia said that the forthcoming child might be classed among madame du Châtelet's miscellaneous works.[161]

[158] In a covering note that accompanied his letter to Machault, Voltaire described himself as a "zealous and perhaps a little talkative citizen" and asked that the letter be returned to him. This suggests that he planned to be zealous and perhaps a little talkative in Machault's behalf. See Voltaire to the marquis de Coudray (16 May 1749), *Correspondence*, xvii, 81.

[159] Madame du Châtelet confided the secret to the marquise de Boufflers on 3 April 1749: "I am pregnant, and you can well imagine my distress, how I fear for my health and even for my life, how ridiculous I think it is to give birth at forty, after having spent seventeen years without producing a child. . . ." *ibid.*, xvii, 56.

[160] Voltaire to the comte and comtesse d'Argental, 28 August (1749), *ibid.*, xvii, 146. A letter from the comtesse d'Argental to her husband (?ca. 10 June 1749), provides remarkable insight into Voltaire's state of mind in these months: she describes a visit from Voltaire, his sudden and irrational fury, his abject apologies, his rushing from place to place with nervous tension: ". . . I have never seen anybody so beside himself." This from someone who had known him intimately for years. *ibid.*, xvii, 89-90.

[161] The remark appears in a letter to Algarotti, 12 September 1749. See

Then, on 10 September 1749, the time for jesting was over. Shortly after giving birth to a daughter, Voltaire's divine, irresponsible Emilie suddenly died. Plunged in despairing apathy, Voltaire was in no mood for politics, whatever Machault's predicament. The Cirey years, for all their alarums, misunderstandings, and resentments, had been years of peace and hard work; madame du Châtelet, for all her limitations, had been Voltaire's indispensable goad, nurse, critic, and friend. Voltaire had great recuperative powers, but he needed months to recover his spirits. As it happened, they were the months in which Machault and the clergy did little more than spar for position; both parties were waiting for June 1750, when the quinquennial Assembly of the Clergy was to meet in Paris. In February, Barbier rightly predicted that this session of the Assembly would provide the forum for a great debate on the *vingtième*.[162]

By the spring of 1750, installed in the Paris house of his beloved niece, Voltaire was ready for the Assembly.[163] And the Assembly was ready for him and all other opposition; it had excellent arguments, widespread support, and the unwitting aid of the Paris masses. In May 1750, they rioted against the brutality of the police and the tax policy of the ministers.[164]

---

ibid., xvii, 164n. In numerous biographies and studies of eighteenth-century men and ideas, the remark has been mistakenly attributed to Voltaire. For a recent example see Wilson, *Diderot*, 102, who bases himself on Brandes' biography of Voltaire.

[162] *Journal*, iii, 120.

[163] We now know that this beloved niece, fat, unreliable, pleasure-loving madame Denis, had been her uncle's mistress since the early 1740's.

[164] In the spring of 1750, under the orders of the comte d'Argenson (cordially hated by his brother, the diarist) and of Berryer, the *lieutenant de police*, the Paris police rounded up a large number of persons with no fixed or respectable profession—beggars, vagabonds, prostitutes—in an effort to wipe out begging. Rumors spread among the anxious public that the captives would be deported to the French colonies; other rumors, that the police were holding some individuals for ransom or were kidnapping working-class children whom they caught in the street on their way to buy food for their families. These rumors were in part false and in part exaggerated, but police brutality was very real. Talk spread in town of a march on Versailles, and the riots were repressed with characteristic harshness.

D'Argenson noted bluntly on 28 May, "Never have there been such cruel ministers under such a kind king; I know them all."[165] The prelates were hopeful that in the question of their immunity the kind king would prevail over his cruel ministers.

But the *vingtième* was an explosive issue. It confused traditional alignments—the bishops, usually in the king's party, were now in opposition—and gave encouragement to anticlericalism among the educated bourgeoisie. Conflict between church and state was not new in France; patronage, relations with the Papacy, tax privileges, and sometimes even religious questions had stirred up intermittent dissensions for centuries. In earlier days, dissenters had had no alternative to obedience; except to a few pagan *libertins* and recalcitrant Jansenists, the decrees of the authorities had been final. Yet seventeenth-century controversies had never been resolved, and continued to plague the eighteenth: Louis XIV had firmly adopted the Gallican position in the declaration of 1682 and meekly compromised with the ultramontanes later. More firmly, he had tried to suppress the Jansenists. The severe Augustinian theology of Arnauld, Pascal, and Nicole was condemned again and again by king, prelates, and popes; the convents at Port Royal were dissolved and then razed in 1709; four years later, Pope Clement XI promulgated the Bull *Unigenitus*, popularly known as the *Constitution*, which condemned 101 Jansenist propositions drawn from Quesnel's *Réflexions morales sur le Nouveau-Testament*, and Louis XIV spent much of the time that remained to him

---

These incidents, soon brought under control, suggest the great propaganda problems of the *thèse royale* among the lower classes: to the workers and to the *Lumpenproletariat* the state was not a machine for creating welfare but simply an enemy, taking the dismal form of the brutal policeman or the rapacious tax collector. To these groups in France, Machault's tax program was not "progressive" but just another kind of exploitation. On the other hand, respectable bourgeois, secure from police brutality, exempt from some taxes, disdainful and afraid of the vagrants who made the streets unsafe, favored the policy of the ministry both in its attempt to repress unrest and to make the privileged corporations pay.

[165] *Journal et mémoires*, VI, 205.

securing acceptance of the Bull. Yet Jansenism was not to be extirpated.

In the Regency, and under Louis XV, religious controversies continued and became more dangerous to the state: they had become political, and lent support to a growing anticlerical party. When Barbier made his much-quoted remark that the city of Paris was Jansenist from head to toe, he did not mean that respectable Parisians shared Pascal's austere doctrine of the hidden God, but that they resented the submission of the bishops to the Papacy, applauded the parlements' resistance to royal policies, and hated the Jesuits.[166] And these political Jansenists were making themselves heard. Under Louis XIV, there had been little but muffled grumbling; now a strange new phenomenon, public opinion, was becoming a force in French politics. "The powerful command," observed Duclos in his brilliant *Considérations sur les moeurs*, published in the year that the clergy was debating Machault's decrees, "the intellectuals govern, for in the long run they form public opinion."[167] And this public opinion, although perhaps not irreligious, was largely anticlerical. Barbier, who was neither a good Christian nor a philosophe, spoke for many educated Frenchmen in his support of the *vingtième*: "There is much talk of making ecclesiastics pay a twentieth of their goods and their income. That would have several good results. First, we would really know the extent of ecclesiastical revenues, which make up too large a part of the wealth of this kingdom. Secondly, it would make them contribute to the expenses of the state like other subjects, which would be just. . . . Thirdly, it would give relief to the lower clergy which is now being oppressed by the bishops. . . ."[168]

Machault was not insensitive to public opinion; he adroitly courted and fostered it with his edicts and his propaganda pam-

---

[166] Philippe Sagnac calls this new Jansenism "a ferocious Gallicanism." *La formation de la société française moderne*, II, 134.

[167] Charles Pinot-Duclos, *Considérations sur les moeurs*, 138.

[168] September 1749, *Journal*, III, 101-102.

phlets. While the representatives of the clergy were gathering in Paris in May 1750, they were rudely greeted by an anonymous polemic, simply entitled *Lettres*, probably written by the elderly and respected lawyer Charles Bargeton upon the instigation of Machault. The pamphlet bore an aggressive epigraph from Seneca, *Ne repugnate bono vestro*—Do not refuse your goods. It argued, with a wealth of historical detail and anticlerical venom, that the clergy, the most useless estate in France, could under no circumstances be excused from contributing its share to the public treasury.[169] On 1 June, the *conseil* ostentatiously ordered *Ne repugnate* suppressed, widely publicized its order and did nothing to enforce it. Barbier assumed, probably correctly, that the suppression "was designed to prejudice the public, which does not read such books, against the church."[170]

Ne repugnate was the first drop in a shower of pamphlets, satires, handbills, and impolite *bon mots*. The Assembly of the Clergy answered the jokes and the songs with its traditional arguments: the church is not of this world; its property belongs to the poor; its privileges are ancient, well-founded, and should not now be roughly handled by profane hands. The clergy was doing its duty by making contributions to the state of its free will; its Assembly voted the *don gratuit* with pious regularity, and its dioceses collected the contributions for the treasury; it could not degrade its love offering into an enforced tribute. The Assembly respectfully reminded the king that Louis XIV—and Louis XV himself—had repeatedly exempted the clergy from taxation, and had affirmed and reaffirmed that ecclesiastical property would always remain immune.

Louis XV was willing to give up the word if he could retain

[169] The pamphlet was attributed to a number of parlementarians, and Bargeton is only the most probable author. It was a powerful work, deeply disturbing to the clergy, playing all the variations possible on the Biblical passage, "Render therefore unto Caesar the things which are Caesar's." Marion, *Machault*, 241-251.

[170] June 1750, *Journal*, III, 145. Barbier was much impressed with *Ne repugnate*.

the thing. In a declaration of 17 August 1750 he insisted that the clergy contribute its usual *don gratuit* and add a contribution of 7,500,000 livres, to be paid in five annual installments. This was a concession, since it left the division and the collecting of the contribution to the clergy, but for all its silence on the *vingtième*, the declaration insisted on the principle of secular control over church finances. D'Argenson thought that the declaration of 17 August was a decisive victory for the clergy,[171] but the Assembly did not agree. On 10 September it formally transmitted remonstrances to the king. "This is really the caste spirit," wrote Barbier.[172] He was right: *esprit de corps* had overridden the sense of public responsibility. The Assembly remained defiant and compelled the king to dissolve it on 20 September. The ecclesiastics returned to their dioceses—still unsubmissive, still unrepentant, still untaxed.

Voltaire witnessed only the first part of this Assembly; toward the end of June he had left for Prussia. But before his departure he had been neither idle nor silent; doubtless encouraged by the state of public opinion, he had grown more radical in his views—or at least in his public pronouncements. In his letter to Machault of 1749 he had supported the *vingtième* on the moderate ground that all classes in society should contribute to public expenditures. In May and June 1750 he supported it on the extreme ground that the clergy was rich and useless, that it commanded without obeying, and consumed without producing. He imagined a dialogue between an Indian philosopher and a Turkish palace guard, a bostangi. While the two men were talking of profound matters, "About twenty beautiful two-footed animals passed by, wearing a short cloak over a long tunic, a pointed hood on their heads, a rope belt on their loins.

'These are some well-made big fellows,' said the Indian. 'How many of them do you have in your country?'

[171] 23 August 1750, *Journal et mémoires*, VI, 247.
[172] September 1750, *Journal*, III, 172.

'Nearly a hundred thousand of different kinds,' answered the bostangi.

'Fine fellows to work on beautifying Cashmir!' said the philosopher. 'How I would like to see them, spade, trowel, square rule in hand.'

'So would I,' said the bostangi, 'but they are too great saints to work.'

'What do they do?' asked the Indian.

'They sing, they drink, they digest,' said the bostangi.

'How useful to the state!' said the Indian."[173]

An even more playful contribution to the pamphlet war was Voltaire's parody of a decree from the Papal Inquisition, anticipating by half a year the condemnation of Bargeton's *Ne repugnate*: "Antichrist has already come, said Antichrist already has sent several circular letters to the bishops of France, in which he has had the audacity to treat them as Frenchmen and subjects of the king. . . . He strives to prove . . . that the clergy form part of the body politic, instead of affirming that they are essentially its masters . . . he suggests that those who have a third of the revenue in the state owe at least a third in contributions; forgetting that our brethren are made to have everything and to give nothing. Said book, in addition, is notoriously filled with impious maxims drawn from natural law, the law of nations, the fundamental laws of the kingdom, and other pernicious prejudices which have the evil tendency of strengthening royal authority, increasing the circulation of species in the kingdom of France, assisting the poor clergymen who up to now have been oppressed by the rich in saintly fashion."[174]

More serious and far more controversial than these amusing

[173] *Des embellissements de la ville de Cachemire*, XXIII, 478.
[174] *Extrait du décret de la sacrée congrégation de l'Inquisition de Rome, à l'encontre d'un libelle intitulé 'Lettres sur le vingtième,'* XXIII, 463. Voltaire dates this "condemnation" 20 May 1750, which may be the date of publication. On 25 January 1751, Rome in fact condemned the *Lettres*; in the same condemnation it included Voltaire's major contribution to the controversy, *La voix du sage et du peuple*. Marion, *Machault*, 264, 314.

productions is *La voix du sage et du peuple,* which Voltaire published as the Assembly of the Clergy was convening.[175] One of his first and most characteristic political works, it served as a model for many of his later pamphlets: it is brief, pungent, witty, and elliptical. Yet despite its calculated omissions and general language, contemporary readers had no hesitation in understanding it as a partisan statement of the royal position on the *vingtième.*[176]

Significantly, *La voix du sage* opens with a reminiscence of d'Argenson's *Considérations:* "The excellence of a government consists of protecting and containing equally all callings in a state." As for the church, it should "contribute to the expenditures of the state in proportion to its revenues." To grant immunity to any group is an injustice; for the clergy to demand it is an impudence. "The government that would permit a certain number of men to say, 'Those who work should pay; we should not pay anything, because we are idle,' would be fit for Hottentots. The government in which citizens could say, 'The state has given us everything, and we owe it nothing but prayers,' would outrage God and men." One thing that men owe to society is offspring; in vigorous support of the edict restricting *mainmorte* (too vigorous for most readers), *La voix du sage* demanded that the state "return to the laws of nature imprudent men and women who are vowed to the extinction of society."

As could be expected from a proponent of the *thèse royale,* Voltaire supported his argument with references to earlier struggles between sovereign and privileged bodies. Only a "single

[175] *La voix du sage* appeared late in May or early in June 1750; it was attributed to Voltaire with little difficulty. D'Argenson wrote on 10 July 1750 that "it is said to be by Voltaire." *Journal et mémoires,* VI, 222.

[176] Within a year over a dozen imitations and refutations appeared in France; they were all condemned on 21 May 1751. In the light of his later writings, *La voix* appears as a significant work, but students of Voltaire have either treated it unhistorically by quoting it out of context, or neglected it entirely. In his exhaustive eight-volume biography, Desnoiresterres finds no room either for the pamphlet or for Voltaire's political activities in the years 1749-1750. Marion's *Machault* is a brilliant exception.

power" can produce sound government and avoid anarchy: "There ought not to be two powers in a state." French history demonstrates the truth of this maxim: "The happy years of the monarchy were the last years of Henri IV, the years of Louis XIV and Louis XV, when these kings governed by themselves." In resting its claim for immunity on the theory of divided sovereignty, the church abused "the distinction between spiritual power and temporal power"—the former deserved respect but no authority, the latter deserved both respect and authority.[177] In a word, "The prince must be absolute master of all ecclesiastical regulations, without any restriction, since those ecclesiastical regulations are a part of the government; and just as the father of a family prescribes to the preceptor of his children the hours of work, the kind of studies, etc., so the prince may prescribe to all ecclesiastics, without exception, all that has the least bearing on the public order."

This was radical doctrine, and Voltaire knew it. That is why he thought it prudent to defend the philosophes who advocated or supported such doctrine against the inevitable charge of subversiveness, and to associate the interests of the philosophes with the interests of the king: "The best thing that can happen to men is for the prince to be a philosopher. The philosophic prince knows that the more progress reason makes in his state, the less damage will be done by disputes, theological quarrels, enthusiasm, superstition; hence he will encourage the progress of reason." These tactical lines have often been quoted to lend plausibility to the thesis that Voltaire envisaged some sort of philosopher-king whom he would guide, like a modern Plato. This interpretation overlooks the time and the purpose of *La voix du sage*. Voltaire knew that Machault was supported at court chiefly by madame de Pompadour and opposed chiefly by the *dévots*; he knew, too, that powerful personages were

[177] In *Fragment des instructions pour le prince de****, Voltaire denounced the "insolent absurdity of the two swords" doctrine. xxvi, 443. See chapter vii for Voltaire's use of similar arguments against the French nobility.

growing increasingly resentful and suspicious of the "philosophic sect." Like a good chess player, Voltaire preferred a
strong counterattack to a solid defense; he insisted that the
philosophes spoke for the public good, that their radical proposals were the radical cure recommended by a sage physician
to a seriously ill patient, that they were loyal citizens; he denounced the *dévots*, Jansenists, and Jesuits alike, as fanatical
madmen, regicides, and instigators of rebellion: "There is in
this world not a single example of philosophes who have opposed the laws of the prince; there is not a single century in
which superstition and enthusiasm have not caused troubles
which horrify us."[178] Voltaire could not expect Louis XV to be
a philosopher-king, but he could expect that the king might be
persuaded to carry out what he had promised to carry out.

There is something a little pathetic about Voltaire's earnest
defense of the philosophes as a group. Anticlerical they were to
a man, but in the fight over the *vingtième* they remained silent
or ambiguous. Montesquieu's *Esprit des lois*, which circulated
openly in Paris in 1750, gave comfort to neither king nor clergy.
It specifically defended the privileges of the clergy in a monarchy
as a bulwark against despotism, but its religious views gravely
offended all wings of clerical opinion and were hardly suitable
for ecclesiastical propaganda against Machault.[179] Diderot's
position is uncertain. His article "Autorité politique," which he
published in the first volume of the *Encyclopédie* in 1751,
mixed liberal and absolutist opinions—it called at the same
time for limited power and submission to authority.[180] Most of

---

[178] *La voix du sage et du peuple*, xxiii, 466-471. When he was seeking
to impress authority, Voltaire made himself sound as loyal and as conservative as possible. His assertion that philosophes cannot be subversive,
like his assertion that books can never do anybody any harm, are tactical
pronouncements designed to disguise his radicalism.

[179] The Jansenist *Nouvelles ecclésiastiques* and the Jesuit *Journal de Trévoux* castigated Montesquieu, and both the Sorbonne and the Roman Inquisition investigated the book at length. Joseph Dedieu, *Montesquieu,
l'homme et l'oeuvre*, 184-185.

[180] Among Diderot's correspondence no letters have been preserved for
1750; Wilson points out that the article on "Autorité politique" was widely

the others—d'Alembert, Rousseau, Holbach—were too young, too busy, too detached to participate in this political debate; the shock troops of radicalism that Voltaire was leading into battle consisted mostly of himself and some minor figures like Toussaint and Chauvelin.[181]

It would of course have made no difference to the outcome if the philosophes had formed a full-fledged party. The real battle was waged at court and in the superstitious mind of Louis XV. For over a year, Machault, madame de Pompadour, and their allies among prominent administrators, urged the king to carry through his tax reforms, while the king's family, the Archbishop of Paris, and other leading clergymen urged him to abandon them. Finally, his timidity, conservatism, and fear of damnation won out over his pride, accesses of courage, and need of money: on 23 December 1751 he withdrew his declaration of 17 August 1750.[182] His surrender was complete and unconditional. The king thought that he had surrendered to God; the bishops thought that he had surrendered to them. In fact, the king's retreat was a first and irrevocable step in surrendering public opinion to the philosophes.

A great victory, Nietzsche has observed, is a great danger; indeed, there are some victories which it is best not to win or at least not to exploit. The clergy's successful defense of its privileges did much to arouse latent anticlericalism, but the bishops, flushed with triumph and heedless of danger, exacerbated hostility against them by the affair of the *billets de confession*. Despite the authority of the crown and the bishops, under-

---

considered daring (*Diderot*, 142-143), but it can have had no impact on the debate over the *vingtième*.

[181] It was Toussaint who published *Les moeurs*, a secular and anticlerical book, in 1748; Chauvelin was a parlementarian who became an important enemy of the Jesuits during their "expulsion" in 1762.

[182] Marion observes that the two pamphlets which most energetically defended the king's tax policy, Bargeton's *Lettres* and Voltaire's *Voix du sage*, were both condemned by Rome. "He was forbidden under pain of excommunication to own or read them; how then follow the policy which was highly recommended in them?" *Machault*, 314.

ground discontent with the Bull *Unigenitus* had persisted, even though in 1730 the king issued an edict making the Bull, already the law of the church, the law of the land. Beginning in the 1740's, some bishops ordered priests to refuse the sacraments to unrepentant Jansenists; in 1746 Christophe de Beaumont, Archbishop of Paris, instructed his clergy to refuse the last rites to any dying Christian who could not show a *billet de confession*, a statement attesting that he had confessed to a priest loyal to the Bull *Unigenitus*. To excited Jansenists and anti-Jesuit parlementarians, this was a most un-Christian obstruction of the road to salvation, and the *billets de confession* caused vehement debates which reached a climax after the king's surrender in December 1751.[183] In 1749, a Parisian curé had refused the last rites to a prominent Jansenist; in 1751, a councillor at a Parisian court suffered the same refusal; in 1752 an aged priest of known Jansenist leanings died without the sacraments; in 1753, the parlement of Paris vigorously remonstrated with the king, only to be exiled for its fervor. This bald recital of facts cannot convey the popular turbulence over the *billets*, turbulence that was not appeased until the mid-1750's, when Catholics could once again die in peace, whether they accepted *Unigenitus* or not. "In the war between the parlements and the bishops," wrote Voltaire to d'Alembert in 1756 with commendable impartiality, "reasonable people have the game in their hands. . . ."[184]

Although he had been out of France since June 1750, Voltaire continued to do his best for the reasonable people. Busy as he was at Potsdam, he always found time to follow French affairs with close attention,[185] and his political writings of these

[183] Voltaire was under the mistaken impression that the clergy deliberately precipitated the affair of the *billets de confession* as a diversion from the embarrassing affair of the *vingtième*. *Précis de siècle de Louis XV*, xv, 377. Marion has proved this to be an error. *Machault*, 330-331.
[184] 13 November (1756), xxxix, 131.
[185] See Voltaire to d'Argental, 15 October (1750) from Potsdam: "The adventure of . . . the bishops does not contribute little to making me love France." *Correspondence*, xviii, 181.

years all draw their energy from the *vingtième* crisis. The most ambitious among them, *Pensées sur le gouvernement*, reads like a new edition of the notorious *Voix du sage*.[186] It is full of reminiscences and even direct quotations from the earlier work, and like *La voix du sage*, the *Pensées* must be read as a commentary on French politics rather than a defense of absolutism in general. The much quoted remark, "It is very natural to love a dynasty that has reigned for almost eight hundred years," is an expression of the *thèse royale* and is aimed at the defenders of feudal privileges in France;[187] again, "A king who is not contradicted can hardly be evil," alludes to experiences of Henri IV, Louis XIV, and Louis XV with the parlements and the Assembly of the Clergy. It is not a statement of principle—had Voltaire been writing about England, he would have said the opposite.[188]

[186] *Pensées sur le gouvernement* was first published in 1752 and then reissued in somewhat revised form in 1754 and 1756. Two other political works of these years, *Dialogue entre un plaideur et un avocat* and *Dialogue entre un philosophe et un contrôleur général*, also hark back to the *vingtième*. In the first, Voltaire suggests that the domination of a single religion destroys sovereignty, which should be undivided and indifferent to religion:
"The Litigant: 'But it seems to me that in England there is only one law and one measure.'
The Advocate: 'Don't you see that the English are barbarians? They have the same measure, but in recompense they have twenty different religions.'
The Litigant: 'You tell me something that astonishes me. What! people who live under the same laws don't live under the same religion?'
The Advocate: 'No, and that proves clearly that they are devoted to their outcast views.'
The Litigant: 'Could it not also be that they believe the laws are made for the outside of men and religion for the inside?' " xxiii, 496.
In the second dialogue, Voltaire calls French ecclesiastics beggars who exact contributions from the people in the name of God, and then go to dine in fine mansions where they live at their ease. xxiii, 504.
[187] *Pensées sur le gouvernement*, xxiii, 528. Far too much has usually been made of this statement, innocent enough in context.
[188] *ibid.*, xxiii, 529. This statement, again, is a reminiscence of *La voix du sage*, as is evident from this passage in the *Pensées*: "After the adventure of the duc de Lauzun, Louis XIV did not act with rigor against a single person at his court: that is because he was absolute." *loc.cit.* See above, p. 136.

Stimulated as well as irritated by Montesquieu's *Esprit des lois*, Voltaire carefully distinguished between absolutism and despotism, and made clear in the *Pensées* that support of the first did not mean support of the second: "Despotism is the abuse of monarchies, as anarchy is the abuse of republics. A prince who imprisons or executes his subjects without justice or due process of law is nothing but a highway robber who is called 'Your Majesty.' "[189]

He was much too adroit and much too cautious to call the French Majesty a highway robber, but the remark suggests that he reserved the right to be critical of his king. It can hardly be repeated too emphatically that Voltaire's royalism was strategic and political rather than doctrinaire; it was a plea for a strong executive and against a strong aristocracy; it was, above all, an attack on privilege and on a clergy subservient to Rome.

In this polemic, Voltaire was not without support. Since the sixteenth century, Gallican Christians had sought to enhance the power of the French crown at the expense of the Papacy; since the early eighteenth century, anticlerical Christians—and there were many of them in France—had sought to enhance the power of the French crown at the expense of the French clergy. But *La voix du sage* was too drastic for them; with its secular conception of the state, with its assumption that the clergy was a group of public servants to be hired and fired at will, the pamphlet went far beyond the most radical Gallicans.[190] *La voix du sage* was a defense of Machault, but its position was so extreme as to embarrass the minister. To compare ecclesiastics to teachers whose "hours of work" and "program of study" should be fixed by the state was to preach dangerous doctrine: it deprived Roman Catholicism of its claim to be the only true religion, and transformed the King of France from the eldest son of the church into its master.

[189] XXIII, 530. As I have shown, d'Argenson drew the same distinction in his *Considérations*.
[190] See Marion, *Machault*, 264.

Hence *La voix du sage* made Voltaire unpopular with the very political party in whose behalf he had written it. *La Bigarrure*, a contemporary newsletter, reported that the pamphlet was written on orders of the court and that Voltaire was spirited away to Prussia to shield him from the wrath of the clergy.[191] But that report is as improbable as the contrary report, spread by his detractors, that Voltaire escaped to Prussia from a court angered by his misplaced zeal.[192] His real reason for leaving was

[191] See XXIII, 466n. That French clergymen were furious with Voltaire is, of course, beyond question—but they were right to see in him an implacable enemy. Constance Rowe writes that he was hounded by "royal leeches and clerical hypocrites" (*Voltaire and the State*, 53), but such Whiggish name-calling is hardly to the point. The clergy was attempting to protect an interest that Voltaire had begun to attack and would continue to attack. His later anticlerical pamphlets are little but echoes of his writings on the *vingt-ième*. See *Idées de la Mothe le Vayer* (date of writing and publication are both uncertain; Beuchot assigns the latter to 1767): "Which is the dangerous religion? Is it not obviously the religion that, establishing incomprehensible dogmas, necessarily gives men the urge to explain these dogmas each in his own manner, necessarily excites disputes, hatreds, civil wars? Is it not the religion that, calling itself independent of the sovereign and the magistrates, is necessarily in combat with the magistrates and the sovereign? Is it not the religion that, choosing its head outside the state, is necessarily in an open or secret war with the state?" XXIII, 489.

Of even greater interest is the article "Lois civiles et ecclésiastiques," in the *Dictionnaire philosophique*, published in 1764: "Let no ecclesiastical law have force unless it has the express sanction of the government. . . . Let the magistrate alone permit or prohibit work on holidays; it is not for priests to prohibit men from cultivating their fields. Let everything concerning marriage depend solely on the magistrate; let the priests limit themselves to the august function of blessing it. . . . Let all ecclesiastics be submitted in all law cases to the government; they are subjects of the state. Let us never have the ridiculous shame of paying to an alien priest the first year's revenue of a piece of land that citizens have given to their fellow-citizen, a priest. Let no priest ever be able to deprive a citizen of the smallest prerogative under the pretext that the citizen is a sinner, for the sinner-priest should pray for sinners, not judge them. Let magistrates, laborers, and priests pay equally for the expenses of the state, for they all belong equally to the state." (pp. 289-290). This article was written in the safety of Ferney, but it does little more than to spell out the implications of *La voix du sage*.

[192] Thus Rowe: ". . . he was speeded off to Prussia less by the persuasion of King Frederick than by the scathing almost revolutionary pamphlet, *La voix du sage*." *Voltaire and the State*, 52-53. In his *Mémoires*, the mendacious Marmontel tells still another version which is wholly unpolitical: Voltaire was first tempted to go to Prussia because of his disgust with literary

that after the death of madame du Châtelet there was little to keep him in France, not even his niece, madame Denis.

This is not to say that the fiasco of *La voix du sage* was not a bitter disappointment to Voltaire. In August 1750, he complained to the duc de Richelieu from Potsdam that his pamphlet had attempted "to sustain the rights of the king. But the king hardly cares to have his rights sustained."[193] It is a wistful and an accurate comment on French politics at mid-century, and, in view of the king's surrender to the clergy in December 1751, a prescient prediction. Whether a more energetic king could have imposed fiscal reforms on the church of France must remain an unanswered question. But it is certain that while the course of action advocated by Machault and his supporter Voltaire might have failed, the course of action—or rather inaction—that Louis XV adopted instead could not but fail. Voltaire sought to save the Old Regime by transforming it. In refusing to transform it, Louis XV was leading it to ruin. As he moved comfortably toward Potsdam in the early summer of 1750 to visit the King of Prussia, Voltaire must have asked himself whether a Frederick on the French throne would not have done better.

---

squabbles in Paris, and was finally lured to depart in haste because he was read a poem of Frederick's that compared him to a setting, and a wholly insignificant young poet to a rising sun. The only trouble with all these stories is that they are contradicted by the plain evidence of the correspondence. Voltaire negotiated with Frederick throughout the spring, and these negotiations were completed in May of 1750. See chapter III.

[193] (ca. 31 August 1750), *Correspondence*, XVIII, 144; in a long letter of apology for his "desertion" of France. Careful to protect his anonymity, Voltaire does not allude to *La voix du sage* by name, but only as a pamphlet "which people attribute to me."

III

PRUSSIA:
SPARTA IN A COLD CLIMATE

You must know my Prussian king, when he was but a man, lov'd passionately yr. englhigh gouvernement. But the king has altered the man, and now he relishes despotik pouver, as much as a Mustapha, a Selim or a Solyman.
　　　　　　　　　—VOLTAIRE to Fawkener, ca. June 1742

1. THE SALOMON OF THE NORTH

DURING Voltaire's years at Cirey, madame du Châtelet had only one serious competitor for her lover's attention, Frederick of Prussia.[1] Like most private matters in the eighteenth century, the friendship between prince and poet was exceedingly public and aroused widespread interest in Voltaire's own day. In our day, it has established his reputation as a partisan of enlightened despotism; Frederick, more than any other ruler, is supposed to embody Voltaire's ideal. Voltaire's royal friendships, we are told, reveal the essence of his political philosophy, a proposition that deserves more careful examination than it has received.

It was the Prussian Crown Prince who began the friendship in 1736 with an ardent letter, the letter of a disciple to a revered master: "I find beauties beyond number in your works.... One cannot imitate Voltaire, short of being Voltaire himself.

---

[1] Voltaire's affair with madame Denis was kept strictly secret and never threatened to remove Voltaire from his association with madame du Châtelet. Frederick was a much greater danger.

In these moments I feel that the advantages of birth and the phantom, greatness, with which vanity deludes us, are good for little or rather for nothing. . . . If my destiny should not favor me enough to be able to possess you, at least let me hope that I shall one day see the man whom I have admired from afar for a long time.''[2]

The summer when this letter was written and received, was a critical time both for Frederick and for Voltaire. The crown prince, then twenty-four, had just occupied his own castle in the domain of Rheinsberg. It was an immense liberation for him: after trying all his life to please a stern father he could now for the first time please himself. He was a sensitive, secretive young man who had been compelled to take an interest in things that bored him, and to suppress an interest in things that fascinated him; he was an aesthete whose father ridiculed him as a dandy, a scholar who had to buy and read his large library in secret. Only six years before, he had sought to flee to England, but the escape had been cruelly frustrated. Now he could flee to Rheinsberg; he could have music and paintings and novels and French verses. And he could try to "possess" Voltaire.

He opened his campaign at an auspicious time, when Voltaire was going through one of his periods of panic. The censors were making serious difficulties over his comedy, *L'enfant prodigue*, and over his poem, *Le mondain*; the bookseller Jore was trying to blackmail him with documentary evidence that Voltaire had written the *Lettres philosophiques*. This conjunction was not lost on Voltaire. "These persecutions on one hand," he wrote to Thieriot on 27 November 1736, "and a new invitation from the Prince of Prussia and from the Duke of Holstein on the other, at last force me to leave. I shall be in Berlin soon."[3] And less than two weeks later he complained to Cideville, using more excited exclamation points than usual:

[2] 8 August 1736, *Correspondence*, v, 212-214.
[3] *Correspondence*, v, 331.

"I have spoken to you of persecutions in my letter. Do you know that *Le mondain* has been treated as a scandalous work, and can you imagine that they are using this miserable excuse to crush me? What a century we are living in! And after what a century! To accuse me of a crime for having said that Adam had long fingernails, and to treat that seriously as a heresy! I assure you that I am outraged; friendship must have great power over my heart, for otherwise I would have sought a retreat far from here, like Bayle and Descartes."[4]

Time and distance did not mellow Voltaire's impressions of these events. When he moved to Prussia in the summer of 1750, he told his closest friends, the d'Argentals: "You will say that it was fifteen years ago, that all this is past. No, my angels, it happened a day ago, and these atrocious injustices are always recent wounds." Perhaps Voltaire did not remember the "atrocious injustices" of 1736 accurately, but they had come to acquire a reality of their own. His sufferings had been slighter in fact than they became in memory, but it was memory, not fact, that governed his conduct.[5]

Voltaire thus looked to Frederick as a possible protector. He could not be certain whether adroitness, influential friends, and money—and he had all of these in abundance by the 1730's—could keep him out of the Bastille.

Si le ciel t'a fait roi, c'est pour me protéger,

he wrote in his tragedy *Mérope*, doubtless thinking of his relationship with the philosophic prince.[6]

A French writer finding refuge with the Prussian king—this idea should not be discounted as Voltaire's extravagance. Diderot expressed the same idea quite independently in one of

[4] 8 (December 1736), *ibid.*, v, 347-348. See also Voltaire to Thieriot, 24 November 1736, *ibid.*, v, 325.

[5] 28 August (1750), *ibid.*, xviii, 135; see Voltaire to the duc de Richelieu (ca. 31 August 1750), *ibid.*, xviii, 140-146. Voltaire's overstatements are similar to Dickens' experiences in debtors' prison and his later use of these experiences.

[6] *Mérope* is of 1743; it thus dates from the late Cirey period. The line is in act iv, scene 2. iv, 235.

his earliest philosophical works, *La promenade du sceptique* (1747). He imagines a dialogue between an author who wants to enlighten the public and a friend who urges him to suppress his radical manuscript: "Religion and government are sacred subjects which it is not permitted to touch. . . . It is better to be a bad author who is left alone than to be a good author who is persecuted." A mutual friend resolves this debate by proposing that the author place himself under the protection of the "philosopher-prince" of Prussia: "Pass into his state with your work, and let the bigots rage." This was a suggestion the author could accept: "This advice was in accord with my tranquility, my interests, and my vices."[7]

Voltaire's friendship with Frederick was in accord with his tranquility and his interests, but also with his vices. Correspondence with a crown prince, and especially such a crown prince, flattered Voltaire's vanity. In 1740, after the crown prince became king, and in 1748, after Voltaire had failed to conquer the French court, his friendship with Frederick became even more valuable. A bourgeois poet, disdained at Versailles, was being courted from Potsdam by a king who was one of the most extraordinary figures in an extraordinary century: a statesman, general, poet, metaphysician. "I did not fail to feel attached to him," wrote Voltaire, "for he had wit and charm, and what is more, he was king, which, given human weakness, is always a great seduction. Ordinarily, we men of letters flatter kings; this one praised me from head to toe."[8]

This singular prince touched more than vanity in Voltaire; again and again, Voltaire confessed to an overwhelming attraction: "How does one resist a victorious king, a poet, musician, and philosopher, who affected to appear to love me! I believed that I loved him!"[9] Writing to his niece, madame de Fontaine, from Berlin, Voltaire called Frederick an old passion: "He

[7] *Oeuvres complètes*, I, 181, 184-185, 187.
[8] *Mémoires*, I, 17.
[9] *ibid.*, I, 36.

turned my head."[10] And he told the duc de Richelieu, again from Berlin, "I gave myself to him out of passion, out of infatuation, and without reflection."[11]

This is hyperbolic language, but it was a hyperbolic century, and the effusions of Voltaire to his friends, like the effusions of Voltaire to Frederick, must be discounted. These most urbane of correspondents peppered their letters with exaggerations that seem cloying today, but were ritual formulas then. The king called the poet the Apollo of the French Parnassus, and the poet called the king the Salomon of the North, but Voltaire reduced such language to its proper value with a single pointed phrase: "Epithets cost us nothing."[12] He anticipated by a century Disraeli's celebrated *mot* that "Everyone likes flattery; and when you come to Royalty you should lay it on with a trowel."

"Hypocrisy" is a word that is used much too freely; Reinhold Koser, a distinguished biographer of Frederick, has said that beneath these honeyed epithets there was a real elective affinity.[13] The two men had much in common: energy, wit, malice, love of literature, interest in philosophical speculation, a gift for intrigue, impatience with stupidity, and contempt for supernatural religion. There were times when Voltaire distrusted Frederick and when Frederick despised Voltaire, and there were times when both had good reasons for their feelings. But each knew his friend and the world well enough to appreciate the other's virtues, although never as much as the other's vices.

Interest, vanity, affection, admiration—these were the elements in Voltaire's friendship for Frederick. And, perhaps ex-

[10] 23 September (1750), *Correspondence*, XVIII, 167.

[11] 31 August 1751, *ibid.*, XIX, 39.

[12] *Mémoires*, I, 14. Voltaire's hyperbole appears measured politeness compared to the effusions of other eighteenth-century writers. Grimm wrote to Catherine the Great that he wanted to be counted among her dogs, and that he was a mere worm created to crawl at her feet. Dimitri S. von Mohrenschildt, *Russia in the Intellectual Life of Eighteenth-Century France*, 134. Diderot, much less given to flattery, called the moment he received Voltaire's first letter to him "one of the sweetest moments of my life." Denis Diderot, *Correspondance*, Georges Roth, ed. (1955), I, 75.

[13] Reinhold Koser, *Geschichte Friedrichs des Grossen*, II, 267.

cept for affection, they were also the elements in Frederick's friendship for Voltaire. This was no one-sided bargain; Frederick, too, derived tangible benefits from it. For Frederick, as for most cultivated men, Voltaire was Europe's greatest living poet, the successor to Corneille and Racine. Frederick had read, repeatedly and avidly, whatever work of Voltaire his agents could procure for him— the *Histoire de Charles XII* in 1732, the *Henriade*, the *Lettres philosophiques*, the plays.[14] To be singled out by such a poet, to receive letters from him—and what letters!—to answer them in kind, all this was gratifying nourishment to the talented prince whose abilities had been stifled and whose affections had been starved at home.

Their correspondence soon became intimate, but correspondence was not intimacy enough for Frederick. When the crown prince became king he renewed his invitations with greater insistence and greater authority. The king's first letter to Voltaire, written on 6 June 1740, a week after his accession, breathes a tone of camaraderie that would have melted the most unfeeling of men: "I beg you, see in me only a zealous citizen, a philosopher who is a bit skeptical, but a friend who is truly faithful. For God's sake, write to me only as a man, and join me in despising titles, names, and external glitter."[15] Voltaire showed this private letter to his friends with even greater pride than he had shown the others. He met the King of Prussia three months later, in September 1740, near Cleves; in November and December, while Frederick was contemplating his attack on Austrian Silesia, Voltaire visited Rheinsberg and Berlin. He talked about poetry, listened to concerts, shared intimate suppers with the king. But these and later visits were only preliminaries: Frederick wanted to "possess" Voltaire, and he found his opportunity only after 1749—after the death of madame du Châtelet.

[14] See Frederick's first letter to Voltaire, 8 August 1736.
[15] *Correspondence*, x, 145.

His negotiations with Voltaire were concluded in May 1750, while the French clergy was gathering in Paris for its Assembly. Voltaire may not have been afflicted with the canonical vice of avarice, but his thrift bears a striking resemblance to it; he asked the king to advance his expenses.[16] Frederick complied, comparing himself with Jupiter showering gold on Danaë, and, in the same letter, Voltaire with Horace, who liked to "unite the useful to the agreeable."[17] In a charming reply, Voltaire pleaded guilty with unabashed good nature:

Votre très-vieille Danaé
Va quitter son petit ménage
Pour le beau séjour étoilé
Dont elle est indigne à son âge.
L'or par Jupiter envoyé
N'est pas l'objet de son envie;
Elle aime d'un coeur dévoué
Son Jupiter, et non sa pluie.
Mais c'est en vain que l'on médit
De ces gouttes très-salutaires:
Au siècle de fer où l'on vit,
Les gouttes d'or sont nécessaires.

Voltaire wrote these lines on 9 June 1750;[18] the next day he left Paris. His long stay with Frederick began as a spectacular success and ended as a spectacular failure. He reached Potsdam late in July, and was greeted by the king as his "only Apollo."[19] Voltaire was enchanted with Frederick, who had transformed "a sad Sparta into a brilliant Athens."[20] Frederick gave Vol-

---

[16] But in his letter of 8 May (1750), *Correspondence*, xviii, 61-62, Voltaire makes it clear that he intended to repay the money.

[17] 24 May 1750, *ibid.*, xviii, 72-73. Voltaire liked to say that Frederick scratched with one hand while he protected with the other. See Voltaire to Frederick, 26 June 1750, *ibid.*, xviii, 92.

[18] *ibid.*, xviii, 79.

[19] See Besterman's note, *ibid.*, xviii, 104n.

[20] Voltaire to the marquis de Thibouville, 1 August (1750), *ibid.*, xviii, 109. He liked the Sparta-Athens image and used it repeatedly. See Voltaire

taire the post of a chamberlain, the *pour le mérite*, and, remembering his Danaë, a generous salary; he asked permission of Louis XV to attach Voltaire to his court—a permission that was granted with insulting rapidity on condition that Voltaire divest himself of his post as historiographer. In France no one could understand Voltaire's "desertion."[21] To his courtiers Louis XV said that this made one madman more at the court of Prussia and one madman less at his own court.[22] From Potsdam the madman reported that he was happy: he spoke without constraint, he was at liberty to complete his *Siècle de Louis XIV*, he attended philosophic suppers, made witty conversation, and corrected Frederick's writings.

But brilliant Athens turned out to be, after all, only a sad Sparta in disguise, and the King of Prussia, for all his Athenian polish, a Spartan martinet. Voltaire assured his correspondents that he and *Fédéric le grand* were made for each other, but like two tenors in an opera company, they were the kind of friends who love each other most when one is on tour. Voltaire had long had good reason to distrust Frederick. In 1741 he had written the comtesse d'Argental: "I still don't know if the King of Prussia deserves the interest we are taking in him: he is king—that makes one tremble."[23] Two years later, exasperated

to Princess Louise Ulrica of Prussia, 22 December (1743), *ibid.*, XIII, 154. In this elegant age of the classical allusion, it was probably a commonplace. Frederick used it himself: "Under Frederick I Berlin was the Athens of the North; under Frederick William she became the Sparta." Quoted in Penfield Roberts, *The Quest for Security* (1947), 63.

[21] Friends like the d'Argentals were wounded, admirers like Lord Chesterfield were puzzled, while his many enemies were greatly pleased. There was much justice in Voltaire's complaint to madame Denis: "It is amusing that the same men of letters of Paris who wanted to *exterminate* me only a year ago, now declaim against my removal, and call it desertion. It seems they are angry at having lost their victim." 13 October (1750), *ibid.*, XVIII, 180. See also *ibid.*, XVIII, 174n. It did seem rather odd to make Voltaire give up his post of historiographer and give it to Duclos at the very time that Voltaire was completing the greatest history of France yet written.

[22] D'Argenson, 25 August 1750, *Journal et mémoires*, VI, 249.

[23] 13 March (1741), *Correspondence*, XI, 56.

by clumsy French efforts to convert Voltaire into a spy at his court, Frederick committed a *petite trahison* against the Apollo of the French Parnassus: he conveyed into the hands of the French government a purported letter of Voltaire's, filled with offensive remarks against Louis XV and other high personages. "My intention," Frederick admitted candidly, "is to embroil Voltaire so thoroughly in France, that nothing will remain for him to do but to come to me."[24] The letter was a forgery, and the plot neither worked nor remained secret; Voltaire discovered it and acknowledged that the favor of a treacherous king was dangerous.[25]

Yet, dangerous as it was, Voltaire continued to seek it, although not always without dignity. He knew that Frederick was a cynic, and told him so: "Sire, Your Majesty makes beautiful verses, but you mock at the world."[26] But until he went to Prussia in 1750, he did not know how deep that cynicism went. In 1749 Frederick told his intimate Algarotti that he despised Voltaire but needed him to study French elocution: "One can learn good things from a scoundrel. I want to know French, what do I care about his morals?"[27] In November 1750, after a brief three months at the Prussian court, Voltaire sensed this royal indifference. "So they know in Paris, my dear child," he wrote to madame Denis, "that we have played *La mort de*

[24] Frederick to Friedrich Rudolf, Count von Rothenburg, 17 August 1743, *ibid.*, XIII, 46. For the forgery and other details of the plot, see Besterman's note, *loc. cit.* The phrase "little treason" is the king's own. See Besterman's note, *ibid.*, XIII, 96n.

[25] Voltaire to Amelot, then French foreign minister (5 October 1743), *ibid.*, XIII, 95-96.

[26] 26 January 1749, *ibid.*, XVII, 17. One of Voltaire's favorite terms for Frederick was "coquette"; upon his first departure from Berlin, 2 December 1740, he used it in a little farewell poem to the king himself. See *ibid.*, X, 355.

[27] Besterman's note, *ibid.*, XVII, 164n. Most German historians of Frederick have associated themselves with the king's contempt for Voltaire's supposed moral failings—a regrettable surrender of independent judgment. Surely it was not a moralist who wrote these lines to Algarotti, praised Voltaire to his face and defamed him to his back, caressed with one paw and scratched with the other.

César in Potsdam, that Prince Henri is a good actor, has no accent, is very amiable, and that we have pleasure here? All that is true; . . . But . . . the suppers of the king are delicious; there we talk reason, wit, science; there liberty reigns; he is the soul of it all; no ill humor, no cloud, at least no storms. My life is free and occupied; but . . . but . . . opera, comedies, carrousels, suppers at Sans Souci, war manoeuvers, concerts, studies, reading; but . . . but . . . the city of Berlin, large, much easier to traverse than Paris, palace, theatres, affable queens, charming princesses, beautiful and well constructed maids of honor, the house of madame de [Tyrconnell] always full and often too full; . . . but . . . my dear child, the weather is beginning to get pretty cold."[28] Two weeks later he explained his mysterious language: "I saw a touching, pathetic, and even highly Christian letter that the king deigned to write to d'Arget on the death of his wife. I learned the same day that his majesty had made an epigram against the deceased; that doesn't fail to make you think."[29] He was becoming fearful: "They give me the velvet paws more than ever; but . . ."[30]

The weather was indeed getting pretty cold, and Voltaire did nothing to raise the temperature. During the winter of 1750 to 1751, he became mired in a confused lawsuit with the Berlin banker Abraham Hirschel over some dubious speculations. Frederick took advantage of the unsavory affair to express his disdain for a poet whom he had long affected to admire, and to adopt the improbable pose of a "German who says what he thinks."[31]

[28] 6 November (1750), *ibid.*, XVIII, 197.
[29] Voltaire to madame Denis, 17 November (1750), *ibid.*, XVIII, 210.
[30] Voltaire to madame Denis, 24 November (1750), *ibid.*, XVIII, 218.
[31] Frederick to Voltaire, 28 February 1751, *ibid.*, XIX, 77. Eighteenth-century politeness was a powerful civilizing agent, but it exacted its price: it made the expression of hostility very difficult. One can sense, again and again, correspondents smarting under the obligation to suppress hostile feelings. Both Voltaire and Frederick often were angry with each other, but the man of letters could not afford the luxury of telling his friend so. The king could.

For the moment the candid German did not think the time ripe for a break. Neither did Voltaire. His friends begged him to return to France, to face the predictable and limited displeasure of Paris rather than the unpredictable and much more dangerous displeasure of Potsdam. Their advice was affectionate and rich in common sense, but they were amateurs in literature. Voltaire, just as affectionate, perhaps sometimes lacked common sense, but he was a professional man of letters with an enormous respect for his craft. He was reluctant to leave Prussia while he was supervising the publication of his collected works, and without finishing, after twenty long years, his *Siècle de Louis XIV*. These chores were part, an important part, of his métier; they were more important to him than pleasure, comfort, and even friendship. "The longer I advance in the career of my life," he wrote to Hénault in August 1751, "the more I find work necessary. In the long run it becomes the greatest of pleasures, and takes the place of all the illusions we have lost."[32]

Voltaire's hope that he could maintain good relations with Frederick was one illusion he had not yet lost. It was dissipated in September 1751 by La Mettrie, "the king's atheist," the irresponsible, good-natured, gourmandizing materialist philosopher who was Frederick's reader. The king, La Mettrie told Voltaire, was getting ready to discard his most distinguished guest. "I shall need him another year at the most; one squeezes the orange and one throws away the peel." True or false, the re-

[32] 15 August (1751), *ibid.*, xx, 12. The most revealing letters concerning Voltaire's return are d'Argental's hard-headed and moving letter of 6 August 1751, *ibid.*, xx, 3-4 ("He [the king] is a coquette who, in order to keep several lovers, makes none of them happy. . . . You went in search of liberty and you have submitted to the greatest constraint"); Voltaire's reply, 28 August (1751), *ibid.*, xx, 31-32; and Voltaire's long letter to the duc de Richelieu, 31 August 1751, *ibid.*, xx, 35-40, "You will tell me that I am a pedant and you will be right, but one must never abandon what one has begun, and perhaps you will not be annoyed to see my *Siècle*. You know very well that there is not one little censor of books [in Paris] who would not have made a merit and a duty out of mutilating or suppressing my work." (p. 37).

mark stunned Voltaire: "A king who has won battles and provinces," he wrote to madame Denis, "a northern king who makes verses in our language, a king, finally, whom I did not seek out, and who told me that he loved me! Why did he make so many advances to me? . . . I have done what I can not to believe La Mettrie." Yet he could not bring himself to leave Prussia: "When a man has started something he must finish it; and I have two editions on my hands. . . ."[33] Struggling to dismiss La Mettrie's gossip, he compared himself to a cuckold who trusts his wife, and to a man falling from a steeple who says to himself in midair: "Good, provided it lasts."[34]

It did not last. Voltaire resolved the conflict between his urge to stay and his urge to leave just as several years before, at the court of Louis XV, he had resolved a similar conflict— by precipitating an explosion. In 1752 the head of the Prussian Academy, Maupertuis, a distinguished physicist, geometer, and explorer, opinionated, avid of notoriety, brilliant and unstable, became embroiled with the Dutch mathematician König, his friend and fellow Academician, an intelligent and pitiless controversialist. König dared to question Maupertuis' hypothesis that nature always acts economically on a "principle of least action"; he cited an unpublished letter to prove that Leibnitz had been the first to enunciate the principle but had wisely refused to make extravagant deductions from it. Stung, incapable of taking scientific criticism objectively, Maupertuis challenged König to produce the original Leibnitz letter and, when he could not do so, induced his Academy to accuse König of forgery. It was a highhanded proceeding; König promptly resigned from the Berlin Academy and published an

[33] 2 September (1751), *ibid.*, xx, 43. Koser dismisses the remark as improbable and calls it the malicious mischief of an amoral person. *Geschichte Friedrichs des Grossen*, ii, 272. Koser may be right, but Frederick's behavior in these years makes the remark far less improbable than Koser suggests.

[34] Voltaire to madame Denis, 29 October (1751), *Correspondence*, xx, 71.

Appeal to the Public in which he acidly conceded Maupertuis' claim to originality: what was true in the principle of least action was in Leibnitz, what was untrue in it had been added by Maupertuis.

Voltaire was delighted. He had known both König and Maupertuis since the days of his scientific researches at Cirey, and he disliked them both. Now he threw himself into the controversy with feverish and heedless pleasure. Voltaire's motives, as always, were mixed. He liked to make mischief; he had an old grievance against Maupertuis for his amorous conquest of madame du Châtelet; perhaps he resented his eminence in Prussia. But above all he was outraged at the arrogant persecution of König, and he felt obligated to protest in the name of free intellectuals. In his first published contribution to the controversy, he said Maupertuis stood condemned for "abusing his position by depriving men of letters of their liberty, and for persecuting an honest man whose only crime is not to agree with him."[35] And a week later he told a friend: "If he were a Newton he wouldn't be permitted to be impertinent in an Academy, and to act there as a tyrant."[36]

Voltaire knew that such pronouncements must intensely irritate Frederick, who took great pride in his Academy, but he courted that irritation. When the King of Prussia entered the squabble with a crude pamphlet attacking Voltaire as a vile scribbler, the storm signals were up, but Voltaire ignored them. Impudently taking advantage of the royal permission to print another work, he published a devastating lampoon against Maupertuis, the *Diatribe du docteur Akakia*. The philosophic king, acting like a most unphilosophic censor, had the pam-

[35] Voltaire to *Bibliothèque raisonnée*, 18 September 1752, published under the title *Réponse d'un académicien de Berlin à un académicien de Paris, Correspondence*, xxi, 72. The lines most offensive to Frederick were the concluding sentence: "Several members of the Berlin Academy have protested against such shocking conduct, and would have left the Academy which M. Maupertuis dishonors and tyrannizes over, if they did not fear to displease the king who is its patron." *loc. cit.*

[36] Voltaire to countess Bentinck, 25 September (1752), *ibid.*, xxi, 75.

phlet publicly burned by the hangman, and melodramatically sent the ashes to Maupertuis.

Voltaire was now cured of his infatuation for the King of Prussia. In December 1752, appalled at Frederick's authoritarianism, and sensing the inevitable, he sent a "little dictionary for the use of kings" to madame Denis: "*My friend* signifies *my slave. My dear friend* means *you are less than nothing to me.* By *I shall make you happy* understand *I shall tolerate you as long as I need you. Dine with me tonight* signifies *I shall make fun of you tonight.*"[37] On 23 March 1753, Salomon and Apollo said farewell to each other as coolly as three years before they had greeted each other warmly. The celebrated friendship seemed at an end, but their correspondence was renewed during the Seven Years' War and continued until Voltaire's death in 1778. The two men never saw each other again, but grudgingly and often cynically they pursued their dialogue, as two civilized men surrounded by savages recognize their affinity despite their mutual distrust.

The student of Voltaire's political ideas who examines this singular friendship must begin with one harsh fact: much as Frederick invited Voltaire to treat him as an equal, much as the two men had in common, they were not equals. The poet needed the prince more than the prince needed the poet. Given Voltaire's circumstances and the limitations of his character, he could not reasonably be expected to advise the King of Prussia to abdicate, or to share his power, in the name of philosophy. Voltaire was not likely to tell Frederick much that Frederick might not want to hear.[38]

[37] 18 December (1752), *ibid.*, xxi, 180. On 28 January 1753 he wrote to La Virotte, translator of several English works on science: "I have never denied my attachment for him; I have had an enthusiasm of sixteen years, but he has cured me of that long disease." *ibid.*, xxii, 53.

[38] I am not suggesting that Voltaire's attitude toward the King of Prussia was the best of all moral attitudes or even the only possible one. Perhaps a sturdy independence, coupled with a refusal to go to Prussia, would

In his conversations and in his correspondence with Frederick, therefore, Voltaire voiced political ideas that were commonplace and predictable. Even more striking than their mild tone is the rarity of Voltaire's allusions to political questions. When they first met near Cleves in 1740, the two men talked of "the immortality of the soul, freedom [of the will], and Plato's androgynes." In Potsdam they discussed superstitions and the first articles of the *Dictionnaire philosophique;*[39] in their letters they debated each other's writings, the drama, and freedom versus determinism. Frederick and Voltaire were far more deeply engaged by persons, poetry, and philosophy than by politics. Their colloquies were thoughtful and sometimes brilliant, but there is little evidence that here was a modern Aristotle instructing a modern Alexander.[40]

---

have been superior. But the question that is of interest here is, what significance do Voltaire's relations with Frederick have for Voltaire's political philosophy?

[39] *Mémoires,* I, 17, 28; see XVII, vii.

[40] Since it is generally accepted that Voltaire thought of himself as a philosophic guide to the King of Prussia, it is important to weigh the evidence carefully. Thus Constance Rowe writes: "In August 1736, when this prince first chose him as a philosophic master, Voltaire saw and seized what seemed to him an incredible opportunity. Here was his long-awaited chance to influence a monarch to benefit humanity. . . . The two correspondents met [in 1740], and Voltaire, the so-called skeptic, came away convinced that the prince he had trained for the kingship would prove to be a civilizer of infinite possibilities." *Voltaire and the State,* 42, 43. Gaxotte goes even further: "It was whispered in Paris that the philosopher was already on the road to Berlin and would be made first minister on his arrival. First minister of the king of Prussia? And why not? . . . In the *Ode to the King of Prussia on the Occasion of his Accession* Voltaire had slipped in a discreet hint. . . ." *Frederick the Great,* 193. The discreet hint of which Gaxotte speaks is in the first stanza of the poem:

> Est-ce aujourd'hui le jour le plus beau de ma vie?
> Ne me trompe-je point dans un espoir si doux?
> Vous régnez. Est-il vrai que la philosophie
> Va régner avec vous?

VIII, 443.

This is not much to go on. The "philosophie" in the poem is ambiguous, and there is no hard evidence that Voltaire expected to become Frederick's minister. What is much more likely is that he expected a different kind of invitation, perhaps to join the Berlin Academy.

This is not to say that Voltaire eschewed the role of preceptor to a prince who was eighteen years his junior and who professed to worship him. But Voltaire's instructions, interspersed with genial admissions that power politics is a tough and amoral business, were little more than exhortations to decency and humaneness. In his first letter to the crown prince, Voltaire set the tone: "Believe me, the only truly good kings have been those who began, like you, by educating themselves, by knowing mankind, by loving truth, by detesting persecution and superstition."[41] After the philosophical prince had become the warrior king, Voltaire continued to extol the blessings of peace and deprecate the glories of war:

> Grand roi, j'aime fort les héros,
> Lorsque leur esprit s'abandonne
> Aux doux passe-temps, aux bons mots:
> Car alors ils sont en repos,
> Et ne font de tort à personne.[42]

He had little hope that he could transform Frederick into a peace-loving monarch, but he tried to make him feel guilty about waging war:

> Je vous aime pourtant, malgré tout ce carnage
> Dont vous avez souillé les champs de nos Germains,
> Malgré tous ces guerriers que vos vaillantes mains
> Font passer au sombre rivage.
> Vous êtes un héros, mais vous êtes un sage;
> Votre raison maudit les exploits inhumains
> Où vous força votre courage;
> Au milieu des canons, sur les morts entassés,
> Affrontant le trépas, et fixant la victoire,
> Du sang des malheureux cimentant votre gloire,
> Je vous pardonne tout, si vous en gémissez.[43]

[41] (ca. 1 September 1736), *Correspondence*, v, 231.
[42] (ca. 15 June 1743), *ibid.*, XII, 245.
[43] 26 May (1742), *ibid.*, XII, 47. For some sarcastic lines on Frederick's invasion of Saxony in 1756, see *Au roi de Prusse*, x, 557-558.

Voltaire wrote these lines in May 1742, a year and a half after Frederick had shocked European opinion by his invasion of Austrian Silesia. Almost four months later, the two men met at Aix-la-Chapelle, after Frederick had made a separate treaty with Austria, leaving the war as treacherously as he had entered it. Voltaire took the occasion to lecture the king, to tell him candidly that he was held in abhorrence all over Europe and would have to work twenty years to re-establish his good name.[44]

Such poems and such lectures have given Voltaire the reputation of a pacifist, of an idealistic dreamer whom no realistic monarch need take seriously. It is true that Voltaire waged a lifelong war on war, but he was not strictly speaking a pacifist. He denounced war as robbery, the desire to reap what one has not sown;[45] he argued that the soldiers and civilians who are its victims usually have no idea of its cause and no stake in its outcome;[46] he suggested that war impoverishes the victors as much as the vanquished, and that its only beneficiaries are insanely ambitious princes, war contractors and their mistresses, and fanatical priests who bless what they should curse: "Every murderer's chief has his colors blessed and solemnly invokes God before he goes to exterminate his fellowman. . . . Everyone marches gaily to crime under the banner of his saint."[47]

---

[44] From an eyewitness report of the conversation by the baron Pöllnitz, as given to Valori, the French ambassador to Prussia. Quoted in Fernand Baldensperger, "Les prémices d'une douteuse amitié: Voltaire et Frédéric II de 1740 à 1742," *Revue de littérature comparée*, x, 260-261. Baldensperger considers the report authentic, and I see no reason to doubt his judgment.

[45] *Dieu et les hommes*, xxviii, 130. See: "I know that only the Tartars ever had reason to make war, and that was to have good wine and pretty girls." Voltaire to Jean-Robert Tronchin, 23 June (1759), *Correspondance avec les Tronchin*, 407.

[46] *Micromégas*, xxi, 119; *Sur la paix de 1736*, viii, 434.

[47] *Dictionnaire philosophique*, article "Guerre," 230-231. See *Siècle de Louis XIV*, xiv, 525; Voltaire to Helvétius, 19 January (1761), xli, 158-159; Voltaire to the duchesse de Saxe-Gotha, 31 July 1761, xli, 382. "The decisive and complete battles have been neither complete nor decisive. But what is complete is the misery of nations. And what has been decided is

But while heroism is cant, and while war, in a word, is madness, Voltaire did not deny a nation the right to military self-defense. He did not have an invincible aversion to the use of war as an instrument of policy, and on occasion he even rationalized aggressive war when waged by a favorite prince.[48] It was his considered opinion that war was an inevitable evil, and the opinion that he ascribes to Duplessis-Mornay in the *Henriade* was his own:

> D'un oeil ferme et stoïque il regarde la guerre
> Comme un fléau du ciel, affreux, mais nécessaire.[49]

Despite Voltaire's concessions to realism, tough-minded historians have sometimes been contemptuous of his pacific insinuations to Frederick; they have argued that he was giving advice that the king either could not use or did not need. It must be admitted that the king took the poet seriously only in literary matters. When Voltaire urged Frederick to pursue his political aims by peaceful means, the king disregarded the advice, sometimes with the disdain of the man of affairs for the unworldly poet, sometimes with the tragic pose of a philosopher whom brutal reality leaves no choice: "I am a galley slave chained to the vessel of state."[50]

Yet Voltaire's preaching of Enlightenment humanitarianism

---

that we are madmen." Voltaire to Jean-Robert Tronchin, 4 October (1758), *Correspondance avec les Tronchin*, 349; "We shall be able to take Madras, we shall lose Canada, and at the end of seven or eight years of war we shall be seven or eight millions poorer than before." Voltaire to the same, 23 June (1759), *ibid.*, 407.

[48] For the "official" Voltaire, blessing the colors of France, see his poem on Fontenoy, and *Eloge funèbre des officiers qui sont morts dans la guerre de 1741*, XXIII, 250; for his blessing the colors of Catherine's Russia, see especially *Sur la guerre des Russes contre les Turcs*, VIII, 490. It may be added that these exceptions weigh but lightly in view of his great antiwar chapter in *Candide*, XXI, 141-143.

[49] VIII, 157.

[50] Frederick to Voltaire, 5 March 1749, *Correspondence*, XVII, 38. The King of Prussia is here lamenting his inability to take time off for poetry, but the remark applies with equal force to his inability to take time off for humanity.

was not irrelevant, either to the realities of politics or to a man of Frederick's character. Once in power, Frederick revealed himself as a worthy successor to his boorish father—niggardly and authoritarian, efficient and hard-working, wholly dedicated to Prussia's territorial growth, financial stability, and military might. But he also admired French culture, sought to emulate French men of letters, and craved their applause. I suspect that he admired and despised Voltaire much as he admired and despised himself. By superb self-discipline he had transformed the flute-playing aesthete into the austere commander, but his excessive pride in his toughness, cynicism and supreme independence suggests that he feared being soft, sentimental, and in need of affection. Voltaire sensed this ambivalence and sought to exploit it, not always without success.[51]

For while *raison d'état* had undisputed primacy in the battlefield of international politics, humanitarianism had some opportunity for play in domestic affairs, especially when it did not conflict with the requirements of high policy. "In the area of domestic politics," writes Friedrich Meinecke, "it was not so hard to arrive at a reassuring concordance of *raison d'état* and enlightenment ideal."[52] In the *Anti-Machiavelli*, which Frederick wrote with Voltaire's editorial assistance before the responsibility of kingship weighed upon him, his leading theme is still the harmony of princely virtue and princely interest, while in his political testaments, more revealing than all his other writings because they were destined only for the eyes of his

[51] Friedrich Meinecke expresses a similar idea in more metaphysical language: "The contradiction between idea and interest . . . did not let him rest. Now [in the *Anti-Machiavelli*] it was to be thoroughly eliminated, the evil Machiavelli was to be banished conclusively from the world and from his own soul. For who could fail to recognize that he was conducting a secret dialogue with himself and the instincts that burned within him?" *Die Idee der Staatsräson*, 363. See *ibid.*, 375 on the "ambivalent demon" driving the King of Prussia.

[52] *ibid.*, 355. Meinecke is too kind to Frederick when he asserts that for him the "highest task" of the state included "making the people happy and enlightening it." *ibid.*, 354.

successors, Frederick unhesitatingly affirms the precedence of power over welfare. It is only when the testaments deal with justice, religious policy, and internal improvements, that these icy documents touch upon the happiness of the Prussian subject; and it was in these areas that the preachments of Voltaire could exert their influence.

The first of the two political testaments was composed between April and July 1752, while Voltaire was still at the Prussian court, although evidently without his knowledge. The prince, Frederick tells his successor, must govern by himself, reduce all threats to his pre-eminence from the princes of the blood or the aristocracy, establish a sound system of finances, keep a disciplined and effective army, encourage industry, improve communications, foster commerce, avoid Utopian adventures in foreign policy, and round out his territory. The gravest obstacles to Prussian greatness are its unfavorable geographical position, its scattered territories, its many enemies, and its poverty. Hence military, diplomatic, and economic policy must all be coordinated under a single sovereign and directed toward a single goal, "the strengthening of the state and the growth of its power."[53]

Frederick's loving attention to the details of military and economic affairs, his unrelieved rationalism, and his utilitarian conception of humanitarian policies make this testament a remarkable document. Politics, he argued, is the science of choosing the appropriate means for the attainment of a rational interest, and both means and interest can be understood by reasonable men. This rationalism extends to the prince himself; he must overcome irrelevant motives: pride, ambition, the desire for revenge, even affection for his dynasty. It is in this sense that "the ruler is the first servant of the state."[54]

[53] Friedrich der Grosse, *Die Politischen Testamente*, "Das Politische Testament von 1752," 42. In a famous paragraph, Frederick defends the statesman's right to "political reveries." *ibid.*, 63.
[54] *ibid.*, 42. Elsewhere, Frederick calls himself the first minister of the

There is less Voltaire in Frederick's testament than Voltaire would have liked to see. The only obvious allusion to Voltaire's writings appears in a section on religion: "I am neutral between Rome and Geneva," a sign that Frederick remembered the *Henriade*.[55] Elsewhere, Frederick overlaid Enlightenment philosophy with a cynical practicality. He suggests that the prince ought to be humane and tolerant for the simple reason that humanity and tolerance pay. In his contemptuous appraisal of human nature—an appraisal against which Voltaire never ceased to protest—Frederick reduced all human motives to two: "fear of punishment and hope for reward."[56] Punishment can therefore be rational rather than savage, religious policy can be tolerant rather than sectarian: "Catholics, Lutherans, Calvinists, Jews, and numerous other Christian sects live in Prussia and live peacefully with each other. If from mistaken zeal the ruler should get the idea of giving preference to one of these religions, parties would form at once and violent squabbles would break out. Gradually, persecutions would begin, and finally the followers of the persecuted religion would leave their fatherland, and thousands of subjects would enrich our neighbors with their industry and increase their population."[57] The sections on law and on internal improvements are just as humane and just as businesslike. They suggest that the philosophes used sound tactics when they stressed the utility of humane policies and gave practical justifications for generous actions; it was language that absolute princes could understand.

---

people, the first magistrate of the nation, etc. For a collection of examples, see Meinecke, *Staatsräson*, 387n.

[55] "Das Politische Testament von 1752," 36. The line from the *Henriade* runs: "Je ne décide point entre Genève et Rome." viii, 66.

[56] "Das Politische Testament von 1752," 37. See Frederick to Voltaire, 25 December 1737: "The original principle of virtue is interest." *Correspondence*, vi, 293.

[57] "Das Politische Testament von 1752," 35. Meinecke rightly suggests (*Staatsräson*, 356) that the coincidence of toleration and *raison d'état* rested on Frederick's conviction that in the eighteenth century the Prussian king was in a strong internal position and had little to fear from plots and cabals.

But Frederick's perfunctory treatment of humanitarianism and his failure to use Enlightenment rhetoric do not demonstrate his indifference to the ideals of the philosophes. It has been shown that Frederick's legal reforms antedate Montesquieu's and Voltaire's legal writings. True; yet, intellectually, morally, and emotionally Frederick was dependent on the philosophes. What Frederick learned from them was not a specific code but a general temper—anticlerical, empirical, humanitarian. What they gave him was not advice but approval.[58]

Nor was that approval wholly misplaced: while Frederick's reforms were less dazzling than they appeared on paper and than the philosophes proclaimed them to be, they were impressive enough. Frederick's father, frugal, efficient, brutal and antiintellectual, had greatly improved Prussia's army, doubled the public revenues, firmly and intelligently established a Prussian bureaucracy. On the other hand, he ruled over his beloved army without pity, interfered in the judicial process to impose death sentences where courts had given lesser sentences,[59] compelled his officials to build, at their own expense, houses in areas designated by the king, and neglected the Berlin Academy. Frederick II kept the assets and reduced the liabilities of his father. Even in the early years of his reign, punctuated as they were with exhausting wars, he proclaimed freedom of conscience ("Religions must all be tolerated . . . for here everybody must be saved in his own fashion"), re-established the Berlin Academy, invited an impressive collection of foreign scientists to Prussia, founded a French journal for politics and literature, sent his

[58] German historians have consistently underestimated Frederick's psychological dependence on Voltaire and other educated Frenchmen. The philosophes formed what sociologists call a "reference group" for the Prussian king; their approval of his actions was a significant gratification for him. If it had not been, would Frederick have resumed correspondence with, and flattery of Voltaire, whom he had roundly denounced and claimed to despise?

[59] Katte, who had helped Frederic escape in 1730, was condemned to imprisonment by a court martial, but Frederick William I changed this to a death sentence. This is not the only instance of his interference.

architect Knobelsdorff to France and the Netherlands to further his education, commissioned his *Kapellmeister* Graun to collect an operatic troupe in Italy, recalled the philosopher Christian Wolff from the exile imposed by Frederick William I, controlled the price of grain, took an immediate and practical interest in commerce and manufacturing, prohibited brutality against cadets, abolished compulsory recruiting for the army, ordered Cocceji to initiate studies for a new legal code, ended the church's right to grant dispensations for marriages of relatives, and suppressed torture, which he had long execrated.[60] He meant what he said when he wrote to Algarotti shortly after the end of the first Silesian war: "My peacetime activity must be as useful to the state as had been my concern for the war."[61]

Voltaire's early enthusiasm for his royal admirer was thus surely justified, as justified as his later disillusionment. He had expected great things from Frederick, but the glib adversary of Machiavelli had proved to be one of his aptest pupils. "If Machiavelli had had a prince as disciple," Voltaire wrote in his malicious *Mémoires* of 1759, "the first thing that he would have recommended to him would have been to write against him."[62]

How much do these fluctuating opinions prove about Voltaire's political philosophy? There is widespread agreement that Voltaire, in Leo Gershoy's words, "was by conviction and temperament an enthusiast of enlightened despotism. . . . To put the authority of the enlightened prince behind the accomplishment of Voltairian reforms was the real essence of his political credo."[63]

[60] The edict of 3 June 1740 excepted only high treason and mass murder, but a supplementary edict of 1755 suppressed torture altogether. Under the old practice women who had murdered their offspring were compelled to sew the leather sack in which they were later drowned. Frederick II substituted a simple death penalty. It is evident from his letter to Voltaire, 11 October (1777), L, 285, that even here Frederick's humanitarianism was colored by utilitarian considerations: Prussia was strong enough to be able to dispense with torture.

[61] 18 July 1742, Arnold Berney, *Friedrich der Grosse*, 234-235.

[62] I, 17.

[63] In the same passage, Gershoy writes about Voltaire: "His *Age of*

Appraisals such as these—and there are many—make an unwarranted logical leap from the realistic acceptance of a form of government to a theoretical preference for it. They are vitiated by their failure to consider the social and legal position of the man of letters in the eighteenth century. The philosophes sought favor with enlightened rulers, for such favor brought handsome benefits. Monarchs gave them salaries, bought their libraries, provided them with audiences for their plays, subscribed to their literary periodicals, lent them prestige, and offered them protection from harassment.

These associations between monarchs and philosophes, usually initiated by the former, awakened in the latter the urge to give political instruction, and to use their patrons as instruments of humanitarian ideals. The enlightened rulers did not stifle this urge. They invited the philosophes to speak their mind, to treat them as equals, and to give them candid advice which they claimed they could not get from flattering courtiers. Such treatment created some false impressions among the philosophes: steeped in classical literature, they were all too easily tempted to imagine themselves, at least on occasion, in the role of a Plato or an Aristotle, and to imagine their royal friends as a Numa or a Lycurgus. But such self-dramatization and self-deception are not the same thing as a conscious preference for enlightened despotism as the best of all possible governments.

Louis XIV can hardly be considered a hostile treatment of the *grand monarque*. His praise of Frederick and his well-rewarded admiration for Catherine were notorious. If he was excited to enthusiasm over the government of China and its civilization, it was because he was convinced that the greatness of that country stemmed from the practical application that the responsible classes made of the teaching of its sages, such as Confucius. If he set great store by the English constitutional arrangement, it was for the benefit of the French middle classes that he courageously extolled the conquest won by their English compeers. . . . [He was] a property-conscious liberal. . . ." *From Despotism to Revolution,* 64-65. This makes Voltaire at once an insincere flatterer of monarchs, a bourgeois liberal, a supporter of absolutism. It is of course precisely the point of this book to show Voltaire as a relativist, but his relativism cannot be fairly epitomized as "enlightened despotism."

Like most intellectuals, the philosophes needed an audience and desired to wield influence, but they had widely differing and sometimes self-contradictory political philosophies. They were realists: they were unwilling to insult their protectors or to tell their patrons to go out of business, but few of them were doctrinaire advocates of absolutism. Indeed, they could never agree among themselves precisely who was an enlightened monarch. Voltaire admired Frederick of Prussia and Catherine of Russia; Diderot distrusted the first, and Mercier de la Rivière, the second. Nor could they ever agree on a clear-cut definition of "enlightened despotism": was it the authoritarian centralism of Joseph II? the aristocratic conservatism of Frederick the Great? the administrative decentralization of Leopold of Tuscany?[64]

The hesitations and ambivalences of the physiocrats, usually cited as the most ardent and the most consistent advocates of this doctrine, further illuminate the confusions inherent in it. As rationalists, the physiocrats rejected despotism as arbitrary and surrounded the ruler with constitutional safeguards; as educated reformers, they were too skeptical of the political maturity of the lower classes to envisage their participation in politics, at least for the present. As aristocrats, they advocated "legal despotism"; as Enlightenment philosophers, confident of the possibilities of human nature, they treated this form of government as a transitional expedient. Although they justified absolute monarchy and a strong state, their justification was pragmatic: effective government is necessary to run the admin-

[64] The dilemma of Du Pont over Joseph II is characteristic: "The Emperor is hard to judge. When one observes what he has done and is doing daily for his country, he is a prince of the rarest merit. . . . But on the other hand when one takes a look at his political attitude toward his neighbors, his avidity for war, his desire for aggrandizement, the partition of Poland, the invasion of Bavaria, the plots against the Turkish Empire, his disrespect for old treaties, his inclination to decide everything by force, then the noble-minded eagle is only a terrible bird of prey." Quoted by Heinz Holldack, "Der Physiokratismus und die Absolute Monarchie," *Historische Zeitschrift*, CVL (1932), 533.

istrative machinery, but it must justify itself by results, and it must always be subject to the goad of criticism. In assigning a large and ever-growing role to public opinion, the physiocrats made the leap from authoritarianism to liberalism.[65] They sometimes regretted that they had introduced the word "despotism" into their political creed; picturesque, remembered only too easily, it did them a serious injustice. "That devil 'despotism'," wrote Turgot to Du Pont, "will forever stand in the way of the propagation of your doctrine."[66]

Unlike the physiocrats, who were much given to theorizing, Voltaire never explained his position on the doctrine which they had invented and which made them so uneasy. But his most strongly held political convictions, his support of the rule of law and of free expression, directly contradict authoritarianism in any form. And the Prussian version, the type of philosophic absolutism that Voltaire knew best, rested on an aristocratic principle that he opposed all his life. Frederick was unshakeable in his belief that the lower classes are governed, and will always be governed, by the crudest kind of self-interest, and he embodied this conviction in his rigidly hierarchical state. His rule was absolute, but like Louis XIV he was not a leveling absolutist. He thought of himself as the first among aristocrats, surrounded himself with the Prussian nobility, and reserved to it the highest bureaucratic, judicial, ministerial, and military posts. The bourgeoisie was confined to making money and obeying orders. Frederick's state was thus a "marriage of aristocracy and bureaucracy";[67] it was at once modern and feudal, a medieval structure in the service of rationalist ends. Its effec-

[65] It is said that Louis XV once asked Quesnay what he would do if he were king. Quesnay answered: "Nothing." Asked further, who would govern then, Quesnay said without hesitation: "The laws." See Fritz Hartung, "Der aufgeklärte Absolutismus," *Historische Zeitschrift*, CLXXX (1955), 21.

[66] Quoted by Michel Lhéritier, "Rapport général: le despotisme éclairé, de Frédéric II à la Révolution française," *Bulletin of the International Committee of Historical Sciences*, IX, 188.

[67] Leonard Krieger, *The German Idea of Freedom*, 22.

tiveness, almost its very survival, depended upon the monarch who was at the controls.

Voltaire, advocate of the career open to talents, bourgeois opponent of powerful aristocracies, hopeful champion of education and the eventual diffusion of enlightenment among all classes, did not, and could not, make such a caste society the "real essence of his political credo." He found much to admire in Frederick's Prussia: the king's rationalism, his anticlericalism, his effective bureaucracy, his humane domestic legislation. But Voltaire's admiration, created by affection and affinity, exaggerated by prudence and servility, was much less for a social and political organization than for the man who headed it. Never was his hostility to theory, his failure to penetrate to general principles of politics, more damaging to his judgment than in his attitude toward Frederick's Prussia. It is not true to say that Voltaire accepted enlightened despotism, a system of government that undertook reforms at the expense of freedom. What is true is that he never thought enough about it to reject it categorically; he never achieved Rousseau's insight that a stratified absolutism like Frederick's, which offered the middle classes no political education, was an authoritarian defense against constitutionalism and civil liberties, rather than a transitional step toward them.

In the end Voltaire's disapproval of Frederick was, as his approval had been in the beginning, a personal judgment. The King of Prussia had mistreated him, and that was enough to make him "the most dishonest man alive," whose "greatest talent is to lie like a lackey."[68] What was perhaps worse, the King of Prussia had missed his unsurpassed opportunities to be the protector of philosophy and the destroyer of Christianity.[69]

[68] Voltaire to madame Denis, 22 August (1753), *Correspondence*, XXIII, 151.

[69] See: "If he had had more daring, he would have destroyed the House of Austria and the Christian religion." *Notebooks*, 324; "He would have been a hundred times better as the protector of philosophy than as the disturber of Europe. He has missed a fine vocation." Voltaire to d'Alem-

For all his pretenses, Frederick was no true Athenian. In September 1752, while Voltaire's favor at the Prussian court was waning rapidly, he wrote to d'Alembert: "There are absolutely no resources here. There are a prodigious number of bayonets and very few books. The king has greatly embellished Sparta, but he has transported Athens only into his study."[70] When Voltaire left Sparta half a year later, he was done with monarchies, but not with monarchs.

2. THE SEMIRAMIS OF THE NORTH

Voltaire observes somewhere that it is a good thing to have a crowned head up your sleeve. After the fiasco in Prussia his stock of royalty was perilously low, and it remained low for nearly a decade. He was therefore delighted when Catherine, Empress of all the Russians, turned to him in the early 1760's, after he had retired to Ferney. Voltaire was far prouder of this acquisition than the empress's actions and character warranted; his correspondence with Catherine shows him at his least admirable. For the sake of a queen, an ambitious and energetic woman who skillfully disguised her ruthless procedures behind humanitarian rhetoric, Voltaire stifled his critical judgment and gave his discerning taste a holiday.

Other philosophes, too, greatly overestimated her—Grimm told her that he cried like a calf when he got her letters, and Diderot went all the way to St. Petersburg to argue with her—but their naïveté does not absolve Voltaire, who took great pride in his practical sense and his intimate knowledge of Russian history. Catherine was never central in his affections or to his political thinking, and perhaps not too much should be made of his involvement with her. Still, Voltaire's relations

---

bert, 25 April 1760, XL, 366; "If he were able to live quietly and as a philosopher, and to spend on *écraser l'inf* . . . one hundredth part of what it has cost him to butcher everybody, I feel I could forgive him." Voltaire to the same, 15 September (1762), XLII, 237.

[70] 5 September (1752), *Correspondence*, XXI, 55.

with Catherine display the depths to which a violent partisan can descend, and the injustices that a *littérateur engagé* can commit for the sake of his cause.

It was half policy, half ignorance that made Voltaire Catherine's devoted agent. The major flaw in his association with Frederick had been his dependence; the major flaw in his association with Catherine was his lack of accurate information, compounded by a deliberate refusal to learn the truth. Unfamiliarity sometimes breeds admiration. Voltaire never saw Russia or Catherine—the wily empress knew better than to invite her formidable friend—and he never grasped her problems or her policies. Had he visited St. Petersburg, the tough-minded and well-informed diplomatic representatives of Western powers would have enlightened him. Living near Geneva as the "Old Invalid of Ferney," he had to depend on Catherine's word, on the enthusiasm of his fellow philosophes, and on the reports of friends who were more rhapsodic than reliable.

When Catherine was proclaimed empress on 28 June 1762 after the deposition of her husband, Czar Peter III, few observers rhapsodized about her. Her hold on the throne was so uncertain that diplomats predicted her speedy fall. "It is certain," the Prussian ambassador reported to Frederick II soon after the *coup d'état* against Peter III, "that the reign of the Empress Catherine is not to be more than a brief episode in the history of the world."[71] It seemed a reasonable prediction. Catherine had been born a German foreigner and a Lutheran heretic; she had come to power through a palace revolt and was likely to be deposed by one; when her incompetent husband was murdered on 6 July 1762, she was widely believed to have ordered, abetted, or at least condoned the assassination; the Russian law of succession made her claim to the throne weaker than that of either her son Paul or Prince Ivan, who had briefly been czar in 1744.

Two powerful political factions close to the court, the "con-

[71] Gershoy, *From Despotism to Revolution*, 108.

servative" and the "modern" nobility, made Catherine's position
even more precarious. After the death of Peter the Great in
1725, the Russian nobility had acquired undisputed predominance in the state. It controlled local government, limited royal
authority through aristocratic institutions, obtained the exclusive
privileges of owning land and serfs, and was granted exemption
from military service. Upon Catherine's accession, the nobility
sought assurances that these prerogatives would remain intact.
It was a passive and conservative program, acceptable to most of
the aristocrats, who stubbornly despised the urban bourgeoisie
and disdained capitalist enterprise. But there were progressive
landowners who were increasingly attracted to investment and
trade, and these pro-capitalist aristocrats, eager to establish a
commercial and political alliance with the middle class, urged
the creation of a mercantilistic government that would foster
commerce, protect investments, rationalize relations between
landowners and serfs, and be secured against what they called
royal despotism by a permanent council of state. As in France,
aristocratic class interests masqueraded behind constitutionalist
pronouncements. The proposed shackles on royal power were
rationalized as essential to the happiness of all Russians; in fact
they were essential only to the happiness of aristocratic mi-
norities.

These noble factions, half allied, half in conflict, were dangerous to Catherine primarily because she was determined to defy
them both. She meant to rule, to create a bureaucratic absolutism that would make the nobility the servants of the state, as in
Prussia, and not its masters, as in eighteenth-century France.
The economic program of the modern nobility was acceptable
to her, but she wanted to realize it under her auspices.

Catherine had set herself a hard task, but she was as determined as a *condottiere* and had about as many scruples.
She had married the feeble Crown Prince Peter because she
wanted to be an empress. "I myself felt little more than indifference towards him," she confessed in her candid *Memoirs*,

"though I was not indifferent to the Russian Crown."[72] She had once assured her friend Sir Charles Williams, the English ambassador, "I shall perish or govern."[73] In the early 1760's, it was by no means certain which would happen.

In her peril, her policies were of necessity devoted to strengthening her hold on the throne, and to continuing the construction of an absolute state begun by Peter the Great. Her actions, both those applauded and those censured by the philosophes, were in themselves neither conservative nor liberal. They were moves in the game for power. At home, Catherine appeased both noble parties by granting them unprecedented rights over the serfs, and by promising concessions that she did not mean to grant. Abroad, she shrewdly enlisted the philosophes to present her version of events in Russia. She was bold because she dared not be timid. "The fear of losing what she has had the audacity to take," reported Breteuil, the French ambassador, "continually manifests itself in the conduct of the empress."[74]

In western European capitals, her conduct was not approved —royal assassins are censured, especially when they are not expected to stay in power. Voltaire, who became her most distinguished catch, at first maintained a cautious reserve. Catherine broke through it by a series of nicely calculated and pleasingly inexpensive moves. In August 1762 she induced a Genevan adventurer seeking his fortunes in Russia, François-Pierre Pictet, to send Voltaire a report on the late Czar Peter's inadequacies, debaucheries, and habitual drunkenness. The Russian people, Pictet wrote, had done well to rid themselves of such a man, and to substitute for him "the greatest empress who has ever reigned in the universe."[75] Voltaire, an expert in exaggerations,

[72] *The Memoirs of Catherine the Great* (ed., 1955), 66.
[73] Georg Sacke, *Die gesetzgebende Kommission Katharinas II, Jahrbücher für Geschichte Osteuropas*, Beiheft 2, 50.
[74] A. Kizevetter, "Catherine II (1762-1796)," *Histoire de Russie*, eds. Paul Milioukov et al., II, 537.
[75] Pictet to Voltaire, 4 August 1762, XLII, 197. Pictet, nicknamed the "giant" in Geneva, was a *docteur en droit* and a popular actor in Voltaire's

was not impressed; he sent Pictet a reply so unsatisfactory that it could not be shown to Catherine.[76]

Shrewd and undaunted, Catherine now proceeded to offer Diderot's *Encyclopédie* an asylum in Russia—a generous gesture she could well afford since she could be certain that it would not be accepted.[77] Then she took an interest in the Calas family—a delicate bit of flattery for Voltaire, who had become obsessed with the Calas case early in 1762. Finally, in 1765, she bought Diderot's library, leaving him in possession during his lifetime. This purchase was a work of supererogation: by now, Voltaire had been completely won over by the philosophic empress. "All those who have been honored by the bounty of Your Majesty," he told her shortly after, "are my friends; I am grateful for what you have done so generously for Diderot, d'Alembert, and the Calas family. Every man of letters in Europe ought to be at your feet."[78]

Not every man of letters in Europe agreed with Voltaire, but he declared himself ready to defend the "Semiramis of the North" against all criticism. "I can boast to you," he wrote madame du Deffand, "of being a little in her good graces. I am her knight before and against everybody. I know very well that she is being reproached with some bagatelle concerning her husband; but these are family affairs in which I don't interfere. . . ."[79] It is a tasteless and cruel remark, and it deeply

---

amateur theatricals. Voltaire knew him well enough to lend him 10,000 *livres*. See *Correspondance avec les Tronchin*, 481.

[76] See Pictet to Voltaire, 19/30 November 1762, XLII, 287.

[77] See Voltaire to Jean Shuvalov 25 September (1762), and his letters of the same date to d'Alembert and Diderot. XLII, 246-247, 249-250. Grimm reported the offer on 1 January 1763. *Correspondance littéraire*, v, 199-200. In the summer of 1762, Catherine also asked d'Alembert to become tutor to her son, the Grand Duke, an offer that he rejected.

[78] XLIV, 74-75.

[79] 18 May (1767), XLV, 267-268. See her sarcastic reply, 26 May (1767), XLV, 274. Madame de Choiseul and Horace Walpole shared madame du Deffand's disapproval. See Desnoiresterres, *Voltaire et J.-J. Rousseau*, 379-381. Incidentally, while Voltaire used the term "Semiramis of the North" freely in speaking of Catherine, he never addressed her with it. His own

shocked madame du Deffand and her friends, but it is not quite as callous as it appears, because Voltaire believed Catherine innocent of the little bagatelle.[80] The skeptical Voltaire could be the most credulous of men when his will to believe was stirred into action.

It may be added that to believe Catherine was more than a sign of credulity: few rulers have had a better grasp of the art of mystification. In 1767, Catherine published an *Instruction*— a mixture of proposed legislation, constitutional theory, and legal code—and summoned a legislative commission to debate it. Experienced diplomats dismissed the commission as a hypocritical charade; sympathetic philosophes greeted it as an assembly that would lead Russia toward the rule of law. The diplomats were closer to the truth than the philosophes: the commission was a political move designed by Catherine, as the English *chargé d'affaires* put it, "to strengthen Herself still more, knowing the restless dispositions of Her subjects."[81] Voltaire, less cynical than the envoy and also less well informed, hailed Catherine as a legislator in the great tradition: "I have read the preliminary instruction that you were good enough to send me. Lycurgus and Solon would have signed your work, but they would not have been able to do it. It is frank, precise, equitable, firm, and humane. Legislators have the first place in the temple of glory, conquerors come behind them."[82] Such

---

play *Sémiramis* has some unfortunate allusions to a woman who kills her husband for the sake of a throne.

[80] Voltaire to Jean Shuvalov, 13 August (1762), XLII, 208: "I admit that I fear my heart is corrupted enough not to have been as much scandalized by that little scene as a good Christian should be. A very great good can come from this little evil. Providence is as the Jesuits used to be: it uses everything. And anyway, when a drunk dies of colic, that will teach us to be sober." He takes a similar line to d'Argental, 23 January (1768), XLV, 506. In his notebook he wrote: "Today 19 January 1766 Count Rewusky assured me that Peter III died only from having continuously drunk punch in his prison." *Notebooks*, 335. He tried to get others to accept this convenient version of the Czar's death. See Voltaire to Choiseul, 1 April 1768, XLVI, 1-2.

[81] Sacke, *Die Gesetzgebende Kommission*, 81.

[82] Voltaire to Catherine, 26 February 1769, XLVI, 263. Diderot was more

a legislator deserved unstinted support throughout Europe. "I have another favor to ask you," Voltaire wrote to d'Argental early in 1768, "that is, for my Catherine. We must re-establish her reputation in Paris. . . . I beg you, say much good of Catherine."[83]

Voltaire pronounced himself impressed with the legal sections of the *Instruction*; he was silent on its political theory, but clearly it impressed him as well.[84] Like Louis XV, Catherine was confronting a powerful aristocracy, and like Louis XV, she opposed her *thèse royale* to the aristocratic *thèse nobiliaire*. "The monarch must be sovereign," she wrote in the first draft of the *Instruction*, in accents reminiscent of Voltaire's *Voix du sage*. "His power cannot be divided."[85] Royal power exists for the purpose of directing men's actions toward felicity under the rule of law. The aristocracy, Catherine added boldly, is an honorific estate with no special political prerogatives.[86]

The *Instruction* shows that Catherine wanted to confirm her power, not share it with an aristocratic council or a popular as-

---

skeptical; he wanted the Russian government to make some definite move toward constitutionalism. Mohrenschildt, *Russia in the Intellectual Life of Eighteenth-Century France*, 81-82.

[83] 23 January (1768), XLV, 506.

[84] See Voltaire's comment of 1777: the government of Russia, he said against Montesquieu, is not despotic. Rather, "it seeks to destroy anarchy, the odious prerogatives of the nobles, the power of the magnates, and not to establish intermediate bodies or to diminish its authority." *Commentaire sur l'Esprit des lois*, xxx, 439.

[85] Sacke, *Die Gesetzgebende Kommission*, 64. She explained the need for this absolutism by Russia's unique situation. In some secret instructions of 1764, she told one of her top officials: "Some think that when they have lived in this or that country for a while, we must constitute everything, everywhere in accord with the policies of their favorite country. . . . The Russian empire is so large that any political order other than autocracy (*Selbstherrschaft*) would be harmful"—a relativist, pragmatic absolutism of which Voltaire would have strongly approved. *ibid.*, 60.

[86] In view of Catherine's rejection of a strong aristocracy, it is misleading to say, "Catherine made no attempt to conceal her indebtedness to Montesquieu and Beccaria." G. P. Gooch, *Catherine the Great and Other Studies*, 94. She admired Montesquieu's legal philosophy but not his political philosophy.

sembly. The commission did not make a code of laws; it debated over procedure, and voted Catherine the title "Mother of the Country." The English *chargé d'affaires* reported that "the power of Her Imperial Majesty increases every day, and is already arrived to such a degree, that this prudent Princess thinks herself strong enough to humble the Guards, who placed her upon the throne."[87] After more than a year of ceremonious and subservient wrangling, most of the deputies left the commission to intervene in Poland and to fight in Catherine's first war against the Turks. Those who remained continued their earnest debates in subcommittees. Voltaire was eager to be patient; in June 1771 he told Catherine that he had just been rereading the *Instruction*, "the most beautiful monument of the century."[88]

He continued to serve the creator of this monument with unabated and uncritical devotion. During the Turkish wars, he cheered Catherine on to Constantinople, and gave wide publicity to her letters, which were really tendentious communiqués in disguise.[89] When Catherine prepared to intervene in Poland, Voltaire lent himself to her designs by writing propaganda in her behalf and upon her instructions. Catherine, he wrote, does not want an inch of foreign territory; her foreign policy is wholly philosophic: "Not only is that princess tolerant, but she wants her neighbors to be tolerant. This is the first time that supreme power has been employed to establish free-

[87] Sacke, *Die Gesetzgebende Kommission*, 156.
[88] XLVII, 465.
[89] Sacke has proved that Voltaire published many of Catherine's letters in journals such as the *Journal encyclopédique* or the *Gazette de Berne*, and that he incorporated in his writings information she conveyed to him. He seems to have been a little self-conscious about his role as a celebrant of war, as well he might be. "Your Majesty will tell me," he wrote to Catherine on 20 July (1770), "that I don't think philosophically enough, and that peace is the greatest of goods. No one is more convinced of this truth than I am. . . ." XLVII, 144. In *Le tocsin des rois*, a propaganda pamphlet he wrote at Catherine's request in 1771, he explained that the Turks deserved to be beaten since they were the enemies of all Europe. The pamphlet is as feeble as this reasoning. XXVIII, 465-468.

dom of conscience. This is the greatest epoch I know in modern history."[90] The greatest epoch came to an end in 1772, when Voltaire, Catherine's self-appointed dupe, was shocked by the first partition of Poland.[91] It did not cure him. In the great peasant rebellion of 1773-1774, led by the Don Cossack Pugachev, Voltaire professed to be more concerned with her safety against the "brigand" than with the appalling conditions of the peasantry which had caused the gigantic *jacquerie*. Catherine had coolly sacrificed her peasants, Russia's largest and politically most expendable class, to the landlords; she had increased their servile dues and their labor obligations, and tightened the masters' legal authority over them. While in legal theory the noble landlord was responsible for the well-being of his serfs, in the thirty-four years of Catherine's reign only twenty landlords were punished for cruelty to serfs—a sign not of the nobles' kindness but of their immunity. These were great years for the Russian nobility and terrible years for the Russian peasant. "The peasant millions," says G. T. Robinson, "were hardly likely to forget the 'Golden Age of the Russian Nobility'—but they would perhaps remember it by some other name."[92]

In the all-important peasant question Catherine stifled whatever humane instincts and absolutist energy she had. Here the enlightened autocrat was neither enlightened nor autocratic, but surrendered to the political pressures of an exclusive, narrow-minded, and insensitive nobility. Yet most of this Voltaire did not know; his unswerving support of Catherine cannot be fully explained as a mixture of flattery and infatuation. Catherine adroitly deceived Voltaire on the nature of her situation and the

[90] *Lettre sur les panégyriques*, XXVI, 314. He wrote several other propaganda pamphlets for Catherine, all equally unfortunate.

[91] There has been much debate over Voltaire's conduct in this affair. It has been suggested that he must have known of the partition in advance, and it is true that some of his letters written not long before the event sound suspiciously like that. Still, it would be consistent with his character to have deceived himself willfully as to the true state of affairs—not that this makes his part in Catherine's Polish intervention any more honorable.

[92] *Rural Russia under the Old Regime*, 33.

extent of her reforms. She continuously referred to her *Instruction* as a code of law, exaggerated her toleration in Poland, pretended to share Voltaire's interest in several sensational miscarriages of justice. It was easier to see Catherine's flaws from St. Petersburg than from Ferney, just as it is easier to see them today than it was in the middle of the eighteenth century.[93]

But after allowances have been made for Voltaire's lapses in taste, failures in judgment, and gaps in information, there remains something in his conception of Catherine's role that can be characterized only as support of enlightened despotism. It illustrates, once again, his political pragmatism: benevolent autocracy may not be appropriate to Western countries, but it is appropriate to a country whose population is still close to primitive conditions. The Russians, far more than the French, the English, or even the Prussians, can and indeed must be civilized by a legislator.

For eighteenth-century historians, barely liberated from the idea that Providence guided historical events, the legislator was an almost superhuman figure. They saw him as the embodiment of human energy, wisdom, and rationality, as the founder of states, the preceptor of his country, the father of his people. "The legislator," wrote Rousseau in the *Contrat social*, published in the year Catherine came to power, "is the engineer who invents the machine. . . ." He must have supreme abilities and

[93] For self-advertisement of her *Instruction*, see Catherine to Voltaire, 1765, xliv, 18-19, and 29 June/9 July 1766, xliv, 333. For the Polish intervention, see Voltaire to comte de Voroncov, Russian envoy to the Hague, 25 August 1767, xlv, 360; Voltaire to Prince Gallitzin, 7 October 1767, xlv, 398. For the law cases, see Sacke, *Die Gesetzgebende Kommission*, 28. Sacke has shown that while Catherine did contribute to the Calas family, she gave Voltaire the mistaken impression that another case, that of the chevalier de La Barre, was being discussed in the legislative commission, when in fact it was not even mentioned.

Nevertheless, self-deception does not fully account for Voltaire's behavior—some of it was plain bad faith. He was shrewd enough, for all his limited information, to have doubts concerning Catherine's communiqués. See Albert Lortholary, *Les "philosophes" du xviiie siècle et la Russie*, 130.

supreme confidence: he should "feel himself capable . . . of changing human nature."

The more primitive—that is to say, for the philosophes, the less French—the country, the more significant the role of the legislator. Voltaire was prepared to argue that "almost nothing great has ever been done in the world except by the genius and firmness of a single man combating the prejudices of the multitude";[94] he was prepared to argue, further, that political consequences depend chiefly on the determination of leaders: "Let us repeat, then, that one can do everything; that the great fault of almost all those who govern is that they have only half-wills and half-means."[95]

In his mordant study of the philosophes' infatuation with Russia, Albert Lortholary compares such views to Carlyle's Great-Man conception of the historical process.[96] This stricture seems to me unhistorical: Voltaire wrote his histories nearly a century before Carlyle, long before the disciplines of economic and social history had even been invented. Surely there was exaggeration, and naïve exaggeration in the statement, "For Russia, see Peter the Great." But it was not solely hero worship or historical naïveté to attribute great powers to eighteenth-century monarchs. This was before universal literacy, before universal suffrage, before organized political parties, in an age in which the political public was small. Of course, rulers, then as now, operated within a framework of social, economic, and political pressures. Yet it was still an age of dynastic politics, of sudden shifts caused solely by individuals in positions of power. Indeed, if Voltaire had needed any proof of this truth, it would have been dramatically supplied to him by Russian events in 1762,

[94] *Essai sur les moeurs*, XII, 161, in a passage praising the contribution of Prince Henri the Navigator to the prosperity of the Portuguese empire. See: "We can see after the death of Henri IV, how the power, respect, manners, spirit of a nation often depend on a single man." *ibid.*, XII, 572.
[95] *Questions sur l'Encyclopédie*, article "Vénalité."
[96] *Les "philosophes" du* XVIIIe *siècle et la Russie*, 66.

while the Seven Years' War was still raging. In January, the Empress Elizabeth died, and her successor, Czar Peter III, immediately made peace with Prussia, saving Frederick the Great and leading to the end of the war. The energies of highly placed individuals still counted for much.

Moreover, Voltaire wrote at least some of his histories mindful of Bolingbroke's maxim that history is philosophy teaching by examples. In Russia, the lesson could never be preached too emphatically: "It is sovereigns," Voltaire told Catherine in a rhymed epistle in 1771, "who form the character and customs of men."[97] The first modern legislator in Russia, a figure who fascinated both Catherine and Voltaire, had been Peter the Great. Before his accession, Voltaire said in his *Histoire de Charles XII*, "The Muscovites were less civilized than the Mexicans when they were discovered by Cortez." Educated by the Genevan, Le Fort, Peter "resolved to be a man, to command men, and to create a new nation."[98] He traveled incognito, worked in Holland, observed in France, and returned to Moscow bringing artisans and Western civilization. He rebuilt the capital, created a commercial fleet, established colleges, schools, libraries; he constructed cities, reformed the church, and subjected proud ecclesiastics to the state. The greatness of his achievement was marred only by his personal failings. "A single man changed the greatest empire in the world"; yet, "he civilized his people and he was a barbarian."[99]

[97] *Epitre à Catherine II*, x, 438.

[98] XVI, 157, 159. These lines, be it noted, were written while his relations with Russians were still disinterested.

[99] XVI, 161, 164. I need hardly point out that this greatly exaggerates Peter's personal achievement. But it is worth noting that as realistic a statesman as Frederick the Great counted it as Peter's achievement that he "made men, soldiers, ministers, out of a people of savages." *Histoire de mon temps* (1746), quoted in Meinecke, *Staatsräson*, 415.

Voltaire returned to the theme of Peter the Great in the 1740's, with *Anecdotes sur le czar* (1748), a relatively objective performance; in 1757 he began to write *Histoire de l'Empire de Russie sous Pierre le Grand* at the instance of the Empress Elizabeth. Of all his command performances, this is the worst by far. It covers Peter with praise and wholly

He had been a barbarian, but he had more than a half-will and half-means; he had begun what Catherine must finish. The task that remained was great, hence it required absolute authority held in check only by reason and humanity—in a word, enlightened despotism. It is significant that when Voltaire sought epithets for Frederick of Prussia, he used historical figures, statesmen rather than legislators: Salomon, Marcus Aurelius, Trajan. But when he sought epithets for Catherine of Russia, he used legendary supermen or creators of commonwealths whose achievements no matter how real, had risen into legend: Solon, Lycurgus, and that fabulous Babylonian queen, Semiramis. With all his enthusiasm for the warrior-queen, Voltaire preferred Catherine in the role of Lycurgus. "Your Majesty will once again put on the dress of legislator," he wrote her in 1771, "after having put off that of amazon."[100]

It is easier to smile at such extravagance than to assess its political consequences. It cannot be emphasized too much that Catherine courted Voltaire and that, to win him, she had to do more than to send hyperbolic messages. At the turn of this century, radicals sometimes scorned liberal social legislation as "ransom legislation"—insincere and politically motivated acts of appeasement. Acts of appeasement they were, but in ransoming the ruling class from the working class, the former transformed society in behalf of the latter. Similarly, the reputation of enlightened despot imposed upon the ruler certain obligations which he had to discharge if he wished to retain the epithet "enlightened" and to lighten the burden of "despot." As with Frederick, Catherine's performance was much less im-

---

neglects the criticisms. Voltaire did not like his own performance; the other philosophes were appalled at it: d'Alembert said it made him want to vomit; Grimm said it showed that Voltaire had no vocation for history; Frederick II derisively castigated Voltaire's "venal pen"; Diderot thought it was unworthy and commonplace. See Lortholary, *Les "philosophes,"* 50-51; Grimm, *Correspondance littéraire,* IV, 308-310; Langer, *Friedrich der Grosse,* 57; Diderot to Sophie Volland, 20 October (1760), *Lettres à Sophie Volland,* I, 157-159.

[100] 9 February (1771), XLVII, 349.

pressive than her reputation among the philosophes, but she secured important although not fundamental reforms in education, commercial policy, local government, and penal laws—for all her subjects except, of course, the peasants. The old order was too strong for her. She could compromise with the nobility and associate it with her aggressive foreign policy, but she did not have the power to enforce social and economic reforms that directly offended its interests.

This is not to say that she had no liberal instincts. She used Voltaire because she needed him, incidentally paying a great tribute to the stature and influence of the philosophes. But she used him, too, because she admired him and his principles. She referred to him, when she could afford to, as a standard, and even, despite her realism, as an inspiration. After Voltaire's death she wrote to Grimm, with whom she was informal and candid: "He was my master; it was he, or rather his works, that formed my intellect and my judgment . . . I am his pupil; when I was younger, I loved to please him; before I was satisfied with any action it had to be worthy of being reported to him, and I informed him of it immediately. . . ."[101]

But she did not always inform Voltaire correctly, and she was not Voltaire's best pupil. Even the most benevolent observer of his career must regret that he did not listen to his recurring doubts about her. When reports reached him in August 1764 that Prince Ivan, a possible rival for the Russian throne, had been assassinated, he wrote ruefully to d'Alembert: "I believe that we must moderate a little our enthusiasm for the North; it produces strange philosophies."[102] It was excellent advice to give, but he did not take it himself. He was far too fond of having a crowned head up his sleeve.

[101] Catherine to Grimm, 1 October 1778, I, 454. It is obvious that at least some of this is posturing; after all, it was likely that even her most private letters to Grimm circulated among the elect in Paris.

[102] 7 September (1764), XLIII, 313. D'Alembert replied on 4 October that he was a little tired of Catherine getting rid of so many people and then saying publicly that she was sorry but of course she had had nothing to do with it. XLIII, 337.

IV

GENEVA:
CALVIN'S THREE CITIES

1. PATRICIANS

VOLTAIRE's breach with the King of Prussia made him as unwelcome in Potsdam as he was in Paris. He proceeded westward
in leisurely stages—Leipzig, Gotha, Cassel—and in June 1753
reached the Free City of Frankfurt, ostensibly beyond Frederick's jurisdiction. But in this Imperial City Voltaire felt, for
the last time, the scratch of Frederick's paw. Flouting international law and good manners, the King of Prussia had Voltaire
arrested, searched, detained for over a month in a dismal inn,
just to get back a copy of his *Oeuvres du philosophe de Sans
Souci*, a mélange of historical essays, epic poems, obscene verses,
malicious epigrams against influential personages all over Europe.
The coarseness of Frederick's agents, which the king publicly
condemned and privately condoned, made La Mettrie's gossip
plausible after all: the King of Prussia had squeezed the orange
and was throwing the peel away. "Here then is Voltaire, who
does not seem to know where to lay his head! . . ." sententiously
wrote Montesquieu, who had never liked him. "Sound judgment
is better than brilliance—*Le bon esprit vaut mieux que le bel*

185

esprit."[1] David Hume was more charitable. "The fate of poor Voltaire," he wrote, "will terrify all men of Genius from trusting themselves with his Prussian Majesty, who, tho' one of the most illustrious Characters of the Age, is too much a rival to be a very constant Patron."[2]

The fate of poor Voltaire seemed sad indeed. His efforts to obtain permission to return to Paris were fruitless,[3] and for a year and a half he led the life of an elegant vagrant. Restlessly he visited Colmar, Strasbourg, Lorraine—a moody guest, a celebrated vagabond in search of a home. In long letters to his niece, he poured out his passion for her and his sense of isolation. "It is hard to be such an old bird and to have no nest."[4]

Then, in the winter of 1754-1755, the old bird found a nest in Geneva. Voltaire bought a house—rather, the banker Jean-Robert Tronchin bought it for him—and gratefully called it *Les Délices*.[5] Eleven years before, in unconscious prophecy, he had told the French foreign minister that he would rather live in a Swiss village than enjoy the dangerous favor of the Prussian king.[6] He would have saved himself much suffering if he had chosen the village over the king before his disgrace forced him to do so.

Les Délices was truly a delight. It looked upon the placid

[1] Montesquieu to the abbé de Guasco, 28 September 1753, *Oeuvres complètes*, ed. André Masson, 3 vols. (1950-1955), III, 1474.

[2] Hume to the abbé Le Blanc, 24 October 1754, *Letters of David Hume*, I, 207.

[3] See Voltaire to madame Denis, 13 September (1753), *Correspondence*, XXIII, 177-179.

[4] Voltaire to madame Denis, 30 August (1753), *Correspondence*, XXIII, 161.

[5] "It is amusing," Voltaire wrote to the duc de Richelieu, 13 February (1755), "that I own land in the only country where I am not permitted to acquire it." XXXVIII, 345. Genevan law reserved ownership of land to citizens, and citizenship to Protestants.

[6] Voltaire to Amelot de Chaillou (5 October 1743), *Correspondence*, XIII, 95-96. Switzerland was not a new enthusiasm. As early as 8 May 1739 he had written Johann Bernoulli, the Swiss mathematician, that he planned to write the history of the Swiss people, a people that had made such impressive efforts to be free. *ibid.*, IX, 131.

lake and the energetic city of Geneva; it was a convenient carriage-ride from the lordly homes of the Genevan patricians who soon accepted Voltaire's splendid hospitality. Best of all, it was in the territory of the Republic of Geneva. It was, or seemed, an ideal haven where Voltaire could indulge in two of his favorite occupations: meticulously supervising the publication of his writings and meticulously pampering his health. Geneva had philosophes who ministered to both these needs: the brothers Cramer, an enterprising publishing firm, deeply impressed Voltaire with their probity, their craftsmanlike competence, their sociability, and their patience. These were qualities which Voltaire, plagued with a succession of sharp and careless printers, could not but admire.[7] And there was Théodore Tronchin, a fashionable physician, who would try to keep Voltaire alive. But Voltaire gloomily assured his friends that he would not require the doctor's services for long: he had come to Geneva to die.

This was more than a hypochondriacal lament. Voltaire was thin, depressed, given to fits of panic. Copies of *La pucelle*, with crude and obscene alterations, were spreading through France and reaching Geneva. For a while friends observed an unwonted caution, even timidity, in Voltaire's relations with the authorities. His successive failures in France and Prussia were having their effect.

But as always, his magnificent resiliency came to his aid. Like many a city dweller before and after him, he discovered that he loved the country. "I am so happy that I am ashamed of it," he wrote to Thieriot on 27 May 1756.[8] And as his equilibrium returned, his aggressiveness returned as well. He was filled with a new sense of political mission. "He had reached the threshold of old age," as Lytton Strachey said, "and his life's work

---

[7] "The Cramers are my brothers; they are philosophes." Voltaire to Damilaville, *Lettres à Cramer*, xi. With an author as perfectionist as Voltaire, who constantly rewrote his manuscripts on galleys, the Cramers doubtless needed to cultivate the philosophic quality of patience.

[8] XXXIX, 47.

was still before him"—the work of a reformer.[9] "To overturn
the colossus," he boldly told d'Alembert in December 1757,
"we need only five or six philosophers who understand each
other."[10]

This fresh combativeness was in no way dampened, but
rather enhanced, by Voltaire's disappointed discovery that
Geneva, too, harbored the colossus. He soon learned that for all
its natural beauties, sophisticated patricians, reasonable pastors,
Geneva's reputation as a home of liberty and toleration was
undeserved.

Like most educated Europeans, Voltaire had been misled by
the Genevan genius for self-advertisement. Even Rousseau,
then the Republic's most illustrious son, had lent himself to
the comedy: in 1754 he had dedicated his *Discours sur l'inégalité*
to the Republic of Geneva. In that country, he wrote, equality
and inequality were happily combined in conformity with
natural law; it was neither too large nor too small for good
government; the interest of sovereign and citizen were the same;
everyone was subject to the rule of law, and all citizens had the
right to make the laws: "May a Republic, so wisely and happily
constituted, last forever, as an example to other nations, and
for the happiness of its own citizens!"[11]

In March 1755, not long after he had settled at *Les Délices,*
Voltaire gave further circulation to this misconception with a
paean to Genevan liberty:

> Mon lac est le premier: c'est sur ces bords heureux
> Qu'habite des humains la déesse éternelle,
> L'âme des grands travaux, l'objet des nobles voeux,
> Que tout mortel embrasse, ou désire, ou rappelle,

[9] *Books and Characters,* 172.

[10] XXXIX, 318-319.

[11] *Oeuvres,* I, 75. In his *Considérations,* d'Argenson gave a rapid survey
of the governments of Europe, with a two-page chapter that lumped together all the Swiss states. "Switzerland," he wrote, "is a country of complete equality among citizens." (p. 45).

Qui vit dans tous les coeurs, et dont le nom sacré
Dans les cours des tyrans est tout bas adoré,
La Liberté.

And liberty was made sweeter by fraternity:

> On ne voit point ici la grandeur insultante
> Portant de l'épaule au côté
> Un ruban que la Vanité
> A tissu de sa main brillante,
> Ni la fortune insolente
> Repoussant avec fierté
> La prière humble et tremblante
> De la triste pauvreté.
> On n'y méprise point les travaux nécessaires:
> Les états sont égaux, et les hommes sont frères.[12]

Rousseau, of course, should have known better. Events soon compelled Voltaire to learn: in July 1755, the Genevan government suppressed Voltaire's hymn to its liberty (an act of poetic injustice),[13] and in the same year, the Genevan Consistory pointedly reminded him that theatrical performances were not permitted in Calvin's republic.

Still, Voltaire had no desire to abandon Geneva; at least there were more philosophes in that city than anywhere else.[14] Instead of moving he multiplied his refuges: he acquired property in Lausanne, and nearby at Tourney and Ferney in France. "I have made myself freer in buying land in France," he justified himself to Jean-Robert Tronchin, "than I was when I only had my hut in Geneva and my house in Lausanne. Your magistrates are respectable, they are wise, the good society of Geneva is equal to that of Paris; but your people is a little arrogant

---

[12] L'auteur arrivant dans sa terre, près du lac de Genève, x, 364, 365.

[13] Some lines in the poem were thought to offend the memory of a Duke of Savoy, something to which the Genevans, long in dread of Savoy, were very sensitive. See Lettres à Cramer, 3-4n.

[14] Voltaire to Pierre Rousseau, 24 February 1757, xxxix, 180.

and its pastors are a little dangerous."[15] It was the letter of one worldly patrician to another.

The letter suggests, too, that Voltaire was beginning to understand that, whatever people said, Geneva was an oligarchy. In building the stronghold of European Protestantism, Calvin and his successors had built three cities, not one. The overwhelming majority of Geneva's 25,000 inhabitants were political pariahs. In law, this disfranchised majority was divided into three groups: the peasants, the so-called Subjects; the immigrants who had been granted the right to live in Geneva on sufferance, the Inhabitants; and the native-born descendants of these immigrants, the Natives. In practice, Subjects, Inhabitants, and Natives formed one interest group, and in popular parlance they had one name—Natives. They had no vote, no right to practice the liberal professions or to become officers; their economic activities, circumscribed as they were, were further hemmed in by petty regulations; they were compelled to pay burdensome and humiliating taxes; only a few Natives were allowed to buy citizenship every year. A small minority of Genevans, no more than 1,500 men, engrossed all civic rights. That minority, too, was divided—between the Burghers (Genevans who had acquired the rights and privileges of citizenship) and the Citizens (descendants of the Burghers, who alone could hold political office). But this division was bridged by common privileges and common interests: Burghers and Citizens alone had the right to vote; Burghers and Citizens sought to prevent the Natives from swamping them.

Yet, with all their common interests, the privileged minority of active citizens was split by social and economic conflict. A small, powerful patriciate, consisting of a handful of old families such as Voltaire's friends the Tronchins, confronted a larger bourgeoisie, ostensibly sovereign Burghers and Citizens, actually having little more political influence than the Natives.

---

[15] 13 December (1758), *Correspondance avec les Tronchin*, 364. See also Voltaire to Thieriot, 24 December 1758, xxxix, 558.

These legal, social, and economic cleavages reflected Geneva's changing position as a center of immigration. From the fifteenth century on, inhabitants of neighboring states had migrated to this prosperous community. With the advent of Calvinism and the concurrent persecution of heretics in France, refugees streamed into Geneva. They were well received—Calvin himself had traveled this road; many of them were admitted to citizenship and came to form Geneva's elite. A hundred and fifty years later, the revocation of the Edict of Nantes brought a new flood of immigrants, but now the Genevans were less hospitable. They forgot their refugee past and remembered only that they were threatened by the newcomers, who were for the most part skilled artisans and professional men; they discouraged the French refugees from settling in Geneva, imposed heavy taxes on those who stayed, reserved for themselves the most lucrative and most reputable professions, and made it almost impossible for the new Inhabitants to acquire citizenship. In 1600, it had cost 80 florins to buy citizenship; around 1650, the price had risen to 500 florins, and by 1700 to 4,000 florins—an enormous sum.[16] The body of Genevan citizens grew at an ever-decreasing rate: in the sixteenth century, 3,222 heads of families had acquired the privilege of becoming Burghers of the Republic of Geneva; from 1700 to 1782, the number had declined to 730.[17]

When Voltaire purchased *Les Délices*, most Natives were third- and fourth-generation Genevans. Born in the Republic, loyal to its institutions, industrious and thrifty, at home in its religious and moral climate, perhaps more genuinely Calvinist than the Burghers and Citizens who refused them political existence, the Natives smarted in their status but patiently accepted it. They did not raise their voice in protest until the

[16] *Histoire de Genève des origines à 1798*, 358. Great as that sum appears, its real size was somewhat reduced by inflation.

[17] Francis d'Ivernois, *An Historical and Political View of the Constitution and Revolutions of Geneva*, 22.

endemic conflict between patriciate and bourgeoisie erupted in the 1760's.

The Genevan constitution, which like the English constitution was a series of edicts and constitutional practices, did not recognize a distinction between patriciate and bourgeoisie. Rousseau's haven of equality had no aristocracy; Burghers and Citizens of Geneva, rich and poor, were politically equal. But the Genevan government consisted of a set of councils that lent itself to—indeed, seemed to invite—the manipulation of a majority by a tightly organized oligarchy. The largest of these councils was the General Council in which every Burgher and Citizen was entitled to vote. In its annual meeting, it elected the four syndics and other magistrates, debated domestic and foreign affairs, and ratified proposals for legislation. But the real power of the General Council had sharply declined during the Calvinist revolution of the 1530's. Two smaller councils, the Council of Two Hundred and the Council of Twenty-Five, came to divide legislative, executive, and judicial powers between them.

In 1543, their powers and practices were confirmed by Calvin's Political Edict, which provided that the Council of Two Hundred would elect the members of the Council of Twenty-Five, that the Council of Twenty-Five would return the courtesy by electing the members of the Council of Two Hundred, that the Council of Two Hundred would present a list of eight candidates from which the General Council must appoint the four syndics, and that the two smaller councils alone had the power to initiate legislation. After this sweeping edict, confirmed by a supplementary edict in 1568, the General Council, the voice of the people, was in practice silent—it could reject nominations and proposals, but no more. In 1570 it even surrendered the precious right to levy taxes. Leading families learned to treat the government of the city as their private property. They named close relatives to important posts, stifled criticism of their actions by stigmatizing and punishing it as sedition. Some syndics remained in office for half a century or more.

It was inevitable that the two smaller councils, too, would struggle for predominance; it was equally inevitable that the Council of Twenty-Five would emerge as the effective instrument of government. Geneva was like a holding company: a few families controlled the Council of Twenty-Five, through which they controlled the Council of Two Hundred and, in turn, the General Council. The patriciate tightened its hold through intermarriage, nepotism, bribery at elections, violations of tenure rules, and the use of intimidation and violence. Since it held the chief positions in the Republic, the patriciate could dictate policies, interpret the laws in its own way, prosecute its enemies, and shield its friends.

By 1700, the social and political predominance of the patriciate and the political emasculation of the bourgeoisie were almost complete. Sumptuary laws, designed by the church to keep all in the paths of righteousness, were used to underline class divisions by permitting luxuries to the patriciate which were prohibited to the bourgeoisie; the Consistory was a welcome ally to the aristocracy. It became possible for members of the Council of Twenty-Five to remain in office even though the Council of Two Hundred had failed to reappoint them; it became possible for one leading family to place eight of its members in the two smaller councils; it became possible for the son of a syndic to sit as a member of the Council of Two Hundred although he was only sixteen. The aristocracy deliberately underscored its exclusiveness by withdrawing into its own quarters in the city, by rarely associating with the ordinary citizens, by developing its own salons, tastes, and dress. The old custom of electing two syndics from the lower and two from the upper city was silently dropped.

This aristocratic isolation had social advantages but political disadvantages. It greatly strengthened bourgeois resentment and, at the same time, kept the patriciate in relative ignorance of popular discontents. As the patricians grew more exclusive, the number of talented, energetic, proud, and wealthy Burghers who were not among the privileged grew as well. Their resentment was fed by the French refugees who came to Geneva after the revocation of the Edict of Nantes; by 1700, wrote d'Ivernois eighty-two years later, "These distinctions, this marked separation, recalled to the people's remembrance the equality established by the laws; they saw it more and more destroyed by the inequality of fortunes; they at last resolved that it should not be lost."[18]

In 1707, bourgeois malcontents, irked by a squabble over taxes, resolved that the equality established by law should not be lost. Moving from grumbling to action, they proposed a constitutional program which included publication of all edicts and limitation on the number of persons one family could place in the governing councils. The patriciate's reply was to make token concessions, to treat the bourgeois party with disdain, and to arrest Pierre Fatio, its leader. Fatio was executed after a secret trial for sedition; his followers were ruthlessly exiled and deprived of their citizenship rights. For the moment the oligarchy had been saved, but at a price: the patriciate, rather than give in to the demands of the bourgeoisie, had called in troops from Berne and mediators from Berne and Zurich.

When civil conflict broke out again in 1734, it lasted longer, was more violent, and again required outside mediation. After an armed clash on 21 August 1737 in which a dozen Genevans were killed, Zurich, Berne, and France offered to settle the civil war; on 8 May 1738 the General Council approved the proposals of the "illustrious mediation" by the overwhelming vote of 1316 to 39. The rhetorical victory belonged to the bourgeoisie: the *règlement* provided that the General Council had the right to declare peace or war; to approve or reject legislation, including new taxes and fortifications; to elect or reject the magistrates; and to make representations to the magistrates, a pro-

18 *Historical and Political View*, 26.

vision that the bourgeoisie interpreted as a sweeping power to supervise administration. The chief ideologist of the bourgeoisie, Micheli Ducrest, had proclaimed throughout the troubles that the people of Geneva alone was sovereign, and that only the body in which it assembled—the General Council—could be called the sovereign legislator of the Republic. But the real victory was won by the patriciate: the *règlement* also provided that "nothing shall be laid before the Council of Two Hundred that had not been previously dealt with and approved by the Council of Twenty-Five, and nothing shall be laid before the General Council that had not been previously dealt with and approved by the Council of Two Hundred."[19] The people of Geneva had been solemnly granted what it had always possessed: the right to approve the acts of the magistrates. Micheli Ducrest bitterly but accurately protested that the *règlement* chained the sovereign and delivered him into the hands of twenty-five masters.[20] Spokesmen for the twenty-five masters, including the international lawyer Jean-Jacques Burlamaqui, continued to claim that the Council of Twenty-Five was a separate order, of equal rank with the General Council, and that Geneva was a mixed state, an "aristo-democracy."

The settlement of 1738 did not change Geneva's aristocratic character, but the middle class embraced it with joy. Weary of strife, anxious for accommodation, the bourgeoisie felt safe now that its right to make representations to the magistrates was guaranteed. Moreover, there was general prosperity in Geneva, and in prosperity issues of political principle lose their urgency. Events were to show that the prosperity of the bourgeoisie was more secure than its liberties: the magistrates continued to govern with a high hand, to evade the obligation of publishing all edicts, to manipulate criminal procedure in their favor.

[19] John Stephenson Spink, *Jean-Jacques Rousseau et Genève*, 27.
[20] *ibid.*, 28. D'Ivernois, a contemporary, has a different interpretation of the *règlement* of 1738: he argued that it was substantially favorable to the popular party, but that its provisions were twisted by the patriciate in the 1740's and 1750's. *Historical and Political View*, 117-132.

This continued rule of an oligarchy conflicted more and more with economic realities. The spread of the watch-making industry brought moderate affluence to ever larger numbers of Genevans, even to Natives. And with affluence came the desire for education, recognition, and political participation. Rousseau was mistaken to accuse Voltaire in 1760 of "ruining" Geneva.[21] Voltaire's presence was an occasion, not the cause, of the civil strife of the 1760's.

Still, to have Voltaire in the neighborhood was not exactly a soothing influence. His purchase of Ferney, a mere half-hour's ride from Geneva, did not bring his withdrawal from polite Genevan society. Their elegant carriages followed Voltaire from *Les Délices* to Ferney, for while some of the patricians professed to distrust his character, all admired his dinners, his conversation, and above all his amateur theatricals. Voltaire was devoted to the theatre; he wrote great dramas, offered exciting private productions, and consented to act in his own tragedies. To his aristocratic guests these were more than gracious acts of hospitality; they were a sign that Voltaire was taking a political position on the side of his natural allies, the Genevan patriciate, French in training, in sympathy, in culture, skeptical of the Protestant ethic, ashamed of what it privately called Calvin's "murder" of Servetus. Nothing gratified Genevan magistrates more than crying for five acts over a Voltairian tragedy; nothing gratified Voltaire more than watching them cry—except, perhaps, crying a little himself.

But against such innocuous debauchery stood the Genevan bourgeoisie, upholding Calvinist asceticism with wounded dignity. It was the people who were not invited to Voltaire's parties who decried him as a source of corruption. "I realized," Rousseau remembered later, with characteristic inaccuracy, "that [Voltaire] would work a revolution in the city, and that if I

---

[21] 17 June 1760, *Correspondance générale*, ed. Th. Dufour and Pierre-Paul Plan, 20 vols. (1924-1934), v, 135.

returned I should find in my native land the tone, the airs, and the customs which were driving me from Paris. . . ."²² The theatre, in a word, was a symbol of inequality, cherished by the patriciate and hated by the bourgeoisie. When the inevitable quarrel over the theatre finally erupted, Voltaire quite naturally became a symbol for the upper, Rousseau for the middle class.

The precipitating event was d'Alembert's visit to *Les Délices* in August 1756. There he met the leading citizens of Geneva: savants, magistrates, bankers, pastors. He charmed and was charmed. In his article "Genève," published in the seventh volume of the *Encyclopédie* in October 1757, he paid grateful tribute to the manners, the intelligence, the morality of the Genevans. Their ministers, he wrote, have pure morals, faithfully obey the law, refuse to persecute dissenters, and worship the Supreme Being in a worthy manner: "Several ministers do not believe at all in the divinity of Jesus Christ . . . their religion is a perfect Socinianism." Such a people, led by such divines, could well tolerate a theatre in its country. While troupes of professional actors sometimes had a pernicious impact on the morals of the community, the civilizing influence of the drama made such risks worth taking. "Theatrical representations," he said with gentle irony, "would form the taste of the citizens and would give them a finesse of tact, a delicacy of feeling, which is very hard to acquire without this aid."²³

²² *Confessions*, Book VIII. In fact, Rousseau was very pleased to have Voltaire near Geneva; in his letters of 1756 and even later, he spoke to (and of) Voltaire with the greatest respect and even admiration.

²³ D'Alembert's remark concerning the "Socinianism" of the Genevan ministers, although moderate and far from unjust, created a great stir: it expressed publicly what many of them were willing to say privately. On 12 April (1756) Voltaire had written to Cideville that "the reasonable Christianity of Locke is the religion of almost all the ministers." XXXIX, 21. When they professed themselves outraged by d'Alembert's article, Voltaire wrote a long, admirable letter to Théodore Tronchin: "M. d'Alembert has the courage to tell you that you approach this simple and divine cult, and you would have the cowardice to take it in bad part? . . . Almost the whole English parliament thinks like you." 15 January (1758), *Correspondance avec les Tronchin*, 308.

The Calvinist bourgeoisie, the *parti anticomédien*,[24] was outraged but helpless until Rousseau's *Lettre à Mr. d'Alembert sur les spectacles* appeared in October 1758. It was a relentlessly long refutation of d'Alembert's suggestion, a tortuous defense of Rousseau's own conduct and philosophy. The drama, he wrote, is as immoral as the actors who perform it; the theatre offers escape and debases virtue; comedies would give Geneva "the most terrible disorders; they would serve as the instrument of factions, parties, private vengeances."[25]

As it turned out, it was Rousseau's *Lettre* on the drama, rather than the drama itself, that served as the instrument of factions and parties. "Before the appearance of d'Alembert's article," Paul Chaponnière tells us, "the partisans and adversaries of the theatre only defended their opinion, and that opinion only depended on their taste or their principles. . . . But after Rousseau's *Lettre* . . . the question of the theatre, which had become a political affair, cleanly separated the classes: it was no longer a question of pleasure but of the right to see or to play the drama. The iron gates of Ferney seemed to open only before carriages. . . . The movement unleashed by Rousseau was followed by all those who saw in the theatre a privilege implicitly reserved to the aristocracy, hence an injustice."[26]

The quarrel over the theatre ran its course, as quarrels will, but it was a warning that the earlier accommodations between patriciate and bourgeoisie had been no more than truces, and that all was not for the best in the best of all possible republics.

The warning was borne out in 1762, and this time it was Rousseau rather than Voltaire or d'Alembert who precipitated the conflict. Early that year, Rousseau published two of his masterpieces, *Emile* and the *Contrat social*. Both books bore his

[24] The phrase is by Jean-Louis Du Pan, member of the Council of Twenty-Five. *Lettres à Cramer*, 27n.

[25] J.-J. Rousseau, *Lettre à Mr. d'Alembert sur les spectacles*, 162-163. Rousseau was certain that Voltaire had had a hand in d'Alembert's article "Genève," but he ostensibly directed his refutation to d'Alembert alone.

[26] *Voltaire chez les Calvinistes*, 161-162.

name on the title page, thus violating one of Voltaire's most cherished (and most sensible) principles. *Emile* was an immense popular success in France; it was further advertised by its condemnation and burning by the parlement of Paris on 11 June. Acting with unwonted and inappropriate haste, obviously under pressure from France, the Genevan Council of Twenty-Five condemned both *Emile* and the *Contrat social* on 19 June, prohibited the importation of copies, ordered the seizure of copies already at booksellers, and decided to have Rousseau arrested if he entered Genevan territory.

In view of the enduring place which the *Contrat social* holds in the history of political theory, a profound examination of the relation of authority to liberty, ranking with Machiavelli's *Prince* and Hobbes' *Leviathan,* the Genevan government's reasons for condemning it are at once amusing and instructive: they reveal once again the many dimensions of a great book. Geneva's attorney general, Jean-Robert Tronchin, a cousin of the banker, told the Council of Twenty-Five that the *Contrat social* reiterated the ideology of the Genevan bourgeoisie. It affirmed the absolute sovereignty of the people, considered all institutions of government its servants, recommended periodic popular assemblies, refused to recognize reciprocal obligations between governors and governed. Were these not the pernicious ideas of Micheli Ducrest?[27] "The *Contrat social*," Tronchin wrote later, "is hence not a Utopia . . . it was made for us, it is our government that is its principal object."[28] Voltaire read the book in the same way: "In a little booklet . . ." he told d'Alembert late in 1763, "[Rousseau] took the part of the people against the magistrates too strongly; hence the people, very gratefully, has taken the part of Jean-Jacques in its turn."[29]

But the people was slow in expressing its gratitude. For al-

[27] Spink, *Rousseau et Genève,* 51. The name Micheli Ducrest was apparently not mentioned in the session of the Council of Twenty-Five, but it is evident that it was on the minds of its members.
[28] *Lettres populaires,* of 1765, quoted *loc.cit.*
[29] 28 September 1763, XLII, 582. Rousseau took the same view.

most a year the bourgeoisie, unpolitical and timid, did not come to the aid of its champion. His only vocal defender was Colonel Charles Pictet, member of the Council of Two Hundred, who printed a letter accusing Voltaire of having caused the condemnation of Rousseau, and the Council of Twenty-Five of having acted in fear of France and out of a desire to efface the bad impression made by d'Alembert's article "Genève." For exercising his freedom of speech in the haven of liberty, Pictet was sentenced by the Council of Twenty-Five to an apology, and was deprived of his membership in the Council of Two Hundred as well as his citizenship rights for a year. The trial, whose legal details became a rallying point for bourgeois discontent, was conducted by the Council of Twenty-Five in the absence of a syndic, since all four syndics had to disqualify themselves for being too closely related to Pictet or to the attorney general. It was another example of the tyranny of Geneva's twenty-five masters.

Voltaire watched, remembered, and said nothing—or almost nothing: he protested to Pictet and to the Genevan government that he had had nothing to do with Rousseau's condemnation.[30] And to his brethren in France he maligned Rousseau with that special aversion the believer reserves for the apostate: Jean-Jacques Rousseau, deist, author of that brilliant *Profession de foi du vicaire Savoyard* which Voltaire wished he had written himself, was more pernicious than the Frérons of this world. He had seen the light and rejected it, he was an ex-philosophe. "Jean Jacques is the scourge of philosophers. He writes against them and will get them hanged."[31]

[30] See *Lettres à Cramer*, 87n; in 1766, when he would have had a better reason to complain of Voltaire's treatment of Rousseau, Pictet apologized to Voltaire for having given in to an "erroneous prejudice." Chaponnière, *Voltaire chez les Calvinistes*, 197-198. It is extremely probable that Voltaire was innocent of this particular infamy: he denied it to the Tronchins, who certainly would have known of it. See *Correspondance avec les Tronchin*, 578n.
[31] Voltaire to Gabriel Cramer (September 1762?), *Lettres à Cramer*, 89.

This is why Voltaire was so blind to Rousseau's genius. "This social or unsocial contract," he wrote to Damilaville on 25 June 1762, "is remarkable only for a few coarse insults to kings from the citizen of the town of Geneva."[32] This, too, is why Voltaire was initially so indifferent to Rousseau's fate. "Since this bastard of Diogenes' dog is unhappy," he wrote to Gabriel Cramer in July 1762, being coarse himself this time, "we must forgive him. But if he comes to Geneva, he will be even more impudent and more foolish than he had been in his village near Paris. That man fits neither into a republic nor into a kingdom nor into society."[33]

But Voltaire's second thoughts were often more sensible and more humane than his first. He had once said of himself that he was a devil, but a good devil; when the apathetic Genevan bourgeoisie was finally stung into action by Rousseau's abdication of his citizenship, the good devil applauded heartily. Rousseau's abdication had the effect he had hoped for: on 18 June 1763, a day before the anniversary of the condemnations, a delegation submitted to the first syndic a "Very Humble and Respectful Representation of Citizens and Burghers of Geneva." Its grievances were the old grievances of 1707 and 1734 in a new form: the judgment against Rousseau had been irregular and illegal; the tribunal that had convicted Pictet had sat illegally; the confiscation of 24 copies of *Emile* from Genevan booksellers invaded property rights. The Council of Twenty-Five rejected the representation a week later, admitting no wrongdoing and no need for remedial action. The bourgeoisie, thoroughly aroused, made further representations through the summer. Voltaire delightedly informed his friends that these were great days: "There are two thousand members in the parish of the Savoyard vicar. . . . God be blessed—toleration is winning in Geneva."[34] And at last he rose above the personal and immediate to the universal,

[32] XLII, 142.   [33] *Lettres à Cramer*, 84.

[34] Voltaire to Damilaville, 26 August 1763, XLII, 557; Voltaire to the duchesse de Saxe-Gotha, 30 June 1763, XLII, 512.

above his association with the patricians to the issue itself: "Don't you bless God to see the people of Calvin take Jean-Jacques' part so loudly? Let us not consider his person, let us consider his cause. The rights of humanity have never been better sustained. . . ."[35] Let us not consider his person, let us consider his cause—surely the old devil had some good in him.

2. BOURGEOIS

The representations of the bourgeoisie, energetic if a little belated, deeply gratified Voltaire, but they also alarmed him. The patricians, used to autocratic pre-eminence, stubbornly refused to make any concessions whatever. On 21 August 1763, Voltaire wrote prophetically to the duc de Richelieu: "It is pleasant enough to see a whole people demand reparation for Jean-Jacques Rousseau. . . . You will soon hear people talk about the city of Geneva, and I think that you will be obliged to be arbiter between the people and the magistrates, for you are guarantors of the laws of this little town."[36] A few weeks later, the Council of Twenty-Five offered a startling interpretation of the Genevan constitution: it claimed a veto power, the *droit négatif*, over ill-founded or frivolous representations. The bourgeoisie indignantly insisted on its right to have all its representations heard and examined. It was from this exchange that the parties took their names: the patricians became the *Négatifs*; the bourgeois, the *Représentants*.

Voltaire's friends, guests, bankers, fellow actors, were all *Négatifs*; as the intimate of kings and aristocrats, as the cultivated dramatist, the friend of the ubiquitous Tronchins, Voltaire's proper place was with the patriciate.[37] And through 1763

[35] Voltaire to Damilaville, 23 August 1763, XLII, 553.

[36] XLII, 551.

[37] The power of the Tronchin clan evidently greatly alarmed the bourgeoisie. D'Ivernois said in 1782: "This family, devoted to France, where they were already laying the foundation of the credit to which they aspired, were trying every means to lord it in Geneva. Two of the family were members of the senate, and a third had recently been elected attorney general." *Historical and Political View*, 166.

and 1764 he kept to his place at least in public. In September 1763 one of his friends, the attorney general Jean-Robert Tronchin, published a reasoned statement of the *Négatifs*' position, the *Lettres écrites de la campagne*; a year later Rousseau replied, justifying himself and the bourgeoisie in his *Lettres écrites de la montagne*. This was a brilliant performance, an occasional pamphlet that far transcended its occasion.

Unfortunately, Voltaire was in no mood to do justice to its brilliance. Rousseau irresponsibly endangered Voltaire by identifying him as the author of the *Sermon des cinquante*, a vehemently anti-Christian pamphlet that Voltaire had so far successfully attributed to La Mettrie.[38] Voltaire had an attack of fury fed by an attack of panic; he launched a vile, anonymous denunciation, the *Sentiments des citoyens*, which revealed scurrilous details, true and false, about Rousseau's private life, and piously denounced him as an enemy of Christianity who deserved capital punishment.

His controversy with Rousseau postponed but did not prevent Voltaire's public defection from the Genevan aristocracy. When it came, it deeply annoyed his friends in Geneva and greatly surprised his friends in Paris,[39] yet it was a logical, almost an inevitable, defection. Voltaire, the empiricist, had been studying

[38] See Voltaire to d'Argental: "He tells the Council [of Twenty-Five] that I wrote the *Sermon des cinquante*. Ah! Jean-Jacques, that is not acting like a philosopher: it is infamous to be an informer, it is abominable to denounce one's confrère." 10 January 1765, XLIII, 433. It was neither infamous nor abominable to push off the pamphlet on La Mettrie, who had been safely dead since 1751.

[39] In May 1768, Grimm wrote in the *Correspondance littéraire*: "For over two years he has found himself abandoned by all his friends and he no longer receives anybody from town, since he tried, very maladroitly, to play a role in the troubles, and since he sacrificed his true friends and his essential interests to the party of the people." Chaponnière quotes this passage, *Voltaire chez les Calvinistes*, 225, and comments sarcastically: "Decidedly, the patriarch was getting old." The Tronchins were of course furious. Théodore Tronchin told Boswell: "He is very amiable, but is never the same for two days . . . he is mad. I call any man mad who has no fixed principles." *Boswell on the Grand Tour*, 314.

the facts of Genevan life, and the better he knew them, the more sympathetic he felt toward the cause of the bourgeoisie.

On its side, the bourgeoisie was learning much about Voltaire. Supposedly in retirement at Ferney, he was more active than ever. "I must comment on thirty-three pieces," he wrote to the comtesse d'Argental on 2 January 1763, "translate from Spanish and English, search for anecdotes, revise and correct all the proofs, finish the *Histoire générale* and that of *Czar Pierre*, work for the Calas, make tragedies, retouch them, plant and build, receive a hundred strangers, all of this with deplorable health. . . ."[40] He might have added that he was making the final corrections in his one-man *Encyclopédie*, the *Dictionnaire philosophique*, and urging on the brethren to *écraser l'infâme*. Some of these activities were of no interest to Genevan burghers; others, had they known of them, they would have found abhorrent. But in the midst of his literary and propagandist labors, Voltaire was working for the Calas family and pleading for toleration and legal reform in his *Traité sur la tolérance*. More and more the symbol of luxury and impiety was transforming himself into the fighter for lost causes. Although Voltaire's connections were entirely among the rich, wrote d'Ivernois a little pompously, "his sentiments were too elevated to permit him to espouse their petty passions."[41]

For several years, Voltaire ostentatiously employed his elevated sentiments on behalf of one Robert Covelle, Citizen of Geneva, a young man of limited intelligence and evidently inadequate caution. On 23 February 1763 the Consistory found Covelle guilty of having fathered an illegitimate child, and sentenced him to ask God's pardon on his knees. Covelle asked for a week to think it over, and then refused to comply with the humiliating penalty. In this defiance of the clerical authorities, Covelle was aided by Voltaire, who found the case irresistible. He ceremoniously greeted Covelle as *monsieur le*

[40] XLII, 316.
[41] *Historical and Political View*, 187.

fornicateur—a salutation which the simple young man accepted as an honorific title—and began a campaign for abolition of genuflection.

This trivial and absurd case had its constitutional as well as its humorous aspects. Covelle's partisans were incidentally asserting the sovereign legislative power of the people. *Génuflexion*, a pamphlet probably written by Voltaire, curtly declared itself in favor of popular sovereignty: "The citizen, member of a republic, must only be governed by laws that he himself has made; it is this that constitutes his liberty."[42] The war of Covelle raged intermittently for six years and ended in a victory for Voltaire's party: genuflection was abandoned in February 1769. Voltaire was establishing himself as the champion of the persecuted—in Geneva as well as in France.

It is not an accident that Voltaire's growing radicalism in Genevan politics came after 1762, after he had cast himself in a new role as the conscience of Europe. When he attacked *l'infâme*, *l'infâme* not unnaturally fought back, and he was reminded more than once that he and Rousseau were fighting the same battle. On 19 March 1765, the parlement of Paris suppressed Voltaire's *Dictionnaire philosophique* and Rousseau's *Lettres écrites de la montagne* in the same decree. Ill-matched as they were, the Apollo of the French Parnassus and the

[42] Spink, *Rousseau et Genève*, 57. The pamphlet was published at Neufchâtel, not Geneva, on 28 March 1764, and suppressed by the Genevan authorities on the next day. Voltaire's authorship of the pamphlet is not certain, but it is as probable as Covelle's paternity of Catherine Ferboz's child. Chaponnière has no hesitation in attributing *Génuflexion* to Voltaire (*Voltaire chez les Calvinistes*, 210), but it appears neither in Bengesco's bibliography nor in any edition of Voltaire's works that I have seen. The story of Covelle's reception at Ferney was first retailed by Grimm, *Correspondance littéraire*, 1 November 1768, VIII, 201-203. To judge from one severe remark, Voltaire did not view the Covelle affair simply as a class issue, but expected to have some patrician support for his campaign. "I flatter myself," he wrote to Théodore Tronchin, "that you are not among those who want to see fornicators kneel. Rid yourself of all such sorry matters." (Probably spring 1764), *Correspondance avec les Tronchin*, 600.

Bastard of Diogenes' dog were allies in the war against the old order.

As a writer, Voltaire had always been sensitive to attempts to stifle his and his friends' political and religious views. Now, in the 1760's, freedom of opinion became an offensive weapon for him: the colossus of fanaticism could be overturned only by an informed public opinion, the public could be well-informed only if it could read the philosophes without interference, hence the first and perhaps the most important battle must be the battle against censorship. It was a battle that Voltaire had fought all his life; he was fighting it with ever great vigor in the 1760's, with all the eloquence and cunning at his command. Tirelessly he reiterated the old themes: humanity is an association of brothers groping for light; in our ignorance we must learn to subject everything, including our methods of inquiry and the values by which we live, to rational and critical scrutiny; all forces that limit or thwart inquiry are the forces of darkness, the enemies of humanity.[43]

Now, at Ferney, he decided that the Genevan patricians, attractive as some of them were as individuals, only too often ranged themselves on the side of darkness. The Council of Twenty-Five, the spokesmen for the patriciate, had suppressed Voltaire's first Genevan work, *L'auteur arrivant dans sa terre*, in the summer of 1755. In the following year, Voltaire had warned his publisher Cramer against distributing the *Poème sur le désastre de Lisbonne* and *La loi naturelle* in Geneva: "I doubt whether the preachers would be content with certain

---

[43] As usual, Voltaire mingled the interest of his craft with the interest of civilization as a whole. "The life of a man of letters is liberty," he had written to Cideville on 15 September (1733), *Correspondence*, III, 142. But he was equally certain that the liberty of men of letters would be mirrored in the liberty of the public as a whole. Ernst Cassirer points out that for Voltaire this demand for freedom of opinion is central. But Cassirer overlooks his device of making himself appear harmless when he quotes without comment Voltaire's remark that there are no dangerous books and that censorship is therefore unnecessary. *Philosophy of the Enlightenment*, 251-252.

sermons."[44] Nor were they content with other sermons: early in 1759 the Council of Twenty-Five condemned *Candide* for being "filled with dangerous principles concerning religion and tending to the depravation of morals."[45] Voltaire piously accepted the decree: "Since I find this work very contrary to the decisions of the Sorbonne and to the Papal decretals," he told Jean-Robert Tronchin, "I maintain that I had no hand in it." He added, alluding slyly to *Candide*, that he was building a château "more beautiful than that of M. le baron de Thunder ten Trunckh. It is ruining me, but I hope that the Bulgarians won't come there."[46]

But the Bulgarians were at the door. The philosophes had been thrown on the defensive in France. Damiens' insane attempt to assassinate Louis XV in January 1757 had brought the savage decree of 16 April 1757, which threatened the death penalty for authors convicted of attacking religion or the state. The decree was not enforced, but it was a grim warning. D'Alembert, alarmed by the outcry over his article "Genève," abandoned the *Encyclopédie* in January 1758; in July, Helvétius' *De l'esprit* reminded all the *dévots*, if they needed reminding, of the length to which pernicious modern doctrines could go. Less than a year later Omer Joly de Fleury, the French attorney general, suppressed the *Encyclopédie* in its entirety as the source from which Helvétius had taken his dangerous ideas.[47]

And in Geneva, the Bulgarians were interfering with Voltaire. He had begun the *Dictionnaire philosophique portatif* at Potsdam in 1752, where he had shown the first articles to Frederick, and completed it at his leisure at *Les Délices* and at Ferney. The first edition, printed by the faithful Cramers, appeared in August 1764. Here were other sermons to displease the Genevan

[44] Voltaire to Gabriel Cramer, 25 (February 1756), *Lettres à Cramer*, 10.

[45] *ibid.*, xxi.

[46] 12 March (1759), *Correspondance avec les Tronchin*, 384.

[47] Wilson, *Diderot*, 333-334. However, work on the *Encyclopédie* continued.

pastors. The Consistory promptly called the government's attention to the book, and in September the Council of Twenty-Five ordered all copies seized and the book burned. Voltaire denied his brain child and reprinted it: "A magistrate came politely to ask my permission to burn a certain *Portatif*; I told him that his confrères were at perfect liberty to do so provided they did not burn my person, and that I took no interest whatever in any *Portatif*."[48]

In truth, he never took a greater interest in, never lavished more loving care on any other work. The *Dictionnaire philosophique* contained little that was new. Deists and skeptics and humanitarians had been preaching its lessons for a century: true religion needs no doctrine or ritual; all man needs to know is that there is a just God who wants men to love each other; theological disputes that no one understands cause cruelty and bloodshed; fanaticism is a disease created by superstition; there is nothing more pernicious in a state than a powerful church; the Bible and the traditions of the Catholic church are filled with contradictions and absurdities.

These were old preachments, even for Voltaire, and yet the publication of the *Dictionnaire philosophique* was a major event in the intellectual history of Europe. Like the *Lettres philosophiques*, published thirty years before, the Dictionary was a bomb thrown at the Old Regime. It is the most personal of creations; no one but Voltaire could have written it. It is light in touch, witty, erudite, prejudiced and limited in its vision, often wise, sometimes foolish, always entertaining. From its first article, "Abbé," to its last article, "Vertu," the *Dictionnaire philosophique* uses all the techniques that Voltaire had mas-

[48] Voltaire to d'Argental, 23 December (1764), XLIII, 408. On 12 February 1765, Voltaire advised the Council of Twenty-Five that Geneva was being swamped by pernicious brochures, including a *Dictionnaire philosophique* and "other follies which people have the insolence to attribute to me. . . ." Desnoiresterres, *Voltaire et Rousseau*, 344. Grimm reports that the *Dictionnaire philosophique* was immensely popular in Paris and very hard to get. *Correspondance littéraire*, 1 September 1764, VI, 65.

tered: sarcasm, pathos, irony, eloquence, slyness. He gives a detailed exposition of the reasonable theology of the Unitarians and then lamely "refutes" it in the name of Roman Catholicism; he lists contradictory positions of church fathers on the Trinity and other Christian mysteries and then sarcastically comments that he accepts Christian doctrine because infallible councils and popes have pronounced it true; he attacks the Biblical Jews, the chosen people, for their barbarity and brutality and then suggests that his readers draw their own conclusions about the Christian religion which is the child of Judaism; he extols the laws of nature as outlined by great pagan philosophers and then contrasts their teachings with the bloodthirsty practice of Christians.[48a] He repeats himself without becoming repetitious; he has one theme and many variations, all interesting. Altogether, the *Dictionnaire philosophique* is a devastating book.

But with all this activity, Voltaire did not neglect Geneva—indeed, the Genevans did not let him neglect it. Rousseau's *Lettres écrites de la montagne* had told the Genevan bourgeoisie what it had not wanted and yet needed to know: that the Burghers and Citizens of Geneva were sovereign in law and impotent in fact. "In the General Council, your sovereign power is chained: you can act only when it pleases your magistrates, and speak only when they interrogate you. . . . If you are sovereign masters in the assembly, you are nothing after you leave it. Four hours each year you are subordinate sovereigns, the rest of your life you are subjects, handed over without reservation to the discretion of others."[49]

In early 1765, the bourgeoisie, stirred up by Rousseau, tried to attain real power. In January, the General Council threatened to go on strike, and then confined itself to electing the syndics with 500 to 600 abstentions as a sign of protest; in March, the General Council refused to legalize a tax on wine that had been

[48a] See Appendix III, "Voltaire's Anti-Semitism."
[49] *Lettres écrites de la montagne,* letter VII.

levied illegally on orders of the Council of Twenty-Five; through the spring and summer, it launched remonstrances and pamphlets. The bourgeoisie was marshaling its arguments for the inevitable day that outside mediation would begin.

But the bourgeoisie were Rousseauians without Rousseau. In February 1765, Jean-Jacques Rousseau had told his friends that he was withdrawing from the Genevan controversy and would no longer answer their letters.[50] Hesitantly, reluctantly, but remembering Covelle, cherishing the *Traité sur la tolérance*, cheered by the vindication of Calas in March 1765,[51] Rousseau's friends turned to Voltaire. He received them well, for he now looked upon the Genevan patriciate, with only a few exceptions, as "sixteenth-century pedants," and upon the ordinary citizens as men of "intelligence and reason."[52] On 11 October 1765, he confessed to d'Argental that he had for a long time thought the patriciate worthy of French protection, but that he had been wrong: "The Council [of Twenty-Five] has acted against all the laws on more than one occasion."[53] Having once enlisted his support, the *Représentants* found Voltaire a sturdy sympathizer. "The divisions in Geneva will soon explode," he told Damilaville on 16 October, in an important statement of his new position. "It is absolutely necessary that you and your friends spread the word among the public that the citizens are right against the magistrates. For it is certain that the people only want liberty, while the magistrature has ambitions for absolute power. Is there anything more tyrannical, for instance, than to take away the freedom of the press? And how can a people call itself free when it is not permitted to think in its writings?

[50] Rousseau to Chappuis, 2 February 1765, *Correspondance générale*, XII, 292-293. In December 1765, Rousseau wrote d'Ivernois a long and remarkable letter urging his friends to accept Voltaire's good offices. *ibid.*, XIV, 358-359.
[51] "They are intoxicated at Geneva . . . over the success of our lawsuit." Voltaire to Damilaville, 17 March (1765), XLIII, 493.
[52] Voltaire to d'Argental, 26 October (1765), XLIV, 91.
[53] XLIV, 83.

Whoever has power in his hands wants to put out·the eyes of those who are subjected to him; every village judge wants to be a despot: the rage to dominate is an incurable malady."[54] In Geneva, although apparently not in Russia or France, power corrupted.

Voltaire was partisan, but he was also pacific. Through October and November he invited both *Représentants* and *Négatifs* to Ferney for discussions that might lead to conciliation. Conciliation was needed: on 1 November 1765, the General Council met to elect Geneva's officials for the coming year and refused to accept any of the proposed candidates. "A large party of Citizens is still very bitter against the big wigs . . ." wrote Voltaire on that day. "There are men of merit in either party, but they are incompatible merits. I receive one and the other as best I can; I limit myself to that."[55]

But Voltaire had to be wary; the *grandes perruques* were his old friends, and his desertion had deeply wounded them. Hence he let it be known that his status as a foreigner, his poor health, his retiring disposition all made it impossible for him to intervene in Genevan politics. On 13 November he told Jacob Tronchin, a member of the Council of Twenty-Five, with uncharacteristic modesty: "I am far from thinking that I could be useful; but I have an idea (perhaps I am wrong) that it is not impossible to reconcile spirits," largely by bringing the parties together at Ferney.[56] On the same day he asked d'Argental to inform the duc de Praslin, French foreign minister, that he was passive and neutral.[57]

[54] xliv, 89. See Voltaire to d'Alembert, 16 October (1765): "The Council and the bourgeois are more divided than ever, and I believe that the Council is wrong, since the magistrates always want to extend their power, and the people limits itself to not wishing to be oppressed." xliv, 87.
[55] Voltaire to de Florian, xliv, 97.
[56] xliv, 107.
[57] xliv, 108-109. He told d'Argental in the same letter that things are seldom as they appear from afar: French representatives who came to Geneva were greatly surprised to learn of the moderation of the bourgeoisie and of the excesses of the Council. On 20 November he wrote a note to

Having assured everybody that he could not possibly meddle, Voltaire meddled happily. On 21 November Jean-Louis Du Pan, patrician, member of the Council of Twenty-Five, and an old friend, wrote in some distress: "He makes proposals, has prejudices, and listens to no one. With the best of intentions he cannot help but do us harm."[58] On the same day, the Council of Twenty-Five politely told Voltaire that his negotiations with the Genevan parties were at an end.

In asking Voltaire to stop doing what he wanted to do, the Council behaved like King Canute trying to hold back the waves. He wanted to help, and he was certain that he could help. On 27 November he reported to d'Argental: "Several members of the Genevan Council and several Citizens have come to me in turn, and have explained to me the subject of their divisions. I have taken the liberty to propose accommodations to them. There are several articles on which they could come to terms in a quarter of an hour; there are others which would take time, and above all more information than I have. My only merit, if it is one, is to play a role diametrically opposed to that of Jean-Jacques, and to seek to extinguish the fire which he has puffed up with his little lungs. I have put on paper a little plan of pacification. . . . Please, give yourself the pleasure or the boredom of reading my little chimera; I do not want to present it to the interested parties until you have told me it is reasonable. I think it should first be shown to two lawyers in Paris, to find out whether it violates public or international law. . . . If M. le duc de Praslin approves of this plan, I shall then propose it to the Council of Geneva, and that will be a preliminary to the peace which M. Hennin [the new French resident] will make upon his arrival. I shall not meddle in anything

the foreign minister directly, asking him to read his letter to d'Argental, and characteristically signing it: "The old Swiss who lives only for himself." XLIV, 115.
[58] Chaponnière, *Voltaire chez les Calvinistes*, 219.

as soon as M. Hennin comes; I only prepare the ways of the Lord."[59]

Voltaire's "little plan of pacification" is an informed document; Voltaire had read and listened well. Reasonably enough, it treats as the central question the dichotomy between the legal sovereignty and the political impotence of the General Council, a dichotomy introduced at the time of Calvin and last confirmed in the *règlement* of the 1738 mediation. The Citizens, said Voltaire, are "sovereign legislators," but their representations are only too often "rejected purely and simply" by the Council of Twenty-Five.[60] Not all representations deserve to be weighed, but not all of them should be rejected out of hand. The point is to find a constitutional method for distinguishing frivolous from serious grievances. Voltaire proposed a simple solution: when 700 Citizens, supported by three lawyers of a university of their choice, demand the interpretation of an obscure law, the improvement of an inadequate law, or the enforcement of a neglected law, the Council of Twenty-Five shall take the representation to the Council of Two Hundred and the first syndic shall convoke the General Council for action. Voltaire's figure of 700, approximately half the number of Citizens and Burghers in the Republic, was a compromise. When he discovered that the Citizens thought it too large and the Council of Twenty-Five too small, he was convinced that the figure was sound.[61]

On the other grievances of the *Représentants*, Voltaire's plan was resolutely optimistic: the ruling patriciate had undertaken in

[59] XLIV, 121. In his letter, Voltaire gave d'Argental elaborate instructions as to who should and should not see the plan. He was anxious to keep it from M. Crommelin, Genevan *chargé d'affaires* at the French court, a strong partisan of the patriciate. This instruction alone shows Voltaire's awareness that his "little plan" was more favorable to the bourgeoisie than to the patriciate.

[60] Voltaire's *Propositions à examiner pour apaiser les divisions de Genève* was first published by Fernand Caussy, *Revue bleue*, ve série, IX (4 January 1908), 13-15.

[61] Voltaire to d'Argental, 28 November (1765), XLIV, 122.

1738 to print all the laws under which the Genevans lived. "This necessary code" had not yet appeared and ought to appear promptly. Again, the magistrates had repeatedly imprisoned citizens by simple administrative procedure, without trial and without public hearing. It was better for a guilty man to escape than for an innocent man to suffer imprisonment: the Citizens of Geneva deserved guarantees against such tyrannical practices.[62] These were the major issues, and Voltaire insisted that it would be possible to conciliate them all without outside mediation.

While he was compiling, distributing, and arguing for his plan, Voltaire found time to write *Idées républicaines,* one of his most widely quoted political pamphlets. It is that ideal polemic which embodies two dimensions, the particular and the universal. Students of Voltaire, paying no attention to its origins, have usually cited it as an eloquent expression of eighteenth-century liberalism. Grimm announced it in January 1766 as Voltaire's "word on the quarrels dividing the Republic of Geneva," and praised it for offering sensible ideas and wise proposals "without entering into the details of the Genevan bickering."[63]

Both interpretations are correct, but both are incomplete: *Idées républicaines* is a propaganda pamphlet for the *Représentants,* the public counterpart to Voltaire's privately-circulated plan. To ignore its Genevan roots is to reduce its pronouncements to vague, well-meaning generalizations in favor of republicanism and against a powerful clergy. At the same time, *Idées républicaines* uses the "Genevan bickering" to develop a liberal

[62] There was only one point on which Voltaire dissented from the bourgeois party line: recalling the case of Colonel Pictet, Rousseau's defender, the *Représentants* demanded that the General Council name a temporary syndic whenever the regular syndics had to disqualify themselves from presiding over a trial. Voltaire rejected this as too cumbersome, and suggested instead that in the event of disqualification an inferior magistrate take the place of the syndic.

[63] *Correspondance littéraire,* 15 January 1766, vi, 474-475.

position applicable anywhere. To ignore this larger meaning is to reduce it to a fugitive and occasional piece. It is precisely the dual aspect—particular and universal, concrete and abstract—that gives *Idées républicaines* its significance.

It is thus possible—indeed, necessary—to read the pamphlet in two ways. In castigating Geneva for condemning Rousseau's *Contrat social*, Voltaire is defending free thought everywhere: "We burned this book. The operation of burning it was perhaps as odious as that of writing it. There are things that a sage government should ignore. If this book was dangerous, it needed to be refuted. To burn a rational book is to say, 'We do not have enough intelligence to reply to it.' "[64] In making invidious comparisons between the Genevan Consistory and practices in England, Voltaire supports free speech in general: "In a republic worthy of its name, the liberty to publish one's thoughts is the natural right of the citizen. He can use his pen as he uses his voice: it should no more be forbidden to write than to talk; and the offenses committed with the pen should be punished like the offenses committed with the word: that is the law of England, a monarchy, but a country where men are freer than they are elsewhere, since they are more enlightened."[65]

Repeatedly, *Idées républicaines* alludes sympathetically to the grievances of the *Représentants*. In criticizing the Genevan magistrates for keeping edicts secret and for exercising arbitrary

[64] XXIV, 424. See Appendix II, "The Date of Voltaire's *Idées républicaines*."

[65] XXIV, 418. During the summer and fall of 1765, Voltaire published a series of "letters" which he attributed to various persons, including, in a characteristic bit of humor, Covelle. These letters begin with religious questions, but by the tenth letter, Voltaire is discussing Genevan affairs, in accents only too familiar to readers of *Idées républicaines*. Thus, on England's freedom: "Let us uphold the liberty of the press, it is the basis of all other liberties; through it we enlighten each other. Every citizen can speak to the nation in writing, and every reader can examine at leisure, and without passion, what his compatriot is telling him. . . . This is how the English nation has become a truly free nation. It would not be free if it were not enlightened; and it would not be enlightened if every one of its citizens did not have the right to print what he wants." *Questions sur les miracles*, XXV, 419.

judiciary power, Voltaire speaks for the rule of law in universal terms: "A criminal code is absolutely necessary for citizens and magistrates. . . . The law that permits imprisoning a citizen without a preliminary inquiry and without judicial formalities would be tolerable in times of trouble and war; it would be cruel and tyrannical in times of peace."[66] And in advocating the rule of law and popular sovereignty, Voltaire uses language familiar and congenial to Genevan bourgeois: "The magistrates are not the masters of the people; the laws are master. . . . We have the right, when we are assembled, to reject or approve the magistrates and the laws that have been proposed to us. . . . Civil government is the will of all, carried out by a single person or by several, in accord with the laws that all have supported."[67] Popular sovereignty, says Voltaire in a phrase reminiscent of his "little plan," is particularly important when laws are in dispute: "When a law is obscure, all must interpret it, for all have promulgated it. . . ."[68]

In extracting universal meaning from particular incidents, Voltaire even makes use of Covelle: "An ecclesiastical assembly that would presume to make a citizen kneel before it, would play the role of a pedant who corrects children, or of a tyrant who punishes slaves. It is to insult reason and law to pronounce these words: *civil and ecclesiastical government.* We must say, *civil government and ecclesiastical regulations,* and these regulations can only be made by the civil power."[69] Rarely has so weighty an Erastian argument been based on so hilarious an example as the Covelle case!

Voltaire did not hesitate to draw a lesson from his own experience, of course without using names. Alluding obliquely to his inability to buy land on Genevan territory, he makes a plea

[66] XXIV, 424, 417.
[67] XXIV, 421, 416.   [68] XXIV, 417.
[69] XXIV, 415. See *Questions sur les miracles,* "Dixième lettre," by "Covelle": "You wanted to make me kneel. . . . You knew then that I do not kneel except to God, and you learned that pastors are not magistrates. . . . We can accept you or reject you: hence we are your sovereigns." XXV, 409.

for toleration: "If a republic has been formed in wars of religion, if in these troubles it has expelled from its territory the sects that were enemies to its own, it has conducted itself wisely, for at that time it considered itself like a country surrounded by persons infected by the plague, afraid that the pest would be imported. But when such times of vertigo are over, when tolerance has become the reigning dogma of all *honnêtes gens* in Europe, is it not a ridiculous barbarity to ask a man who has just established himself and brought his wealth to our country, 'Monsieur, what is your religion?' Gold and silver, industry, talents have no religion."[70]

This is the political program of the *Idées républicaines*. The Geneva visualized in the pamphlet is a liberal republic: all citizens elect their magistrates, approve the laws, supervise their enforcement; they enjoy free speech, even in the sensitive areas of religion and politics;[71] they can give their religious and aesthetic predilections free reign; there is free access to the professions and a general atmosphere of equality, limited only by certain restrictions on the political rights of the Natives. This is not Geneva as it was, but the Geneva that a *Représentant* endowed with wide sympathies would like to see: "We have never known that odious and humiliating distinction of nobles and commoners, which originally meant only lords and slaves. Born as equals, we have remained such; and we have given the dignities, that is to say, the public burdens, to those who seemed to us most fit to sustain them."[72]

[70] xxiv, 418.

[71] See also *Questions sur les miracles*, "Dixième lettre": "There are two important things that people never talk about in slave countries, and which all citizens should discuss in free countries: one is government, the other is religion." xxv, 409. Again, "Treizième lettre," by "Covelle": "We must be jealous of the rights of our reason as of those of our liberty, for the more reasonable beings we shall be, the freer we shall be. My dear compatriots, Citizens, Burghers, Natives, and Inhabitants, take good care of them; we must not be deceived either concerning our religion or our government." xxv, 418-419.

[72] *Idées républicaines*, xxiv, 415.

In outlining his egalitarian republic, Voltaire once again strikingly reveals his relativism. In Russia, Voltaire was supporting enlightened despotism with his admiring letters to Catherine; in France, he was supporting constitutional absolutism by taking the king's part in his protracted controversy with the parlements. And in Geneva, he was supporting liberal republicanism by supporting the bourgeoisie. "Let us insult neither monarchies nor republic," he wrote in *Idées républicaines* against Rousseau's dogmatism. "We must defy all those general rules which exist only under the pens of authors."[73] Indeed, in *Idées républicaines* Voltaire praised the republic as the "most tolerable" form of government, since it "approaches most closely the natural equality of men."[74] But monarchies, too, could realize the purposes for which governments are instituted among men. What was important to Voltaire was not the form of government but its substance. Did it oppose the pretensions of aristocrats and ecclesiastics? Did it practice toleration? Did it operate under the rule of law, or was it at least moving toward it? If so, it was a good government.

The Geneva of 1765 was far from being a bad government, but it was far from ideal, too. It was a small republic, well-regulated in many respects, but, Voltaire said in *Idées républicaines*, it was troubled by partisan passions. Still, there was a remedy for these passions: ". . . Reason, which will finally make itself heard, when the passions are weary of shouting. Then the two parties relax their pretensions a little in fear of worse. But time is needed."[75] Time, and men of good will: "It is perhaps useful to have two parties in a republic, because then one

---

[73] XXIV, 422, 419-420.

[74] XXIV, 424. As I have already suggested, Voltaire did not use the word "republic" as we would use it, but in the eighteenth-century sense (accepted by Kant as well as John Adams) of "constitutional regime." Thus to Voltaire England, Sweden, and Poland were "republics under a king." *Dictionnaire philosophique*, article "Patrie," 336. And in *Siècle de Louis XIV*, Voltaire refers to the English opponents of James II as "republican royalists." XIV, 296.

[75] XXIV, 419.

watches over the other, and men need supervisors. It is perhaps not as shameful as people think that a republic has need of mediators; that proves, too, that both parties possess much intelligence, much information, a great sagacity in interpreting the laws in different senses. . . ."[76]

In the late fall of 1765, the word "mediators" was a specific and, for the bourgeoisie, a none-too-pleasant allusion to the likelihood that the patriciate would once again call in outsiders. But it implied something else as well: mediation could after all be private, and Voltaire just happened to have a most suitable mediator in mind—himself.

Voltaire served his allies too well. The plan of pacification, like *Idées républicaines*, was a moderate and sensible document —it did not advance beyond the political program of Micheli Ducrest and Jean-Jacques Rousseau. Yet the *Représentants* flinched before it: when M. Hennin showed them Voltaire's plan on 19 December 1765, some objected to its conciliatory tone, more objected to its daring. Voltaire had ventured into enemy territory and had been fired upon by his own troops. One hint was enough; from now on the *Représentants* had to do without him.

But Voltaire did not withdraw from Genevan politics. On 6 January 1766, the Council of Twenty-Five formally asked France, Zurich, and Berne to mediate the Genevan dispute. In the general excitement, the Natives, hitherto so timid and unpolitical, gathered up enough courage to address statements of their grievances to the mediators. In vain French and Genevan authorities pleaded with Voltaire to keep out of this new embroilment. By the spring of 1766 Voltaire had assumed a new role, more radical than any he (or for that matter Rousseau) had ever taken. He had become the adviser and advocate of the Natives, nothing less than a democratic movement.

Eleven years before, Voltaire had sung Genevan equality:

76 XXIV, 426.

Les états sont égaux, et les hommes sont frères.

To the intense exasperation of his former associates, patricians and bourgeois alike, the Old Invalid of Ferney was taking his own rhetoric seriously.

3. NATIVES

Voltaire the democrat—it seems an unexpected and even faintly ludicrous idea. He was an aristocrat or, rather, a bourgeois with aristocratic friends, aristocratic correspondents, aristocratic tastes, aristocratic aspirations, who was (as his enemies said with some plausibility) as snobbish to his inferiors as he was servile to his superiors. Moreover, did he not often voice an unconquerable contempt for the *canaille*? How could he lend his support to an aggregation of men whom he must have despised as incurable barbarians?

And yet Voltaire's association with the Genevan Natives was too intimate to be mere playfulness, too enduring to be mere rancor against *Négatifs* and *Représentants*. There was something in the Natives as much as in the evolution of Voltaire's political ideas that made their alliance possible and even natural.

In the works of his early years Voltaire had expressed his disdain of *le peuple* with a laconic dogmatism that left no room for argument. In two of his tragedies, *Oedipe* and *La mort de César*, he described the "people" as unjust, vacillating in adversity, changing from hatred to love in a day;[77] in the *Henriade* he called it fanatic, inconstant, cruel, a "ferocious and blind monster";[78] in the *Siècle de Louis XIV*, condemning the Dutch mob that had murdered the De Witt brothers in August 1672, he concluded curtly: "The populace is the same nearly everywhere."[79]

He did not tire of these clichés even after he had moved to

[77] II, 83; III, 330. [78] VIII, 46, 67-68, 91, 121, 184n.
[79] XIV, 258.

Geneva. "It is not a question of preventing our lackeys from going to mass or to the sermon," he wrote to d'Alembert in December 1757, "it is a question of tearing fathers of families from the tyranny of impostors, and to inspire the spirit of toleration."[80] Again, he told d'Argental in 1765, "We will not tolerate the absurd insolence of those who say, 'I want you to think like your tailor and your laundress' ";[81] and d'Alembert in 1767, "As for the *canaille*, I don't concern myself with it; it will always remain *canaille*."[82] Late in 1762, Voltaire entered into correspondence with La Chalotais, *procureur général* of the parlement of Brittany and vigorous opponent of the Jesuits, over his plan for modernizing French education. Voltaire liked the plan, including its aristocratic reservations: "I thank you for proscribing study among day-laborers. I, who cultivate the earth, petition you to have laborers, not tonsured ecclesiastics."[83]

These are authentic Voltairian accents, the accents of the self-satisfied grand seigneur with a limited social imagination, the condescending gentleman-farmer with excessive pride in his practicality. But they are not the only accents. In the draft of a letter intended for the *Lettres philosophiques*, Voltaire characterized the English *peuple* as healthy, prosperous, and free; as we have seen, he found nothing absurd in the phrase, "the majesty of the English people."[84] He admired Dutch simplicity and dignity; he was pleased and astonished to see the rulers of the state walking in the streets like ordinary men, without serv-

---

[80] XXXIX, 319.

[81] 27 April (1765), XLIII, 545. Voltaire expressed similar opinions in *Essai sur les moeurs*, XI, 398; see also Voltaire to Damilaville, 19 March (1766), XLIV, 248; Voltaire to Frederick the Great, 5 January (1767), XLV, 10.

[82] 4 June (1767), XLV, 285. Incidentally, Voltaire used the term *canaille* as a general *Schimpfwort*, rather than as simply a derogatory term for the masses. He applied it to journalists, dramatists, ecclesiastics. See Voltaire to d'Argental, 1 September (1752), *Correspondence*, XXI, 51.

[83] 28 February (1763), XLII, 404.

[84] See "Projet d'une lettre sur les Anglais, à M. ***," *Lettres philosophiques*, II, 259; and above, chapter I.

ants, and he praised the Dutch for establishing a government based on equality.[85]

He did more. Retirement gave Voltaire his first good opportunity of observing ordinary men in action: Genevan craftsmen repaired his country homes, and Genevan farmers cultivated his soil. What is more, Genevan watchmakers read his books. And his observations led him to draw distinctions: *le peuple* was not simply a brutal, uneducated, uneducable mass. Since Protestantism and the city were far less pernicious than Catholicism and the country, a Protestant, urban *canaille* was far more civilized than a Catholic, rural *canaille*.[86] Voltaire was ready to idealize rural beauties, but not rural inhabitants; he came to see that the ordinary citizen in Geneva, London, or Amsterdam had a far greater opportunity of enlightening himself than a French or a Russian peasant.

Even more important than differences springing from religion or location were differences of class. In a dialogue inspired by the contest over the *vingtième*, Voltaire noted that "the populace always remains in the profound ignorance to which it is condemned by the need to gain its livelihood. . . . But the middle order is enlightened. This order is rather large; it governs the magnates, who think sometimes, and the little people, who do not think at all."[87] By "the little people who do not think at all" Voltaire meant "the populace who have only their arms to live." He doubted whether "that order of citizen will ever have the time and the capacity to instruct themselves; they will die of hunger before they become philosophers. . . ."[88] Indeed, he said flippantly to d'Alembert, "We have never pretended to enlighten shoemakers and servants; that is the job of the apostles."[89] More seriously, he told Linguet who had

[85] Voltaire to the marquis d'Argenson, 8 August (1743), *Correspondence*, XIII, 32-33.
[86] See *Essai sur les moeurs*, XI, 226.
[87] *Un philosophe et un contrôleur général des finances*, XXIII, 502.
[88] Voltaire to Damilaville, 1 April (1766), XLIV, 256.
[89] 2 September (1768), XLVI, 112.

written him that all is lost once the people knows that it has some intelligence: "In what you call people, let us distinguish the professions that demand a respectable education from those that only demand manual labor and daily toil. The latter class is the more numerous. All it will ever want to do for relaxation and pleasure will be to go to High Mass or to the tavern—there is singing there, and it too can sing. But the more skilled artisans who are forced by their very profession to think a great deal, to perfect their taste, to extend their knowledge, are beginning to read all over Europe. . . . The Parisians would be astonished if they saw in several Swiss towns, and above all in Geneva, almost all those who are employed in manufacture spending in reading all the time that they cannot devote to work. No, monsieur, all is not lost when one puts the people in a state to see that it has intelligence. On the contrary, all is lost when one treats it like a herd of cattle, for sooner or later it will gore you with its horns."[90]

Voltaire wrote this letter in March 1767, almost a year after he had become active in behalf of the Genevan Natives. It characterizes both the extent and the limits of Voltaire's liberalism with unusual clarity. Like other eighteenth-century liberals, Voltaire followed Locke in accepting some forms of equality and rejecting others.[91] The philosophes, hopeful (but not very hopeful) that all men could be enlightened, spoke of a far-off time when all men would be truly equal. But the abysmal poverty of the French proletariat, rural and urban; the apathy created by want, staggering taxes, bias of the courts; the absence of a tradition of education or taste for reading—all this made

[90] 17 March 1767, XLV, 163-164.

[91] "Though I have said . . . 'that all men by nature are equal,' I cannot be supposed to understand all sorts of equality. Age or virtue may give men a just precedency; excellency of parts and merit may place others above the common level; birth may subject some, and alliance or benefits others, to pay an observance to those whom nature, gratitude, or other respects may have made it due; and all this consists with the equality which all men are in, in respect of jurisdiction or dominion one over another. . . ." *Second Treatise of Civil Government*, paragraph 54.

the demands for universal education and equal suffrage appear like the dream of a Utopian. Even Rousseau acknowledged that equality did not mean equality in all things.[92]

Clearly, equality was a vague term which could mean much or little. It is noteworthy that for Voltaire, the older he grew the more precise and more inclusive it became. In his *Discours en vers sur l'homme* (1734-1737) he had advanced the threadbare notion that all men are equal because all suffer the same fate, and because the rich can be as bored, as miserable, as ill, as the poor:

> Avoir les mêmes droits à la félicité,
> C'est pour nous la parfaite et seule égalité.[93]

And in the first draft of the poem he fatuously advised men to accept the class into which they had been born, forgetting that one M. de Voltaire, born François-Marie Arouet, had chosen social mobility for himself:

> Quiconque en dirigeant la course de sa vie
> Ecoute prudemment la voix de son génie,
> N'entend point dans son coeur les cris du repentir:
> Enfermé dans sa sphère il n'en doit point sortir.[94]

But Geneva made him more sympathetic to the lower orders. He came to understand that the poor had no obligation to be content with their lot just because they were born and died in pain, like kings. The exploitations of imperialists, the burdens

[92] Despite this concession, which appears most prominently in the early *Discours sur l'inégalité*, Rousseau was of course far more radical on this point than the other philosophes. No man, he wrote, should be rich enough to buy another man, no man be poor enough to have to sell himself. "The social state is advantageous to men only when all have something and none too much." *Contrat social*, book I, chapter 9.

[93] IX, 380.

[94] Voltaire to Thieriot, 13 November 1738, *Correspondence*, VII, 448. He later changed the last line to read, "Enfermé dans sa sphère il n'en veut point sortir," which is not much better. Voltaire to Thieriot, 24 (November 1738), *ibid.*, VII, 460. This line appears in an early edition but not in the final version of the poem.

of unequal taxation, the waste of the idle rich were forms of inequality for which neither human nature nor social necessity gave any excuse. Inequality, wrote Voltaire in the *Dictionnaire philosophique*, is an evil, but it is a necessary evil: "On our unhappy globe it is impossible for men living in society not to be divided into two classes; one of the rich who command, the other of the poor who serve. . . . The human race, such as it is, could not subsist unless there were an infinitely large number of useful men who possess nothing at all. . . . Equality is thus at once most natural and at the same time most chimerical."[95]

This view is still ideological, but it is not threadbare. Voltaire makes the important concession that inequality is an economic rather than a metaphysical necessity; it is in no way part of a hierarchical universe, but results from want pitted against scarce resources. Writing before the industrial revolution, Voltaire did not see that an expansion of productivity might do away with the necessity for "useful men who possess nothing at all." But limited as his vision was, the writings of his later years suggest that the number of the poor and the uneducated could at least be reduced. Enlightenment was a gradual process, spreading from the solid burgher to the artisan, from the artisan to the apprentice. Education was therefore not merely a matter of capturing the "principal citizens" for philosophy; little by little the lower classes, too, must be included in philosophic propaganda.[96] "I am pretty old," wrote Voltaire in *L'homme aux quarante écus*, "I like to repeat my stories sometimes, to inculcate them better in the heads of the little fellows for whom I have been working such a long time."[97] Indeed, the vast number of popular political and anticlerical pamphlets he pro-

[95] *Dictionnaire philosophique*, article "Egalité," 176, 177. That the complacent clichés of his early years had not wholly left him becomes clear from a comparison of this article with the *Discours en vers sur l'homme*.
[96] See Voltaire to Helvétius, 2 July (1763), XLII, 514; Voltaire to Damilaville, 13 April (1766), XLIV, 265.
[97] XXI, 334. On the question of educating the masses, see below, chapter v, section 3.

duced in the last quarter-century of his life are in themselves a commitment to education, and hence to growing equality among men.

Clearly, Voltaire's opinion of the *petits garçons* underwent a distinct evolution. He never wholly gave up his distrust of the masses; his remarks, even of his last years, sometimes betray petulance and caprice. But to a surprising extent he overcame the tenacious social prejudices of his youth. By the time he began to devote himself to the Genevan Natives his social philosophy was more radical than most liberal bourgeois thought of his century.

There can be little question that this evolution was slowed down by the aristocratic presuppositions of his classicism. His neoclassical view of human nature, most prominently displayed in his tragedies, rejected the Christian view of man as sinful after the Fall. But it retained a dualism between reason and passion: reason orders, directs, and restrains the passions; the passions, although not evil by nature, are undisciplined and easily seduced into folly.[98] Voltaire applied this conception of human nature to social classes. Broadly speaking, he identified the masses with passion, the educated classes with reason. That is why he used terms about *le peuple* that are usually applied to the passions of individuals—fickle, ferocious, foolish. In guiding, shaping, refining the passions, education reduces fickleness, ferocity, and foolishness. However, as long as the masses are uneducated, rational persuasion can mean little to them. Voltaire knew that the educated could serve what he called the forces of darkness—were not his most implacable opponents

[98] See this striking passage in *Traité de métaphysique* (1734): "It is quite certain that some men are freer than others, for the same reason that we are not all equally enlightened, equally robust, etc. Freedom is the health of the soul; few people have this health fully and continuously. . . . We fortify it by accustoming ourselves to making reflections, and this exercise of the soul makes it a little more vigorous. But whatever effort we make, we can never reach the point of making our reason sovereign over all our desires." XXII, 218-219.

educated men?—but they could sometimes listen to reason. The masses could not.[99]

This was a neat scheme, but real life kept breaking into it: Voltaire's experience compelled him to admit that his fears were exaggerated. As artisans and apprentices proved to Voltaire that they too had rationality, his doctrinaire distrust receded. Perhaps the *canaille* was not doomed to remain *canaille* forever.

Voltaire did not reach this moderate position easily or early. He had to undergo a lengthy political education before he could accept the masses as educable and as potential participants in the political order. In this education, the artisans of Geneva had played a prominent part. When in March and April 1766 several articulate Natives came to consult him, Voltaire was ready for them.

In *Idées républicaines,* Voltaire had taken the position that the Natives could be "associated" with other citizens: "Should those who have neither land nor house in this society have a voice in it? They have no more right to that than a clerk paid by merchants has the right to regulate their commerce. But they can be associated by rendering services or by paying for their association."[100] Those words, written in the late fall of 1765, were still the words of a *Représentant* face to face with the unenfranchised majority of Genevans. By April 1766 Voltaire had gone beyond them. The Natives told him that they had serious grievances which they could not legally bring to the attention of the government, since regulations did not permit them to hold meetings or to submit petitions. They made

[99] In thus projecting a theory of human nature upon social classes, Voltaire may very well have been projecting his fears of his own emotions upon the outside world.

[100] xxiv, 425. Constance Rowe quotes the phrase about associated citizenship as an example of Voltaire's "unfailingly progressive outlook." *Voltaire and the State,* 108. Hardly. It is the outlook of a *Représentant* which Voltaire himself promptly overcame.

up three-fourths of the Genevan population, and as watchmakers they sustained Geneva's prosperity. Was it too much to ask for admission to the General Council, for free admission to citizenship for a limited number each year, for equal conditions of admission to the liberal professions? Voltaire thought not.

He addressed his visitors as if he were their attorney, asking them to supply him with legal and historical information that would buttress their case. Once in possession of his facts, he edited a *Compliment* and a *Requête aux médiateurs*, and guided the Natives through their negotiations with paternal solicitude. As political novices, the Natives were divided and indecisive. Some hoped to be granted their rights by indulgent patricians; others had similar hopes from the bourgeoisie; the most independent among them presented their case directly to the mediators and to the Genevan government. They pleaded their cause awkwardly, timidly, maladroitly; the mediators, busy with the dissensions between *Négatifs* and *Représentants*, were indifferent to these new petitioners; the Council of Twenty-Five spoke for respectable people, Genevans and mediators alike, when it rebuffed the Natives' proposals as "criminal and audacious."[101]

Voltaire was not disheartened—he continued his efforts for several years, although not without obstructions from the Natives themselves. Some of them did not trust him enough, others trusted him too much: one Barraud, wig maker, insisted that Voltaire read his comedies. This was too much. "Make wigs, monsieur Barraud," Voltaire told him. "Make wigs."[102] He found the Natives hard to command: they begged him for advice and disregarded it; they begged for his leadership and did not follow it. In these annoying circumstances, the aristocratic general showed more patience with his democratic troops than anyone might have expected.

But the Natives were only the least of Voltaire's troubles.

---

[101] Jane Ceitac, *Voltaire et l'affaire des Natifs*, 60.
[102] Chaponnière, *Voltaire chez les Calvinistes*, 232.

When he had sided with the *Représentants* against the *Néga-tifs*, his patrician friends had been disappointed. Now that he was siding with Geneva's political pariahs, patricians and bour-geois were at one in condemning his conduct as reprehensible. On 5 May 1766 the Council of Twenty-Five officially com-plained to the duc de Choiseul, and Choiseul tersely warned his friend: "Don't meddle in this quarrel in any way what-ever."[103] Charles Bonnet, lawyer and scientist, wrote to his famous friend, the scientist and philosopher Haller: "Candide, after having served the *Représentants* in his venomous writings, had tried to rouse up the simple Natives."[104] Even Hennin, who admired Voltaire, told him caustically, "What do you care by whom and how [Geneva] will be pacified, provided its beef is tender and its fish fresh? Once again, I beg you for the sake of your repose and for that of your friends, forget that there are a Council and *Représentants* in the neighborhood of Fer-ney."[105] De Beauteville, chief French mediator, thought he knew the cause of Voltaire's meddling: Candide was getting senile. "I don't want to excuse M. de Voltaire," he wrote to Choiseul, "but permit me, monsieur le duc, to point out to you that he is almost seventy-three years old. . . . His behavior, as ab-surd as it is ridiculous, is more deserving of pity than anger."[106]

To counteract this anger and this pity—it is hard to say which he found more offensive—Voltaire wrote brilliant and menda-cious letters. "The Natives say that I am taking the part of the bourgeois," he told d'Argental on 12 May 1766, "the bourgeois are afraid that I am taking the part of the Natives. The Natives and the bourgeois claim that I have had too much deference for the Council. The Council says that I have had too much friendship for the Natives and the bourgeois. The bourgeois, the Natives, and the Council don't know what they want, what

[103] *Correspondance avec les Tronchin*, 663n.
[104] Ceitac, *Voltaire et les Natifs*, 57.
[105] 5 May 1766, XLIV, 283.
[106] Chaponnière, *Voltaire chez les Calvinistes*, 234.

they are doing, what they are saying. . . . I have therefore declared to Councils, bourgeois, and Natives that since I am not churchwarden of their parish, it does not become me to meddle in their affairs and that I have enough affairs of my own."[107] D'Argental did not believe his friend, but that did not matter —he loved Voltaire even in his democratic folly. The anger of the Tronchins was more dangerous and harder to appease.[108]

As usual, Voltaire had his attacks of panic and then, afraid of being thought afraid, he defied his former friends by continuing to aid the Natives. He greatly enjoyed being called "the illustrious protector" by the disinherited whom even Jean-Jacques had ignored, and he relished the pleasure of exercising his generosity and of feeling his power.[109] His former allies, the *Représentants*, he told the Natives, were disguising the most self-centered class interest behind liberal constitutional talk: "They only want liberty for themselves."[110]

He was right. The bourgeois were far too busy wrangling with the patricians to apply their liberal rhetoric to the Natives. The patriciate, on the other hand, found it useful to pose as the protectors of these industrious artisans, and at their insistence the mediators included some minor concessions to the Natives in the plan of pacification which was presented to Geneva in November 1766.

If the Natives were displeased, the *Représentants* were appalled by the mediators' proposals. With unwonted spirit, the bourgeois rejected them in December 1766. Offended by this act of independence, the mediators withdrew, and France began

[107] XLIV, 288-289.
[108] See Voltaire's long letter to Théodore Tronchin, half apology, half defiance, 3 September 1766. *Correspondance avec les Tronchin*, 660-665.
[109] I owe this apt phrase to Chaponnière, *Voltaire chez les Calvinistes*, 235.
[110] Reported in his memoirs by Isaac Cornuaud, one of the Natives' leaders. Desnoiresterres, *Voltaire et Genève*, 58. It is amusing to note that Voltaire told the Natives in April 1766 that they were like flying fish who are eaten by birds of prey when they fly, and by big fish when they dive. A year before he had used the same image to describe men of letters. Ceitac, *Voltaire et les Natifs*, 58.

to apply economic and diplomatic pressure—forms of persuasion that failed to persuade the *Représentants*. Nor were they persuaded by a *Prononcé* of the mediators, published in November 1767, which simply restated the *plan de pacification*. They rejected the *Prononcé* in February 1768.

Tension rose in the city, but it was dissipated by a compromise in the following month, and on 11 March 1768 the General Council acclaimed an Edict of Conciliation by the impressive majority of 1,204 to 37. The *Représentants* had reason for acclamation: the magistrates promised to abstain from arbitrary police and judicial procedures, the General Council was authorized to elect some members of the Council of Two Hundred and to veto the re-election of four members of the Council of Twenty-Five. Thus the principle of popular election of magistrates, abandoned since the sixteenth century, was restored into constitutional practice.

This edict fulfilled a substantial part of the political program advanced by the *Représentants* since the 1730's; it accepted most of the proposals advanced in Voltaire's "little plan" in November 1765. But what would have satisfied Voltaire in 1765 no longer satisfied him in 1768. Now he was urging full civic equality for the Natives. On this score the Edict offered some concessions. The Natives obtained the right to practice the liberal professions, the right to become master artisans, the right to have twenty of their number purchase citizenship in 1768 and five every year after that. This limited success angered them; the alternatives that now remained were resignation or violence.

Resignation became harder and harder to sustain. An outpouring of pamphlets testifies to the Natives' unenviable position: a Native who had gone fishing—a pleasure legally reserved to Burghers and Citizens—was sent to jail; another Native was banished from Geneva for ten years because he refused to add the humiliating term "Native" to his signature; in July 1769 the Council of Twenty-Five abrogated most of the commercial privileges extended to the Natives the year before; three months later two bourgeois attacked a Native in his home and received light punishment for their assault.

The combination of bad faith of the governors and insults to the governed finally brought violence to Geneva. On 15 February 1770, after a Native had been condemned to six months' house arrest for singing satirical songs in a café, Natives demonstrated, paraded, and clashed in the streets with armed burghers and local gendarmes. By evening three Natives had been killed. "I don't like . . . to have people killed in the streets without knowing why . . ." wrote Voltaire to d'Argental on 19 February 1770. "Although I have written many tragedies, these tragic scenes at my door seem abominable to me."[111]

They were abominable, but the government was implacable. A week after the clashes, the Council of Twenty-Five exiled eight leaders of the alleged "Native plot" without the formality of a trial, violating once again the legal forms it had so often promised to respect. To the other Natives it promised forgiveness. Many Natives meekly submitted, but the more determined turned to Voltaire for help.

That "infamous man" who took "such pleasure in doing evil"—as he was characterized by an exasperated patrician[112]— had not forgotten his Natives. Early in 1767, he had proposed to the duc de Choiseul that France found a port in the county of Gex, near Ferney, which would divert commerce from Geneva. Like Goethe's aged Faust, Voltaire dreamed of constructing a new city for free men. Plans went forward slowly: Choiseul was interested in building Versoix, "Voltaire's city of tolerance," but it was hard to finance construction of houses and to obtain toleration for Protestants on French soil. When a number of

[111] XLVI, 565.
[112] J.-P. DuPan to Freudenreich, 22 February (1770), Ceitac, *Voltaire et les Natifs*, 170. Apparently some infuriated *Représentants* threatened during the troubles of 15 February to go out to Ferney and kill Voltaire. See Chaponnière, *Voltaire chez les Calvinistes*, 242.

Native families left Geneva in the troubles of February 1770, some found shelter in Versoix, others were housed at Ferney.

Voltaire, now seventy-five, threw himself into the new venture with the rancorous zest of a young man. What could be more gratifying than to revenge yourself on Geneva by serving humanity?[113] But as peace was restored, the Genevan government induced most of the Natives to return, and the plan for a port of Versoix collapsed in December 1770, when Choiseul, its warm adherent, was dismissed from the conduct of French affairs.

But some Natives refused to go back, and for them Voltaire constructed a substitute-Versoix at Ferney. He built houses and supported industries for them; watches, silk stockings, and other luxury goods streamed from the new industrial center. Adroitly, Voltaire converted his friends, including Catherine of Russia, into his customers. Ferney became a small, working instance of Voltaire's great principle—the union of free trade with free religion:

> Rien n'est plus selon mon humeur
> Que de voir ces bons hérétiques
> Boire et chanter de si grand coeur
> Avec nos pauvres catholiques.[114]

Shepherding a hundred families of emigrants, supervising their finances, building their houses, guiding their worship, superintending their industry, selling their products, petitioning the French government to relieve the county of Gex of burdensome feudal taxation, re-establishing good relations with patricians on whose good will depended the distribution of his writings in Geneva—all this took much of Voltaire's time. But the man of letters did not forget literature. Throughout the late 1760's and early 1770's, Voltaire wrote dramas, essays, pamphlets, and in many of them we can trace the impress of his

---

[113] "Thus Voltaire satisfied his imperious need for justice and his rancor: such conjunctures are rare." *ibid.*, 238.

[114] Voltaire to the duchesse de Choiseul, 27 August (1770), XLVII, 184.

Genevan embroilments. Not surprisingly, his political writings of these years are the most radical of his life.

The most clearly Genevan of these works is *La guerre civile de Genève*, a not very comical comic epic written in February or March 1767, filled with gratuitous insults to Rousseau, a piquant history of the Covelle case, and allusions to the dissensions in the city. It was the fruit of irritation, not reflection, for controversy with Rousseau always brought out Voltaire's worst, most petty side.

Less obvious and far more valuable is *L'homme aux quarante écus*, a collection of dialogues loosely held together by the man with forty *écus*, a peasant harassed by speculators, cheated by tax collectors, driven to destitution by physiocratic tax policies. It was immensely successful (the little book, published by Cramer early in 1768, went into ten printings in its first year) and apparently immensely dangerous, for on 24 September 1768, the parlement of Paris ordered it burned, and sentenced two booksellers to the pillory for three days and to the galleys afterwards.[115] *L'homme aux quarante écus* is a savage satire on physiocracy, and an equally savage attack on the exploitation of the poor by the rich. It has a happy ending: the ignorant peasant who is the hero of the tale becomes wealthy and makes a reputation as a peacemaker, mediating quarrels while presiding over good suppers. In the course of his literary career, Voltaire had adopted many guises; in *L'homme aux quarante écus* he appeared for the first time as a peasant.

Evidently his sympathy for the lower orders was growing. Late in 1766, in the midst of his agitation for the Natives, he wrote a tragedy, *Les Scythes*, in which he pointedly contrasted the simple republicanism of the Scythe people with the educated Persians:

> . . . ce titre de maître, aux Persans si sacré,
> Dans l'antique Scythie est un titre ignoré:

115 Rocquain, *L'esprit révolutionnaire*, 270.

234

"Nous sommes tous égaux sur ces rives si chères,
Sans rois et sans sujets, tous libres et tous frères."[116]

The allusions were obvious enough, but Voltaire made sure
that nobody missed them: he explained to his correspondents
that the Persians were the French, the Scythes the Genevans
—all free and all brothers.

Voltaire's radicalism is probably best expressed in *l'A,B,C*,
a long dialogue on subjects that can be discussed only in free
countries: ethics, theology, and politics. Voltaire himself
thought of it as a dangerous work and strenuously disavowed
it: he told madame du Deffand that it was "an English roast
beef, very difficult to digest for the many small stomachs at
Paris."[117] Like many exercises of this kind, it is an internal dialogue, defining the limits within which Voltaire's political ideas
fluctuated at this late period in his life. A is an Englishman,
moderate, libertarian, constitutionalist, firmly persuaded that
his government is the best in the world; B is not identified,
but the length of his speeches and his preoccupation with
Montesquieu suggest that he is Voltaire himself;[118] C is a
Dutchman who echoes most of A's opinions.[119]

[116] vi, 278. Voltaire wrote the tragedy in ten days, but that is not the
reason for its failure in Paris, since he rewrote it with care. His powers were
in general as great as always, but his late dramas are rather feeble.
  Writing a play in a few days was not unusual for him. There is a story
about one of his most mediocre efforts: he sent it to d'Alembert for criticism with the comment that he had written it in six days. "Then you
shouldn't have rested on the seventh," replied d'Alembert.

[117] 26 December (1768), XLVI, 207-208. It is an interesting and intelligent work, not surprisingly the favorite of those interpreters bent upon
demonstrating Voltaire's radical leanings, but it does not deserve Constance Rowe's ecstatic praise: ". . . a work in which he discussed with in-
comparable brilliance some of the most baffling questions of all time. . . ."
Voltaire and the State, 100.

[118] His praise of Montesquieu should do away with the persistent myth
that Voltaire wholly failed to appreciate him. *L'esprit des lois*, he writes in
l'A,B,C, "must always be precious to humanity." See xxvii, 325-326.

[119] The notion of "internal dialogue" has become a cliché, smoothing
over all disagreements in a dialogue as internal conflicts. But in *l'A,B,C*,
the range of ideas is relatively narrow, and at one time or another Voltaire
had held all of the ideas expressed.

L'A,B,C, is filled with reminiscences, but there is a new edge in the tone of some of the speeches. A lauds the English government for granting its citizens liberty and property under the rule of law, and evokes no disagreement when he says dramatically, "I warn you that I shall not suffer being bridled without being consulted, that I want to bridle myself and give my vote to know at least who will mount my back."[120] All three speakers oppose serfdom (in his recital of the countries where serfdom still exists, B conveniently omits Russia); all three object to "serfdom of the mind," and agree that full freedom of expression, including criticism of government and religion, is infinitely preferable to a system where "all possible care is taken to make a nation idiotic, pusillanimous, and barbarous";[121] all agree, too, that a good state practices toleration and purifies religion: "This great work was begun almost two hundred and fifty years ago; but men enlighten themselves only by degrees."[122]

These are familiar ideas. What is new is Voltaire's defense of democracy. There is a long diatribe by B, beginning with a characteristic Voltairian injunction: "Let's turn to the facts. I assure you that I could adjust quite easily to a democratic government. . . . All those who have possessions in the same territory have the same right to maintain order in that territory. I like to see free men make the laws under which they live, as they have made their habitations. It pleases me that my mason, my carpenter, my blacksmith, who have helped me to build my lodging, my neighbor the farmer, and my friend the manufacturer, all raise themselves above their trade, and know the public interest better than the most insolent Turkish official. In a democracy, no laborer, no artisan need fear either molestation or contempt. . . . To be free, to have only equals, is the true, the natural life of man; all other ways of life are unworthy artifices, bad comedies, in which one man plays the personage of master, the other that of slave, one that of parasite, and the

---

[120] XXVII, 342.   [121] XXVII, 359.
[122] XXVII, 367.

other that of procurer."[123] While to this outburst there is immediate objection, Voltaire makes these objections feeble expressions of mere class interest. When C argues: "As for myself, I like only aristocracy; the people are not fit to govern. I would not stand for my wig-maker being a legislator; I would rather never wear a wig," A sustains him: "You are a rich man, M. C, and I strongly approve of your way of thinking."[124]

B's diatribe, an energetic expression of Voltaire's democratic sympathies, is confirmed by his other writings of this period. In an article published in the *Dictionnaire philosophique* for the first time in 1767, Voltaire extolled democracy above "all other states, since there everybody is equal, and there every individual works for the happiness of all."[125] And a few years later Voltaire paid democracy another, rather restrained tribute: the crimes of democrats are largely preventive; the people wish only to defend their liberty.[126] The Natives were indeed teaching Voltaire a great deal about politics.

A few scattered observations, playful and carefully hedged, do not add up to a position. They reflect a mood, and the aged Voltaire's flexibility. Voltaire did not become a convinced democrat; he never appreciated or even understood Rousseau's conception of the *volonté générale*. But in his last years in Geneva he learned to respect the political capacities of ordinary people. Like Candide he learned from experience; unlike Candide he learned quickly and did not forget what he had learned. In 1777, the Crown Prince of Hesse visited Ferney. It was a day of celebration: the villagers were paying their master homage because he had just succeeded in freeing them from the salt tax. Moreover, it was Voltaire's feast day. As the smartly uni-

[123] xxvii, 347-348. This is typical Voltaire, including the condescension of "my" carpenter, "my" blacksmith, etc. While Voltaire restricts the universality of his statement with the qualification that only those who have property should vote, he weakens the qualification by including artisans among the active citizens.

[124] xxvii, 348-349.

[125] Article "Lois (des)," 288.

[126] *Questions sur l'Encyclopédie*, article "Démocratie," Part iv, 162.

formed young men of the village paraded past Voltaire, his visitor asked him: "Are these your soldiers?" Voltaire turned to the young prince, whose father was then selling subjects to the English army. "No," he said; "they are my friends."[127]

[127] Caussy, *Voltaire, seigneur de village*, 168.

V

FERNEY:

THE POISONOUS TREE

> Culte, nécessaire; vertu, indispensable; crainte de l'avenir, utile;
> dogme, impertinent; dispute sur le dogme, dangereuse; persécu-
> tion, abominable; martyr, fou.
>
> —VOLTAIRE, notebook entry

1. THE NATURE OF *L'INFÂME*

VOLTAIRE had many faithful friends, from Genevan Natives to
French noblemen, but he was such a witty and tenacious
controversialist that he is known less for his friends than for his
enemies. As he matured into the Old Invalid of Ferney, a new
enemy—or an old enemy with a new name—appeared in his
letters: *l'infâme*. Untiringly he urged the brethren to *écraser
l'infâme*; he was so intoxicated with the slogan that he repeated
it endlessly, sometimes spelling it out, sometimes abbreviating
it, sometimes using it as a signature: "Ecr. linf." One of the
censors who opened his letters was impressed with the style of
that Swiss gentleman, monsieur Ecrlinf: "That M. Ecrlinf
doesn't write badly."[1]

Authentic or invented, the anecdote symbolizes the confusion
over the meaning of *l'infâme*. After two centuries of debate
there remain four distinct interpretations: fanaticism, Catholicism, Christianity, and religion. The writers who restrict *l'infâme*

[1] The story is told, apparently on the basis of a contemporary anecdote,
by Beuchot. See xxxxv, 507-508n.

to fanaticism point out that Voltaire never openly left the faith into which he was born and that he occasionally practiced it, that other educated Catholics objected to fanatical and superstitious displays as violations rather than manifestations of true Roman Catholicism, that he treated his Jesuit teachers with respect and affection, and that his violent diatribes against Christianity may be dismissed as the hyperbole of propaganda.[2] Those who enlarge the term to mean Catholicism call attention to his membership in a masonic order which was Christian but anti-Catholic, his statements that Protestantism is greatly preferable to Catholicism, his friendships with Genevan pastors whose philosophical Protestantism resembled his own religious convictions, his obvious admiration for the freedom and toleration of Protestant countries, his contention that deism had grown naturally from the Protestant Reformation. Those who interpret *écrasez l'infâme* as an attack on supernatural religions in general and Christianity in particular cite the vehemence of Voltaire's assault on doctrines shared by Catholics and Protestants, his conviction that all forms of Christianity are the source of fatal infection, his disappointment in the Genevan clergy, and the famous line in his *Henriade*:

Je ne décide point entre Genève et Rome,

which they take as a rejection of both. Finally, those who expand *écrasez l'infâme*, into a war against all religion stress his Aesopianism, his need to mask his dangerous opinions, his skepticism which they think is ill-disguised behind a polite deism.

All these interpretations have some plausibility, but I regard the last as too extreme, and the first two as not extreme enough. Voltaire had genuine, deep religious convictions; he was an emotional, even a mystical deist. "A miracle, according to the origin of the word," he wrote without irony, "is an admirable thing. In that case everything is a miracle."[3] And as a young

[2] For instances of this and the other three interpretations, see the Bibliographical Essay.
[3] *Dictionnaire philosophique*, article "Miracles," 314.

man, he wrote in his notebook in somewhat uncertain English: "We are commonly unconcerned and careless of all things which deserve our search, and our admiration, but for to make amends we admire the most common objects, and the less whorthy of attention of a wise man. How very few are wise enough to admire the daily birth of ligth and the new creation of all things wich born every day with light; the everlasting regulation of stars, the perpetual miracle of generation, effects of loadstone, of lime burned with water. . . ."[4]

Voltaire's enthusiasm for the Divine Watchmaker, the creator of these miracles of nature, grew more intense with the years. Early one morning in 1774, he asked a Ferney visitor to join him in watching the sun rise. After a strenuous climb the men rested on a hill to survey the magnificent panorama. Voltaire took off his hat, prostrated himself and exclaimed, "I believe, I believe in you!" and again, "Powerful God, I believe!" Then he rose and told his guest drily: "As for monsieur the Son, and madame His Mother, that's a different story."[5]

The implacable enemy of enthusiasts himself an enthusiast— it is an arresting sight. Such demonstrations were rare, but the feelings that inspired them were vivid and lasting. A sense of awe, of man's littleness before the divine greatness, pervades the philosophical works of the 1730's composed under the impact of Newtonianism, the short tales of the 1740's and 1750's, and the polemics of his old age. In Voltaire's universe there must be a supreme being, despite evil, irrationality, and Lisbon earthquakes.

This poetic deism was not a Voltairian invention: it had been preached by French and English freethinkers since the late seventeenth century. When they thought of religion at all, the worldly and debauched associates of Voltaire's youth were deists, and even Christians like Fénelon and skeptics like Fon-

---

[4] *Notebooks*, 35.
[5] The anecdote was first reported by Lord Brougham, *Lives of Men of Letters* (1845), I, 141. It is reproduced in René Pomeau, *La religion de Voltaire*, 410-411, and in an English translation in Alfred Noyes, *Voltaire*, 554-555.

tenelle employed the deist watchmaker argument to prove the existence of God.

Their watchmaker was also Voltaire's, a God of order and love, infinitely removed from the little insects that crawl on this pile of slime, the earth. He was the God who consoled Stendhal's Julien Sorel in prison: "Not the God of the Bible, a petty despot, cruel and filled with a thirst for vengeance . . . but the God of Voltaire, just, good, infinite. . . ." Voltaire often spoke of this God as "commanding" men to love each other, but that was picturesque, anthropomorphic language designed for purposes of propaganda. The real God was beyond ordinary words.

And yet, the inexactitude of Voltaire's language also betrays a need of his own. Voltaire yearned for a mild rather than a severe father; his opposition to the stern theology of Jansenism and the strict Protestant sects was more than rational opposition, it was hatred. Voltaire's God was like Voltaire's ideal king, kind rather than cruel. In his political as in his religious thought we can sense his longing for the loving rather than the repressive authority.

But whatever the reasons for Voltaire's metaphorical language, its significance for morals is unmistakable: the existence of God imposes upon all men an obligation to recognize their littleness, their impermanence, their brotherhood. This recognition, in turn, imposes the obligation of mutual toleration and mutual love. For Voltaire, toleration is thus as much a religious duty as a political goal; it is an affirmation of what is most human in human nature: "It is clear that every individual who persecutes a man, his brother, because he does not share his opinion, is a monster. . . . We must tolerate each other, for we are all feeble, inconsistent, subject to change and error."[6] This tolerance is the fruit of man's rational insight into his condition, the most sublime teaching of natural religion.

[6] *Dictionnaire philosophique*, article "Tolérance," 403, 407. See also the *Poème sur la loi naturelle* and many other places.

A God who imposes such obligations on mankind and only such obligations is not a metaphysical construct emptied of all content. He is real enough, but he is not a Christian God. Precisely when Voltaire gave up that Christian God, precisely when his anticlericalism became anti-Christianity is impossible to determine: there is no sharp line between these two positions. In the elegant world in which Voltaire moved as a young poet, anticlericalism was fashionable. After the death of Louis XIV, high society celebrated its new freedom with adolescent abandon, and its favorite victims were Christians and Christianity. Aristocrats circulated scandalous irreligious poems and tracts in manuscript. They were afraid to publish them, but equally afraid to be thought pious; piety was for peasants and the bourgeoisie. By 1720, wrote the Cardinal de Bernis in his *Mémoires*, "it was no longer considered well-bred to believe in the gospels."[7]

Voltaire was nothing if not well-bred; his anticlerical sallies of the Regency were acts of conformity rather than of defiance. Still, for many years he disguised his real views—a duc de Richelieu could profess deism more safely than a François-Marie Arouet—and modestly claimed to criticize only those political and emotional excrescences that any rational Catholic had to view with abhorrence.[8] It was not until he was securely established at Ferney that the fashionable anticlerical worldling openly became the implacable anti-Christian crusader.

Privately, Voltaire had ceased to be a Christian many years before. French freethinkers had been the first to plant doubt in his mind. His godfather, the abbé de Châteauneuf, taught him the *Moïsade*, a rationalist poem so daring that it could not even be printed clandestinely; the Jesuits (religious men, no matter what their reputation) further prepared him for apostasy by training him in the pagan classics; the society of

---

[7] *Mémoires et lettres*, 2 vols. (1878), I, 41, quoted in Pomeau, *La religion de Voltaire*, 90.

[8] Mario Roustan writes that in the eighteenth century, the French bourgeois was "religious and anticlerical."

the Temple professed a natural religion. The notorious *Epitre à Uranie*, probably written late in September 1722, shows how far Voltaire had departed from the faith of his fathers. In this poem he declares war on the "sacred lies that fill the world," and defies a hateful God who created men to be miserable. The true God is the very antithesis of the God that the Christians worship:

> On te fait un tyran, en toi je cherche un Père.
> Je ne suis pas Chrétien, mais c'est pour t'aimer mieux.[9]

Before he was thirty, then, he could confess that he was not a Christian that he might love God better. His visit to England and his years at Cirey provided him with new ammunition against Christianity: he read the critical deists Tindal and Woolston, and with madame du Châtelet he studied the Bible verse by verse and steeped himself in Biblical exegesis. At Potsdam he worked out the tactics for the inevitable conflict: he drafted the first articles of the *Dictionnaire philosophique* and discussed them with the King of Prussia. But only after he was old, rich, famous, and safe was he ready to *écraser l'infâme*. He conducted petty skirmishes against the clergy of the neighborhood, major battles against Catholic fanaticism in the cases of Calas and de La Barre, and an unceasing war against Christianity in general in a torrent of anti-Christian pamphlets.[10]

His declaration of war was the *Sermon des cinquante*, published in 1762 but written ten years before at Potsdam. It is a scandalous work—it reads as if it had been written to *épater le roi*, to surpass in vehemence the royal cynic of Prussia. It is

---

[9] IX, 364.

[10] René Pomeau develops an interesting schedule for *écrasez l'infâme*: the first stage lasted from May 1759 to May 1761, consisting of guerrilla warfare against neighboring priests; the second stage lasted from September 1761 to January 1764, and concerned the Calas case; the third stage, January 1764 to March 1767 were the years of "heavy artillery," including the *Dictionnaire philosophique*; the fourth stage lasted from March 1767 to the beginning of 1772—these were the years of "great hopes" when the philosophes on European thrones went into action against *l'infâme*; the last stage, from 1772 to 1778, a phase of disillusionment.

also a revealing work—in a few pages it sums up Voltaire's campaign against *l'infâme*: the Bible is the most improbable and contradictory of books; the Pentateuch, ostensibly the work of Moses, reports Moses' death; the miracles reported in it are oriental folk tales; transubstantiation is nonsense. But the Bible is reliable in one respect: it accurately records the moral ideals and practices of the Jews, and those ideals and practices are both horrible. The God of the Jews is vain and selfish, his chosen people is cruel, mendacious, and debauched. Away with such a God, away with such "infamous mysteries!" The true God is not the God of the Christians, he is the loving father of all men. "May this great God who is listening to me, this God who can surely neither be born of a virgin, nor die on the gallows, nor be eaten in a piece of dough, nor have inspired these books filled with contradictions, madness, and horror—may this God, creator of all the worlds, have pity on this sect of Christians who blaspheme him!"[11] No wonder Voltaire attributed this pamphlet to La Mettrie! No wonder he was appalled when Rousseau pointed the finger at him, the innocent invalid of Ferney!

This was the message of *écrasez l'infâme*; it never changed. But since it challenged convictions that men held most tenaciously, Voltaire reiterated his message innumerable times. He understood, better than most writers, that men cannot be persuaded when they are bored, so he reiterated it with different jokes, different dialogues, different demonstrations. The lesson, however, never varied: "Every sensible man, every honorable man, must hold the Christian sect in horror."[12]

To help men hold the Christian sect in horror, he adopted many stratagems. After the *Sermon des cinquante*, which presumably had been written by a materialist, he published the powerful *Extrait des sentiments de Jean Meslier* (1762), which summarized the last will of a parish priest who had died in 1729 and had repented of his Christian vocation on his death-

[11] XXIV, 453-454.
[12] *Examen important de Milord Bolingbroke*, XXVI, 298.

bed. After the *Extrait,* he appeared as a good Catholic in *Traité sur la tolérance* (1763), movingly and moderately pleading for Christian toleration. After the *Traité,* he brought out the *Dictionnaire philosophique* (1764), ostensibly written by many hands. He never tired: in 1767 there appeared the *Examen important de Milord Bolingbroke,* which used Voltaire's work on the Bible of the Cirey years in denouncing Jesus as a Jewish fanatic. A few years later came the *Questions sur l'Encyclopédie* (1770-1772), a larger and even more virulent Philosophic Dictionary. And finally, in Voltaire's eighty-second year, he published *La Bible enfin expliquée* (1776), a long and tendentious exegesis, summarizing decades of research and spleen, and rounding out, with its nice title, the fight against *l'infâme.*

In his eulogy, Frederick the Great said that Voltaire was worth a whole academy. But in his fight against *l'infâme,* Voltaire's versatility appeared in his wit rather than his arguments, which never departed far from the *Sermon des cinquante,* his opening salvo: the theology of the Bible is a nonsensical, indeed a diabolical, invention; the morality preached by the Bible is abhorrent.

Modern Biblical criticism makes Voltaire's arguments appear quaint and largely of historical interest. But the wit remains as fresh and as impudent as ever. Consider *Relation du bannissement des Jésuites de la Chine,* in which a Jesuit tries to explain the Christian mysteries to the Emperor of China:

"Frère Rigolet: 'Our God was born in a stable, seventeen hundred and twenty-three years ago, between an ox and an ass. . . . [his mother] was not a woman, she was a girl. It is true that she was married, and that she had two other children, named James as the old gospels say, but she was a virgin none the less.'

The Emperor: 'What! She was a virgin, and she had children!'

Frère Rigolet: 'To be sure. That is the nub of the story: it was God who gave this girl a child.'

The Emperor: 'I don't understand you. You have just told me that she was the mother of God. So God slept with his mother in order to be born of her?'

Frère Rigolet: 'You've got it, Your Sacred Majesty; grace was already in operation. You've got it, I say; God changed himself into a pigeon to give a child to a carpenter's wife, and that child was God himself.'

The Emperor: 'But then we have two Gods to take into account: a carpenter and a pigeon.'

Frère Rigolet: 'Without doubt, Sire; but there is also a third, who is the father of these two, and whom we always paint with a majestic beard: it was this God who ordered the pigeon to give a child to the carpenter's wife, from whom the God-carpenter was born; but at bottom these three make only one. The father had engendered the son before he was in the world, the son was then engendered by the pigeon, and the pigeon proceeds from the father and the son. Now you see that the pigeon who proceeds, the carpenter who is born of the pigeon, and the father who has engendered the son of the pigeon, can only be a single God; and that a man who doesn't believe this story should be burned in this world and in the other.'

The Emperor: 'That is as clear as day.' "[13]

That was the blasphemous and playful Voltaire. When he came to the morality of God's Chosen People, his playfulness acquired a different edge: "If the style of the Books of the Kings and of Chronicles is divine, it may yet be that the actions reported in these histories are not divine. David assassinates Uriah; Ishbosheth and Mephibosheth are assassinated; Absalom assassinates Amnon; Joab assassinates Absalom; Solomon assassinates Adonijah, his brother; Baasha assassinates Nadab; Zimri assassinates Elah; Omri assassinates Zimri; Ahab assassinates Naboth; Jehu assassinates Ahab and Joram; the inhabitants of Jerusalem assassinate Amaziah, son of Joash; Shallum, son of

[13] XXVII, 4-7. The reader who still thinks of Voltaire as a Christian should read his blasphemies, brutal in their directness, about the Mass, *ibid.*, 10-11.

Jabesh, assassinates Zachariah, son of Jeroboam; Menahem assassinates Shallum, son of Jabesh; Pekah, son of Remaliah, assassinates Pekahiah, son of Menahem; Hoshea, son of Elah, assassinates Pekah, son of Remaliah. One passes over in silence many other minor assassinations. I must admit that if the Holy Ghost wrote this history, he did not choose a very edifying subject."[14]

These two quotations from Voltaire's most active and most optimistic period, the mid-1760's, indicate the strength and the limitations of *écrasez l'infâme*. It was a brilliant and a witty campaign; it was erudite, drawing on a close reading of the Bible and Christian exegesis; it used all of Voltaire's formidable stylistic resources. But it was also cruel and unfair. For all the truth embodied in the slogan, it was a propagandist's half-truth, silent on the civilizing labors of the Christian tradition, silent on the benign behavior of ecclesiastics through the ages, silent on the advancement of learning under the auspices of Christian schools and universities. But that did not matter to Voltaire. *Ecrasez l'infâme* was a good battle cry, and a good cry, says the Statue in Shaw's *Man and Superman*, is half the battle.

Voltaire knew that it was a good cry, and in the 1760's he uttered it again and again in his correspondence with the most reliable of the philosophes: "I finish all my letters by saying *Ecr. l'inf . . .*" he wrote to Damilaville on 26 July 1762, "as Cato always said, 'It is my opinion that Carthage must be destroyed.'"[15] There were times, especially in his last years, when he had doubts that Carthage could in fact be destroyed. As he wrote despairingly on 12 May 1776, "that which is founded on a great deal of money and a great deal of preferment is founded on a rock."[16] But whether he was optimistic or pessimistic, he

[14] *Dictionnaire philosophique*, article "Histoire des rois juifs et paralipomènes," 234.

[15] XLII, 186.

[16] Voltaire to Moultou, L, 15. See Voltaire to Frederick, 29 July (1775): "We would have to overthrow the whole world to put it under the government of philosophy. Hence, the only resource that remains to the sage is to prevent the fanatics from becoming too dangerous." IL, 337-338.

knew, and his friends knew, what he meant when he urged them to help him *écraser l'infâme*: extirpate Christianity.

2. THE ANATOMY OF FANATICISM

But why extirpate Christianity? Why this brutal ridicule of what was most holy to most Europeans? Much of Voltaire's vehemence was an expression of rage—rage against a religion that preached a cruel God and against its lieutenants, "priests, whom I have hated, hate, and I shall hate till doomsday,"[17] executioners in the service of their divine tyrant. Rational debate, Voltaire intimated, was impossible with the Christian: "What shall we put in its place, you ask. What! a ferocious animal has sucked the blood of my kindred; I tell you to get rid of that beast, and you ask me what shall we put in its place!"[18] His rage against fanaticism was fanatic in its intensity: on 24 August of every year, the anniversary of Saint Bartholomew's Day, he ran a fever.[19]

That fever and these words are not the language of detached analysis; they speak of frustration, of fury against harsh authority. Voltaire's intense concern with that authority can be gauged by his preoccupation with Pascal. All his life he tried to discredit the "sublime misanthrope," to teach mankind that Pascal's teachings about the terrible God and hateful humanity were wrong. But he would not have pursued this feverish debate with Pascal if he had not harbored the fear that Pascal might, after all, be right. "Pascal," J.-R. Carré tells us, "is in Voltaire";[20] he represented a part of Voltaire that Voltaire sought to escape and to repudiate. To win a victory over Pascal's the-

[17] Voltaire to Fawkener, 28 November 1752, in English. *Correspondence*, XXI, 155.

[18] *Examen important de Milord Bolingbroke*, XXVI, 299.

[19] Voltaire's oft-repeated statement that he suffered greatly on that day has of course been ascribed to his love for exaggeration. But we have independent evidence that on this point he spoke the literal truth. See Pomeau, *La religion de Voltaire*, 108-110.

[20] *Réflexions sur l'anti-Pascal de Voltaire*, 119.

ology was, for Voltaire, to win a victory over his own anxieties and depressions.

But this explains only part of Voltaire's vehemence against *l'infâme*. Voltaire belonged to an intellectual and polemical movement that thought it necessary to deride Christianity in the harshest terms. As a constructive deist, Voltaire preached a natural religion "as old as creation," uniform in all ages and for all men, in language that was rational, moderate, and sometimes lyrical. As a critical deist, adapting the audacious blasphemies of English deists to French conditions, Voltaire treated Christianity as the enemy of true religion.

For Voltaire, Christianity was dangerous because it was the source of a malignant disorder. Even at its most reasonable, Christianity inculcates superstitions, and superstitions are the germs that cause the religious disease. In its mild form, this disease is enthusiasm; in its virulent form, it is fanaticism, "the rage of the soul," which almost inevitably leads to murder.[21] Voltaire warned that while some superstitions appeared merely picturesque and hence harmless, all were sources of infection. He conceded that the naturalistic pagan cults of antiquity had preached sound morality and rarely indulged in persecution; he conceded, too, that Protestantism had claimed far fewer victims than Catholicism. But even a little superstition is a dangerous thing, and Voltaire's definition of superstition included all existing organized religions: "Almost everything that goes beyond the adoration of a supreme being and of submitting one's heart to his eternal orders is superstition."[22] Crosses, relics, rosaries vulgarize true religion and substitute superstitious sickness for religious health: "The emblems of the divinity were one of the first sources of superstition. Once we made God in our image, the divine cult was perverted."[23]

[21] *Dictionnaire philosophique*, article "Fanatisme," 196; *Questions sur l'Encyclopédie*, article "Enthousiasme," Part v, 150.

[22] *Dictionnaire philosophique*, article "Superstition," 394.

[23] *Homélies prononcées à Londres en 1765*, "Deuxième homélie sur la superstition," xxvi, 330. See: "The sect that seems least attacked by this

The most striking symptom of the religious malady is a sense of certainty, doctrinaire yet uneasy. Voltaire did not make the mistake of dismissing fanatics as hypocrites: their danger lay precisely in their sincerity. The fanatic is sure that he knows what in fact he does not know, cannot know, and does not need to know. But his certainty—and this is what makes it so vicious —masks a disturbing sense of uncertainty. The more men are torn with doubts, the more assertive they become; the more ignorant men are, the more reluctant they are to confess their ignorance: "If you were fully persuaded you would not be intolerant. You are intolerant only because deep in your heart you feel that you are being deceived."[24] Anticipating Nietzsche by over a century, Voltaire saw that cruelty is a symptom of weakness rather than strength: "Only the weak commit crimes. The strong and happy man has no need to be evil."[25] The fanatic hides sickness behind assumed toughness; he seethes with resentment.[26]

Since superstition is the direct cause of fanaticism, the only way to blunt the force of the latter is to reduce the influence of the former: "The fewer superstitions, the less fanaticism; and the less fanaticism, the fewer calamities."[27] Voltaire had little expectation that the endemic disease of superstition could be eradicated, but he hoped that it could be gradually brought under control. Superstition is the antiphilosophic disease, and "the philosophic spirit, which is nothing but reason, has become the only antidote against these epidemics."[28] He emphasized that it was the *only* antidote: religion does not soothe the fanatic,

---

spiritual malady is the one that has the fewest rites. But if with this little ceremonial it is strongly attached to an absurd belief, that absurd belief is alone equivalent to all the superstitious practices observed since Simon the magician. . . ." *Dictionnaire philosophique,* article "Superstition," 397.

[24] *Notebooks,* 452.   [25] *ibid.,* 87.

[26] Voltaire makes the shrewd psychological point that men become fanatics out of "wounded pride." *Dictionnaire philosophique,* article "Persécution," 341.

[27] *ibid.,* article "Superstition," 398.

[28] *Questions sur l'Encyclopédie,* article "Confession," Part IV, 42.

since in his diseased condition he transforms its pacific teachings into fuel for further cruelties; the laws are equally helpless, since the fanatic's insane fantasies are his only law. Hence, the statesman who is dedicated to rooting out fanaticism must first root out superstition, and the only way to do this is to spread the message of the philosophes, a message that is not another dogma but the negation of all dogma. In a phrase, *écrasez l'infâme*.

When Voltaire shifts from psychological analysis to political polemics his tone also shifts, and his diagnosis turns into an indictment. History, he tells his readers, is one long demonstration of the crimes caused by superstition. It was Christian fanaticism that guided the hand of Damiens, the would-be assassin of Louis XV, of Ravaillac, the assassin of Henri IV, and of countless other regicides.[29] It was Christian fanaticism that directly inspired the horrors of Saint Bartholomew's Day, the murder of Servetus by Calvin, the judicial assassination of untold thousands of innocents labeled heretics, witches, and blasphemers. The humane teachings of Jesus have been redefined, perverted, ignored by the infamous church that claims to speak in his name. The pacific truths of the New Testament have been buried under a mountain of subtle distinctions, absurd tales of miracles, indecent grasping for wealth, power, and comfort, and murder upon murder committed for the sake of the victim's soul: "When the Mohammedans kill a sheep, they say, 'I kill you in the name of God.' True motto of religious wars."[30] In a savage article on "Massacres," Voltaire drew up a balance sheet purporting to show the total number of victims of Christianity. His estimate—a conservative estimate, he said—was 9,718,800.[31]

[29] On Damiens, *Précis du siècle de Louis XV*, xv, 393; on Ravaillac, *Essai sur les moeurs*, xii, 560-561; on Clément, assassin of Henri III, *Henriade*, viii, 138n.

[30] *Notebooks*, 258.

[31] *Questions sur l'Encyclopédie*, Part viii, 47-54. In *Dieu et les hommes*, he counted only 9,468,800. xxviii, 232-236.

It was ironic, Voltaire suggested, that these victims had lost their lives over theological conundrums which neither they nor their butchers understood. Take the Trinity: "Here is an incomprehensible question which for over sixteen hundred years has exercised curiosity, sophistical subtlety, bitterness, the spirit of cabal, the rage to dominate, the rage to persecute, blind and bloodthirsty fanaticism, barbaric credulity, and which has produced more horrors than the ambition of princes, which indeed has produced enough. Is Jesus Word? If he is Word, did he emanate from God, is he coeternal and consubstantial with him, or is he of a similar substance? Is he distinct from him, or not? Is he created or engendered? Can he engender in turn? Has he paternity, or productive virtue without paternity? Is the holy ghost created or engendered, or produced? Does he proceed from the father, or from the son, or from both? Can he engender, can he produce? Is his hypostasis consubstantial with the hypostasis of the Father and the son? and why, having precisely the same nature, the same essence as the father and the son, can he not do the same things as these two persons who are himself? I certainly do not understand any of this; nobody has ever understood any of this, and this is the reason for which people have slaughtered one another."[32]

For all its psychological and historical penetration, this indictment is better propaganda than psychology or history. In eighteenth-century Europe, *l'infâme* was far from infamous, and, as Voltaire himself acknowledged, its history did not lack grandeur.[33] He knew, even if he was not willing to concede, that enthusiasm had fostered charitable as well as cruel actions, that supernatural theology had fostered scholarship as well as war. But while Voltaire could introduce some objectivity in his his-

---

[32] *Dictionnaire philosophique*, article "Arius," 33-34.

[33] "It is true that there are no more general persecutions in our day, but we sometimes see cruel atrocities." *Des conspirations contre les peuples ou des proscriptions*, xxvi, 15. He knew, too, that "religion has spilled less blood than politics," but, he added, "the crimes of religion are more remarkable since it was made to curb them." *Notebooks*, 380.

tories, he was not objective in his polemics. Evidently he believed that propaganda cannot be effective without oversimplification, without distortion.

There has been much debate over whether Voltaire's attack on *l'infâme* was "good" or "bad," a debate that is unsolvable and irrelevant. The attack was inevitable. The struggle between the philosophes and the orthodox was not a simple struggle between light and darkness, as the liberals tell us, or between impiety and true religion, as the conservatives tell us. The philosophes had no monopoly on wisdom or impudence; the orthodox had no monopoly on charity or ignorance. The two parties represented two world views. Educated clergymen could make concessions to new ideas; they could express urbane reservations about the foundations of their faith; they could support scientific inquiry. But the philosophes were in no mood, and indeed in no position, to compromise with Christianity. They could infiltrate the bureaucracy, the administration, the parlements, the aristocracy, the bourgeoisie, and even the clergy itself, but by definition Christians could not be expected to espouse the secular ideals of naturalistic morality. Jesuits could attenuate the Christian view of man's fall from grace, they could substitute attrition for contrition, but they could never admit that man was without sin. "The church could forgive much," writes R. R. Palmer, "it could absolve from sin and countenance much latitude in thinking; but it could not forgive those who denied its ability to remove sin, or its right to propound the dogmas by which thinking should be governed. It could not tolerate those who questioned its authority."[34] And to question its authority was precisely what the philosophes did and had to do; accommodation was impossible and war was inevitable.

[34] *Catholics and Unbelievers in Eighteenth-Century France*, 4-5. One intelligent defender of the faith, J. G. Lefranc de Pompignan, observed that the philosophes "would have written less, and their writings would have spread less widely, if Incredulity had not had so many partisans ready to applaud it." Quoted in Pomeau, *La religion de Voltaire*, 338.

Voltaire, after all, was not the only soldier in the army of modernity. He was merely the wittiest. His diagnosis of enthusiasm as a mental disease was familiar to most educated men in eighteenth-century Europe. "Above all, monsieur," wrote Lord Chesterfield to him after reading the *Siècle de Louis XIV* four times, "I am grateful to you for the light in which you place the lunacy and frenzy of the sects! You employ the proper weapons against these madmen or impostors; to employ others against them would be to imitate them: it is with ridicule that they must be attacked, it is with contempt that they must be punished."[35]

Ridicule and contempt were not new weapons in the eighteenth century. A hundred years before Voltaire, Robert Burton advanced a remarkably modern diagnosis of religious emotionalism. In his *Anatomy of Melancholy*, first published in 1621, he both mocks and pities Puritan enthusiasm: the emotional displays of the sectaries are symptoms of a desire for notoriety or of "lamentable and tragical" illness. Politicians and priests ruthlessly exploit this "religious melancholy" by playing upon fear, pride, stupidity, jealousy, frustration, despair, and guilt: "What else can superstition, heresy produce, but wars, tumults, uproars, torture of souls, and despair . . . ?" The cure is partly medical, partly philosophical: "To purge the world of idolatry and superstition will require some monster-taming Hercules, a divine Aesculapius. . . ." And to purge individuals of melancholy will require self-control and creative activity: "Be not solitary, be not idle."[36] The resemblance of Burton's teachings to Voltaire's is startling: did not Voltaire dream of being a Hercules-Aesculapius? Did he not flee despair through society and good works?

[35] 27 August 1752, *Correspondence*, xxi, 62.
[36] Robert Burton, *The Anatomy of Melancholy*, 3 vols. (ed. 1889), iii, 425, 429, 501. Burton thought of himself as a pioneer in the discovery of "religious melancholy" as a "distinct species." He had, he wrote, "no pattern to follow as in some of the rest, no man to imitate." *ibid.*, iii, 348.

Burton's sane humanism was echoed by other English writers. Sir Thomas Browne, in the midst of the civil war, pilloried religious excesses in his *Pseudodoxia Epidemica*; in 1655, while the Puritans were at the height of their power, Meric Casaubon published a searching *Treatise Concerning Enthusiasm* which suggested that religious excitement was "an effect of nature . . . mistaken by many for either Divine Inspiration, or Diabolicall Possession." The Cambridge Platonists, in search of a piety that rational men could accept, carefully distinguished true religion from enthusiasm. "I oppose not rational to spiritual," wrote Benjamin Whichcote, "for spiritual is most rational: But I contradistinguish rational to conceited, impotent, affected CANTING."[37]

The decline of the Puritans after the Restoration made this condescending diagnosis more popular. In *Hudibras*, which Voltaire read, Samuel Butler crudely satirized Puritan worship; Dryden derided the "true old enthusiastic breed" in *Absalom and Achitophel*; Sir William Temple, Swift's friend and protector, lamented that Casaubon had died before he could finish his investigations into "the hidden or mistaken sources of that delusion," enthusiasm;[38] Swift himself traced the hidden or mistaken sources of that delusion to physical and psychological disorders, especially sexual frustration.[39] These literary and scientific studies of the religious disease were easily absorbed into the urbane theology of eighteenth-century Anglicanism, and into the empiricist epistemology of the philosophers. Bishop Hoadly ridiculed religious fervor; John Locke devoted a chapter to it in his *Essay Concerning Human Understanding*. Enthusi-

[37] "Eight Letters of Dr Anthony Tuckney and Dr Benjamin Whichcote," quoted in Ernst Cassirer, *The Platonic Renaissance in England*, 38. Another Cambridge Platonist, Henry More, wrote a whole book on the subject, *Enthusiasmus triumphatus*.

[38] Sir William Temple, *On Poetry, Works*, 2 vols. (1750), I, 234, quoted in John Middleton Murry, *Jonathan Swift* (1955), 80.

[39] See especially *Tale of a Tub* and, among the works appended to it, "The Mechanical Operation of the Spirit."

asm, he wrote, "takes away both Reason and Revelation, and substitutes in the room of it the ungrounded Fancies of a Man's own Brain. . . ."[40]

Sophisticated students of ungrounded fancies, from Burton to Locke, had all England as their laboratory, the sectaries as their most rewarding specimens. French scholars had to be content with somewhat rarer outbreaks of religious hysteria: in the early seventeenth century, the celebrated case of the curé of Loudun, Urbain Grandier, who was burned in 1634 for introducing diabolical possession among a convent of Ursuline nuns; in the late seventeenth century, the Quietist movement led by Madame Guyon; in the early eighteenth century, the Jansenist convulsionaries at the cemetery of Saint-Médard. With increasing boldness, skeptics like François de La Mothe le Vayer and epicureans like Pierre Gassendi questioned miracles, and physicians like Gabriel Naudé ridiculed widely accepted tales of possession: Naudé called the nuns of Loudun victims of "Hysteromanie or rather Erotomanie."[41] Half a century later, freethinkers like Fontenelle and Bayle treated religious frenzy as a species of madness, and dramatists like Molière savagely satirized the *dévots* not so much for their hypocrisy as for their genuine ardor. Chaulieu, Voltaire's mentor in the Temple, attributed belief in the God of Christianity to fears inculcated in childhood,[42] while Formont, Voltaire's urbane friend, warned that the convulsionaries must be treated as sincere.[43]

Hence, in treating most expressions of religious conviction as examples of psychopathology, Voltaire was not an innovator;

[40] Book IV, chapter 19, paragraph 3.
[41] René Pintard, *Le libertinage érudit dans la première moitié du* XVIIe *siècle*, I, 222.
[42] *Ode à M. le marquis de la Fare sur la mort, Oeuvres de l'abbé de Chaulieu*, 2 vols. (1757), II, 154.
[43] Pomeau, *La religion de Voltaire*, 152n. Pomeau records (*ibid.*) the statement of a contemporary journal, *Le glaneur*, 20 August 1731: "For the Parisians a girl tormented by erotic furors is a girl possessed, or a saint having a revelation."

he was working in a well-developed and widely accepted tradition.[44] Indeed, he stands in the middle of the tradition rather than at its beginning. Many of his predecessors, like Locke and Swift, had written against enthusiasm because they sought to purify Christianity of the flaws of excess; Voltaire wrote against enthusiasm because he sought to purify religion of Christianity. He told Boswell that he was a man rather than a Christian. Despite their great divergences of opinion, therefore, Voltaire's closest ally was not Locke but Hume. In words that Voltaire could have written, Hume argued that enthusiasm sprang from "hope, pride, presumption, a warm imagination";[45] and in a significant metaphor that is echoed in Voltaire's writings, Hume concluded: "Examine the religious principles, which have, in fact, prevailed in the world. You will scarcely be persuaded, that they are any thing but sick men's dreams. . . ."[46]

David Hume detested these dreams with the intensity of an ex-Presbyterian who was made to suffer through interminable sermons every Sunday of his early life. But his intensity is mild compared to Voltaire's crusading ardor. "When all Christians will have cut each others' throats; when they will have devoured the entrails of their brothers assassinated for arguments; when only a single Christian remains on the earth, he will look at the sun and recognize and adore the Eternal Being; he will be able to say in his suffering: 'My fathers and my brothers were monsters, but God is God.' "[47] And this was the God for whose sake Voltaire wanted to écraser l'infâme, the God in whose defense he insisted on the extirpation of Christianity.

[44] There is plentiful evidence that Voltaire was familiar with most of this literature. See for instance Lettres à S. A. Mgr Le Prince de ***** sur Rabelais et sur d'autres auteurs accusés d'avoir mal parlé de la religion Chrétienne, xxvi, 468-526, which mentions Lord Herbert of Cherbury, Hobbes, Shaftesbury, Wollaston, Locke, Tindal, Collins, Woolston, La Mothe le Vayer, Saint-Evremond, and many others.

[45] "Of Superstition and Enthusiasm," Works, eds. T. H. Green and T. H. Grose, 4 vols. (1882), III, 145.

[46] Natural History of Religion, Works, IV, 362.

[47] Lettres à S. A. Mgr le Prince de *****, xxvi, 509.

3. THE FUTURE OF CHRISTIANITY

It is ironic that Gibbon, who was no admirer of Christianity himself, deplored as too uncompromising and too demagogic Voltaire's conviction that religion is too sublime a matter to be left to the Christians. "I have sometimes thought of writing a dialogue of the dead," he wrote, "in which Lucian, Erasmus, and Voltaire should mutually acknowledge the danger of exposing an old superstition to the contempt of the blind and fanatic multitude."[48]

Whatever the merits of this complaint, Gibbon's observation is a valuable reminder that Voltaire's anticlerical campaign is intimately involved with, and creates serious problems for, his political philosophy. I have suggested that Voltaire's attitude toward "the blind and fanatic multitude" changed over the years, that unqualified contempt was replaced by grudging respect. But his respect was grudging indeed—Voltaire never wholly liberated himself from the idea that the *canaille* deserved a social religion that was more vulgar than the true faith of the philosophers. Did he not write in the margin of one of his English books, "Natural religion for the magistrates, damn'd stuff for the mob"?[49] Did he not tell Diderot in 1762: "I recommend *l'inf*... to you; it must be destroyed among respectable people, and left to the canaille large and small, for whom it was made"?[50]

The notion of a social religion, a noble lie, is as old as Plato, and has always been popular among the educated men who write the histories, invent the political theories, and administer the laws. "The rabble," says Tacitus, urging the inculcation of superstitions, "know no mean, and inspire fear, unless they are afraid, though when they have once been overawed, they can be safely despised."[51] The opposite view, that men can safely

[48] *Autobiography* (Everyman ed.), 178-179. Gibbon wrote this, frightened by the French Revolution.
[49] Quoted in Dorn, *Competition for Empire*, 211.
[50] 25 September (1762), XLII, 250.
[51] *Annals*, I, 29.

be told the truth, was long in a minority. In the sixteenth century the Paduan scholar Pietro Pomponazzi boldly asserted that men could doubt the immortality of the soul and still be moral; in the seventeenth century Pierre Bayle suggested that a society of atheists could flourish in peace; and in the eighteenth century Holbach denounced religion as a trick of the rulers designed to prevent the ruled from noticing the evils they are forced to suffer. But Pomponazzi, Bayle, and Holbach had few adherents.

The major reason why the noble lie was popular in early modern times was the unbridgeable cleavage between educated and uneducated. Students of enthusiasm were unanimous in treating it as the disease of the poor, the lower classes. Burton argued that the common people, the "giddy-headed multitude," were the most prominent victims of religious frenzy; Casaubon and Swift agreed with him. Hobbes was among the first to suggest that religion had been instituted as a political weapon "to keep the people in obedience";[52] Gibbon urbanely confirmed Hobbes's suggestion: In the Augustan Age, he wrote, "the various modes of worship which prevailed in the Roman world were all considered by the people as equally true, by the philosophers as equally false, and by the magistrates as equally useful."[53] And that was as it had to be and would probably always be: the irrationality of the lower classes made them unfit for anything but superstitious nonsense, their passionate and unruly nature needed to be curbed by simple dogmas.

Voltaire knew all these arguments well. They had been commonplaces among the freethinking aristocrats with whom he had spent his apprenticeship; they were even commonplaces among good Calvinists.[54] Nor was Voltaire surprised to discover

[52] *Leviathan* (ed. 1947), 75.

[53] Edward Gibbon, *The History of the Decline and Fall of the Roman Empire*, ed. J. B. Bury, I, 28.

[54] The *Moïsade* bluntly treated religion as a collection of nonsense spread among a bewildered people to keep it quiet. Shortly after Voltaire arrived in Geneva, the pastor Jacob Vernet wrote to him, on 8 February 1755: "Men need a religion . . . and you see that ours is, by the Grace of God, so simple, so wise, so mild, so pure, that a philosopher could not ask for a

in his historical researches that Asiatic elites—Indian Brahmins and Chinese intellectuals—practiced a simple rational religion while preaching mysteries and superstitions to the common people.[55]

But while Voltaire the historian accepted the dichotomy of esoteric and exoteric religion in class societies—and all societies were class societies—this dichotomy confronted Voltaire the political philosopher with a serious dilemma. As the evangelist of enlightenment, he believed in education; as the evangelist of *écrasez l'infâme*, he preached the extirpation of superstition. But history seemed to teach that the very classes most desperately in need of the liberating influence of philosophy were least capable of profiting from it. To uproot Christianity was the only sound policy, because to do less was to leave intact the source of infection; but it was, at the same time, a Utopian policy, because to adopt it was to deprive the masses of the social restraints without which they could not remain moral beings.

Voltaire faced the dilemma early, and characteristically in dialogue form, but did not then resolve it. "Mr. Loke" and "Diogenes" confront "Moses" and accuse him of having deceived the Jewish people with a mass of "Commonplaces and Absurdities." "Moses" accepts the charge but skillfully defends himself: "I was the Leader of an ignorant and superstitious People, who would never have heeded the sober Counsels of Good Sense and Toleration, and who would have laughed at the Refinements of a nice Philosophy. It was necessary to flatter their Vanity by telling them that they were the favour'd Children of God. . . . By such Contrivances I was able to attain my Ends and to establish the Welfare of my Countrymen. Do you blame me? It is not the business of a Ruler to be truthful, but

---

more reasonable one. . . ." Protestantism was a most useful adjunct to the civil authority. Pomeau, *La religion de Voltaire*, 31, 290.

[55] The same holds true of Europe. In *Relation du bannissement des Jésuites de la Chine*, Voltaire has the Jesuit explain to the Chinese emperor that the Catholics begin to convert people by preaching their doctrine first to the children of the lower classes, and then to the women. XXVII, 4.

to be politick; he must fly even from Virtue herself, if she sit in a different Quarter from Expediency." Such rational willingness to "*sacrifice* the Best, which is impossible, to a *little Good*, which is close at hand," completely wins over "Diogenes": "There is no viler Profession than the Government of Nations. He who dreams that he can lead a great Crowd of Fools without a great Store of Knavery is a Fool himself." But "Mr. Loke" is not to be convinced so easily: "If Men were told the Truth, might they not believe it? If the Opportunity of Virtue and Wisdom is never to be offer'd 'em, how can we be sure that they would not be willing to take it? Let Rulers be *bold* and *honest*, and it is possible that the Folly of their Peoples will disappear." But he is argued down; history, prophecy, common observation are invoked against him. "So long as it endures," Diogenes tells him, "the World will continue to be rul'd by Cajolery, by Injustice, and by Imposture."[56]

But in this matter, as in so many others, life at Ferney raised Voltaire above the prejudices current in his circle. Despite recurrent doubts and serious reservations he became more and more insistent that "Mr. Loke" might be right. When in the 1760's he turned his attention to the cases of Calas and de La Barre, he found depressing evidence that cruel sentences had been in part forced on the courts by ignorant and superstitious mobs.[57] He noted privately that "the little people will never reason. . . . The people is between man and beast,"[58] and he joked about the lower classes with his intimates. Mallet du Pan, then a young Genevan patrician ardently supporting the Natives, reports that he was dining at Ferney while d'Alembert

[56] "A Dialogue between Moses, Diogenes, and Mr. Loke," first printed by Lytton Strachey, *Books and Characters*, 133–135. I accept Alfred Cobban's point that this is almost certainly a pastiche written by Strachey himself. But Strachey, one must admit, has captured Voltaire's argument, and manner, perfectly.

[57] See below, chapter VI. See also *Dictionnaire philosophique*, article "Convulsions," 149, which deals with the Jansenist hysteria at the cemetery of Saint-Médard in the late 1720s: "And after all that we dare to make fun of Laplanders, Samoyedes, and Negroes!"

[58] *Notebooks*, 381.

and Condorcet were making antireligious remarks. Voltaire stopped them, sent the servants out of the room, and said, "Now, messieurs, you may continue. I was only afraid of having my throat cut tonight. . . ."[59]

The anecdote is amusing and may even be true. But it should not be taken too seriously. Even in the 1760's Voltaire sometimes expressed the opinion that men are not fit to govern themselves, and that a belief in God is useful to le peuple. Nor could he agree with Bayle that a society of atheists could function smoothly. Such a society could work only, Voltaire observed, if it were a small colony of philosophers.[60] But the note of "Mr. Loke," becomes more and more prominent. Voltaire conceded that the "unthinking masses" might be incapable of distinguishing true from false religion,[61] but he insisted at the same time that it was sound policy to try to enlighten everyone: "We know that our enemies have been crying for centuries that one must deceive the people; but we believe that the lowest people are capable of knowing the truth."[62] Fanaticism can be exterminated only by the diffusion of reason, not by the diffusion of superstition.[63]

It follows that pious frauds practiced on the masses are not only immoral but also politically stupid. "It is a profound but little discussed question," he wrote in a brief sarcastic essay, "up to what point the people, that is to say nine human beings out

[59] Emile Faguet, Dix-huitième siècle, 215.

[60] See Questions sur l'Encyclopédie, article "Athée, Athéisme," Part I, xxx.

[61] "It is a matter of indifference to the unthinking masses whether we give them truths or errors to believe, wisdom or madness; they will follow one or the other equally; they are only blind machines. It is not that way with the thinking masses; they observe sometimes; they begin by doubting an absurd legend, and unhappily they take that legend for religion itself; then they will say, 'There is no religion,' and will abandon themselves to crime." Notebooks, 313.

[62] Epitre écrite de Constantinople aux frères, xxvi, 575.

[63] Remarques pour servir de supplément à l'Essai sur les moeurs et l'esprit des nations, xxiv, 569. See the somewhat more tentative earlier statement: "Perhaps there is no other remedy for this contagion [fanaticism] than finally to enlighten the people itself." Précis du siècle de Louis XV, xv, 394.

of ten, should be treated like monkeys. The deceiving party has never examined this delicate question closely, and for fear of miscalculation, it has accumulated as many phantoms as possible in the heads of the deceived party."[64] But to accumulate phantoms instead of dispelling them is itself a grievous miscalculation: the triumph of reason benefits the rulers as much as the ruled.[65]

Voltaire's rule that a sane belief in God prevents crime applied to princes as well as to ordinary men—if religion was an opiate, it was for the classes as much as for the masses. He insisted that sovereigns who are atheists are as dangerous to mankind as sovereigns who are bigots.[66] Unlike Frederick the Great, who said that it did not matter whether the prince was religious, Voltaire feared unbelieving kings and courtiers: ". . . it is absolutely necessary for princes and people that the idea of a Supreme Being, creator, governor, rewarder and avenger, be profoundly graven in all minds."[67]

It may be confessed that Voltaire's protestations against pious frauds are less than convincing. There is something complacent

[64] *Jusqu'à quel point on doit tromper le peuple*, xxiv, 71. For other denunciations of the noble lie in the 1760's, see *Dictionnaire philosophique*, article "Fraude," 207-211; *Traité sur la tolérance*, xxv, 100-192; *Réflexions pour les sots*, xxiv, 121-124; *Fragment d'une lettre de Lord Bolingbroke*, xxiv, 155-157; *Dieu et les hommes*, xxviii, 243.

[65] See *Dieu et les hommes*, xxviii, 244. Characteristically, Voltaire tried to sell this enlightened social policy as safe. He reassured princes that an enlightened people was more likely to obey the laws and less likely to start a revolution than an unenlightened one. This reminds us of his tactics of advocating freedom of the press on the ground that printed matter could never be dangerous!

[66] *Homélies prononcées à Londres en 1765*, xxvi, 329. See, "An atheist king is more dangerous than a fanatical Ravaillac." *Histoire de Jenni*, xxi, 573. He obviously had Frederick the Great in mind. See his letter to the comtesse de Lutzelbourg, 14 September (1753): "I am very glad you admit a divinity; that's what I tried to persuade a king to believe who does not believe in one, and who acts accordingly." *Correspondence*, xxiii, 181.

[67] *Dictionnaire philosophique*, article "Athée, athéisme," 43. In the same article (p. 42) we find: "It is beyond question that in a civilized city it is infinitely more useful to have a religion, even a bad one, than to have none at all." The quotation is a sound warning that the interpreter who argues that Voltaire was always consistent will get into trouble.

and unpleasantly utilitarian about his reiterated argument that popular belief in a rewarding and avenging God is a good thing for society; there is something uncritical in his easy acceptance of the fallacy that without the expectation of eternal rewards for good behavior nearly all men will become the prey of their antisocial passions. Voltaire continually affirms that men must be told the truth, and continually praises the social efficacy of lies.

Still, Voltaire has been much misinterpreted on this point. "If God did not exist, one would have to invent him," probably the most notorious line Voltaire ever wrote, is not a cynical injunction to rulers to invent a divine policeman for their ignorant subjects. Rather, it is part of a vehement diatribe against an atheist, written in the midst of Voltaire's dialogue with Holbach.[68] Another remark has been similarly misused: "I want my attorney, my tailor, my servants, even my wife to believe in God, and I think that I shall then be robbed and cuckolded less often."[69] Despite its reputation, this is the declaration of a believer who has previously declared his own certainty that God exists, not the disillusioned observation of a worldling who distrusts mankind.[70]

[68] The familiar version occurs in a recent, well-informed study by Elinor G. Barber, *The Bourgeoisie in 18th Century France*, 49: ". . . Voltaire, who is said to have remarked that if God did not exist, it would be necessary to invent Him for the masses. . . ." He did make the remark, and God was not for "the masses" alone. Here are the decisive lines:

> Si les cieux, dépouillés de son empreint auguste,
> Pouvaient cesser jamais de le manifester,
> Si Dieu n'existait pas, il faudrait l'inventer.
> Que le sage l'annonce, et que les rois le craignent.

A *l'auteur du livre des trois imposteurs*, x, 403. For Voltaire's own comment on his offending line, see *Discours de Me Belleguier*, xxix, 10, and Voltaire to Frederick-William, 28 November (1770), xlvii, 265-266.

[69] *L'A, B, C*, xxvii, 399-400. For a misinterpretation of this phrase, see Harold J. Laski, *The Rise of European Liberalism* (1936), 214.

[70] Another notorious pronouncement of Voltaire's, much quoted against him, is, "When the populace begins to argue, all is lost." It appears less obnoxious when it is read in its context: "Confucius said that he had known people incapable of science, but none incapable of virtue. Hence one should preach virtue to the commonest people. But one should not waste

It cannot be emphasized too much that Voltaire, creator of a popular God, believed in a God himself, and that the God of *le peuple* resembled his own. But resemblance is not identity: Voltaire's polemical theology introduces an anthropocentrism and anthropomorphism that he tried to keep out of his own beliefs. "The simpler the laws are," Voltaire wrote in his notebook, "the more the magistrates are respected; the simpler the religion will be, the more one will revere its ministers. Religion can be simple. If the Protestants have got rid of twenty superstitions, they can get rid of thirty. . . . When enlightened people will announce a single God, rewarder and avenger, no one will laugh, everyone will obey."[71]

This conception of God, announced by enlightened people, affirms things that Voltaire really thought doubtful, unknowable, or improbable: that the individual soul is immortal, that man is important to God, that God acts as a judge.[72] This divine policeman who observes and judges human actions is not Voltaire's true God. At the same time—and this is important—he is not the God of Christianity: he does not treat his children as fallen from grace; he does not embody himself in history; he does not perform the miracle of the Incarnation or any other miracles.

Here is the first step in Voltaire's escape from his dilemma

---

one's time over examining who was right, Nestorius or Cyril, Eusebius or Athanasius, Jansenius or Molina, Zwingli or Oecolampadius. Please God that there had never been good bourgeois infatuated with such disputes! We would never have had wars of religion, we would never have had Saint Bartholomew. All quarrels of this kind were started by idle folk who were in comfortable circumstances. When the populace begins to argue, all is lost. I agree with those who would make good laborers of foundlings, rather than theologians." Voltaire to Damilaville, 1 April (1766), XLIV, 256.

[71] *Notebooks*, 381. The *dieu rémunerateur et vengeur* frequently appears in his later writings, but not yet in the writings of the Cirey period. He is thus the fruit of his reflections on popular religion. Pomeau, *La religion de Voltaire*, 201.

[72] Voltaire's uncertainty is a constant theme. In 1777 he told a visitor: "At last God is calling me. But what God? I know nothing about that." *ibid.*, 412.

between the need for enlightenment and the need for a social religion: a popular religion is necessary, but it must not be Christianity. Voltaire's "noble lie" might be called a "noble white lie"; it is a crude deism which rejects mysteries, saints, relics, pilgrimages, transubstantiation or consubstantiation, church hierarchies. Such a religion is oversimplified, but since it is free from superstitions it is not harmful. It avoids the danger of disillusioning the thinking masses with fairy tales: "Let us propose to them a God who is not ridiculous, who will not be dishonored by old wives' tales; they will adore him without laughing and without a murmur."[73] If statesmen had only been wise enough to preach this religion rather than superstitions, how much better the world could have been: "If they had contented themselves with a simple religion, a majestic cult, without mixing it up with superstitions, miracles; with a saintly morality and without casuists; with counsel without the desire to dominate; if, finally, they had not made of Christianity a tax on consciences, extorted by inquisitors, torch in hand. . . ."[74]

It was obvious to Voltaire that his popular religion must avoid this sanguinary path. That is why he found Rousseau's civil religion so abhorrent. On 18 August 1756, four years before Rousseau told Voltaire that he hated him, he sent Voltaire his celebrated letter on Providence, outlining a program for a civil profession of faith, imposed by the laws, proscribing fanaticism and inculcating toleration: "I should like to see a moral code in every state, a kind of profession of civic faith, containing positively the social maxims that everybody would have to accept, and negatively the intolerant maxims that everybody would have to reject, not as impious but as seditious." The code embodying this profession of faith would be "the most useful book ever written"; Rousseau invited Voltaire to compose

[73] *Fragment d'une lettre de Lord Bolingbroke*, xxiv, 156.
[74] *Notebooks*, 381. This explains another notebook entry: "Religion is not a check, it is on the contrary an encouragement to crime. All religion is founded on expiations." *ibid.*, 313. Here "religion" refers to supernatural religion rather than Voltaire's, which was not built on expiations.

this "catechism of the citizen," and crown with this work "the most brilliant career which a man of letters has ever traversed."[75]

Voltaire was flattered by the compliment but repelled by the program. He liked its final form even less: in the *Contrat social*, Rousseau prescribed banishment for those who did not accept the civil religion, and the death penalty for those who falsely swore that they believed in it. This appeal to force revolted Voltaire. "All dogma is ridiculous, deadly," he scrawled in the margin of his copy. "All coercion on dogma is abominable. To compel belief is absurd. Confine yourself to compelling good living."[76]

Voltaire refused the task for which Rousseau considered him so brilliantly equipped because he disliked compulsion and because he hoped that the people would not need a popular religion forever. In time they would transcend even Voltaire's noble, simple, majestic lie. And this is the second step in Voltaire's escape from his dilemma: the religion of *le peuple* is an expedient which will wither away as enlightenment spreads. Again and again, Voltaire lovingly used one of his favorite images, the diffusion of light to larger and larger areas, from philosophes to the educated classes, from the educated classes to the bourgeoisie, from the bourgeoisie to the people. "Men are governed by reigning opinions, and opinions change when the light extends itself."[77] He saw many hopeful signs: "The pure adoration of the Supreme Being is today beginning to be the religion of all respectable people; it will soon descend to the sound part of the masses." Who will begin to purify religion? "The men who think. The others will follow."[78] Men will discard superstitions as a convalescent discards his crutches: "Reason has already made so much progress . . . that it will be easy to uproot by degrees all the superstitions that have brutalized

[75] C. E. Vaughan, ed., *The Political Writings of Jean Jacques Rousseau*, 2 vols. (1915), II, 163-165.

[76] Havens, *Voltaire's Marginalia*, 68.

[77] *Idées de la Mothe le Vayer*, XXIII, 491.

[78] *Le dîner du comte de Boulainvilliers*, XXVI, 555.

us."[79] Progress may be slow, but it is real; the philosophe, the lieutenant of history, aids this progress by unmasking superstitions, slowly and patiently.

There are occasional passages, much quoted by Catholic admirers of Voltaire, that indicate Voltaire's desire to maintain churches within the body politic. "I would like you to extirpate *l'infâme*; that is the great point," he once wrote to d'Alembert. "It must be reduced to the state in which it is in England. . . ."[80] A few years later, Voltaire had A, the Englishman, say in *l'A,B,C,*: "A good respectable religion, *mort de ma vie*, solidly established by act of parliament, completely dependent upon the sovereign—that is what we need. And let us tolerate all the others."[81] Even Gustave Lanson has deduced from such pronouncements that Voltaire envisaged a kind of tolerant Catholicism for France.[82]

But these scattered observations will not carry so heavy a burden. Voltaire strenuously opposed payments to, and residual jurisdiction of, the Papacy; he persistently advocated absolute national independence in religious matters, the complete political impotence of the clergy, full submission of ecclesiastics to civil laws, the abolition of celibacy, the payment of priests by the state, the closing of monasteries. This is complete Erastianism: the priesthood is a profession, and a relatively insignificant profession at that. "Nothing is more useful than a curé who keeps registers of births, giving copies to the magistrate, who takes care of the poor, who makes peace in families, etc., etc. Nothing is more useless than a cardinal. . . ."[83] Let the

[79] *ibid.*, 553-554. "Up to what point does politics permit us to ruin superstitions? . . . That depends on the prudence of the physician. Can there be a nation free of all superstitious prejudices? That is to ask: can there be a nation of philosophers? . . . Magistrates will prevent superstitions of the people from being dangerous. . . ." *Dictionnaire philosophique,* article "Superstition," 398.

[80] 23 June (1760), XL, 437. The passage is exploited in Noyes, *Voltaire,* 492.

[81] XXVII, 365.   [82] *Voltaire,* 183.

[83] *Notebooks,* 375. On occasion Voltaire even advocated separation of church and state, but as Pomeau points out, such texts are rare. Gen-

ministers of the Christian rites have "consideration without power."[84] This is not a doctrine that a good Catholic can support.

In fact, Voltaire's repeated allusions to England as a country that has solved church-state relations supports rather than refutes his radicalism. In England, religion was no longer powerful, but even in England, this desirable state of affairs had been achieved only after a long struggle. It took time "to cure the malady thoroughly . . ." wrote Voltaire in the name of Bolingbroke. "The fruit is not yet quite ripe enough to be gathered."[85] But it will be gathered in time. Voltaire told Helvétius in 1763 that the English had discovered the correct method of crushing superstitions; they published the truth about religion again and again; they wrote short simple tracts suitable to the crudest intelligence; they avoided metaphysical speculations which nobody could understand. French philosophes ought to adopt this method: "It is both effective and agreeable to throw ridicule and horror on theological disputes, to make men feel that morality is beautiful and dogma impertinent, and to be able to enlighten at once the chancellor and the shoemaker."[86]

This did not mean the immediate elimination of public worship. "Let us meet four times a year in a grand temple with music," Voltaire told Boswell, "and thank God for all his gifts. There is one sun. There is one God. Let us have one religion. Then all mankind will be brethren."[87] Voltaire, the Anglomaniac, believed that England had made great progress toward such a faith, at once so rational and so respectful to the true God. Indeed, England was the model for the civilized world. "After having weighed Christianity before God in the scales of truth," wrote Voltaire-Bolingbroke, "it must be weighed in the

erally, he contented himself with advocating complete subjection of the church to the state.

84 *Dictionnaire philosophique*, article "Religion," 369.
85 *Fragment d'une lettre de Lord Bolingbroke*, XXIV, 155, 157.
86 2 July (1763), XLII, 513-514.
87 *Boswell on the Grand Tour, Germany and Switzerland*, 304.

scales of politics. Such is the miserable condition of man that the true is not always the advantageous. It would be dangerous and unreasonable to do all at once with Christianity what we did with Popery. I hold that in our island we should allow the hierarchy established by act of parliament to persist, always submitting it to civil legislation and preventing it from doing harm. It would doubtless be desirable to overthrow the idol, and to offer God purer homage, but the people is not yet worthy of it. For the present it is enough to contain our church in its limits. The more laymen are enlightened, the less harm priests will be able to do. Let us try to enlighten even them, to make them blush for their errors, to lead them gradually to becoming citizens."[88]

This is an important passage, one of the most important that Voltaire ever wrote, but it has been neglected. No other words sum up more forcefully the drift of his religious policy. With all his doubts about the *canaille*, with all his fears of overturning established institutions, with all his hesitations and discouragements, he saw the process of enlightenment as a progressive emancipation from the idol of Christianity. The idol could not be overthrown now, the people was not yet ready for the pure religion, but the passage of time and the teachings of the philosophes would make even shoemakers worthy of deism.

More: they *must* become worthy, not only for their own sake, but for the sake of civilization. Christianity, Voltaire told his readers in a staggering array of metaphors, is a virulent infection, a terrifying madness, a bloodthirsty monster. In *Galimatias dramatique*, Voltaire imagined himself as one of his favorite persons, a Chinese official. After listening to the religious disputations of a Jesuit, a Jansenist, a Quaker, an Anglican, a Lutheran, a Puritan, a Moslem, a Jew, the official has them all put in an insane asylum.[89]

Voltaire was desperately serious: in the last decades of his

[88] *Examen important de Milord Bolingbroke*, XXVI, 299-300.
[89] XXIV, 75-77.

life he wished a plague on all their houses. The crimes of Christianity were not an accident but the essence of Christianity. They were not the poisonous fruits of a sound tree; the tree itself was poisonous: "We must cut off by the roots a tree that has always carried poisons."[90] No compromise was possible. Shortly after he bought Ferney, and while his antireligious campaign was shifting into high gear, he wrote a correspondent that he destroyed only in order to build.[91] He was referring to his estate, but he carried his conviction into the slogan with which he now began to sign his letters. "*Ecrasez l'infâme*" meant that one must destroy Christianity before one could build a rational society.

[90] *Le dîner du comte de Boulainvilliers*, xxvi, 550. See Voltaire to d'Argental, 3 October (1752): "There is a big tree in France which is not the tree of life, which extends its branches to all sides, and which produces strange fruit." *Correspondence*, xxi, 84.

[91] Voltaire to de Brosses, 5 January (1759), xl, 7. See also Voltaire to Thieriot, 10 December (1738), xxxv, 67: "I know how to hate because I know how to love."

VI

FERNEY:
THE MAN OF CALAS

Si on a peint la justice avec un bandeau sur les yeux, il faut que
la raison soit son guide.

—VOLTAIRE, *Prix de la justice et de l'humanité*

1. TRIALS AND ERRORS

IN THE MIDDLE of March 1762, two months after Voltaire had
cast his first stone at Christianity with the *Sermon des cinquante,*
a French visitor to Ferney told him a harrowing tale of *l'infâme*
in action. With dramatic suddenness, the tale converted Voltaire into a legal reformer, and his abstract, benevolent demands
for justice and the rule of law into a concrete program.

This was the visitor's story: about 9:30, on the evening of
13 October 1761, Marc-Antoine Calas, eldest son of a Toulouse
cloth merchant named Jean Calas, was found hanged in his
father's shop. At first, his family insisted that Marc-Antoine
had been murdered by a stranger who had somehow gained
access to the house; after the Calas family were arrested, they
testified unanimously that Marc-Antoine had dined with them,
had left after dinner to go downstairs to the shop, and had
there committed suicide.

The family had good reason to deny that Marc-Antoine had
killed himself: in French law, a suicide was subjected to an
ignominious mock trial, dragged nude through the streets by

the heels, and hanged as an infamous criminal. But their inconsistent testimony, no matter how justified by circumstances, confirmed the magistrates' ready suspicion that Marc-Antoine has been assassinated by his family. "In this case lying was an act of paternal piety," Voltaire said later.[1] Unfortunately the worthies of Toulouse were eager to believe that for a Calas paternal piety included murder: the Calas family were Huguenots, and only too many Frenchmen were sure that Protestants were in the habit of assassinating apostates. The rumor spread that Marc-Antoine had been about to convert to Catholicism, and that his family had strangled him to prevent him from embracing the faith of all true Frenchmen. Marc-Antoine was buried as a Catholic and celebrated as a martyr.

The *canaille* of Toulouse had circulated the report of ritual murder, and the officials of the city were not rational enough to find the report absurd. But while they were willing to believe that Huguenots were capable of such a fanatical enormity, the authorities did scrupulously observe most of the trial procedure laid down in the Criminal Ordinance of 1670 for the guidance of all French courts. They interrogated scores of witnesses, questioned the accused privately and separately, reconstructed the crime in the Calas house, requested local priests to read to their congregations a *monitoire*—a public invitation for witnesses to come forward.[2] Much of the testimony they admitted into evidence was hearsay based upon hearsay, but that violated only common sense, not French legal procedure.[3] David de

[1] Voltaire to Damilaville, October (1762), XLII, 274.

[2] There were some irregularities in the conduct of the Calas case: the arrest, the sentence of the local magistrates, the wording of the *monitoire*, all departed from the explicit instructions of the Criminal Ordinance of 1670. But the eventual conviction of Jean Calas did not result from these breaches of regular procedure; it is extremely probable that he would have been convicted even if all the proprieties had been observed.

[3] "One Massaleng, a widow, gave evidence that her daughter had told her that le sieur Pagès had told her that M. Soulié had told him that la demoiselle Guichardet had told him that demoiselle Journu had made a statement from which she (Journu) had inferred that *le père* Lerraut, a Jesuit, had been the confessor of Marc-Antoine Calas. When the reverend

Beaudrigue, the magistrate who had arrested the Calas on the night of Marc-Antoine's death, pursued them with little pity and with less evidence, but he was only doing his duty as he understood it. The Calas case educated Voltaire because it dramatized the failings of the French legal code rather than the far less important failings of provincial magistrates.[4]

On 9 March 1762, after painstaking and repeated deliberations, the parlement of Toulouse, sitting as an appellate court, condemned Jean Calas to die at the stake. He was first to suffer the *question ordinaire* and *question extraordinaire* which were intended to secure confession of the murder and incrimination of accomplices. On the following day, Jean Calas was publicly broken on the wheel, but through his ordeals he reaffirmed his innocence with stoic serenity. David de Beaudrigue, conscientious to the last, pressed his victim to confess in the face of death, but Jean Calas only turned his head away. A little later, he was strangled by the executioner.

This was the Calas case, a provincial trial of an inconspicuous merchant, which Voltaire transformed into the most celebrated of *causes célèbres* of the eighteenth century. "Do you have reliable news on Calas . . . ?" he inquired of a Genevan correspondent on 27 March 1762, still incredulous that a man could be condemned for what he was rather than for what he had done. "Was he guilty or innocent? On one side or another, this is the most horrible fanaticism in the most enlightened century. My tragedies are not so tragic."[5] Guilty or innocent, Jean Calas offered new and depressing evidence of the need to *écraser*

---

father Lerraut was summoned he showed that the whole of this was without foundation." F. H. Maugham, *The Case of Jean Calas*, 87.

[4] It is important to be clear on this point. Constance Rowe writes: "Theoretically, all individuals charged with a civil or criminal offense were entitled to a fair trial by jury." *Voltaire and the State*, 99. If she were right, Voltaire's intervention in legal cases would merely have involved protests against individual miscarriages of justice by individual magistrates, rather than a thoroughgoing indictment of the whole French legal system. But, as the balance of this chapter will show, she is mistaken.

[5] Voltaire to Camp, *Correspondance avec les Tronchin*, 569.

l'infâme. "For the love of God," Voltaire exploded to d'Alembert two days later, "render as execrable as you can the fanaticism that has led a father to hang his son, or that has led eight *conseillers du roi* to break an innocent man on the wheel."[6] He did not then think it impossible that Jean Calas had murdered his son for religious reasons. Were not good Calvinists almost as imbecilic as good Catholics?

But to Voltaire the Calas case was more than a horror story suitable for philosophic propaganda—it was an enigma, made more enigmatic by the scarcity of documents, the secrecy imposed on the trial by French procedure, and the reluctance of local officials to give information. Voltaire was a propagandist, but he liked to conduct his campaigns with facts—dramatized, simplified, tailored, but still facts. "It is useful to investigate matters thoroughly," he told d'Argental when he first became interested in the Calas case;[7] but the truth seemed deeply buried in the mud of conjecture and prejudice. He made inquiries in Toulouse and in Paris; interrogated members of the Calas family who had succeeded in fleeing to Geneva; asked Jean Calas' widow to swear by her faith (that "imbecilic" Calvinist faith) that her family was innocent.

Once again, Voltaire was meddling. His influential French friends assured him that Calas was guilty, and warned him not to interfere in a case that had been decided in accord with accepted procedure. But their opinion had little weight, and their warning no success. Voltaire's inquiries satisfied him that Jean Calas had died an innocent victim of a monstrous miscarriage of justice. Much in the case remained obscure, but Voltaire was confident that his information was adequate and his logic good. The notion of a secret Huguenot conspiracy to assassinate apostates was a ridiculous, superstitious canard; nothing in Jean Calas' life hinted at homicidal tendencies; there was not a particle of reliable evidence that Marc-Antoine had con-

[6] XLII, 79.
[7] 27 March (1762), XLII, 76.

templated conversion to Catholicism—no priest ever came forward to claim that he had instructed him or given him communion; there was on the contrary good evidence that Marc-Antoine had been a morose young man, thwarted in his ambitions for a legal career by the exclusion of Huguenots from that profession in France, resentful of being compelled to work in his father's business; it was highly improbable that an elderly man of sixty-three could single-handedly strangle a young man of twenty-eight, and yet the very court that had sent Jean Calas to his death seemed to subscribe to such an improbable theory by contenting itself with banishing the other defendants from France.[8]

Voltaire was sure that Calas was innocent, but if he was innocent, the French law was guilty of murder. And although Jean Calas could not be revived, his name could be rehabilitated, and his family, dispersed and destitute, could be reunited. "Shout everywhere, I beg you," Voltaire wrote to d'Alembert in September 1762, "for the Calas and against fanaticism, for it is *l'infâme* that has caused their misery."[9] Voltaire himself had been shouting for three months: he had hired lawyers for the Calas family, invited his friends to offer them their protection, collected money for them from his royal and aristocratic correspondents. And he was also doing what he could do better than anyone else: writing and editing memoranda, ostensible letters, memorials. Frenchmen, said Voltaire, shuddered at horrors for a moment and then went to the opera; he would remind them again and again of the realities they wanted to forget.

There were more such realities than even Voltaire suspected. In January 1762, while Jean Calas was still in prison, a case bearing a close resemblance to the Calas affair occurred in Castres, a small town in the jurisdiction of the parlement of Toulouse. Elizabeth Sirven, the youngest daughter of Pierre-Paul Sirven, a Huguenot surveyor, was discovered drowned in

[8] The bad logic of this sentence did not escape Voltaire. See *Lettre de Donat Calas fils à la dame veuve Calas, sa mère*, xxiv, 372.
[9] xlii, 237.

a well. The girl had been moronic and withdrawn, occasionally suffering hysterical seizures which the local nuns had generously interpreted as signs of conversion to the true faith. The same popular prejudice that was about to ruin Jean Calas put the Sirven family under suspicion of murder, but before they could be arrested, the Sirvens prudently escaped to Switzerland; they had their doubts that the magistrates would be satisfied with such rational verdicts as suicide or accident.

Here were more "Calvinist imbeciles" to be protected by Voltaire. After he had assured himself of their innocence, he undertook to clear their name, as he was undertaking to clear the name of Jean Calas. Deprived of their victims, the authorities of Toulouse elaborately executed Pierre-Paul Sirven and his wife in effigy. The Sirven case, Voltaire wrote in wry comment on this farce, "will not have the *éclat* of the Calas case: unfortunately nobody was broken on the wheel. . . ."[10]

But the *éclat* that the Sirven case lacked was supplied by the melodramatic La Barre case, which was the source of Voltaire's greatest fright and greatest fury in his Ferney years. On 28 February 1766, the nineteen-year-old chevalier de La Barre and his young companion Gaillard d'Etallonde, were convicted in Abbeville, near Amiens, of mutilating a wooden crucifix that stood on a bridge, of making blasphemous remarks, and of singing blasphemous songs. Unlike Calas and the Sirvens, the young men were "Catholic imbeciles"; unlike Calas and the Sirvens, they were obviously guilty of some, if not all, of the acts charged against them. La Barre was ignorant, vain, foolish, rustic, and dependent; d'Etallonde was no less ignorant and no less foolish, but he obviously dominated his friend.[11] Both liked to display their daring, to recite blasphemous poems, to punctuate their

---

[10] Voltaire to madame de Florian, 7 November 1765, XLIV, 103.

[11] Voltaire was only partly aware of his clients' limitations. He helped d'Etallonde to obtain a post in the Prussian army and consistently worked for his legal rehabilitation, which was not granted until 1788. When the young man came to Ferney in 1774, he astonished Voltaire with his ignorance. See Voltaire to Frederick, 7 December (1774), IL, 146-147.

speech with obscenities. They were the kind of adolescent who supply the supporter of corporal punishment with strong arguments.

The vandalism against their beloved crucifix had caused great consternation among the pious folk of Abbeville, and the local magistrates were inclined to be severe with these youths whom they suspected of desecrating it. They took testimony from a large number of witnesses, and conscientiously listened to reports—true, doubtful, and false—of the blasphemous behavior of La Barre and his friends. Had the young men not failed to take off their hats to a religious procession? Had they not cursed the virgin and ridiculed the saints? D'Etallonde managed to escape, which left his friend La Barre to bear the full weight of local resentment and superstitious fear. Frederick the Great told Voltaire that he would have sentenced the youths to reading Thomas Aquinas' *Summa Theologica*, a fate worse than death;[12] the court of Abbeville lacked Frederick's frigid sense of humor. It condemned La Barre to do public penance, to have his tongue cut out and his right hand cut off, and to be burned at the stake. The verdict was immediately appealed to the parlement of Paris.

Voltaire heard disquieting rumors about the case in the spring of 1766, during the months he was allying himself with the Genevan Natives. He failed to perceive that it was the weakness of the clerical party and the strength of the philosophes that finally doomed La Barre; to orthodox Christians, the young man's outrageous behavior was a frightening symptom of the spreading influence of materialism, and their fears made them inflexible and pitiless. Against all expectations, the parlement of Paris, intoxicated by rhetorical denunciations of modern impiety, confirmed the barbarous sentence against La Barre on 5 June 1766. Voltaire's policy of Aesopianism was tragically vindicated. "The scene which has just taken place in Paris," he wrote to Morellet, "proves conclusively that the brothers

---

[12] Frederick to Voltaire, 7 August (1766), XLIV, 379.

must carefully hide their mysteries and the names of their brethren. . . . In such baneful circumstances sages must keep quiet and wait."[13]

Voltaire himself, it turned out, was directly implicated in La Barre's impiety. The prosecution had proved that the young man had read the *Dictionnaire philosophique*, the *Lettres philosophiques*, the *Epitre à Uranie*, and the execution demonstrated dramatically that the authorities had not forgotten what influences had shaped La Barre. On 1 July 1766, after prolonged and fruitless torture, the young blasphemer died heroically on the scaffold. His fellow townsmen of Abbeville, who witnessed his end, were less impressed with his heroism than with the dexterity of the executioner. As soon as their applause for the headsman had died down, La Barre's corpse was publicly burned and a copy of the *Dictionnaire philosophique* was thrown into the flames with the body.

In Paris, Grimm, usually so cool, called for a "public avenger, an eloquent and courageous man who will transmit this unexampled and unmotivated cruelty to the tribunal of the public and to the stigma of posterity." This task, he said, was "worthy of M. de Voltaire."[14] But M. de Voltaire met this crisis by eloquence but not courage. He fled to Switzerland and conceived a plan of collecting a body of philosophes in Cleves, under the protection of Frederick the Great. His courage returned as he saw that Voltaire-Socrates (as he called himself) would not be made to drink the hemlock.[15] The fear disappeared; the fury remained. When d'Alembert sent him an amusing letter about the Hume-Rousseau quarrel shortly after La Barre's death, Voltaire reproached him with his levity: "I cannot tolerate that you finish your letter by saying, 'I am laughing.' Ah! My

---

[13] 7 July (1766), XLIV, 330. The parlement of Paris made some minor modifications in the sentence of the Abbeville judges. It spared La Barre the cutting out of his tongue and the cutting off of his hand and changed burning at the stake to beheading. But it added torture as a preliminary.

[14] *Correspondance littéraire*, 15 July 1766, VII, 77.

[15] See Voltaire to Damilaville, 1 July 1766, XLIV, 324.

dear friend, is this the time to laugh? . . . I embrace you in rage."[16] For once his humor failed him: "The atrocity of this act seizes me with horror and anger,"[17] and neither his horror nor his anger ever wholly left him.

Calas, Sirven, La Barre are only the most celebrated in a long succession of "Voltaire's cases." For them he wrote some of his most eloquent and most disinterested pieces of propaganda—the *Traité sur la tolérance* for the Calas, the *Avis au public* for the Sirvens, the *Relation* for the chevalier de La Barre. These and many other pamphlets were not without consequence: the memory of Jean Calas was cleared on 9 March 1765, the third anniversary of his conviction; the Sirvens were rehabilitated in 1771. It had taken two hours to condemn them, said Voltaire bitterly, and nine years to do them justice. His triumphs—or what a grateful public, forgetting the labors of others, insisted on calling his triumphs—increased demands upon his time. As he became known to a wide public that cared nothing for his tragedies as "the man of Calas," other victims of French justice turned to him for help. There was the case of Martin, a farmer accused of murder, executed, then belatedly recognized as innocent through the confession of another man; the case of Montbailli, accused of having killed his mother, executed, rehabilitated as innocent two years later[18]; the case of General Lally, French royal commissioner in India, defeated by the English and executed on vague charges of disloyalty. For all of these men Voltaire wrote pamphlets, memoranda, propagandist letters to his friends; he was converting his rage into productive work.

His frenzy over these miscarriages of justice astonished even those who knew his frenetic temperament. Four years after the Sirven affair, he told d'Argental that his dramas and his interest in Genevan politics were nothing to him; the fight to

[16] 23 July (1766), XLIV, 357. See also Voltaire to d'Alembert, 30 July (1766), XLIV, 366-367.
[17] Voltaire to d'Argental, 16 July (1766), XLIV, 343.
[18] See below, pp. 294-295.

rehabilitate the Sirvens "agitates my whole soul."[19] Eight years after the execution of La Barre he told Condorcet that rage came into his heart and tears into his eyes as he thought "that a single bigot of Abbeville produced all these horrors, a hundred times more hellish than the Calas assassinations."[20] Diderot, who usually found it easy to restrain his admiration for Voltaire, was moved by Voltaire's aid to the Calas: "Oh! *mon amie*," he wrote to Sophie Volland in August 1762, "what beautiful use of genius! . . . Eh! What are the Calas to him? What can interest him in them? Why should he suspend labors which he loves, to occupy himself in their defense? If there were a Christ, I assure you that Voltaire would be saved."[21]

Not all of Voltaire's contemporaries were so sure that he deserved salvation. Some said that he was hiding in a strategic sanctuary in order to attack the Christian religion with impunity. It is true that when Voltaire first became engaged in the Calas and Sirven cases, he was awake to their uses as anticlerical propaganda. It was the Catholic *canaille* that had kept public excitement in Toulouse at a fever pitch, it was superstition that made magistrates believe in ritual murder, it was fanaticism that converted sober judges into brutal torturers. But his activity taught him that *l'infâme* and the French legal system, although inseparable, were not identical. He never lost *l'infâme* from sight, and his efforts at legal reform always had an anticlerical tinge, but George Saintsbury's sneer that "the injustices he combated were somehow always *clerical*,"[22] is as uninformed as it is uncharitable. Voltaire defended Catholics as freely as he defended Protestants; he defended the victims of political chicanery as freely as he defended the victims of religious fanaticism.

Other detractors, like Fréron, accused Voltaire of defending the Calas family for the sake of notoriety. But Voltaire did not

[19] (10 February 1766), XLIV, 215.
[20] 21 January 1775, IL, 202.
[21] 9 August 1762, *Lettres à Sophie Volland*, I, 267.
[22] *A History of the French Novel*, 2 vols. (1917), I, 384.

need the good opinion of others so badly that he must perform good deeds for their sake. He performed them for his own sake. As the champion of the oppressed he was a busy man (there are always so many oppressed and so few champions), and he pursued his tireless activities for what might be called his worldly salvation. At Ferney, rich, old, secure, and famous, he discovered that conscience must be appeased. He was happy even when he sounded gloomy: he strewed his correspondence with his favorite lament, *sauve qui peut*, with a gusto that suggests the playful tone of his pessimism. But happiness must be paid for. It was not enough to indulge in a vague, diffused benevolence, wishing all humanity well; it was necessary to be benevolent to specific people with specific troubles.[23]

Sometimes in his later years Voltaire professed an epicurean indifference to the evils of this world: "Let heroes slaughter each other and let us live tranquilly," he wrote; and "In any case, let us always live very quietly and let men be as insane, as evil, and as unhappy as they want to be"; and again, "We must amuse ourselves a little although men are unhappy elsewhere for it is not just that the whole globe should be grieving."[24] But this philosophy of sublime indifference did not convince the man he most needed to convince, himself. "I am ashamed to be so happy amid so many disasters," he wrote to Jean-Robert Tronchin on 31 October 1759,[25] and this remark, both the happiness and the shame, provides the clue to Voltaire's humanitarianism. Man can be happy and deserving at the same time if he acts energetically and continuously in behalf of those who are less happy than he. For the Christian, salvation depended on

[23] I am here following the ideas of Nietzsche and Scheler on the role of resentment in benevolence: the more general the love of humanity and the greater the urge to return good for evil, to love one's enemies, the larger the component of hatred in supposed love. Voltaire did not love his enemies, and he returned evil for evil.

[24] Voltaire to Jean-Robert Tronchin, 30 October (1756), *Correspondance avec les Tronchin*, 177; Voltaire to the same, 5 February 1758, *ibid.*, 319; Voltaire to the same, 29 March (1757), *ibid.*, 212.

[25] *ibid.*, 436.

unmerited grace; for Voltaire it depended upon works. Each intervention in a legal case brought him closer to that earthly salvation that is contained in the comforting certainty that one is entitled to be happy.

2. CRIMES AND PUNISHMENTS

The Calas case was a small event with large consequences. It awakened Voltaire's passion for legal reform; it dramatized for the French the deficiencies of their legal system; it started Voltaire on an inquiry into the law that culminated in the *Prix de la justice et de l'humanité,* the most comprehensive and the most radical of his legal works, written in 1777 when he was eighty-two.

Voltaire had not been indifferent to legal questions before 1762, but his concern had been sporadic and perfunctory. The Calas case, moving and mysterious, supplied the impulse that focused his aversion to injustice on French law, and converted him into a crusader. In one sense at least, Voltaire resembled the public he was trying to educate: he reveled in the concrete, he was left cold by the purely theoretical. The rehabilitation of the Calas was dramatic. In 1762, the Calas family had been in disgrace, unhappy, dispersed; in 1763, the *conseil d'état* opened the revision of the trial; in 1764, the *conseil privé du roi* set aside the verdict; in 1765, the Calas family were finally pronounced innocent. They were indemnified, and the sentences of the parlement of Toulouse ordered stricken from the record. Like the public, Voltaire rejoiced in these stirring events; unlike the public, Voltaire could discern the general in the particular. The case had taught him that the crime against Jean Calas was not merely the crime of a fanatic named David de Beaudrigue or the *canaille* of Toulouse, but the crime of a code that made injustice more probable than justice.

The code that governed French courts until the Revolution was the *Ordonnance criminelle* of 1670, one of Colbert's most ambitious and least impressive enterprises. The magistrates who

wrote the Criminal Ordinance were more interested in law enforcement than in law reform; they sought order and clarity,
not humanity. Of all the participants in the preliminary discussions, only one, Guillaume de Lamoignon, made a case for
humanity to defendants and leniency of punishments, but his
advice was ignored.[26] "In several points, the Criminal Ordinance
seems to have been directed solely to the ruin of the accused,"
wrote Voltaire in one of his rare criticisms of the code.[27]

With customary conservatism, the lawyers who drafted the
ordinance of 1670 modeled it closely upon the ordinance of
1539, which had codified the repressive procedures characteristic
of the late Middle Ages. "Until the fifteenth century, the death
penalty and serious mutilation were used only in extreme cases
to supplement the complicated and carefully differentiated systems of fines, but now they became the most common measures.
. . . Even the methods of execution become more brutal. The
authorities were constantly devising new means by which to
make the death penalty more painful."[28]

This growing harshness resulted from an increased need to
repress the turbulent lower classes, especially the rootless urban
proletariat, and to protect private property in an age of urban-
ization. Colbert and his colleagues wanted a system that repressed offenses economically and, at the same time, deprived
the French aristocracy of whatever seigneurial privileges still
remained to it. This program, a combination of political absolutism and class justice, was modern enough, but the religious
features of the code were far from modern. The ordinance of
1670 still treated sins as crimes and crimes as sins: the criminal
was an outcast from society. Executions were public festivals,
entertainments for the spectators who could legitimately dis-

[26] See Voltaire's praise of Lamoignon's humanity, *Précis du siècle de
Louis XV*, xv, 419.
[27] *Commentaire sur le livre des délits et des peines*, xxv, 572-573.
[28] Georg Rusche and Otto Kirchheimer, *Punishment and Social Structure*, 19.

charge their cruel impulses, and purifications of the community.[29] Sorcery, blasphemy, heresy, were not private offenses demanding expulsion from the visible church, but grave public crimes demanding dreadful punishment. The state of Louis XIV and of Colbert avenged not only men but God. Church and state were two arms of a single body of believers, and in French law this alliance of ecclesiastical and secular power manifested itself in laws against religious error, in the *monitoire* which made the church an agent of the prosecution, and in the inquisitorial procedure which assumed that criminals, like sinners, carried a moral infection dangerous to the body politic. Respectable and otherwise kindly persons could glory in the wide power of the law and the cruelty of punishment. There was no reason to spare those whose very existence threatened the stability of the Christian community.

In the 1670's such high-sounding justifications were little more than rationalizations of judicial stupidity and of unsparing exploitation of the poor. Politically they made sense, but morally they were anachronisms, sanctioned by power and tradition. A secular jurisprudence could, of course, also be brutal, but in fact the apostles of secularism—Montaigne and Grotius, Hobbes and Locke, La Bruyère and Bayle—were also the apostles of humanitarianism. In the eighteenth century their pioneering explorations of a humanitarian jurisprudence were used and expanded in the systematic legal writings of Montesquieu, Beccaria, Voltaire, and later Bentham.

Voltaire's borrowings from his predecessors furnish an illuminating commentary on his character and his method of work. Montesquieu pleaded for lenient punishment, liberal treatment of dissent, the elimination of numerous acts from the canon of crimes, and for rational and humane procedures. Yet, despite

[29] That this kind of cruelty had not yet died out in Voltaire's time is evident from the spectacle of Damiens' execution in 1757. Prominent persons, especially ladies, paid high prices for good seats to watch Damiens being drawn and quartered. See Voltaire's detailed account, *Histoire du parlement de Paris*, XVI, 98-99; and *l'A,B,C*, XXVII, 341.

the grace of the *Lettres persanes* and the cogency of the *Esprit des lois*, Montesquieu's legal writings apparently made little impact on Voltaire: he read them too early, when they had mere abstract or literary significance for him. It was different with Cesare Beccaria's *Trattato dei delitti e della pene*, which Voltaire studied in the original late in 1765. A Milanese jurist, a brilliant disciple of the philosophes, Beccaria was the first eighteenth-century theorist to develop a coherent modern theory of crimes and punishments—secular, humane, utilitarian. Voltaire readily acknowledged his indebtedness to the *Trattato*. Fresh from the triumphant vindication of Jean Calas, in the midst of his struggle for the Sirvens, he could apply Beccaria's universal principles in particular cases.

His *Commentaire sur le livre des délits et des peines* (1766) was a token of his gratitude to Beccaria, but since he learned even more from experience than he learned from books, he passed beyond the position he took in the *Commentaire* in the years that followed. As late as 1770 he could write that he would have condemned Ravaillac to be quartered, "without regrets";[30] in *Prix de la justice et de l'humanité* he urged the abolition of torture and the most sparing use of the simple death penalty. But this growing radicalism did not alter the legal philosophy he developed in the early 1760's: repression is necessary but it must be rational. Voltaire's land of Eldorado in *Candide* has no prisons, but then Eldorado is a Utopia. The only justification for repression is political rather than moral or religious; its aim is not the manufacturing of saints or vengeance upon sinners, but rather the securing of a social order at minimum cost to society in general and to the criminal in particular. Voltaire adopted Vauvenargues' businesslike definition of crime as an act that injures society: "This truth should be the foundation of all criminal codes."[31]

"This truth" had a radical influence on Voltaire's philosophy

30 Voltaire to Philippon, 28 December 1770, XLVII, 305.
31 *Relation de la mort du chevalier de La Barre*, XXV, 515.

because Voltaire was a secularist: so-called crimes against religion do not injure society. For a Christian rationale, Voltaire substitutes a secular rationale: "natural law" is adequate to teach men which acts must be prohibited. In addition to being a convenient anti-Christian slogan, this "natural law" is a generalization from history: experience tells us that society cannot survive if it permits theft, murder, or treason to go unchecked. It tells us further that there are exceptional circumstances that force the law-maker to enlarge his basic list with what Voltaire ingeniously calls "local offenses."[32]

Thus Voltaire establishes the nature of crime. His definition places him in the liberal legal tradition, with its emphasis on property rights, its separation of law and religion, its assumption that some things are too important and others too unimportant to be the proper business of criminal legislation. From this definition Voltaire concludes that the French legal code is cruelly out of date, for it proscribes a number of acts that are not crimes at all. This was a conclusion that Voltaire drew with pleasure, since it permitted him to be humane and anticlerical at the same time.

The most absurd of imaginary crimes were crimes against the Catholic church. Take "heresy," nothing but "erroneous opinion," an innocuous action branded as a heinous offense by

[32] *Dictionnaire philosophique*, article "Délits locaux (des)," 162-163; *Relation*, xxv, 510. *Délits locaux*, by their very nature, should be treated leniently. Diderot takes the same position on natural law and crime. See his attack on chastity, monogamy, and other Christian virtues, ending with this eloquent peroration: "Would you like to know what is good and what is bad in all times and places? Pay close attention to the nature of things and actions, to your relations with your fellow creatures, to the effect of your behavior on your own well-being and on the general welfare. You are mad if you believe that there is anything in the universe, high or low, that can add or subtract from the laws of nature. Her eternal will is that good shall be chosen rather than evil, and the general welfare rather than the individual's well-being. You may decree the opposite, but you will not be obeyed. By threats, punishment and guilt, you can make more wretches and rascals, make more depraved consciences and more corrupted characters. People will no longer know what they ought or ought not to do." *Supplement to Bougainville's "Voyage,"* in Diderot, *Rameau's Nephew and Other Works,* eds. Jacques Barzun and Ralph H. Bowen, 209.

French law. Voltaire conceded that suppressed sects have been dangerous to public order, but only because of their suppression, not because of their heresy: "If you want to prevent a sect from overthrowing a state, use tolerance."[33] Even more innocent than heresy was the "crime of preaching,"[34] a prohibition directed against Protestant ministers. Under the act of 1685 that revoked the Edict of Nantes, pastors were threatened with death, while Huguenots who continued to practice their religion faced a life sentence on the galleys or in prison. This ordinance was more than a threat. In the 1740's and 1750's hundreds of Huguenots were sent to the galleys, and hundreds of Protestant families lost their children to monasteries and nunneries or had their property confiscated. In February 1762, three weeks before Jean Calas was executed, the Huguenot pastor François Rochette was hanged in Toulouse with a placard on his chest, stigmatizing him as a "minister of the so-called Reformed Religion." Three Protestants who had tried to free Rochette from prison were decapitated.[35] They were the last Huguenot martyrs in France,

---

[33] *Questions sur l'Encyclopédie*, article "Hérésie," Part VII, 10; see *Commentaire*, xxv, 543-545; *Prix*, xxx, 346-349. This sentiment had earlier been expressed by Locke: "The magistrate is afraid of other churches, but not of his own, because he is kind and favorable to the one, but severe and cruel to the other. These he treats like children and indulges them even to wantonness. Those he uses as slaves, and how blamelessly soever they demean themselves, recompenses them no otherwise than by galleys, prisons, confiscations, and death. These he cherishes and defends; those he continually scourges and oppresses. Let him turn the tables. Or let those dissenters enjoy but the same privileges in civils as his other subjects, and he will quickly find that these religious meetings will be no longer dangerous. For if men enter into seditious conspiracies, it is not religion inspires them to it in their meetings, but their sufferings and oppressions that make them willing to ease themselves." A *Letter Concerning Toleration* (ed. 1955), 53-54.

[34] *Prix*, xxx, 566. Voltaire advocates (*ibid.*) that marriages between persons of different religions be legalized.

[35] Voltaire's efforts in Rochette's behalf were perfunctory at best, but Rousseau, equally informed, did nothing. In *Traité sur la tolérance* Voltaire reports that since 1745 eight Huguenot preachers had been hanged in France. xxv, 59. Some pastors were smuggled out of France, and there are indications in Voltaire's correspondence that he participated in this humane smuggling.

but not the last victims of a jurisprudence that invited the Catholic church to impose its doctrines on the public law.

For those who were still not convinced that such jurisprudence was irrational and barbarous, Voltaire offered in evidence the crime of sorcery. He reported that as recently as 1749 a woman had been burned as a sorceress in Germany, and he estimated that in the course of centuries Christian tribunals had assassinated over one hundred thousand persons on this charge. When we think of these judicial massacres, he wrote, and of the infinitely larger number of innocents burned as heretics, our part of the world appears "like a vast scaffold covered with executioners and victims, surrounded by judges, myrmidons, and spectators."[36] Like all other brain children of fanaticism, this so-called crime of sorcery was a phantom: as soon as courts stopped convicting people of it, the crime simply disappeared. By including sorcery in its code, France only displayed its backwardness. "Let us look at Prussia, England, Holland, Venice, and let the intolerant nations blush."[37]

And then, what could be more backward than to treat suicide as an infamous crime? Like Montesquieu, Voltaire defended man's right to end his own life: "The republic will do very well without me after my death, as it had done very well before my birth. I am discontented with my house, I leave it on the chance of not finding a better one. But you! What madmen you are to hang me by the feet when I am no longer alive! And what thieves you are to rob my children!"[38]

This was the Stoic speaking. When it came to adultery, bigamy, incest, sodomy, Voltaire spoke as the urbane Epicurean, with an amused indifference to the perversities of his fellow men. He was tolerant of homosexuals, although inclined to make jokes about them. With malicious appreciation Voltaire recorded in his *Mémoires* than Frederick II was equally tolerant

[36] *Commentaire*, xxv, 554; see *Prix*, xxx, 549-554; *Avis au public*, xxv, 520-521.

[37] *Prix*, xxx, 566; see *Commentaire*, xxv, 553-554.

[38] *Prix*, xxx, 543; see *Commentaire*, xxv, 567-569.

—perhaps, indeed, more tolerant than a man should be: "Some provincial judges wanted to burn some poor peasant accused by a preacher of a gallant intrigue with his she-ass. No one is executed without the king's confirmation of the sentence, a very humane law that is practiced in England and in other countries; Frederick wrote at the bottom of the sentence that in his state he permitted freedom of conscience and of b. . . ."[39] In France there was no freedom of "b. . . ." In July 1750 Raynal reported the summary treatment given homosexuals and prostitutes in Paris: "The parlement of Paris, which rarely makes examples of severity in certain genres, has had two men burned for the sin of nonconformity, and, in the same week, has had seven or eight women publicly whipped for the contrary sin."[40] Voltaire did not think of "nonconformity," or of its opposite, as a sin. Acts that offended respectable Christians need not be (and, Voltaire implied mischievously, probably were not) crimes. At worst they were minor offenses.[41]

This was an advanced position to take; when it came to "crimes" of which he himself might be accused, notably blasphemy, Voltaire became markedly cautious. He cannot have believed that men could insult God; his God was beyond human feelings. Yet he thought it safer to classify blasphemy as a local offense rather than as a wholly innocent act. He contrasted the humanity of the ancient Romans toward blasphemers with the depressing brutality of French practice: "Montesquieu has said, 'We must honor the divinity, not avenge it.' Let us weigh these words. They do not mean that we must give up maintain-

---

[39] I, 28.

[40] *Correspondance littéraire*, I, 450. The report is confirmed in detail by Barbier who adds the pertinent observation that the two workers who were executed had no influential friends to get them off. *Journal*, III, 148-149.

[41] On adultery, see *Questions sur l'Encyclopédie*, article "Adultère," Part I, 49-58. On bigamy, see *Prix*, xxx, 563. On incest, see *ibid.*, xxx, 566-567. On homosexuality, see *Dictionnaire philosophique*, article "Amour nommé Socratique," 18-21. While he was still a young man, he saved the abbé Desfontaines (who became one of his greatest enemies) from almost certain death for this offense by his intervention.

ing public order; they mean, as the judicious author of *Délits et des peines* has said, that it is absurd for an insect to believe that it can avenge the Supreme Being."[42] His circumspection was characteristic. He was trying to persuade a wide public, still largely Christian, that the French law must be drastically reformed, and his proposals were radical enough without the additional imputation that he was spreading materialism. "One cannot do everything at once," he wrote in a revealing tactical statement. "Hercules could not clean the stable of King Augeas in a day."[43]

To Voltaire, the most loathsome object in the Augean stable of French law was the theory of vindictive punishment. Death, often with brutal accessories, was the standard penalty for a wide variety of offenses. In practice the brutality was highly selective: the laws, as Beccaria and Rousseau understood, were made by and for the rich, and enforced against the poor. "The government of the old regime," Tocqueville tells us, "which in its dealings with the upper classes was so lenient and so slow to take offense, was quick to act and often harsh to a degree where members of the lower orders, peasants especially, were concerned. Of all the many records I have examined, not one mentions the arrest of bourgeois under instructions of the Intendant. Peasants, on the other hand, were constantly arrested in connection with the levies of forced labor or the militia; for begging, for misdemeanors, and countless other minor offenses."[44]

This point Voltaire did not see, or saw only very inadequately. He was far less concerned with the class character of justice than with its irrationality, and like most of the philosophes he put his humanitarian program in utilitarian terms: harshness and cruelty are not merely inhuman, they are uneconomical. Montesquieu and Beccaria had already suggested that severity of punishment, far from reducing crime, increased it. Voltaire

[42] *Commentaire*, xxv, 548.
[43] *Questions sur l'Encyclopédie*, article "Aranda," Part ii, 66.
[44] *The Old Regime*, 133.

adopted their suggestion: "I ask you if we could not diminish the number of offenses by making punishments more shameful and less cruel."[45] The defenders of the old order believed that respect for law stemmed solely from fear; the philosophes believed that this respect could be created by more positive feelings.[46]

Severity causes crime because the criminal who knows that he will be executed for a minor offense is tempted to eliminate a witness whose testimony will cost him his life. "Everything that is excessive in the laws tends to the destruction of the laws."[47] Voltaire added coolly that leniency was most useful: it kept the offender alive to do forced labors, a sentiment characteristic of bourgeois liberalism in the eighteenth century, and shared by the radical Rousseau. "Let the torments of criminals be useful," said Voltaire. "A hanged man is good for nothing, but a man condemned to public works still serves his country and is a living lesson."[48]

This was proportionality, a chilly, commercial kind of humanity. Yet its practical effect was far more humane than its utilitarian formulation would suggest. The European law codes of the eighteenth century abounded with severe and brutal punishments, and the introduction of proportionality could only result in the marked reduction of sentences. Voltaire, for example, opposed as excessive the confiscation of a convicted person's property, a penalty which in France followed conviction

[45] Prix, xxx, 586.

[46] See Voltaire's observation that in England the nation respects the laws because it has participated in making them. ibid., xxx, 584.

[47] Commentaire, xxv, 561; see Essai sur les moeurs, xi, 415; Prix, xxx, 535-538.

[48] Dictionnaire philosophique, article "Lois civiles et ecclésiastiques," 290. See Commentaire, xxv, 555-556; Prix, xxx, 545; Fragment des instructions pour le prince royal de *****, xxvi, 445. Voltaire's repeated remark that begging should be suppressed, in conjunction with this cold demand for proportionality, stamps him—at least on this issue—as a bourgeois ideologist. How strongly this view was held is evident from Rousseau's remark in the Contrat social: "There is not a single evil-doer whom one cannot render good for something. One has the right to put to death, even as an example, only the man one cannot preserve without danger." Voltaire's marginal comment: "bon." Havens, Voltaire's Marginalia, 51.

for murder, suicide, and other crimes. Confiscation, said Voltaire curtly, is robbery of the innocent by the state.[49] The death penalty was an even more flagrant example of disproportionate punishment. Voltaire denounced it as savage, wasteful, and stupid to condemn a person to death for forgery, for theft, for smuggling, and for arson.[50] Life was God's most precious gift; to deprive a person of it, no matter how guilty, was to assume an awful responsibility, a responsibility that must be hedged with precautions and exercised with the nicest discretion. "I do not propose the encouragement of murder, but the means of punishing it without a new murder."[51]

With this critique of the death penalty Voltaire placed himself in irrevocable opposition to the philosophy that had informed the ordinance of 1670. Punishment should be a deterrent, not vengeance; social control should be exercised economically, not harshly; morality should be treated as a private rather than a public matter. In article after article, the ordinance seemed to say that it was better to convict the innocent than to acquit the guilty; ever since *Zadig*, Voltaire had preached that it was better to let a guilty man escape punishment than to convict the innocent. In his view of justice, as in his view of God, Voltaire infinitely preferred kindness to cruelty.

3. PROCEDURES AND PROBABILITIES

In 1771 Voltaire wrote in a little pamphlet about the Montbailli case: "If a married couple, sleeping in the antechamber of their mother while she falls dead of apoplexy, are condemned as parricides, despite the sentence of the first judges, despite the conclusions of the Attorney General, despite the absolute lack of proofs and the unvarying denial of the accused, who is the man who must not tremble for his life? It is not a question here of a judgment rendered in accord with a rigorous and

---

[49] *Commentaire*, xxv, 570-572; *Prix*, xxx, 542-543. *André Destouches à Siam*, xxvi, 99.
[50] *Commentaire*, xxv, 567; *Prix*, xxx, 535, 540, 545.
[51] *Prix*, xxx, 540.

harshly interpreted law; it is an arbitrary judgment pronounced in defiance of the laws and of reason. One can see no justification for it but this: Die, for that is my will."[52]

"Who is the man who must not tremble for his life?"—this question reaches the heart of Voltaire's case against the French legal system. Continuously, almost systematically, that system offended against the rule of law. Under the rule of law the private citizen faces uniform procedures, rational methods of inquiry, penalties that apply to all, the absence of *ex post facto* legislation. All these permit him to predict the legal consequences of his acts. He knows what is legal and illegal; he knows, if he is committing a crime, what kind of crime he is committing, and (at least approximately) what kind of penalty he will receive if he is caught; he knows that another man committing the same crime would receive a similar sentence; he knows, finally, that if he is arrested for a crime that he has not committed, his chances of being declared innocent are excellent. But the French law permitted, indeed almost invited, what Voltaire called arbitrary judgments "pronounced in defiance of the laws and of reason." The Criminal Ordinance, Voltaire said in 1766, "is the only law that is uniform in the whole kingdom."[53] This circumspect and temperate estimate neglects to mention the defects of Colbert's code. An ill-matched collection of medieval survivals and later royal edicts, of Germanic, canon, and Roman law, it hardly deserved to be called a code. It permitted local customs, which it had presumably superseded, to be continued in force; it gave judges wide latitude in imposing torture or sentence; it failed to define some offenses while meticulously defining others, like sorcery. With terrifying regularity, the Criminal Ordinance sounded the notes of repressive and capricious authority: "Die, for that is my will."

---

[52] *La méprise d'Arras*, xxviii, 435. The last phrase—*telle est ma volonté* —is a parody of the royal formula of assent. Voltaire succeeded in clearing Montbailli's name (alas, posthumously), and in securing the acquittal of madame Montbailli.

[53] *Commentaire*, xxv, 573.

It was not easy to persuade the French public (which shuddered at horrors for a moment and then went to the opera) that it should substitute the rule of law for the rule of tooth and claw, that it should introduce a code that was rational, precise, and simple. As a reformer, Voltaire appreciated the practical significance of legal procedure; as a literate propagandist who knew his public, he was aware that such technical matters do not readily lend themselves to dramatic treatment. His passion for the concrete helped him to solve this literary problem. The legal polemics of his last fifteen years add up to a vivid arraignment of the Criminal Ordinance of 1670, but they succeed in being interesting and even entertaining. They illustrate the most technical points of procedure with some spectacular instance of a miscarriage of justice.

The Criminal Ordinance (this is the first count in Voltaire's arraignment) was so loosely drawn that magistrates had long since ceased to respect its vague rules. He cited the improper arrest of Jean Calas and the *monitoire* which implied the guilt of the Calas family contrary to the rule laid down in the Ordinance.[54] He cited the execution of the chevalier de La Barre, which had been based on a law that did not apply to him—a flagrant violation of the principle *nulla poena sine lege*.[55] He cited the execution of General Lally five years after he had lost Pondicherry to the British in 1761, for having "betrayed the interests of the king, of the state, and of the Company of the Indies," for "abuse of authority, vexations, and exactions." These phrases, Voltaire rightly argued, were vague, loose, equivocal; they hinted darkly at treason but merely meant that the French government was displeased with the policies of one of its officials. Voltaire had sarcastically suggested after the execution of the British admiral Byng that it might be useful to shoot an officer once in a while *pour encourager les autres*, but such proceedings bore little resemblance to the principle of the rule

[54] *Histoire d'Elizabeth Canning*, xxiv, 402. *Mémoire de Donat Calas*, xxiv, 388-389.
[55] *Relation*, xxv, 511.

of law that "there must be a precise law [that was violated,] and precise proofs," before there can be a conviction.[56]

Indeed (and this was Voltaire's second count) French procedure showed little regard for the accused. A person who was suspected of a crime was imprisoned in one of those "cesspools of infection" that Voltaire thought too cruel even for convicted criminals. Under French law, preliminary imprisonment was not considered to be a punishment, but Voltaire, remembering that the Calas family had spent months in chains, that prisons were foul dungeons run by venal officials, cut through this legalistic rationalization to the unpalatable truth: "Prison is a torment, no matter how short a time it lasts."[57] When an accused person escaped, he forfeited his property even if he was later proved innocent, and even before the trial had been completed. But, asked Voltaire, what could we expect an innocent man to do? He was face to face with a procedure that seemed expressly designed to convict him; he was shut in a pestilential hole perhaps for months, incommunicado, in irons, as if he had already been condemned. "O judges! Do you want the innocent accused person not to escape? Make it easier for him to defend himself."[58]

It was indeed hard for the accused to defend himself—this was the third count of Voltaire's arraignment. Under the rules of the Ordinance witnesses were interrogated secretly and separately, and the accused was questioned privately by the judge, and strictly prohibited from communicating with anyone, even a lawyer.[59] Until the prisoner confronted the witnesses against him, he might not even know for what offense he was being held.

[56] *Fragments historiques sur l'Inde, et sur le général Lally*, XXIV, 158. Voltaire reports (*loc.cit.*) that one of the judges said: "There was no single crime. . . . We based the judgment on his conduct as a whole." Lally was, in fact, not guilty of treason. He was the scapegoat for French mismanagement and French losses.

[57] *Prix*, XXX, 583.

[58] *Commentaire*, XXV, 575.

[59] On the other hand, persons accused of some minor crimes, like fraudulent bankruptcy, were permitted to communicate with an attorney. The inhuman logic of this provision did not escape Voltaire. *Le cri du sang innocent*, XXIX, 380.

But confrontation, as Voltaire noted, was a farce played to harden suspicion of guilt into certainty. The prisoner, ill-treated, ill-fed, fearful, often uncertain or wholly uninformed of the charges against him, was led from his dungeon to face the witness, narrowly restricted in the rebuttals he could offer or the questions he could ask. And the witness had every incentive to hold fast to his story: the Ordinance provided that witnesses who withdrew their deposition or who changed their testimony in essential particulars could be prosecuted for giving false witness. Thus whether the testimony was true, partly true, or false; whether it was an eyewitness report or a rumor; whether it had been given from a sense of duty, from malice, ignorance, or the desire for notoriety, it was likely to remain on the record. "In France we punish a witness who disavows [his testimony] after the *recolement,* that is, after his second secret interrogation," wrote Voltaire. "Punish him if he has allowed himself to be corrupted, but not on the mere supposition that he could be corrupted."[60]

The secretive character of French procedure gave a trial the Gothic atmosphere of a mysterious nocturnal combat; but, Voltaire argued, the object of a legal proceeding should be the discovery of the truth. To deny an accused the aid of an attorney is to fly in the face of nature, which teaches us that we should have recourse to others when we are too ignorant or too weak to help ourselves.[61] To try a person in secret, to permit judges to give their verdicts in secret, and to permit them to keep secret the reasons for their decisions, is to obstruct justice during the trial and to prevent justice after the trial if a judicial error has been committed. The Calas case had furnished Voltaire with a lesson in the meaning of secrecy. Unable to obtain the official records of the case, he had been compelled to make laborious and expensive inquiries, and to decide whether Calas was innocent or guilty on the basis of unofficial, inadequate, and fre-

[60] *Prix,* xxx, 580.   [61] *Commentaire,* xxv, 576.

quently contradictory reports.[62] Not long after that experience, Voltaire began to plead that the proceedings, the record, the verdict of a criminal trial should all be made public, as they were in England. "Justice is depicted with a bandage over her eyes, but must she be mute?"[63]

Voltaire's Anglomania, never wholly dormant, proved most useful in his writings on French law. Perhaps the most charming example of his sentimentalized picture of English legal procedure is the *Histoire d'Elizabeth Canning et des Calas*, which he wrote in July or August 1762, shortly after he had completed the *pièces originales*, the memoranda and declarations that the Calas family sent to the authorities and to influential private citizens. The *pièces originales* were moving documents, but d'Alembert informed Voltaire that they were almost unknown in Paris.[64] If the volatile French public wanted comedy rather than sober documents of injustice, Voltaire would give them the second in the guise of the first.

Hence Voltaire's tale of Elizabeth Canning: in 1753, young Elizabeth disappeared from her home in London for nearly a month. She returned thin, ill, almost without clothes. Questioned by anxious relatives and neighbors she told a story of having been kidnapped, taken to a house of prostitution ten miles from London, threatened and mistreated, kept on bread and water, until at last she had made her escape. As the girl regained her weight and her beauty, her neighbors filed a complaint against the persons she identified as her kidnappers; her circumstantial account, reinforced by the dubious testimony of a frightened servant, led a London court to condemn nine persons to be hanged.

After reporting this unlikely tale, Voltaire drew the moral:

[62] On 12 May 1762, one of Voltaire's informants wrote him from Montpellier about his inquiries into the Calas affair: "The magistrates, who ought to put the truth in the light of day, are obstinately silent." Quoted by Athanase Coquerel, fils, *Jean Calas et sa famille*, 218n.

[63] *Lettre de Donat Calas fils, à la dame veuve Calas, sa mère*, XXIV, 375.

[64] D'Alembert to Voltaire, 31 July (1762), XLII, 191.

"Fortunately, in England no trial is secret, since the punishment of crimes is designed as a public instruction to people, not as a private vengeance. All interrogations are made with open doors, and all interesting trials are printed in the newspapers." Before the execution could take place, a report of the trial fell into the hands of a "philosopher named Ramsay," who found the business preposterous. He published a small pamphlet in which he argued that Elizabeth Canning's story did not make sense—who would keep a young prostitute on bread and water when it was her business to please?—and that jurors ought to use common sense in arriving at a verdict. His reasoning convinced the sheriff and the jury, and the case was reviewed. Elizabeth Canning was found to have committed wholesale perjury—in reality she was a "little rascal who had gone away to have a child"—and the wrongfully condemned were saved. Voltaire concluded that such a happy ending was possible in England but not in France, and he made his invidious comparison more powerful by appending a sober account of the proceedings against the Calas family.[65]

This account, laced with the piquant touches of eroticism that were Voltaire's specialty, was based on a trial that had aroused much interest in London in 1753, but Voltaire's version greatly oversimplified and often distorted the case. It is not certain why Voltaire introduced these distortions. Perhaps the exact truth eluded him; more probably he wanted to draw a simple moral for a public easily bored by complexity. That is probably why Voltaire described the girl as beautiful when in fact she was plain; why he reported that nine persons had been condemned to death when actually it was only one; why he converted Elizabeth into a villainous little tart when in fact she had clearly not been pregnant and there was genuine mystery about her disappearance; why he attributed the reversal of the verdict to the labors of one philosophe when there had been a lively war of pamphlets and a series of complicated legal

[65] *Histoire d'Elizabeth Canning et des Calas*, XXIV, 399-402.

maneuvers. The exact truth, supposing that Voltaire knew what it was, would have weakened and confused the point he wished to make: in trials, secrecy has pernicious and often irreparable consequences.[66]

The Canning case provided some incidental illumination on another point of French procedure, the review of sentences. The Ordinance provided that sentences must be carried out promptly: the parlement of Toulouse had condemned Jean Calas on 9 March 1762 and he was executed on the following day. It was theoretically possible to appeal for royal intervention, but such intervention was rare; despite fervent appeals, Louis XV did not reverse or mitigate the barbarous sentence against the chevalier de La Barre.

In contrast, Voltaire pointed out, English law provided for an interval between sentence and execution, and for royal assent to each death sentence. It was the delay caused by this salutary provision that enabled the philosopher named Ramsay to read the record of this trial, write his pamphlet, persuade sheriff and jury, and save the lives of nine innocent people. Publicity itself was of inestimable value since it permitted rational supervision of the legal process by the community. But to the accused, publicity was of real use only if it was accompanied by a delay in the execution of the sentence and by royal review. Voltaire urged Frenchmen to import this provision of English law, and he put his case on the high ground of humanity: "Never allow a citizen to be executed," he advised an imaginary prince, "be he the lowliest beggar in your state, until his trial has been sent to you, so that you can have your *conseil* examine it. This wretch is a man, and you are accountable for his blood."[67]

[66] It is thus beside the point to criticize Voltaire's inaccuracies in his account of the Canning case as proof that he was a careless reporter, as is done in an otherwise flawless, and exciting, treatment of the case by Lillian de la Torre, *Elizabeth is Missing*, which tries to explain the mystery—I shall not say how.

[67] *Fragment des instructions pour le prince royal de *****, xxvi, 444. See *Commentaire*, xxv, 557; *Déclaration de Pierre Calas*, xxiv, 397; *La méprise d'Arras*, xxviii, 426.

French courts were only too casual with the blood of the accused, crippling the defense not only with an archaic trial procedure but also with an equally archaic and irrational system of obtaining proof. This was the fourth count of Voltaire's arraignment. The Ordinance of 1670 treated confession by the suspect as conclusive proof of guilt; "complete proof," usually requiring two eyewitnesses, was only slightly less definitive. Lower in the hierarchy of certainty were proofs of the second rank, such as incriminating documents or clues—*indices*. The weightier clues, *indices nécessaires*, were sufficient to secure conviction; slighter clues, the *indices prochains*, were treated as "half-proofs"; and suspicious indications, *indices éloignés*, such as confused answers or a trembling voice, entitled the magistrates to pursue their investigations.

If the magistrates lacked conclusive proof of guilt, but if they believed on the basis of *indices prochains* or *indices éloignés* that guilt was probable, they could draft a *monitoire* and subject the suspect to torture. From the trembling of a voice to burning at the stake was more than one step, but not many more.

The *monitoire*, to Voltaire a hateful reminder of the Inquisition,[68] was a list of questions prepared by the prosecution, asking all who had information on a case, "by hearsay or otherwise," to come forward and testify. It was posted on walls and solemnly read in all churches on three successive Sundays. On its final reading the *monitoire* was "fulminated": the faithful were warned that all who had withheld pertinent evidence would be excommunicated.

Voltaire rightly pointed to the demagogic uses of such an awesome device. The formidable circumstances of the reading and the threat of eternal damnation inflamed men's imaginations, excited fear, intimidated those who dared to defend the accused, and allowed gossips to disguise their exhibitionism as obedience to religion. In the La Barre case, said Voltaire, more

68 *Le cri du sang innocent*, xxix, 380.

dramatically than accurately, the *monitoire* had created an outcry over blasphemies that the public had long forgotten: "The public scandal was only in the procedure itself." He conceded that in exceptional circumstances a *monitoire* might be useful, but for the most part it invited malice, encouraged jealousy, protected ignorance, and exerted an irresistible pressure on the superstitious: "You are threatened with hell if you do not put your fellowman in danger of his life."[69]

Monitoires were designed to obtain information from witnesses; torture, euphemistically known as "the question," was designed to obtain information from the accused. Sometimes, torture was prescribed purely as punishment; more often, as with Jean Calas, it was prescribed partly as punishment, partly as an attempt to obtain a confession and revelations about accomplices.

The prominent place of confession in French law, the tacit assumption that a defendant was guilty until proved innocent (indeed, sometimes he was treated as if he were guilty even after he had been proved innocent), made the "question" a logical and almost indispensable procedure to the lawyers who drafted the Criminal Ordinance in 1670. Montaigne, and later Bayle, Fontenelle, La Bruyère, and Montesquieu, had put forward the obvious argument that torture was as absurd as it was barbarous: it would wring confessions from the innocent who were weak, and protect the guilty who were strong. The Ordinance disregarded this reasonable objection. Carefully it specified two major types of torture: the "preparatory question," designed to secure a confession, was applied before the final sentence; the "provisional" or "preliminary question," designed to obtain information about accomplices, was applied after the death sentence. The preparatory question was subdivided into two types, the "question with proofs reserved," which kept the accusations alive even though the defendant remained steadfast in his denials, and the "questions with proofs not reserved," which could purge the defendant of all suspicion. The preliminary question was subdivided into the "ordinary" and the "extraordinary question," hyperboles which designated different kinds and degrees of torment. "In the books which take the place of a code in France," wrote Voltaire with a fury made tremendously impressive by deliberate repetitions, "we encounter nothing but those terrible words: preparatory question, provisional question, ordinary question, extraordinary question, question with proofs reserved, question with proofs not reserved, question in the presence of two attorneys, question in the presence of a doctor, of a surgeon, question which one gives to young girls provided they are not pregnant. It seems that all these books were composed by the executioner."[70]

It may be admitted—and the many detractors of the philosophes have insisted on it—that it would be absurd to speak of a reign of terror or of mass torture in the France of Louis XV. Except in occasional flights of rhetoric, Voltaire also conceded that brutality had greatly declined. But the sufferings of Calas and La Barre were not isolated or particularly shocking instances; most Frenchmen accepted them rather casually, and torture had formidable defenders in the legal fraternity. Jean Calas was subjected to the ordinary and the extraordinary question—his arms and legs were pulled apart gradually, and he was compelled to swallow enormous quantities of water—before his limbs were broken on the wheel with an iron bar. The chevalier de La Barre suffered similar torments. Against such treatment Voltaire's rage can hardly be called excessive. In pamphlet after pamphlet he told the French public what humanitarians from Montaigne to Montesquieu had said before him: torture does not and cannot produce the truth; its torments, far more dreadful than a simple death sentence, are all too often imposed on

---

[70] *Prix*, xxx, 581. The only instance in which torture might be justified, according to Voltaire, was in the case of Ravaillac, the murderer of his beloved Henri IV. Marcello T. Maestro rightly points out that this is an unfortunate concession on principle, but I suspect that it was partly tactical. See *Voltaire and Beccaria as Reformers of Criminal Law*, 122-123.

those who have not yet been found guilty; countries like Russia, England, Prussia, Hesse, have abolished torture and reduced the crime rate at the same time.[71] In England, where needless cruelties had often been perpetrated, persons convicted of high treason could still be tortured, but the inhuman provisions of that law were not enforced. "It took time before that nation learned to join pity to justice. The time has come at last."[72] Thanks to Voltaire and the brethren, it was soon to come to France, although after Voltaire was dead. Two royal declarations, of 1780 and 1788, finally abolished all forms of torture.

The dreadful methods by which a French court obtained proofs were made more dreadful by the methods by which it weighed them. This was the fifth count in Voltaire's arraignment. Neither the *monitoire* nor torture could be used in the absence of suspicious clues. But there was wide variety of the use of *indices* in different jurisdictions which in itself was a sign that French rules of evidence were irrational. The parlement of Toulouse, of infamous memory, placed heavy reliance on "half-proofs," a logical monstrosity. "As there are half-proofs, that is to say, half-truths," wrote Voltaire sardonically, "it is clear that there are half-innocent and half-guilty persons. So we start by giving them a half-death, after which we go to lunch."[73] He noted that the magistrates of Toulouse went even beyond half-proofs in their quest for certainty: "They admit quarter-proofs and eighth-proofs. For example, they may consider a hearsay a quarter, a vague hearsay an eighth, in such a manner that eight rumors which are only an echo of an ill-founded report can become a complete proof."[74]

[71] This simultaneous reduction of the crime rate and abolition of torture showed the absurdity of the traditional defense of the practice. See *Prix*, xxx, 584; *Commentaire*, xxv, 558; *André Destouches à Siam*, xxvi, 98-99; *Questions sur l'Encyclopédie*, article "Question, Torture," Part VIII, 184-189; *ibid.*, article "Supplices," Part VIII, 244-251; *Dictionnaire philosophique*, article "Torture," 408-410.

[72] *Prix*, xxx, 584.

[73] *André Destouches à Siam*, xxvi, 99.

[74] *Commentaire*, xxv, 576. See Voltaire to Damilaville, 23 March (1763), XLII, 435-436.

This liberal use of *indices* invited grave abuses and glaring absurdities. An *indice*, Voltaire rightly pointed out, "is merely a conjecture,"[75] and a string of conjectures cannot logically add up to the complete proof upon which convictions can be based. Even a man caught in *flagrant délit* might have been acting innocently. The identical testimony of two eyewitnesses, which the French law accepted as a complete proof of guilt, might be mistaken and result in judicial errors. If even the supposedly complete proofs were doubtful, how much less reliable were the *indices* upon which persons were tortured and executed in France!

Voltaire the empiricist and skeptic conceded that perfect certainty was never possible and that public order sometimes required the verdict of guilty. He suggested that as a safeguard judges take probabilities into account in every trial. This advice sounds feebler than it is; it is meant as an appeal to common sense. It was common sense that had enabled the philosopher named Ramsay to save nine persons from the malicious perjuries of Elizabeth Canning; common sense would have saved Jean Calas from the outrageous imputation that he had performed a ritual murder upon his son; common sense would have condemned La Barre and his fellow delinquents to a few weeks in prison for their adolescent pranks. In two little-known essays Voltaire proposed an arithmetical method that would enable judges to compare probabilities. "It seems to me that half-certainty no more exists than does half-truth. A thing is true or false, there is nothing in between. You are certain or uncertain. . . . However, one must take sides, and one must not take sides at random."[76] Probabilities point to the truth, they do not establish it: "It is possible that twenty appearances against [the defendant] are balanced by a single one in his favor. This is the case and the only case for the doctrine of probabilism."[77]

[75] *La méprise d'Arras*, xxviii, 432.
[76] *Essai sur les probabilités en fait de justice*, xxviii, 496-497.
[77] ibid., 497. See *Nouvelles probabilités en fait de justice*, xxviii, 577-586; *Questions sur l'Encyclopédie*, article "Certain, Certitude," Part iii,

Voltaire's doctrine of probabilism is the doctrine of moderate, bourgeois common sense. It has the cool utilitarian sound of his doctrine of proportionality, but it rests on the humane doctrine that life itself is valuable. To protect life, Voltaire proposed that death sentences be given only by an overwhelming majority of judges. The Ordinance specified (and here is Voltaire's last count) that all judgments of the last resort be voted by a minimum of seven judges, and by a majority of at least two. Jean Calas had been sentenced to death by a vote of eight to five, and only after one member of the minority had been persuaded to join the majority which, with a vote of seven to six, had been too small to convict him; La Barre's sentence had been confirmed by the parlement of Paris by the slightly larger majority of fifteen to ten. These proportions deeply disturbed Voltaire: "How could men who are not carnivorous beasts ever have imagined that a few votes in the majority could suffice to give them the right to tear a human being to pieces in terrible torments? Would it not need at least the preponderance of three-quarters of the votes? In England all the jurors must be in accord, and that is very just. What an absurd horror to play at life and death of a citizen with the game of six to four, or five to three, or four to two, or three to one!"[78]

These words, Voltaire's testament to legal reform in France, were written near the end of his long life. They show how far he had traveled, from the witty man of letters to the technical critic of legal procedure, from the worldly friend of the great to the disinterested moralist. Most of his life he had been known as the author of the *Henriade* and of *Zaïre*; in his last years, as his plays grew feebler but his humanitarian energies remained strong, they called him "the man of Calas." Diderot

---

190; *Déclaration de M. de Voltaire sur le procès entre M. le comte de Morangiès et les Veron*, xxix, 25-32.

[78] *Prix*, xxx, 556. In *Relation* he proposed a three-fourth vote but argued that unanimity was preferable. See also his severe criticisms of Montesquieu for accepting a two-thirds majority. *Commentaire sur l'Esprit des lois*, xxx, 436-437.

spoke for the general public in *Le neveu de Rameau*: "Voltaire's *Mahomet* is a sublime work. But I would rather have rehabilitated the Calas family." It is a pity that these words were published after Voltaire's death; this warm tribute from such a cool admirer would have given him much satisfaction.

VII

FRANCE:
CONSTITUTIONAL ABSOLUTISM

Je n'ai point de sceptre, mais j'ai une plume.
—VOLTAIRE to madame Denis, 15 October (1752)

1. CONSTITUTIONAL ABSOLUTISM

THESE then are the politics of Voltaire: realistic and serious but rarely solemn, reformist and hopeful but rarely abstract. His assertion that he took no interest in political questions is as untrue as his critics' assertion that his radical program was merely the random energy of a creature of air and flame, the playfulness of an old child who quickly kindles and as quickly tires. Like Shaw's Don Juan he rebelled against a philosophy that looked at the world and found it good, and he cultivated the instinct that looked at the world and found that it could be improved. But unlike Shaw's Don Juan, he believed that it could be improved by political means.

Voltaire's practical political style vividly emerges for the last time in his polemics against the French parlements, the culmination of his life-long fight for the *thèse royale*. His admiration for English institutions, his royalism, his hostility to censors, his hatred of fanaticism, his passion for a humane and rational jurisprudence—all his political convictions, all his rancors and enthusiasms, were enlisted in his last great battle for French absolutism.

Voltaire had left France in 1750 defending the royal cause against the clergy; at Ferney in the late 1760's and early 1770's he defended the royal cause against the parlements, a far more energetic adversary to the crown than the church. The French clergy had forced the king to abandon his tax program, but the church's influence was waning. The philosophes were occupying stronghold after stronghold; by 1770 they had infiltrated the censorship, conquered the *Académie française,* and invaded the administration. Most Frenchmen did not accept the bold materialism of the Holbachian clique and hesitated to accept the more sedate deism of the Voltairians, but they were strongly anticlerical. Unsavory controversies within the church, slyly publicized by philosophic propaganda, had done the faithful much damage.

The expulsion of the Jesuits in the 1760's suggests how little control the crown had over these controversies. Ultramontane, royalist, urbane and sophisticated, the Society of Jesus had long excited the resentment of the Jansenist magistrates. Since Pascal's brilliant and cruelly unfair *Lettres provinciales,* the Jesuits had been a safe target for jokes, rumors, and slander. Even a good Christian could allow himself the pleasure of painting them as servants of a foreign power, sinister intriguers, and probably all pederasts. These dark accusations, some well-founded but mostly imaginary, came to be generally accepted in 1761, after the bankruptcy of a Jesuit house on Martinique. A Marseilles court made the Society financially responsible for the commercial losses of a single mission, and the Jesuits appealed the verdict to the hostile parlement of Paris, which was perhaps as good a sign as any that their celebrated shrewdness was in decline. The Jansenist judges gleefully confirmed the verdict, and initiated a comprehensive investigation into the statutes and political ideas of the Jesuit order. To no one's surprise, the investigators found what they were looking for: the Jesuits preached tyrannicide. Men who followed their maxims,

Voltaire wrote drily, "could gain paradise and the rope."[1] In August 1761 the parlement ordered the burning of twenty-four Jesuit works as irreligious and seditious, and moved to close the Jesuit *collèges*, while the philosophes, many of them products of these schools, fervently applauded. The king and the bishops tried to save the Jesuits, but they succeeded only in postponing their inevitable suppression until the following year.[2]

While Jansenist Christians persecuted Jesuit Christians, unbelievers rejoiced. D'Alembert wrote excitedly to Ferney that the parlements were executioners serving the philosophes without knowing it.[3] Voltaire, far more politically acute than his brethren, was afraid that the parlements were executioners serving no one but themselves, and that the magistrates were right to celebrate the suppression of the Jesuits as a great victory. He had savagely and ungratefully lampooned his old teachers in their prosperity, assiduously spread stories about their politics and their morals. Even the cannibals in *Candide* were Voltairians: they threaten to eat Candide only while they mistake him for a Jesuit.

But now that the French cannibals had eaten the Jesuits, the delicate natural balance that kept the enemies of philosophy and of the state at each others' throats had been disturbed:

Les renards et les loups furent longtemps en guerre:
Les moutons respiraient; des bergers diligents

[1] *Précis du siècle de Louis XV*, xv, 398. "In great affairs, there is always a pretext that is put forward, and a true reason that is hidden. The pretext for the punishment of the Jesuits was the supposed danger of their evil books which nobody read; the reason was the esteem they had long abused." *ibid.*, xv, 399.

[2] The "destruction" of the Jesuits, as it was called, took several years. In 1762, the various parlements suppressed the Society, the Jesuit *collèges* were closed; in 1764, a royal edict expelled the Society from France but permitted Jesuits to remain in the country as secular priests; in 1767, finally, they too were ordered expelled.

[3] Henri Carré, *Louis XV*, 327. Joseph Bertrand calls d'Alembert "more Voltairian than Voltaire." *D'Alembert* (1889), 117. The phrase is more revealing than Bertrand suspects. It suggests, quite rightly, that d'Alembert had Voltaire's political principles but not Voltaire's political sagacity, which permitted Voltaire not to push his principles too far.

Ont chassé par arrêt les renards de nos champs:
Les loups vont désoler la terre.
Nos bergers semblent, entre nous,
Un peu d'accord avec les loups.[4]

Voltaire had no reason to like these wolves. They had burned his books, and after they had chased the foxes, they began to burn people.

Voltaire had observed the growing political influence of the magistrates with dismay. After the regent restored the parlements' right to remonstrate in 1715, they emerged as the supreme enemy of reform. On more than one occasion an angry Louis XV exiled them to their country houses, but his attacks of courage failed to reduce the magistrates' power and only increased their popularity.[5] After the suppression of the Jesuits gave them a monopoly of resistance to the crown, the parlements' conduct fully justified Voltaire's fears: they strengthened their united front and launched demagogic appeals to a public already suspicious of "despotism" and "centralization."[6]

The crown could either surrender or fight. It chose to fight. The political crisis erupted in Brittany in 1764, when the estates

[4] Voltaire to Damilaville, 19 June (1763), XLII, 505. The Jesuits, he wrote to Bianchi, should be "sustained and contained" rather than destroyed. (? end of 1761), XLI, 573.

[5] In 1753, the parlements took an aggressive part in the debate over the refusal of sacraments to Jansenists; against the king's explicit orders, they debated and remonstrated. The robe nobles, Louis XV told his intimates, are an assembly of republicans: "The regent made a great mistake to restore their rights to remonstrate. They will end up by ruining the state!" To stave off that ruin, he dispersed the parlement of Paris in May 1753, but meekly recalled it in October. Carré, Louis XV, 239.

[6] There were perhaps no more than 2,000 robe nobles in the country, but they became more and more exclusive in the eighteenth century. It was precisely the relative recency of their noble status that made them so punctilious and so eager to limit their caste to a few families. Parlement after parlement decreed that new posts carrying nobility be restricted to individuals who belonged to families that were already noble. By the end of Louis XV's reign, the stream of social ascent had become a narrow and obstructed trickle. "The road is blocked in every direction," wrote the young Barnave. The frustrations of a whole generation of ambitious bourgeois are in that sentence. Lefebvre, The Coming of the French Revolution, 41.

refused to levy the royal *corvée* on the ground that the tax illegally infringed time-honored rights; the Breton parlement at Rennes, led by its Attorney General La Chalotais, sustained the estates and went on strike. A violent war of words broke out between La Chalotais and the duc d'Aiguillon, the military governor of Brittany; the central government, determined to enforce obedience, arrested La Chalotais and five other Breton officials. True to their policy of vocal cooperation, the other parlements energetically remonstrated with the king.

It was against this subversion of royal authority that Louis XV launched his celebrated lecture at the *séance de flagellation*. On 3 March 1766, he sternly told the parlement of Paris that provincial affairs were none of its business, that he would not tolerate a "confederation of resistance," that sovereignty and hence the law-making power were his alone, that the authority —indeed, the very existence—of the courts depended on the royal will, and that the parlements had the duty to register decrees if the king insisted on them.

These were powerful words, and they delighted Voltaire who was following matters closely from Ferney. "You have sent me a truly beautiful present in sending me the king's reply to the parlement," he wrote to Damilaville. "It's been a long time since I have read anything so wise, so noble, and so well written."[7] But the king's forceful tone ill concealed his defensive mood. The parlements were no longer afraid of royal bluster. Following their brief exile of 1753, they had perfected a bold aristocratic interpretation of the French constitution which pushed the *thèse nobiliaire* to unprecedented, dizzying heights. They adopted Montesquieu's notion that they were "intermediate powers" indispensable to civic freedom; in the words of one of their ideologists, the lawyer Le Paige, they claimed that "sovereign courts" were as essential to the French constitution as the monarchy itself. They revived the fanciful history of

[7] 12 March (1766), xliv, 243. How much the news elated him can be seen from the other two letters he wrote on the same day.

Boulainvilliers; they asked the crown to acknowledge that the registration of decrees was a legislative rather than an administrative act—a sign of the people's consent, a guarantee that the king's edict did not violate the fundamental laws of France. The French constitution, said the magistrates, adopting the language of natural rights and even of popular sovereignty, was a contract between king and people.[8] Since the people could not speak for itself, the parlements spoke for the people in a single voice: "All the companies of magistrates, known under the name of parlements, compose the court of the king, and are the diverse classes of a single and unique corps, animated by the same spirit, nourished by the same principles, occupied with the same object."[9] To remove magistrates from their posts, to treat the dozen parlements as separate bodies, to compel registration of edicts—all this was to overstep the boundaries of legitimate kingship and to move in the direction of despotism. Such claims sounded old, but in their sheer boldness, they were new; Louis XV significantly denounced them in the *séance de flagellation* as "pernicious novelties" which disregarded "the true fundamental laws of the state."[10] For even the most royalist of lawyers and the most vigorous of kings carefully distinguished between absolutism and despotism. They maintained that the

[8] It should be remembered that during and after the French Revolution the *thèse nobiliaire* was transformed into a weapon of French liberalism, while the *thèse royale* became a weapon of conservatives and authoritarians. But this subsequent history, which makes such present-day royalists as Pierre Gaxotte strong advocates of the *thèse royale,* does not affect my argument in the text.

[9] This is from a declaration of the parlement of Paris. Jules Flammermont, *Le Chancelier Maupeou et les parlements,* 126-127. The parlement of Rouen went so far as to say in 1756 that "no act is vested with the form necessary to give it the force of law if it is not verified by Your parlements, to whom alone belongs the right to communicate to the laws the final form essential to give them authority." *ibid.,* 121.

[10] *Remontrances du parlement de Paris au* xviiie *siècle,* ii, 557. Interestingly enough, when chancellor Maupeou attacked the parlements in 1770, he too insisted that his policy was in no way novel. The royalist position, he said, was based on "principles avowed and defended by our fathers and consecrated in the monuments of our history." Flammermont, *Maupeou,* 140.

crown had a monopoly of the legislative and executive power, but it did not follow that the king could do as he pleased. Advocates of the *thèse royale* from Bodin to d'Argenson subjected the crown to the unwritten fundamental laws of France and assumed, further, that the king would obey the decrees he had made.[11] This legal tradition was perhaps illogical in that it mixes elements from two positions usually treated as incompatible, constitutionalism and absolutism. But logical or not, it was this "constitutional absolutism" rather than naked despotism on which eighteenth-century royalists, including Voltaire, rested their case against the parlements.

This fine distinction between a legitimate and an illegitimate absolutism did not find a wide response. The magistrates' exiles were triumphant processions, their remonstrances were popular manifestos: it was the parlements' position that impressed the general public, and alternately intimidated and infuriated the king. It neither impressed nor intimidated Voltaire—it only infuriated him. He said again and again that he hated the "assassins of Calas," but his enmity to the parlements antedated the execution of Jean Calas and was political opposition more than abhorrence.[12] He condemned the magistrates' interpretation of the French constitution as a defense of archaic institutions and privileges, a verbal counterrevolution. The parlement

[11] Since the fundamental laws were unwritten, the precise nature of the French constitution was legitimately a matter of debate. There was general agreement that the fundamental law consisted (1) of the inalienability of the king's domain (usually interpreted to mean French territory), (2) of the Salic Law, which excluded women from succeeding to the throne, (3) and of the hereditary character of the crown, which kept it Catholic and confined it to legitimate sons of the king. Louis XIV, who knew these obligations well enough when he needed to cite them to escape an onerous duty, violated the last of these when he legitimized his bastards in 1714. Voltaire knew of these violations and admitted that the status of the fundamental laws was far from clear. See *l'A,B,C*, xxvii, 379-382.

[12] "With all of Europe I have abhorred the assassins of the chevalier de La Barre, the assassins of Calas, the assassins of Sirven, the assassins of the comte de Lally. . . . They have produced nothing but evil. As you probably know, I have never been their friend. I am faithful in all my passions." Voltaire to madame du Deffand, 5 May 1771, xlvii, 421.

of Paris, he wrote, "seemed to take the side of the people, but it obstructed the government and seemed to wish to establish its authority on the ruins of the supreme power."[13]

In the late 1760's, the parlements appeared close to success in this enterprise. They persistently refused to register royal edicts, ordered the arrest and trial of royal officials, inundated the country with remonstrances ever more seditious in tone. "This astonishing anarchy could not subsist," wrote Voltaire. "Either the crown must recover its authority, or the parlements must prevail. In such a critical moment, an enterprising and audacious chancellor was needed. He was found."[14]

That chancellor was René-Nicolas de Maupeou, member of an old robe family and former *président à mortier* at the parlement of Paris. He had exercised considerable influence in the government even before Louis XV appointed him chancellor in September 1768—it is probable that he inspired the king's harangue at the *séance de flagellation*—and there was nothing he liked better than to exercise influence. Serious, active, unscrupulous, indifferent to literature and hostile to men of letters, he was a man to fear. Diderot derisively called him "a nobody, without great fortune, without good family, without great talents, who made up for these deficiencies with servility, duplicity, a vengeful spirit, ambition and audacity."[15]

The parlements had good reason to fear their former colleague. So did his present colleagues: the duc de Choiseul, minister of foreign affairs and secretary of war, a powerful court favorite and the king's chief adviser, became the victim of Maupeou's machinations. As soon as he held the chancellor's seals, Maupeou plunged into the congenial tasks of trying to tame the parlements, undermine the position of Choiseul, and muzzle the philosophes.[16] Here was indeed a strange

---

[13] *Histoire du parlement de Paris*, xvi, 106.
[14] *ibid.*, xvi, 107.
[15] "Essai historique sur la police," *Diderot et Catherine II*, 127.
[16] In an autobiographical memorandum that Maupeou submitted to Louis XVI, he acknowledged without apology that he had "severe views"

ally for Voltaire, and the philosophes, who disliked and dreaded Maupeou, were appalled to find Voltaire ready to overlook the chancellor's vices for the sake of his program. But then Voltaire was never particular about his tactical affiliations.[17]

In the spring of 1769, Voltaire supported Maupeou's program, probably upon the chancellor's instigation, with a tendentious *Histoire du parlement de Paris*. It is a relatively minor achievement, but it is a full-scale history, remarkably informative and objective. Voltaire disavowed it immediately and pointed out that a "M. l'abbé Bigore" had written it, but he let it be known that he found this work, which pernicious gossips had falsely attributed to him, a sound and reasonable history.

In the preface, Voltaire-Bigore hinted suavely that earlier historians, including Hénault, had been hampered by their obligations or their prejudices. "Freedom alone knows and tells the truth."[18] It was regrettable (Voltaire wrote without regret) that the truth was not wholly pleasant. In France's perennial conflicts with papal arrogance, the parlement of Paris had served its country well. In the fifteenth century, it had sensibly opposed the payment of annates to the Papacy; in the sixteenth century, after much vacillation, it had accepted Henri IV and "returned to its earlier sentiments of patriotism which have

---

about literature, and had intended to strengthen the censorship to "purify" the profession of letters. Flammermont, *Maupeou*, 606. Pellisson cites a letter from Maupeou to Sartines, 8 December 1773, which shows that Maupeou wanted to make the censorship the last court of appeal, under no obligation to give reasons for rejecting manuscripts. *Les hommes de lettres*, 15.

[17] In *Le neveu de Rameau*, "He," who occasionally speaks for Diderot, says: "You would never have been able to write *Mahomet*, but then you wouldn't have praised Maupeou either."

[18] *Histoire du parlement de Paris*, xv, 445. Despite these bold words, it is evident that once the history was published, Voltaire had one of his attacks of panic. Even to his best friends—d'Argental and d'Alembert—he disclaimed authorship, and contended that only an author who had access to archives could have written this history. This disclaimer only suggests that Maupeou in fact supplied Voltaire with documents. See Desnoiresterres, *Voltaire et Genève*, 382.

been France's firmest ramparts against the enterprises of the court of Rome";[19] in the seventeenth century, it had vigorously supported Bossuet's Gallican declaration; in the eighteenth century, it had risen in justified wrath against the Bull *Unigenitus,* against the refusal of sacraments to Jansenists, and against the Jesuit order. This was an enviable record of service.

Further, Voltaire impartially acknowledged, in many a civil conflict the parlement of Paris had been no more at fault than its opponents. The Frondes had been produced as much by the cruelty of Richelieu, the rapacity of Mazarin, the ambition of Condé, as by the irresponsibility of the magistrates; in the ridiculous squabbles between Jansenists and Jesuits, the fanaticism of the Jansenist parlements had been hardly more reprehensible than the obstinacy of the Jesuit bishops.

A prejudiced, unrelieved attack on the parlement would have been much less damaging than this judicious praise: it was the magistrates' occasional service that threw their frequent disservice into pitiless prominence. Voltaire approvingly quoted the self-denying ordinance of a fifteenth-century magistrate— the proper business of a parlement is to administer justice rather than to meddle with political, financial, and military questions[20]—and reminded his readers that unfortunately such rational modesty was rare. Over and over, the parlements had proved themselves reactionary, selfish, divisive, irresponsible, superstitious, and intolerant. They were reactionary, for they had persistently opposed salutary innovations in French life, from the establishment of the *Académie française* to the *Encyclopédie,* from inoculation against small pox to the gratuitous administration of justice. They were selfish, for they claimed to safeguard the traditional rights of Frenchmen, while they defended the interests of only a small privileged caste. They were divisive, for they had instigated religious wars in the sixteenth, civil war in the seventeenth, class war in the eighteenth

[19] *Histoire du parlement de Paris,* xv, 558.
[20] *ibid.,* xv, 481.

century. They were irresponsible, for without a shred of legal jurisdiction, they had tried the dauphin Charles in 1420. They were superstitious, for they had condemned the first printers in France, applauded Saint Bartholomew, and condemned the maréchale d'Ancre to be burned as a witch. They were intolerant, for they harassed men of letters, persecuted Protestants, and tortured the innocent.

This parade of facts, offered soberly, with few tricks of rhetoric and few appeals to emotion, adds up to an unsparing condemnation of the aristocratic position. For the most part the *Histoire* is history; it makes few contemporary allusions, but it makes its contemporary point forcefully: from its medieval beginnings, the parlement of Paris has acquired no legislative or administrative rights. Since it did not have the right to try a peer in 1420, it has no right to try the duc d'Aiguillon in the 1760's; since the parlements were created one by one during the Middle Ages, they have no right to associate themselves into a single corps in the eighteenth century;[21] since the first deposit of laws under Philip the Fair was no more than an administrative convenience, eighteenth-century parlements have no constitutional right to veto legislation. This is the burden of Voltaire's *Histoire du parlement de Paris*. It restates the king's speech at the *séance de flagellation*, at greater length and with more impressive documentation.

The magistrates, persuaded that royal actions would never match royal words, did not choose to take seriously the warning implicit in Voltaire's book. In the summer of 1766 Louis XV had recalled the duc d'Aiguillon and restored the old parlement of Britanny except for its attorney general and his five associates. The Bretons were not satisfied with this partial victory; stirred by La Chalotais' account of his sufferings, they demanded the restoration of all their members, and initiated a

---

[21] Voltaire quotes an edict of Philip the Fair, which, he explains, "makes it evident . . . that these tribunals were established to judge cases, that they all had equal jurisdiction, that they were independent of each other." *ibid.*, xv, 455.

prosecution of d'Aiguillon for a series of sensational and improbable crimes. D'Aiguillon, eager to be cleared, requested a trial by his peers, and such a trial actually began in April 1770 before the parlement of Paris, but the king quashed all proceedings at the end of June and ordered all to observe silence on the case.

But silence was not to be had, for Maupeou was trying to precipitate a crisis. His program of reform and his dependence on madame Du Barry, d'Aiguillon's intimate and Choiseul's enemy, made him decide to move quickly and decisively. He persuaded Louis XV that the crown must finally crush parlementary pretensions, and that Choiseul, the ally of the magistrates, must go. In September, he delivered an offensive harangue to the parlement of Paris, haughtily demanding its dutiful obedience. Two months later, he sent it an edict which stigmatized the magistrates as "victims of the *esprit de système*"[22] and as disseminators of "new ideas" dangerous to the public order, and forbade them to use the terms "unity, indivisibility, classes," to send proceedings concerning one parlement to others, to go on strike by resigning or refusing to sit on cases, to reopen discussion or obstruct administration of edicts that had been registered: "We permit them once again to make such remonstrances or representations they deem fit for the good of Our people and the good of Our service before Our edicts, declarations, or letters patent have been registered. ... *Car tel est notre plaisir.*"[23]

The king's pleasure was not the magistrates' pleasure. Pro-

[22] Voltaire, himself a lifelong opponent of the *esprit de système*, was much amused to see Maupeou denouncing the nobility of the robe for being infected with it. Voltaire to d'Alembert, 19 December (1770), XLVII, 290. It is probable that some of the correspondence between Voltaire and Maupeou has been lost, but we have a flattering letter from Voltaire to Maupeou of 22 August (1770), which proves that they were in direct touch. XLVII, 182.

[23] Flammermont, *Maupeou*, 116-120. As early as September, the parlement of Paris had protested that the chancellor was contemplating changes in the form of government "against the letter and the spirit of the fundamental laws." *ibid.*, 105.

testing that it had always labored to enhance royal authority, the parlement of Paris defied the king, and refused to register Maupeou's edict. But Louis XV could be firm when he had someone to lean on—on 7 December 1770 he presided over a *lit de justice* in which Maupeou delivered an able address restating and clarifying the crown's constitutional position.[24]

Half persuaded that its legal position was untenable, and wholly unwilling to make this fact official by accepting the edict, the parlement continued its resistance, closed its doors to legal business and sent its *premier président* to the king. He was not admitted. Louis XV was now determined to prevail: on 20 December he signed Maupeou's draft of *lettres de juission*, ordering the magistrates to abandon their disobedience. Four days later, Choiseul was dismissed and d'Aiguillon was brought into the cabinet.

Thus the fortunes of politics placed Voltaire in a cruel dilemma which he resolved in characteristic fashion. Cultivated and witty, Choiseul had been an adherent of madame de Pompadour and an enemy to the Jesuits; he, his wife, and his wife's intimate, madame du Deffand, had long been Voltaire's correspondents. During his rivalry with Maupeou, he strongly supported Voltaire's plan to build the free port of Versoix near Geneva. Voltaire had much reason to regret his dismissal, and regret it he did, loudly and unconvincingly.[25] Maupeou, on the other hand, was everything that a man of letters must distrust. But Choiseul had made himself into an instrument of the magistrates, and Maupeou, whatever his character, was the most inventive and the most energetic advocate of the *thèse royale*

---

[24] There is nothing new in this address: the parlements' pretension to "free verification" of edicts, he said, has no place in the French constitution: "When the legislator wants to manifest his desires, you are his organ, and his goodness permits you to be his counsel; he invites you to enlighten him by your intellect, and orders you to show him the truth. Your office ends there." Flammermont, *ibid.*, 141.

[25] "Monsieur le duc and madame la duchesse de Choiseul have been a great loss to me. Whoever depends on the court cannot depend on anything." Voltaire to Bertrand, 7 January (1771), XLVII, 317.

since Machault. So like Byron's Julia, who "whispering she'd ne'er consent, consented," Voltaire, proclaiming that he'd ne'er desert his friend, deserted him.[26]

Politically, at least, Voltaire's choice was wise. Maupeou needed and deserved support. The magistrates continued to refuse to register the edict, and the public, inflamed against the chancellor by libelous brochures, angered by the dismissal of the popular Choiseul, vocally abetted this disobedience. On 3 January 1771, and again a week later, the king repeated his orders; the magistrates agreed to go back to work, but submissively informed their sovereign that they could not register an act that violated the fundamental laws of France. On 20 January, between one and four in the morning, every Parisian magistrate was awakened by two royal musketeers bearing a *lettre de cachet*, which ordered him to signify his obedience or disobedience in writing, "without evasions or dodges."

The proud nobles of the robe were not to be intimidated. An overwhelming majority, protesting its love for Louis XV, replied in the negative. Within the next two days, 165 members of the Paris parlement were deprived of their posts and exiled to the country. Voltaire was pleased but not wholly satisfied: "It is a pretty feeble consolation," he wrote to d'Alembert on 2 February 1771, "that the assassins of the chevalier de La Barre are in their country houses; but we can no longer hope for justice in this world."[27]

[26] Naturally enough, both the duc and the duchesse de Choiseul regarded Voltaire's act as a betrayal. In exile at Chanteloup, the ex-minister was strengthened in this conviction by his immense popularity. Crowds gathered to see him, aristocrats ostentatiously visited him—and François-Marie Arouet, bourgeois poet, had cast in his lot with the dour tyrant who had displaced him! In the face of their anger, Voltaire continued to write his explanations to Chanteloup, but his letters only exasperated him and his friend, madame du Deffand. See Voltaire to duchesse de Choiseul: "I shall die as faithful to the faith I swore to you as to my just hatred against the men who have persecuted me as much as they could, and would still persecute me if they were still the masters." XLVII, 428-429.

[27] XLVII, 340. The remark is inaccurate; fewer than half of the magistrates were exiled to their properties, and some of the elderly judges suffered real hardships on the icy roads to their places of exile. Just how much

This callous and vindictive observation placed Voltaire in the vanguard of a small minority who applauded Maupeou's *coup d'état.* Condorcet, d'Alembert, and to some extent even Diderot, sometimes echoed Voltaire's tone, but none of them had Voltaire's political sagacity, none of them saw as clearly as Voltaire that Maupeou's program was the best, perhaps the only, hope for saving the country from revolution.[28]

The immense and unshakeable popularity of the parlements suggests how little rational political discussion there was in eighteenth-century France. Every single charge of Voltaire's against the parlements could be documented over and over again; the counterrevolution of the robe nobility was what German sociologists have called a "reinfeudation" of society in an age when feudal institutions, feudal exemptions and privileges were becoming more and more damaging to stable government. It should have been obvious that in the midst of prosperity France was nearing bankruptcy, that taxation weighed most heavily on those least able to bear the burden, that trade and industry were crippled by archaic restrictions and absurd

---

the parlementarians suffered, and just how much of it was deserved, depends in a striking degree on the political position of the writer. Flammermont's *Maupeou* has much pathetic description of the deprivations of the magistrates, while the royalist Pierre Gaxotte finds their sufferings comical, and concludes that the king had shown admirable forbearance and that the punishment of the judges had been deserved a hundred times over. *Le siècle de Louis XV*, 460-461. Gaxotte, I think, is right.

[28] Kingsley Martin writes: "The *philosophes*, indeed, had supported the King against the *Parlements*. They favoured 'enlightened despotism' and criticized Louis, not for his despotism, but for his lack of enlightenment." *French Liberal Thought in the Eighteenth Century*, 86. This greatly underrates Voltaire's isolation; it suggests that all the philosophes had the good political sense that, in fact, Voltaire displayed almost alone. Thus Diderot told Catherine II that the parlements did not enjoy public esteem because they did not deserve it, but at the same time he did not approve of Maupeou's program, since the parlements' power to supervise legislation prevented tyranny. *Diderot et Catherine II*, 110, 112, 115. René Hubert has shown that the Encyclopedists, including Diderot, had considerable sympathy with the Germanic theory of the French constitution and were more or less unwitting allies of Montesquieu. *Les sciences sociales dans l'Encyclopédie*, 110-127.

customs barriers, and that fiscal and administrative reforms were overdue.

But it was not obvious, and the central government, which might have explained its policies to gain public support, never explained them. Under Louis XV, the target of flattery and contradictory advice, minister succeeded minister and cabal succeeded cabal. Many of the king's ministers were incompetent, and when they were competent administrators, they were all too often inept politicians, like Turgot,[29] or unpopular, like Machault, or indifferent to public opinion, like Maupeou. The government operated privately, and seldom asked men of letters to come to its aid. The case for its policies was often excellent, but it was rarely made. Catherine II, looking back upon the royal fiasco at the beginning of the Revolution, rightly observed that the king and his ministers had failed to make themselves masters of public opinion.[30]

The magistrates, on the other hand, were united by ties of profession, family, and interest; they knew what they wanted and they were highly sensitive to the public mood. They exploited each bread riot, each grain shortage, each rise in prices, to pose as the defenders of the public interest. They staged spectacular investigations, spread stories about the speculations of royal officials, and resorted to demagogy the crown was too proud or too foolish to refute. To the public, politically uninformed, superstitious, and conservative, the magistrates were the guardians of the general interest, the enemies of the Jesuits, the representatives of the people. It saw the central government at its worst—the dragoon and the tax farmer; it overlooked the government at its best—the intendant. Most Frenchmen lived near the starvation level; their favorite topics of conversation were the price of bread and rumors about government officials

[29] An exception must be made for Turgot's work as intendant of Limoges: there he adroitly explained his tax and road building program to the public and as result had wide public support—an instructive experience.

[30] 10 August 1789, quoted in Lortholary, Les *"philosophes"* et la mirage russe, 308.

making fortunes in the grain market. Magistrates were popular heroes, but representatives of the king all too often appeared as speculators in starvation. The tenacity of this parlementary mystique can be surmised from Tocqueville's comment, made eighty-five years after the event: "When in 1770 the parlement of Paris was dissolved and the magistrates belonging to it were deprived of their authority and status, not one of them truckled to the royal will. . . . In the history of free nations I know of no nobler gesture than this."[31]

It was this attitude that drove Turgot and Voltaire to despair. Turgot tried more than once to rouse the government from its lethargy. "The magistrates have always sought to display themselves as the protectors of the people against the Crown," he wrote, "but the crown would do well to unmask these magistrates and to show them as they really are—as corporations little interested in the well-being of the masses."[32] Maupeou worked against, rather than with, public opinion. For a month after the exile of the Paris parlement he tried in vain to carry on with a makeshift court composed of cabinet ministers and administrative officials, but lawyers refused to serve before this "interim parlement" and even the princes of the blood, usually so docile, protested that an "arbitrary absolutism" was being introduced into the French government. On 23 February 1771, Maupeou therefore proceeded to the second, constructive stage of his *coup d'état*: he published several edicts over the king's signature introducing drastic reforms into the magistrature. They abolished the venality of office and of justice, and greatly reduced the territory and jurisdiction of the parlement of Paris, creating in its place six "superior councils" to administer justice. Voltaire was delighted with this reform. "Nothing is nobler and more useful," he wrote on 27 March 1771, "than the establishment of six sovereign councils. This

---

[31] *The Old Regime*, 116-117.

[32] Quoted in Douglas Dakin, *Turgot and the ancien régime in France*, 71. Dakin shows that this complaint is a persistent theme in Turgot's correspondence.

alone should make the reign of Louis XV precious to the nation. Those who rise up against this benefit are sick people who complain of the doctor who restores their health."[33]

Most Frenchmen were complaining heartily about their doctor: Louis XV was compelled to enforce registration of the February edicts in a *lit de justice* of 13 April. In words that Voltaire might have written, the king praised the Maupeou reorganization for reducing the expense and increasing the certainty of justice. "You have heard my wishes . . ." he concluded dramatically. "I shall never change."[34]

For once in his long reign the king meant what he said. By 1772, more and more lawyers and magistrates consented to serve in the new courts, fewer and fewer libels circulated against the chancellor. Some minor scandals, greatly exaggerated by a hostile public opinion, marred the work of the new courts, but in general the reform appeared successful and promising. At last it seemed possible that the counterrevolution of the robe nobility might be stopped, and that a bureaucratic absolutism, rational and modern, might be imposed on the country.

This was Maupeou's aim, and Voltaire's as well. To achieve it, he followed up his *Histoire du parlement de Paris* with a series of short pamphlets, containing nothing new, and important only as propaganda efforts designed to undermine the popularity of the magistrates. This popularity, Voltaire argued, rested on ignorance of their history, misunderstanding of their function, and susceptibility to their rhetoric. "You seem to be afraid that tyranny might some day take the place of reasonable power," he told the magistrates' partisans, "but let us be even

---

[33] Voltaire to de Rochefort, XLVII, 402. In several other letters of February and March, he extolled the substitution of six councils for the huge parlement of Paris as making justice more efficient. See Voltaire to Veymerange, 25 February (1771), XLVII, 366; and Voltaire to Tabareau, 4 March (1771), XLVII, 374. See also Voltaire's appreciative poem addressed to Maupeou in 1771, X, 588; and the note he added to the *Essai sur les moeurs* in 1775: Maupeou abolished the "infamous venality of judicial office" and the "opprobrious presents" to judges, but alas both were restored in 1774. XII, 203.

[34] J. de Maupeou, *Le chancelier Maupeou*, 121.

more afraid of anarchy, which is only a tumultuous tyranny."[35]
The English estates general, which represent the people of
England, are called a "parliament," but the French bodies with
a similar name are neither estates nor representatives of the
people. French magistrates are exploiting a purely verbal resemblance and are turning the facts inside out: "How do you
begin? By declaring that benefits of the king are oppressions;
by forbidding obedience to the most salutary orders."[36] They
are equally untrustworthy in their interpretation of the French
constitution: it is the king and his ministers who know the
common good, not the parlements, with their narrow *esprit de
corps*; the king is sole legislator and has full authority to call
the nobles together to advise the crown; the parlements' duty
to register decrees is no more than a convenience; the courts
are "respectable organs of the laws, created to follow and not
to make them."[37]

Voltaire found it incomprehensible that the people should
so stubbornly resist the very reforms it needed so desperately,
but he expressed confidence that good sense would conquer
prejudice. "It is raining remonstrances," he wrote hopefully,
but, as it turned out, inaccurately. "People read the first, skim

[35] *L'Equivoque*, xxviii, 424. As with his support of Machault, Voltaire's
support of Maupeou elicited from him some general statements that have
been much misinterpreted. Who has not heard of this apparent defense of
despotism: "I prefer obeying a fine lion, who is born much stronger than I
am, than two hundred rats of my own species." This phrase occurs in a
letter to Saint-Lambert, significantly on 7 April (1771), xlvii, 408. It is
thus not a statement of general preference, but a comment on the contest
between Maupeou and the parlementarians. The "two hundred rats" are, of
course, the magistrates of Paris, exiled three months earlier. Georges Pellissier, *Voltaire philosophe*, 249-250, has some sensible comments on this
remark, but he is an exception.

[36] *L'Equivoque*, xxviii, 423.

[37] *Les peuples aux parlements*, xxviii, 413. Since Voltaire's pamphlets
are nothing more than restatements of what he and others had been saying
for years, I have summarized them in this brief paragraph. His contributions to the Maupeou debate are: *Lettre d'un jeune abbé, Réponse aux
remontrances de la cour des aides, Fragment d'une lettre écrite de Genève,
Avis important d'un gentilhomme à toute la noblesse du royaume, Sentiments des six conseils établis par le roi et de tous les bon citoyens, Les
peuples aux parlements, L'Equivoque*, xxviii, 383 *et seq.*

through the second, yawn at the third, and ignore the last."[38] He predicted that Maupeou would win enduring popularity: "I watch the battle with tranquility . . ." he wrote on 24 June 1771. "I am absolutely sure that the chancellor will carry off a complete victory and that people will love the victor."[39]

But Louis XV died on 10 May 1774, and his successor, who had enthusiastically applauded Maupeou's program when it was first proposed, promptly destroyed it with no less enthusiasm. Before the year was out, Maupeou had been dismissed, the old parlements had been recalled, and the robe nobility was again entrenched in its strategic position.

It has often been suggested that with Maupeou's great *coup d'état*, "the whole of the ancient Constitution of France had been wiped out."[40] This is to exaggerate Maupeou's break with the past and to accept the magistrates' version of the fundamental laws of France. Supplanting the parlement of Paris with six councils was indeed a frontal attack on an ancient institution, but it was largely a defensive measure, a revolution designed to stave off a revolution. In his letters patent of 1673, Louis XIV had almost completely silenced the parlements; in his reforms of 1771, his successor had gone further only because the magistrates had driven him further. "The parlement lost its liberty by its license," wrote Voltaire in his notebook about the events of 1673.[41] He could have written the same words about the events of 1771.

As a proponent of constitutional absolutism for France, Voltaire rejected the widespread assertion that Maupeou's *coup d'état* established despotism in France. It led toward absolutism, but absolutism need not, indeed must not, be arbitrary. It is not only in his play *Les lois de Minos*, which the angry

[38] *Lettre d'un jeune abbé,* xxviii, 383.
[39] Voltaire to Mignot, xlvii, 460.
[40] Kingsley Martin, *French Liberal Thought in the Eighteenth Century,* 82.
[41] *Notebooks,* 97.

duchesse de Choiseul thought had been written to glorify Maupeou, that Voltaire distinguished between the legitimate and the illegitimate exercise of royal authority.[42] The distinction appears as early as 1731 in the *Histoire de Charles XII* and 1734 in the *Lettres philosophiques*, and as late as 1777, in his drama *Agathocle*. The tyrant of Syracuse, Agathocles, hands his throne to his son who in turn renounces power and gives it to the people to whom it rightfully belongs. In a dramatic speech in the last scene, the new, just tyrant descends from the throne:

> Peuples, j'use un moment de mon autorité:
> Je règne . . . votre roi vous rend la liberté.
> (Il descend du trône.)[43]

We should not dismiss this drama of self-abnegation as the Utopian dream of a senile poet: Voltaire had never been an indiscriminate royalist. In his major histories, he had supported the king's cause in France, but he never hesitated to criticize those—like Louis XI, Richelieu, and even Louis XIV—who advanced that cause at the expense of the rule of law. Long before the abbe Sieyès became famous for asserting the claims of the third estate, Voltaire wrote that the third estate was the nation itself,[44] and praised Louis XII for the edict of 1499— "forever memorable"—which ordered people "always to follow the law, despite the orders contrary to law which importunity could wring from the monarch."[45]

Voltaire's constitutional absolutism is patently open to a serious objection: it fails to provide institutions to determine

---

[42] See Prologue, p. 16. For madame de Choiseul's remark on this play, see Desnoiresterres, *Voltaire et Genève*, 401-402.

[43] VII, 430. See the famous couplet from his *Don Pèdre* (1775), in which the king is told:
> Vous n'êtes plus qu'un homme avec un titre auguste,
> Premier sujet des lois, et forcé d'être juste.
> Act II, scene 3. VII, 274.

[44] *Siècle de Louis XIV*, xv, 5; *Histoire du parlement de Paris*, xvi, 12.

[45] *ibid.*, xv, 484-485. See also this interesting observation: "Cromwell never abused his power to oppress the people. He made the nation flourish internally and respected externally. Usurper and not tyrant." *Notebooks*, 110.

whether the king is observing the rule of law, and to resist him if he should disobey it. "Enlightened despotism," as I have repeatedly said, is not an apt phrase to characterize Voltaire's political program, even for France. But his royalism seems to leave him almost defenseless against despotism, enlightened or unenlightened.

It is improbable that Voltaire would have admitted the force of this objection. He was willing to use Maupeou, but his version of good government was not the same as the chancellor's.[46] Maupeou sought absolute centralized power for the sake of reform, unhampered by competing institutions or by criticism. Voltaire too wanted to employ royal power as the engine of reform in France, but as a radical man of letters, with a firm faith in education, he wanted to check and guide that power by the force of public opinion. That opinion was not embodied in formal institutions as it was in England, a country lucky enough to have a real parliament and rudimentary political parties. But public opinion could exercise influence, and as the enlightenment of the middle classes grew, that influence too would grow. Voltaire's persistent demand for free speech in all matters, including religion and politics, envisaged a rational administration, governing through fixed rules and cooperating with a free and informed public.

Moreover, France was faced with a condition, not a theory. The only available institutions to check the crown in 1771 were the parlements and the provincial estates, but Voltaire had no faith in either of them, and modern historians have come to accept his judgment. Not long after Maupeou was dismissed, the parlements' treatment of Turgot gave another,

[46] I cannot emphasize enough that Voltaire's tactical alliances do not necessarily give reliable testimony concerning his permanent preferences. He was even willing on occasion to support the parlements. On 13 November (1765), in the midst of his mediating efforts in Geneva, he reread the Bull *Unigenitus* and wrote to d'Argental: "If I hold an even balance between the Citizens and the Council of Geneva, it is not thus with the quarrels between your parlement and your clergy. I declare myself flatly in favor of the parlement, but I make no promises for the future." XLIV, 109.

conclusive demonstration that they were bodies dedicated to the preservation of privilege rather than to the securing of the general good.

Anne-Robert-Jacques Turgot was a public servant of exceptional intelligence and independence. He was identified with the physiocrats, but he rejected their tenet that land was the only source of wealth; he was counted among the philosophes, but he did not share their hostility to organized religion; he was a Catholic, but he advocated toleration of Protestants. As a young intellectual he had delivered an epoch-making discourse on the theory of progress; as a mature administrator he had served brilliantly as intendant of Limoges. Voltaire was greatly taken with Turgot; he was delighted when Louis XVI took him into his cabinet, first as secretary of the navy, and then in August 1774, in the strategic post of controller general.

It was inevitable that a man as able and as disinterested as Turgot must make powerful enemies. "Woe to France," Voltare wrote prophetically in December 1774, "if he were to leave his post!"[47]

Energetically, Turgot attacked the problems facing the grain trade and initiated some modest reforms of the tax system. Opposition soon arose; it was not only his ability, it was also his policies that endangered his future in the cabinet. His advocacy of toleration aroused the clerical party; his opinionated honesty annoyed the remaining supporters of Choiseul; and his economic and fiscal program offended the vested interests of the privileged classes. Turgot, wrote Voltaire to Condorcet on 26 April 1775, was the greatest man in France, whose policies were being obstructed by "abominable popular and parlementary superstitions."[48]

Superstitions were Voltaire's specialty, and he tried to dispel

[47] Voltaire to de Lalande, 19 December (1774), II, 171. For Voltaire's close interest in Turgot's career, see his letter of congratulation to Turgot, 28 July (1774), II, 42; Voltaire to d'Argental, 23 September (1774), II, 84-85; and Voltaire to d'Alembert, 28 September (1774) II, 89-90.
[48] II, 286.

them in Turgot's behalf, not always adroitly. His *Diatribe à l'auteur des Ephémérides*, circulated in Paris in August 1775, was a vigorous defense of free trade. But it was also, to Turgot's intense embarrassment, a vehement attack on the French clergy.[49] Far from disarming opposition to Turgot, Voltaire's pamphlet stimulated and united it.

Turgot was neither a politician nor a courtier. He was an administrator who knew that he was right and his opponents wrong. Early in 1776 he persuaded Louis XVI to support an expansion of his reform program. The celebrated Six Edicts brought free trade to Paris; suppressed archaic duties on food and unnecessary offices connected with the food trade; destroyed the systems of guilds that hampered the movement of skilled labor, investment, and the growth of technology; and abolished the road tax, the *corvée*.

Naturally, the parlements refused to register such revolutionary measures, and in March 1776 the king ordered them registered in a *lit de justice*. But the staying power of Louis XVI was even less impressive than that of his predecessor. Other ministers were indifferent or hostile; the *dévots* were outraged; the parlements were roused to resistance. Against all this opposition Turgot could do nothing without the king, but the king dismissed him in May and his successor rapidly reversed his policies. "Ah! *mon Dieu*, monsieur, what disastrous news!" Voltaire exclaimed on 15 May. "What will become of us?"[50]

Voltaire's hopes for France had been aroused by Maupeou's ministry, but dashed by Maupeou's dismissal. Turgot had revived them, but French kings seemed unable to learn from ex-

---

[49] The *Diatribe* is in XXIX, 359-370. Excerpts were printed in the *Mercure* in August 1775, but the censor who approved these excerpts for publication was fired. See XXIX, 359n. Long before, Frederick the Great had told Voltaire that he liked to unite the useful with the agreeable. Voltaire proved the truth of this remark while Turgot was in power: after complicated negotiations and much pamphleteering, Voltaire succeeded in getting Turgot to free the county of Gex, where his properties were located, from the tax farming, in return for a single annual contribution.

[50] Voltaire to de Vaines, 15 May (1776), L, 17-18.

perience. "The dismissal of this great man crushes me," Voltaire wrote to Du Pont in June.[51] "I have been in a perpetual depression since we were deprived of the protector of the people and my province," he complained to Condorcet as late as September 1776. "Since that fatal day, I have not followed anything, I have not requested anything of anybody, and I am waiting patiently for someone to cut our throats."[52]

Voltaire was lamenting more than the fall of a man, he was lamenting the fall of the *thèse royale*. In the eighteenth century, Frenchmen could take one of three major political positions: the *thèse nobiliaire*, the *thèse royale*, or Rousseau's democratic theory. But Rousseau's position was Utopian and, in any event, had never been intended for France, and the *thèse nobiliaire* was no more than an ideology for special interests. What remained was the *thèse royale*, and all his life Voltaire had placed his trust in it. "Neither Louis XV nor Louis XVI," Franz Neumann wrote in his brilliant essay on Montesquieu, "could possibly arouse the hope that a monarch could and would have the courage to cut himself loose from all ties with the aristocracy, to wipe out all privileges, to create economic freedom, to put the finances on a sound basis, to establish a reorganization of the administration, clean out the drones, and throw himself into the arms of the masses of the people. . . . Turgot's short-lived administration proved the Utopian character of the *thèse royale*."[53]

The beginning of this statement seems too harsh: for years the only realistic political position in France was Voltaire's. But its conclusion is just: with the dismissal of Turgot the *thèse royale* collapsed, and all positions became equally unrealistic. When Voltaire returned to Paris early in 1778, there was much prosperity and much gaiety, but some kind of revolution was now inevitable.

[51] 15 June (1776), L, 43.
[52] 7 September 1776, L, 81.
[53] "Montesquieu," *The Democratic and the Authoritarian State*, 112.

2. RETURN OF A RADICAL

On 5 February 1778, Voltaire said farewell to "his" villagers at Ferney; genuinely fond of him, and true to eighteenth-century sensibility, they wept to see him go. He had not been to Paris since he had left it over twenty-seven years before to go to Prussia, but he had never really been away: he had furnished gossip for Parisian journals, written dramas for Parisian audiences, and participated in Parisian politics. Montaigne's declaration of love to the city might have been his own: "I am never so exasperated with France that I cease to have a kindly feeling for Paris; she has had my heart since my boyhood. . . . I love her tenderly, even her warts and her blemishes."

And Paris, it turned out, loved Voltaire tenderly, even his warts and his blemishes. His journey was like the progress of a popular monarch, his reception in Paris like the triumph of a victorious general. The waiters in the inns, the officials at the gates, the crowds in the streets, the strangers who intruded on him, the writers, scientists, and diplomats who sought an audience, the old friends and correspondents—d'Argental, Diderot, Turgot, Benjamin Franklin, madame du Deffand, madame Necker, d'Alembert—who had the privilege of a *tête à tête*, joined in saluting the greatest man in France, her leading man of letters, and, more than that, a powerful political force.

The *dévots* sensed the menace of this visitor: priests denounced him from the pulpit; officials searched their files for a *lettre de cachet* that might give them the right to banish him from the city. In vain: Voltaire had every right to be in Paris; indeed, he seemed to own it. On 30 March 1778, his greatest day, he heard d'Alembert eulogize him at the *Académie française*, and in the evening he presided over a representation of his last tragedy, *Irène*. Everyone applauded the play, but no one listened to it: Voltaire rather than his drama was in the center of the stage. After the performance, the actors assembled before the curtains and apostrophized his bust, crowned with laurels. "Voltaire the king," writes Daniel Mornet, "became

Voltaire the God."[54] These are extravagant words, but they do no more than echo contemporary accounts.

The Parisians who applauded Voltaire showed a deeper understanding of Voltaire's significance for French politics than many a later critic who has characterized Voltaire as a conservative or dismissed his political ideas as propaganda for one social class. "We may say," writes André Bellessort, "that the French Revolution began on 10 February 1778, the day that Voltaire entered Paris."[55] We may indeed say so; Voltaire's tumultuous homecoming was a radical demonstration: while Voltaire did not have a program for revolution, his program was revolutionary. Like the other philosophes, he had little taste for violent upheavals and sought gradual reform through persuasion of the powerful and education of the public. "Injudicious reformers," he observed in his notebook, "are like Eson's daughters who killed their father in trying to rejuvenate him."[56] Voltaire was not an injudicious reformer: he lacked the professional revolutionary's sense of alienation, and he had no intention of biting the hand that applauded him.

But it is unhistorical to interpret his moderation as conservatism or as bourgeois ideology. "The changes he demanded were broadly those of the prosperous bourgeoisie . . ." Harold Laski suggests in a widely accepted interpretation. "The world he wanted to build was, of course, an infinitely better world than the one he inherited. But the improvements would have been limited in their benefit very much to the propertied class."[57] There is something in this view: Voltaire's attitude

---

[54] *Les origines intellectuelles de la révolution française*, 226.

[55] *Essai sur Voltaire*, 365.

[56] *Notebooks*, 221. In a late political essay he admitted that revolutions might sometimes be inevitable: "It may be presumed that a constitution which has regulated the rights of the king, nobles, and people, and under which everyone finds his safety, will last as long as human things can last. It may also be presumed that all states which are not founded on such principles will go through revolutions." *Questions sur l'Encyclopédie*, article "Gouvernement," Part VI, 225-226.

[57] *The Rise of European Liberalism*, 215, 216. H. N. Brailsford similarly portrays Voltaire as caught in a conflict: "What he states is authentic

toward equality has the complacent condescension of the man of property; his suggestion that poverty is inescapable shows the limits of his social imagination; his strong sympathies with the economic and social aspirations of merchants, financiers, and industrialists were congenial to the bourgeois world view, as congenial as his demands for rationality in taxation and legislation.[58]

Still, Voltaire's political ideas were by no means "limited in their benefit very much to the propertied class." It is obvious to say that drastic reforms in the old regime would first benefit those groups that were in the best position to take advantage of them. Law reform would be to the advantage of persons wealthy enough to hire lawyers, but poor as much as rich—in fact, more than rich—could benefit from lenient punishments, public trials, presumption of innocence, review of sentences, reductions in the costs of justice. Tax reform would be welcome to bourgeois envious of the exemptions enjoyed by the privileged estates, but poor as much as rich—in fact, more than rich—could benefit from public works and proportionate taxes on property. Again, free speech and toleration would be most significant to those prosperous enough to buy books and educated enough to read them, but as education spread, the benefits of these liberal tenets, too, would spread and result in a

---

middle-class doctrine: but it revolts his humanity. . . . He knows very well that the principles of the middle-class revolution, stated as they were with a bold universality, ought to lead to economic equality. But he sees as clearly that this would conflict with the interests of that class." *Voltaire*, 126-127. This statement implies far more than its author, an admirer of Voltaire's, intends to convey: it suggests that Voltaire deliberately and consciously betrayed his universal principles for the sake of middle-class doctrine.

[58] His celebrated gratitude to England for rewarding bourgeois and bourgeois virtues has been discussed in Chapter 1. His remark, "*Liberty and property*, that is the English cry. . . . It is the cry of nature," has now become a commonplace. *Questions sur l'Encyclopédie*, article "Propriété," Part VIII, 169. The same article suggests (p. 172) that what is good for businessmen is good for the country; and in two letters to Jean-Robert Tronchin, 9 February (1758), and 7 May (1759), he argued that merchants make good public servants. *Correspondance avec les Tronchin*, 320, 392-393.

wide political public. In his age, and in his regime, Voltaire was a radical.

Half a century ago, Gustave Lanson made this point in a few penetrating pages. He listed, one by one, Voltaire's reform proposals and contrasted them with the society into which they were to be introduced. There was the France of Louis XV, with the "capricious despotism of his government, the egotistical and wasteful court, the great corporations (magistrates and clergy) taking greater interest in their privileges than in the general good, the disorder of the finances and the oppressive absurdity of the fiscal system, the scandalous enormity of ecclesiastical revenues and the misery of the parish priest, the chaos of the laws, the confusion and conflicts of authority, the intolerance which condemned Protestants to concubinage or hypocrisy and which sent their pastors to the galleys, the multitude of privileges and regulations which had turned into vexations and calamities for the mass of the people." Compare all this with what Voltaire fought for, to "introduce into that France, which remains Catholic and monarchical, toleration, freedom of the press, proportional taxation, unity of legislation, the reform of criminal procedure, the submission of the clergy to a salary, the development of poor-relief, the principles of government pacific and liberal, the administration hard-working, honest, and solely concerned with acting in behalf of public prosperity"—only then can we understand rather than belittle the significance of Voltaire's politics. What he wanted was "a completely different France . . . a very modern France."[59] Voltaire's radicalism was, in a word, modern. In a regime that was not yet modern, Voltaire was modern in his empiricism, his secularism, his humanitarianism, his hedonism.

It was in tirelessly preaching this modernity to others that Voltaire had a radical impact on French politics. Voltaire was more than a spokesman, he was a creator. He did not merely

[59] *Voltaire*, 189-190.

express articulately what the French bourgeoisie had inarticulately felt: he did more, he told Frenchmen what they must want and that they did not want enough. Most bourgeois were content to make money, some hoped to climb into the aristocracy, but few demanded the abolition of rank or equality before the law. Why demand equality when there was hope that one might some day become a beneficiary of inequality? "Strikingly enough," a close observer of the French bourgeoisie tells us, "there were few expressions of egalitarian sentiments by bourgeois writers of the 18th century. The vast majority . . . supported the anti-egalitarian presuppositions of the structure of French society and of the French government. The bourgeois made no explicit assertions of the equal dignity of all men, nor of the equal right of all men to opportunity for advancement."[60] Hoping to climb, French bourgeois did not wish to destroy the ladder.

But Voltaire did: he had always been the enemy of the enemies of reform. Had he lived a dozen years longer, he would have been amused to see French bourgeois, not always aware of their debt, echoing his sentiments. Through the 1780's, in spite of apparent prosperity, the financial crisis of the monarchy deepened, but the parlements, supported by a public that still believed their rhetoric, defied all attempts to raise new taxes, and instead demanded the calling of the estates general. In 1788, the rebellion of the nobility reached its climax; in the summer the crown surrendered, once again, and agreed to convene the estates in 1789. Then, in September 1788, ten years after Voltaire's death, came the dramatic public awakening. What all his polemics against the *thèse nobiliaire* had failed to do was done by a single declaration of the parlement of Paris; it decided that the forthcoming estates general should vote as they had voted at their last assembly in 1614, by estate rather than by delegate. "Never," wrote one observer, "was a

[60] Barber, *The Bourgeoisie in 18th Century France,* 144.

revolution in opinion so profound; never did enthusiasm turn so quickly to denunciation."[61]

This reversal of opinion in 1788 sheds, in retrospect, an ironic light on the Parisians' reception of Voltaire ten years earlier: in hailing him as *l'homme aux Calas*, in celebrating this revolutionary whom the king was too petty to receive and took weak to expel, they were declaring themselves in favor of his political goals but not of his political strategy, his ends but not his means. Still, Voltaire had high hopes for Frenchmen. On 31 March, elated by his triumph at the theatre, he wrote: "After thirty years of absence and sixty years of persecution, I have found a public and even a theatre audience turned philosophe."[62] And on the next day he told Frederick the Great, "At last men are enlightening themselves."[63]

Voltaire found it cheering to be acclaimed as *l'homme aux Calas*; as a man of letters who had made politics his business he could ask for no tribute more appropriate than this. But as an old dramatist, writing, directing, and acting in his works to the last, he carefully staged his own final scene. Benjamin Franklin and his grandson had come to see Voltaire in February. Voltaire, carefully noting (and reporting) the presence of twenty spectators "who shed tender tears" at the sight, blessed the boy in English: "God and liberty."[64] Soon after that he fell ill. Worn out by celebrations, visitors, and old age, "wrapped up in eighty-four years and eighty-four maladies,"[65] he took to his bed. By the 25th of May lethargy and fever made it clear that his end was near. But on the following day he was told that General Lally, whose name he had fought to vindicate for ten years, had been rehabilitated by the parlement of Burgundy. The news acted on him like a stimulant,

---

[61] Quoted in Lefebvre, *The Coming of the French Revolution*, 44.

[62] Voltaire to madame de Meynieres, L, 383.

[63] 1 April (1778), L, 383.

[64] See Voltaire to Théodore Tronchin, 17 February (1778), L, 366; and Voltaire to the abbé Gaultier, 21 February (1778), L, 372.

[65] Voltaire to Théodore Tronchin, February (1778), L, 365.

and he roused himself to dictate just one more letter. "The dying man revives upon hearing this great news," he wrote to the comte de Lally, the general's son, "he kisses M. de Lally tenderly; he sees that the king is the defender of justice; he will die content."[66] Four days later he was dead. The poet had made his last foray into politics.

[66] (26 May 1778), L, 397.

APPENDICES
AND
BIBLIOGRAPHICAL ESSAY

APPENDIX I

VOLTAIRE AND NATURAL LAW

ONE of the most complicated questions concerning Voltaire's thought is its relation to the natural law tradition. Voltaire wrote a great deal about the law of nature, but his pronouncements must be read in the context of his philosophy and his century. In the first half of the eighteenth century, while Voltaire's political ideas were reaching maturity, the natural law tradition was on the defensive. Natural law had been introduced into Western thought by the Stoics and integrated into theology by Christian philosophers. In the seventeenth century, as skepticism, scientific empiricism, and revived pagan philosophy were beginning to compete seriously with Christian thought, natural law was gradually stripped of its theological associations. It became a set of rules, discovered by reason, which reasonable men would obey and unreasonable men would violate; it could be used to justify absolutism or constitutionalism. In either form, it was a popular device of political theorists, for it offered a standard that transcended and judged mere positive law.

Yet the very philosophers who employed it—especially Hobbes and Locke—also undermined it with their theories of knowledge. Natural law claims to be universally applicable and unconditionally valid. Empiricism, on the other hand, maintains that philosophers cannot legitimately claim universal validity for moral rules. If all knowledge comes to us through the senses, natural law cannot be proved to be generally true; it is no more than one philosopher's social ideals stated in universal terms. Moreover, "Natural Law doctrines begin by asserting the existence of a state of nature"[1] and, usually, of a

[1] Franz Neumann, "Types of Natural Law," *The Democratic and Authoritarian State*, 70. Neumann holds that all natural law philosophers whatever must posit some such state of nature—the condition of man outside the state which imposes positive law on him—to establish the difference of natural from positive law.

343

social contract—conceptions for which there is no empirical evidence. Even when they are treated as logical constructs they do not allow the empiricist to draw universal conclusions from them.[2]

Yet, despite the impact of empiricism, natural law doctrines died hard. They were tenacious because they offered grounds for the assertion of natural rights, not because they were true—ideas that are useful weapons survive even the most devastating refutations. "Those political writers who have had recourse to a promise or original contract as the source of our allegiance to government," wrote David Hume, the most effective opponent of natural law doctrines in the eighteenth century, "intended to establish a principle which is perfectly just and reasonable; though the reasoning upon which they endeavoured to establish it was fallacious and sophistical."[3]

Fallacious and sophistical though it was, the natural law tradition survived into the eighteenth century, but chiefly as rhetoric. The philosophes, with the exception of Helvétius, still dwelt on the moral laws of nature, but more and more candidly they were driven to accept utilitarianism, a moral theory less exciting than the theory of natural rights and, as the French Revolution demonstrated, less useful in times of stress, but a theory that was compatible with associationist psychology, empiricist epistemology, and the emergent science of society.

[2] In his excellent *History of Political Theory*, George H. Sabine entitles his chapter on the philosophes, "France: The Decadence of Natural Law" but rightly stresses the toughness of natural law: "The self-evidence of natural rights was asserted and reasserted, yet the rationalism essential to a system of self-evident principles became continually more remote from the growing empiricism of social studies. An ethical and political utilitarianism, essentially empirical in its implications, was repeatedly crossed with the theory of natural rights in spite of the logical incompatibility of the two positions." (p. 544). I do not accept Sabine's contention, however (a contention widely accepted), that Locke contradicted himself in rejecting innate knowledge in the *Essay* and accepting natural law in the *Treatise on Civil Government*. Locke was fully aware of the problem, and in the *Essay*, I, iii, 13, he carefully distinguished between "innate law," which he rejected, and a "law of nature" found by the use of reason, which he accepted.

[3] *Treatise of Human Nature* (ed. 1951), 549.

Like the other philosophes, Voltaire too celebrated natural law: he wrote a long poem in its praise and constantly alluded to it in his political writings. Yet it is impossible to take his pronouncements literally: he explicitly rejected the theory of knowledge that would make it possible for him to affirm the existence of natural law;[4] he treated the most respectable representatives of the natural law tradition, the international lawyers, with withering and unreasonable contempt as bores, mediocrities, and authors of rubbish;[5] he never showed the slightest interest in the indispensable concomitant to natural law, the state of nature. The most serious defense of natural law he offered, universal consent, was both wrong in fact and unimpressive in theory.[6]

[4] Ernst Cassirer writes: "How does the necessity and immutability of the concept of law agree with the proposition that every idea is derived from the senses and that, accordingly, it can possess no other and no higher significance than the various sense experiences on which it is based? Voltaire clearly grasped this contradiction, and at times he seems to waver as to his decision. But in the end the ethical rationalist, the enthusiast for the original competence and the fundamental force of moral reason, triumphs over the empiricist and the skeptic." *Philosophy of the Enlightenment*, 244. This seems to me to underrate Voltaire's rhetoric and to overrate Voltaire's interest in the theory of knowledge. How is natural law known? Voltaire says repeatedly that God has "engraved it upon our hearts," but that is no more than a metaphor; he does not mean that the discovery of natural law is self-evident, but that it is easy: "It has taken centuries to know a portion of the laws of nature. A day suffices to know the duties of man." *Dictionnaire philosophique*, article "Philosophie," 342. Finally, Voltaire never settles the important question what the natural laws are: he defines them in one place as tolerance, elsewhere as self-defense, and elsewhere as liberty. At times he finds the list in the Bible, at times in universal human experience; at times he draws up veritable catalogues of natural laws, but they are never the same. See: *Dictionnaire philosophique*, article "Tolérance," 401; *ibid.*, article "Lois (des)," 285; *ibid.*, article "Nécessaire," 328; *Essai sur les moeurs*, xi, 155-156; *ibid.*, xi, 307; *l'A,B,C*, xxvii, 381; *Remarques pour servir de supplément à l'Essai sur les moeurs et l'esprit des nations*, xxiv, 574.
[5] Vattel's *Le droit des gens* is "a pretty mediocre imitation." Voltaire to La Chalotais, 28 February (1763), xlii, 405; Grotius writes "rubbish," and is a poor reasoner. *L'homme aux quarante écus*, xxi, 366; *l'A,B,C*, xxvii, 311-314; Pufendorf is not much better. *Questions sur l'Encyclopédie*, article "Droit," Part iv, 255-259.
[6] This was one point on which Voltaire deserted his great teacher Locke, who had rejected consensus: "Show me a country in which it is honest to

The conclusion is therefore highly probable that Voltaire's appeal to natural law is rhetorical.[7] As a realistic social reformer, he is impatient to get to work, suspicious of fine-spun theoretical arguments that divert men from action, angry with debates over the foundations of morality when the evils in society are so patent. As a deist, he had no hesitation in affirming that civilized men everywhere agree on good and evil, right and wrong, and that fruitful discussion should confine itself to the practical question: what are the most efficacious methods of repairing those wrongs that it is possible for human activity to repair? Like other practical men, Voltaire knew what he wanted, and spent relatively little time on fundamentals.

APPENDIX II

THE DATE OF VOLTAIRE'S "IDÉES RÉPUBLICAINES"

DURING the Genevan upheavals of the 1760's, there appeared a slim octavo brochure of 45 pages, *Idées républicaines, par un membre d'un corps.* It was published anonymously, but the

---

rob me of the fruit of my labor, to violate one's promises, to lie in order to hurt, to calumniate, to assassinate, to poison, to be ungrateful to one's benefactor, to beat one's father and mother when they give you food." *Questions sur l'Encyclopédie,* article "Loi naturelle," Part VII, 242. Supposed exceptions are not exceptions at all: "B: It is said that at Lacaedemon one applauded thefts for which men were condemned to the galleys in Athens. A: Abuse of words, logomachy, evasion; one could not commit thefts in Sparta since everything there was held in common." *ibid.,* 241. While priests and other "fakirs" have obscured the obvious, we can learn the rules of natural law in the same way that we learn that two and two are four. "They have all said the same thing: Socrates and Epicurus, Confucius and Cicero, Marc Antony and Amuruth II have had the same ethics." *Dictionnaire philosophique,* article "Juste (du) et de l'injuste," 270.

[7] I do not want to imply that Voltaire consciously deceived his reader. Rather, I think that Voltaire found the rhetoric so convenient that he did not examine it carefully. There are occasions when he breaks through to a simple utilitarianism: "Virtue and vice, moral good and evil, are . . . in all countries that which is useful or harmful to society"; it is rational self-interest put in the most general language. *Traité de métaphysique,* XXII, 225.

master's touch is unmistakable: editors have never hesitated to assign the pamphlet to Voltaire, and to treat it as one of his three or four most important political works. But *Idées républicaines* also appeared without date or place of publication, and there has been an intriguing—and, as I shall show, an instructive—mystery about the time of its composition. The three great editions of Voltaire's works—Kehl, Beuchot, and Moland—date it 1762, while in the rash of unscholarly and unreliable editions that flooded France in the 1820's and later, the pamphlet was redated, without ceremony and without apparent justification, to 1765.[1] The pamphlet, Beuchot explains in a footnote, had appeared "without date, but it must be from 1762, the year of the *Contrat social*, of which *Idées républicaines* is a critique. It seems to me an error to have dated this pamphlet 1765."[2]

Bengesco supported Beuchot's scholarly authority. "In his *Idées républicaines*," Bengesco notes in his *Bibliographie*, "Voltaire criticizes several points of the *Contrat social* of J.-J. Rousseau; now, the *Contrat social* appeared in 1762. . . . The *Idées républicaines* must thus be from the year 1762."[3] Bengesco allowed himself a "?" after his date, but in view of his assurance, this was only a polite nod to modesty.

The combined weight of Beuchot and Bengesco has been sufficient to impress later scholars, partly because the editors who assigned *Idées républicaines* to 1765 spoiled their case (if any) by reproducing the pamphlet with unwarranted cuts and with a wrong title. With one or two exceptions, scholars have caviled neither at Beuchot's reasoning nor at his date.[4]

Yet his reasoning is feeble and his date is wrong. We know that Rousseau's *Contrat social* was burned in Geneva on 19

---

[1] See for instance, *Oeuvres complètes*, Armand Aubrée, 54 vols. (1829ff), XXIII, 139; *Oeuvres complètes*, F. Didot, 13 vols. (1876-1878), V, 596.

[2] *Oeuvres complètes*, XXXX, 567.

[3] *Voltaire. Bibliographie de ses oeuvres*, II, 111.

[4] For exceptions see Chaponnière, *Voltaire chez les Calvinistes*, 215; C. E. Vaughan, *Studies in the History of Political Philosophy Before and After Rousseau*, 2 vols. (1925), I, 262-263n.

June 1762, and that Voltaire censured this act in his pamphlet. But this censure only gives us the earliest possible date of composition—why equate that with the actual date of composition? It would be tempting to ascribe such reasoning to naïveté or carelessness, but such an ascription would be gratuitous and mistaken—Beuchot was neither naïve nor careless. It is far more fruitful to assume that Beuchot and Bengesco (like most of the writers I have criticized in my Prologue) thought of Voltaire as an abstract, flighty poet who could not sustain an interest in political affairs, and whose political writings dealt with contemporary events only on rare occasions. We see what we seek: if Voltaire was indeed what Tocqueville called an "abstract, literary" political thinker, then *Idées républicaines*, a collection of generalities, must have been written in 1762.

However, once the reader studies the pamphlet with the image of Voltaire as a practical, realistic political thinker (the image I have suggested throughout this book), *Idées républicaines* changes its nature: the generalities become specific allusions to the party struggle in Geneva.

As readers of Chapter IV will recall, this is how I read *Idées républicaines*: as a partisan pamphlet, reproducing ideas and demands current among the *Représentants*, and copying, sometimes almost word for word, Voltaire's memorandum *Propositions à examiner pour apaiser les divisions de Genève*. To make the parallels between *Idées républicaines* and the *Propositions* even more evident than they are in the text, I cite a few excerpts from each:

Propositions	Idées républicaines
In a brief preliminary statement, Voltaire writes: "Il y a de l'équité et des lumières dans les deux partis opposés. . . ."	"On a dit mille fois que l'autorité veut toujours croître, et le peuple toujours se plaindre; qu'il ne faut ni céder à toutes ses représentations, ni les rejeter toutes. . . ."

Propositions	*Idées républicaines*
First grievance of the *Représentants*: "Que le conseil d'état (the Council of Twenty-Five) ayant promis suivant le règlement de la médiation, de faire imprimer le recueil entier des lois, ce code nécessaire n'ait pas paru encore."	"Un code criminel est absolument nécessaire pour les citoyens et pour les magistrats. Les citoyens alors n'auront jamais à se plaindre des jugements, et les magistrats n'auront point à craindre d'encourir la haine. . . ."
Second grievance: "Que l'on emprisonne d'office des citoyens sans les avoir entendus."	"La loi qui permettrait d'emprisonner un citoyen sans information préalable, et sans formalité juridique, serait tolérable dans un temps de trouble et de guerre; elle serait tortionnaire et tyrannique en temps de paix."
Fourth grievance: "Que lorsque les citoyens (qui sont souverain législateurs) font une représentation au Conseil des Vingt-Cinq qui a le pouvoir exécutif, cette représentation puisse être rejetée purement et simplement."	"Le gouvernement civil est la volonté de tous, exécutée par un seul ou par plusieurs, en vertu des lois que tous ont portées." "Dans une petite république le peuple semble devoir être plus écouté que dans une grande, parce qu'il est plus aisé de faire entendre raison à mille personnes assemblées, qu'à quarante mille."
And Voltaire proposed that the General Council be convoked by the first syndic: "Quand sept cents citoyens, ap-	"Lorsqu'une loi est obscure, il faut que tous l'interprètent, parce que tous l'ont promulguée: à moins qu'ils n'aient

Propositions	Idées républicaines
puyés de la décision de trois jurisconsultes d'une Université à leur choix, viendront demander ou l'interprétation d'un point de loi déclaré obscur, ou l'extension d'une loi déclarée insuffisante, ou ce qui n'arrivera probablement jamais, l'exécution d'une loi négligée. . . ."	chargé plusieurs expressément d'interpréter les lois."

There are many other suggestions that *Idées républicaines* is about Genevan politics: the covert allusion to the Covelle case, the soothing reference to the value of mediation, the praise of a small republic, "mêlé de démocratie et d'aristocratie. . . ."

It thus becomes extremely probable that *Idées républicaines* was written not in 1762, but in October or November 1765, while Voltaire was negotiating with *Négatifs* and *Représentants* and while he was meditating or writing his *Propositions*.

Fortunately there is some persuasive external evidence to support this thesis: on 15 January 1766, Grimm reported in his *Correspondance littéraire* that Voltaire had published a political pamphlet on the *tracasseries* of Geneva, entitled *Idées républicaines*. With considerable shrewdness Grimm not only identified the pamphlet as Voltaire's, but also as a partisan tract addressed primarily to a Genevan audience.[5] This shrewdness is remarkable, but what is perhaps more remarkable is Bengesco's obtuseness: Bengesco was aware of Grimm's entry but failed to use the clue.[6]

Thus, redating *Idées républicaines* from 1762 to 1765 has more than bibliographical significance. It illuminates Voltaire's technique of exploiting specific issues for the sake of general

[5] *Correspondance littéraire*, vi, 474-475.
[6] *Voltaire. Bibliographie de ses oeuvres*, ii, 112.

statements, and it demonstrates how fruitful it is to think of Voltaire as a practical political pamphleteer.

APPENDIX III

VOLTAIRE'S ANTI-SEMITISM

SOME of Voltaire's worst bankers were Jews. In October 1726, after he had returned to England from his futile search for the chevalier de Rohan, he wrote to Thieriot that he was sick and without funds: "I had about me onely some bills of exchange upon a Jew called Medina for the sum of about eight or nine thousand French livres, rekoning all. At my coming to London i found my damned Jew was broken."[1] A quarter of a century later, in Prussia, he referred in similar terms to another "damned Jew," the *Schutzjude* Abraham Hirschel, with whom he had first been engaged in some illegal speculations and later became involved in an unsavory lawsuit.

This tone runs through Voltaire's writings: Jews are materialists, they are eminently qualified to be usurers, they are greedy, iniquitous, clever, and rootless.[2] "You are calculating animals," he advised them, "try to be thinking animals."[3] Such expressions did not make Voltaire a racist: he deplored the persecution of the Jews, especially by the Spanish and Portuguese inquisitions,[4] and he urged Jews to assimilate themselves to Western civilization by abandoning their dietary laws and their "hatred" of other nations: "But what shall I say to my brother the Jew? Shall I give him dinner? Yes, provided that

---

[1] *Correspondence*, II, 36. The whole letter is in rather adequate English.

[2] For examples see *Dictionnaire philosophique*, article "Ciel des anciens (le)," 139; *ibid.*, article "Catéchisme du Japonais," 91; *Questions sur l'Encyclopédie*, article "Patrie," Part VIII, 125; *La pucelle*, IX, 149; *Essai sur les moeurs*, XII, 163; Voltaire to Cardinal Dubois, 28 (May 1722), *Correspondence*, I, 146-147; Voltaire to Darget, 18 January 1751, *ibid.*, XIX, 53; Voltaire to de Lisle, 15 December (1773), XLVIII, 522.

[3] "Juifs," XIX, 541.

[4] *Henriade*, VIII, 136; *Sermon du Rabbi Akib*, XXIV, 281.

during the meal Balaam's ass does not take it into its head to bray; that Ezekiel does not mix his breakfast with our dinner; that a fish does not come to swallow one of the guests and keep him in his belly for three days; that a serpent does not mix into the conversation to seduce my wife; that a prophet does not take it into his head to sleep with her after dinner, as did that good fellow Hoseah for fifteen francs and a bushel of barley; above all that no Jew make a tour round my house sounding the trumpet, making the walls come down, killing me, my father, my mother, my wife, my children, my cat and my dog, in accord with the former usage of the Jews."[5]

Such accents are, of course, only too familiar, and they are startling only in a free spirit like Voltaire, who transcended so many prejudices and saw through so many shams. The writings of Montesquieu and Lessing demonstrate that philo-semitism was possible for eighteenth-century Europeans, but when it came to the Jews Voltaire was content to mouthe the accepted clichés. He never reached Hegel's insight that if the Jews were, indeed, calculating animals, it was the Christians who had made them so. In fact, on this matter even his empiricism deserted him: he had some Jewish acquaintances[6] and late in life his prejudices were challenged directly. Isaac Pinto, a learned Portuguese Jew who admired Voltaire's work, wrote him a sensible and noble letter, deploring Voltaire's anti-Semitic remarks in an article on "Juifs." Voltaire replied, decently enough, that he would alter the offending passages: "I was wrong to attribute to a whole nation the vices of some individuals."[7] But neither acquaintance nor remonstrance had much impact on Voltaire:

---

[5] *Questions sur l'Encyclopédie*, article "Tolérance," Part IX, 18.

[6] In his notebook he records an anecdote: "Madame Acosta said in my presence to an abbé who wanted to convert her to Christianity: 'Was your God born a Jew?' 'Yes.' 'Did he live as a Jew?' 'Yes.' 'Did he die as a Jew?' 'Yes.' 'All right, then, be a Jew.'" *Notebooks*, 233. Mme Acosta belonged to a family of English Jews with whom Voltaire was friendly during his stay in England.

[7] Voltaire to Pinto, 21 July (1762), XLII, 182.

he never rewrote the passages that offended Pinto, he never re-
canted his rather crude prejudices.

But this is not all. Voltaire's anti-Jewish remarks are a partly
unconscious, partly conscious cloak for his anti-Christian sentiments. "When I see Christians, cursing Jews," he wrote into his
English notebook, "methinks I see children beating their
fathers."[8] Like his admirer Nietzsche over a century after him,
Voltaire struck at the Jews to strike at the Christians. Bossuet
had made the chosen people the center of his so-called universal
history; Voltaire strove for a more genuine universality. "I am
weary of this absurd pedantry," he wrote after an account of
the sanguinary history of the ancient Jews, "which sanctifies
the history of such a people for the instruction of the young."[9]
Bossuet and Voltaire agreed that Judaism was the father of
Christianity, but they drew opposite conclusions: Bossuet, that
he must make Jewish history central; Voltaire, that the paternity
of Christianity was only another argument against it. The Jewish people of the Old Testament, judging from their records
alone, were uncivilized, lecherous, and cruel. The heroes of the
Jews, like King David, had been gangsters and murderers;[10] the
accumulation of broken treaties, assassinations, blood feuds,
adulteries, incests, recorded in the Old Testament led Voltaire
to observe drily that if the Holy Ghost was the author of this
history, he had not chosen a very edifying subject.

The despicable history of the Jews, ancestors and models of
the Christians, permitted Voltaire to draw some devastating
conclusions. Christians profess to despise Jews—what shall we
think of a religion that urges men to imitate them? If the
miracles of the Jews are childish fables, if the *Book of Proverbs*
is a "collection of trivial, sordid, incoherent maxims, without
taste, without selection, and without design";[11] if the *Song of*

---

[8] *Notebooks*, 31, in English; see the similar remark in *ibid.*, 215.

[9] *L'A,B,C*, xxvii, 349-350. For cruelties of the Biblical Jews, see above
all, *Sermon des cinquante*, xxiv, 441-444.

[10] Here is another instance of Voltaire's borrowing from Bayle, who had
written a scathing attack on David in his Dictionary.

[11] *Dictionnaire philosophique*, article "Salomon," 379.

Songs is an "inept rhapsody"[12]—what shall we think of a religion that urges men to believe them to be of divine inspiration? In a word, the vileness and absurdity of the Biblical Jews demonstrates the vileness and absurdity of Christianity.

Moreover, Voltaire showed with grim humor that the Jews of antiquity, superstitious and barbarous as they had been, were at once less superstitious and less barbarous than the Christians. The ancient Jews had not believed in the immortality of the soul, or in the divinity of their Messiah.[13] Now when Voltaire deplored the Jews' failure to rise to such sublime ideas as the God-man or the immortality of the soul, he was of course pretending to censure ideas that he shared with enthusiasm.

Indeed, the Jews were less intolerant than the Christians: the Sadducees among the Jews, wrote Voltaire, denied the existence of angels, even though the majority of Jews believed in them. Still, the Sadducees enjoyed all the rights of citizenship. This, he remarked without sarcasm, is a "beautiful example of tolerance."[14] The Romans tolerated the Jews because with all their stubborn clinging to their superstitions, they did not try to foist their superstitions on others: "The Jews did not want the statue of Jupiter to be in Jerusalem; but the Christians did not want it to be in the Capitol. . . . The Jews adored their God; but they were never astonished that each people had its own."[15] This is why the Jews, for all their failings, would be part of Voltaire's good state. At times he did not seem certain whether he would extend the same privilege to believing Christians.

---

[12] *ibid.*, 383; see also *ibid.*, article "Genèse," 212-225; *ibid.*, article "Miracles," 314-320.

[13] See *Olympie*, act I, scene 1, VI, 98n; *Essai sur les moeurs*, XI, 75; *Histoire de Jenni*, XXI, 569; *Dictionnaire philosophique*, article "Messie," 307.

[14] *Notebooks*, 264; *Traité sur la tolérance*, XXV, 77-78. He held the same opinion privately. See Voltaire to d'Alembert, 13 February (1764), and 1 March (1764), XLIII, 126, 144; Voltaire to Damilaville, 4 March (1764), XLIII, 150.

[15] *Dictionnaire philosophique*, article "Tolérance," 401, 402.

BIBLIOGRAPHICAL ESSAY

GENERAL

BIBLIOGRAPHICAL essays usually begin with the modest disclaimer that they do not pretend to completeness and that it would take another volume merely to list all the works which the author has read. I am happy to adopt this ritual—the literature on Voltaire is enormous, and I have made no attempt to discuss all of it here. I have confined myself to the works that have influenced, informed, or irritated me. Since the point of my book is to place Voltaire in his social and political environment, I have included works on history, law, and political theory which, I trust, will be useful to experts on Voltaire.

Readers in search of titles on Voltaire should consult Mary M. H. Barr, *A Century of Voltaire Study: A Bibliography of Writings on Voltaire, 1825-1925* (1929); "Bibliographical Data on Voltaire from 1926 to 1930," *Modern Language Notes*, XLVIII (1933), 292-307; and "Bibliographical Data on Voltaire from 1931 to 1940," *ibid.*, LVI (1941), 563-582. The exhaustive bibliographies appended to Raymond Naves, *Le goût de Voltaire* (1938) and René Pomeau, *La religion de Voltaire* (1956) are very helpful. For the present state of research on Voltaire, see René Pomeau, "Etat présent des études voltairiennes," *Travaux sur Voltaire et le dix-huitième siècle*, ed. Theodore Besterman, I (1955), 183-200. (All succeeding volumes of this specialized journal, invaluable to scholars interested in Voltaire, are appearing under the title *Studies on Voltaire and the Eighteenth Century*.)

Editions of Voltaire's writings are catalogued in Georges Bengesco, *Voltaire. Bibliographie de ses oeuvres*, 4 vols. (1882-1890), a very useful work of reference despite its occasional errors and omissions. There is a useful *Table* (1953) to this bibliography by Jean Malcolm. Bengesco should be supplemented by the numerous critical editions of individual works that have appeared in the last half century, and by G. L. van

Roosbroeck, "Notes on Voltaire," *Modern Language Notes,* XXXIX (1924), 1-10; Francis J. Crowley, "Corrections and Additions to Bengesco's *Bibliographie,*" *ibid.,* L (1935), 440-441; Desmond Flower, "Some Aspects of the Bibliography of Voltaire," *The Library,* Fifth Series, I (1946-1947), 223-236. See also my appendix in this volume on the date of Voltaire's *Idées républicaines,* which I have expanded, into an article, "Voltaire's *Idées républicaines*: A Study in Bibliography and Interpretation," in *Studies on Voltaire and the Eighteenth Century,* VI (1958), 67-105.

As bibliophiles know to their delight (and cost), there are many editions of Voltaire's writings, but most of them are less scholarly than decorative. Specialists have applied the epithet "great" to three: the so-called Kehl edition, edited by Beaumarchais and others, *Oeuvres complètes,* 70 vols. (1785-1789), (this is the octavo edition; there is also a duodecimo edition of 92 volumes which still turns up in the bookstalls on the Seine); *Oeuvres,* edited by A. J. O. Beuchot, 72 vols. (1829-1840); and the *Oeuvres complètes,* edited by Louis Moland, 52 vols. (1877-1885). Moland's edition is now the vulgate, and I have followed the usual practice of citing from it wherever possible. It is for the most part an excellent edition, relying on Beuchot's unsurpassed scholarship. I have therefore resisted the temptation to cite from more recent critical editions except when absolutely necessary—when Moland nodded, or when I cited material, such as letters, not available to him.

Thus for the *Lettres philosophiques* I used Gustave Lanson's exemplary, fully annotated 2-volume edition (1909); and for the *Dictionnaire philosophique* (which is an indiscriminate mélange in Moland's edition) I used Raymond Naves and Julien Benda's recent, easily available version (ed. 1954). The *Questions sur l'Encyclopédie,* a work separate from the *Dictionnaire philosophique,* was absorbed into the latter by Moland. For the sake of clarity, I have therefore cited from the original edition of the *Questions,* 9 parts in 3 vols. (1771-1772). For

Voltaire's Notebooks, incomplete in Moland, I have used the superb edition by Theodore Besterman, 2 vols. paginated continuously (1952). Mr. Besterman is now at work on what will be the definitive edition of *Voltaire's Correspondence* (1953ff); it is a major scholarly achievement, giving immense help to the specialist and offering immense pleasure to the amateur. At this point (early spring 1958), Volumes 1 to 24 have appeared, reaching to 1754. I have cited all letters to this date from Besterman. As for later letters, I have cited from Moland, or from separate collections of letters not available to Moland, particularly from *Correspondance avec les Tronchin* (1950), ed. A. Delattre; *Lettres inédites à son imprimeur Gabriel Cramer* (1952), ed. Bernard Gagnebin. It should be noted that Besterman is printing additions and corrections to his edition of the *Correspondence* in each issue of his *Studies on Voltaire and the Eighteenth Century.* Many letters have come to light in recent years, and have been published in scholarly journals. For a list of these publications, far too long to be included here, see Pomeau, *La religion de Voltaire,* 466-469. All these letters are, of course, finding their place in Besterman's edition. In 1914, Fernand Caussy supplemented Moland's edition with a volume of *Oeuvres inédites,* I, *mélanges historiques.* Finally, Moland's printing of Voltaire's marginalia is not very satisfactory; I have used the excellent edition of *Voltaire's Marginalia on the Pages of Rousseau* (1933) by George R. Havens.

There are dozens of Voltaire biographies; most, although not all, derive from Gustave Desnoiresterres, *Voltaire et la société française au* XVIIIe *siècle,* 8 vols. (1867-1876). It is out of date now, but it remains an impressive achievement. I shall deal with each volume separately below under its individual title. Among Desnoiresterres' many successors, the most impressive are Gustave Lanson's objective, penetrating, and economical synthesis, *Voltaire* (1906), a justly popular book; André Bellessort's no less penetrating but unfortunately less popular *Essai sur Voltaire* (1925), from which I learned much; and Raymond Naves's skillful, brief *Voltaire, l'homme et l'oeuvre* (1942). In English, John Morley, *Voltaire* (1872, ed. 1909) is a Victorian period piece, vigorous and sympathetic but dated; H. N. Brailsford, *Voltaire* (1935) is well written, well informed, and shrewd, but somewhat limited in its perspective by its author's conviction that Voltaire was a bourgeois ideologist. Georg Brandes, *Voltaire* (English tr. 1930) is an old-fashioned long biography, full of insights; S. G. Tallentyre (pseud. E. Beatrice Hall), *The Life of Voltaire*, 2 vols. (1903) is a characteristic specimen of Voltaire worship: it is uncritical, racy, and the source of many an untrue anecdote.

By far the most impressive book on the philosophes is Ernst Cassirer, *The Philosophy of the Enlightenment* (English tr. 1951), a profound and illuminating work whose stature grows with the years and in comparison with other attempts to deal with the eighteenth century. It is flawed only by its slighting of materialism and a rather conventional chapter on politics. Carl Becker, *The Heavenly City of the Eighteenth Century Philosophers* (1932) is a sparkling and influential (but to my mind completely misleading) essay that links the philosophes to medieval thought. I have undertaken a critique in "Carl Becker's Heavenly City," *Political Science Quarterly*, LXXII (June, 1957), 182-199. Paul Hazard, *La pensée européenne au* XVIIIe *siècle: de Montesquieu à Lessing*, 3 vols. (1946) is an indispensable guide to the period by a scholar who seems to have read everything and grasped everything without, however, acquiring the style for which French *vulgarisateurs* are justly famous. Hazard's earlier *La crise de la conscience européenne, 1680-1715*, 3 vols. (1934) is a highly original survey of the prelude to the Enlightenment. Bernard Groethuysen's sociological study of bourgeois consciousness in France, *Die Entstehung der bürgerlichen Welt- und Lebensanschauung in Frankreich*, 2 vols. (1927-1930) remains controversial, but I, for one, found it most illuminating. Hazard's books contain impressive bibliographies which can be supplemented by D. C. Cabeen, ed., *A Critical*

Bibliography of French Literature, IV, The Eighteenth Century, eds. George R. Havens and Donald F. Bond (1951). Arthur O. Lovejoy has some brilliantly suggestive chapters on the eighteenth century in The Great Chain of Being (1936) and some equally brilliant essays in Essays in the History of Ideas (1948). J. H. Randall, The Making of the Modern Mind (2d ed., 1940) is a stimulating and familiar study whose interpretations of the Enlightenment and the "romantic revolt" I find unconvincing; Basil Willey, The Eighteenth Century Background (1940) has good material on the philosophes' conception of nature. Among Gustave Lanson's many path-breaking articles on the eighteenth century, perhaps the two most important are "Origines et premières manifestations de l'esprit philosophique dans la littérature française de 1675 à 1748," Revue des cours et conférences (26 December 1907-21 April 1910); and "Le rôle de l'expérience dans la formation de la philosophie du xviiie siècle," La revue du mois, IX (January, April 1910), 1-28, 409-429. Daniel Mornet, La pensée française au xviiie siècle (1932) is short and reliable. René Hubert deals with the philosophes' hope that men could control their environment through a science of society in his important Les sciences sociales dans l'Encyclopédie (1923). Among shorter treatments, special mention should be made of Walter L. Dorn's fine chapter and thoughtful bibliography on the Enlightenment in his Competition for Empire, 1740-1763 (1940); and Alfred Cobban's synthesis in the New Cambridge Modern History, VII, The Old Regime, 1713-1763 (1957), ed. J. O. Lindsay. George R. Havens, The Age of Ideas (1955) is built on lifelong, solid scholarship, but is adulatory and unpolitical. Albert Guérard, The Life and Death of an Ideal, France in the Classical Age (ed. 1956) has some sparkling pages on the philosophes.

A whole bibliography could be compiled on the sins of textbook writers. Much the best History of Political Theory in English is by George H. Sabine (2d ed., 1950), but even his treatment of the Enlightenment is sketchy and not wholly satisfactory. Kingsley Martin, *French Liberal Thought in the Eighteenth Century* (2d ed., 1954) is a puzzling book: it offers a lively and useful account of the social and political environment in which the philosophes thought and wrote, but its treatment of individual thinkers, including Voltaire, is far from comprehensive or searching. Henri Sée, *L'Evolution de la pensée politique en France au* xviiie *siècle* (1925) is brief but informative and generally reliable in its judgments. I found Maxime Leroy, *Histoire des idées sociales en France*, i, *De Montesquieu à Robespierre* (1946), full of insight but less than comprehensive.

PROLOGUE
VOLTAIRE'S REPUTATION

In my polemical prologue I dealt chiefly with those interpreters of Voltaire with whom I disagree. But I do not want to convey the impression that I think of myself as the only man in the world who ever understood Voltaire correctly. Indeed, Voltaire has been lucky in the scholars who have devoted themselves to him, and I am deeply in debt to several of them. In addition to the biographies of Lanson and Bellessort, listed above, I have learned much from Georges Pellissier, *Voltaire philosophe* (1908), an accurate, fair-minded, closely argued analysis of Voltaire's ideas; its only shortcoming is its failure to place Voltaire in his historical context. J.-R. Carré, *Réflexions sur l'anti-Pascal de Voltaire* (1935) and *Consistance de Voltaire le philosophe* (1938) are brilliant studies which take Voltaire seriously as a thinker. Norman Torrey, *The Spirit of Voltaire* (1938) explodes many a mischievous canard about Voltaire and is an illuminating summary of his mind and actions, perhaps a little too good-tempered and unpolitical. Paul Sakmann, *Voltaires Geistesart und Gedankenwelt* (1910) sums up the researches of a leading and productive German Voltaire scholar; eminently worth reading, Sakmann's study is however a typical product of German *Geistesgeschichte*—far more metaphysical than Voltaire would have liked.

There is no wholly satisfactory account of Voltaire's politics. As René Pomeau said in 1955 in his article on Voltaire scholarship: all has not yet been said on Voltaire and science, and "tout n'est pas dit non plus sur la politique de Voltaire." *Travaux sur Voltaire et le dix-huitième siècle*, I, 196. Emile Faguet denies Voltaire moral convictions and political consistency in *La politique comparée de Montesquieu, Rousseau et Voltaire* (1902) and *Dix-huitième siècle* (1890), 199-288. Both books, despite many a shrewd hit, are unfair and very misleading. The same criticism applies to Ferdinand Brunetière's anti-Voltaire crusade. See *Etudes sur le xviii siècle* (1911), 1-145; and his articles in *Etudes critiques sur l'histoire de la littérature française*, "Première série," (1888), 181-254; and "Quatrième série," (1891), 267-324. Philip G. Neserius, "Voltaire's Political Ideas," *American Political Science Review*, xx (February 1926), 31-51, is superficial and unrevealing; Therese Winkelmann, *Zur Entwickelung der allgemeinen Staats- und Gesellschaftsanschauung Voltaires* (1916) is a scholarly if a little mechanical German dissertation. There is an excellent brief article on Voltaire's politics (the best article I know) by J. B. Black, in F. J. C. Hearnshaw, ed., *The Social and Political Ideas of Some Great French Thinkers of the Age of Reason* (1930), 136-167. Constance Rowe, *Voltaire and the State* (1955) makes a well-meaning attempt to defend Voltaire against all criticisms; her thesis that Voltaire was a patriot is not tenable.

On the variety of Voltaire's reputation, see in addition to the various biographies the interesting collection of opinions in Pomeau, *La religion de Voltaire*, 7-16. The anonymous character sketch of 1735, edited by R. A. Leigh, is in *Studies in Voltaire and the Eighteenth Century*, II (1956), 241-272. Josef Popper-Lynkaeus, *Das Recht zu Leben und die Pflicht zu Sterben* (4th ed., 1924) is a fascinating and idiosyncratic essay; a vigorous defense of Voltaire's character with abundant quotations from such earlier writers as Goethe, Schiller, Carlyle, and others. Hans Leo Götzfried, "Versuch einer neuen Deutung des Charakters von Voltaire auf Grund moderner psychologischer Forschungen," *Zeitschrift für französische Sprache und Literatur*, LVII (1933) 211-220, keeps less than its title promises: a good psychological analysis of Voltaire is still needed. Much interesting light is thrown on Voltaire's reputation in Germany in the scholarly and detailed study by H. A. Korff, *Voltaire im literarischen Deutschland des* XVIII. *Jahrhunderts*, 2 vols. (1918). For England, see the dissertation by Bernard N. Schilling, *Conservative England and the Case Against Voltaire* (1950). Some of the biographies and critical volumes speculate on Voltaire' influence. See also J. F. Nourrisson, *Voltaire et le Voltairianisme* (1896), R. Fargher, "The Retreat from Voltairianism, 1810-1815," *The French Mind*, ed. Will Moore *et al.* (1952), 220-237, and the whole of European history since the middle of the eighteenth century.

The question of Voltaire's character and reputation inevitably brings up the questions of Voltaire's relation to money and to his enemies. There has been much talk, not all of it informed, concerning Voltaire's "greed." See the hostile study by Louis Nicolardot, *Ménage et finances de Voltaire* (1845), which has now been superseded by two balanced and informative volumes: Léon Kozminski, *Voltaire financier* (1929) and Jacques Donvez, *De quoi vivait Voltaire* (1940). That Voltaire could be petty and spiteful to his enemies—especially literary enemies—is admitted by all but the most infatuated of his admirers. Still, there is much nonsense. Take as a single example (and a good one, since she is intelligent and informed) Nancy Mitford's comment on Voltaire's feud with Maupertuis in Prussia: "he literally killed the poor man with ridicule." *Voltaire in Love* (1957), 59. It must have been a lingering death, for Voltaire's attack on Maupertuis took place in 1752, but Maupertuis managed to struggle on until 1759. Thus myths are made. François Cornou, *Trente années de luttes contre Voltaire et les philosophes du* xviiie *siècle.* Elie Fréron (1718-1776), (1922) has been much praised, largely by persons who seem to think that objectivity consists of believing at least half the charges made against a man you admire. Cornou's book is well researched and does a valuable job of rehabilitating Fréron, but its treatment of Voltaire is exceedingly unfair and often inaccurate. See also Charles Nisard, *Les ennemis de Voltaire* (1853). F. C. Green has a malicious essay on "Voltaire's Greatest Enemy" in *Eighteenth-Century France* (1931), 111-154, which begins (vividly but inaccurately), "Few great men of letters possessed Voltaire's capacity for intense and tenacious hatred: few, too, cultivated to such a fine degree the art of making enemies and of keeping them," and continues in this vein for forty-five pages.

Despite the able work of J.—R. Carré, much still needs to be done on Voltaire's relation to earlier ideas, such as Stoicism. Eugène E. Rovillain, "Rapports probables entre le *Zadig* de Voltaire et la pensée stoïcienne," PMLA, LII (1937), 374-389, is an illuminating beginning, no more. Aram Vartanian, *Diderot and Descartes* (1953) is an interesting but overargued attempt to prove that Descartes had far more influence on the philosophes than they were ready to admit. I am indebted to Charles C. Gillispie for several conversations on this subject and for showing me several as yet unpublished manuscripts. For Stoicism, see the useful books by E. Bréhier, *Chrysippe et l'ancien stoïcisme* (1951); and L. Zanta, *La renaissance du stoïcisme au* xvie *siècle* (1914). S. Sambursky, *The Physical World of the Greeks* (English tr. 1956) is brilliant and very suggestive. On Newton and the philosophes (of great importance for Voltaire) see above all Pierre Brunet, *L'introduction des théories de Newton en France au* xviiie *siècle* (1931). Paul Vernière, *Spinoza et la pensée française avant la révolution,* 2 vols. (1954) illuminates the influence of a thinker to whom Voltaire did not do justice but for whom he had some admiration.

The notion that the philosophes had no sense of history, once widely accepted, is no longer tenable in the light of Wilhelm Dilthey's epoch-making article, "Das achtzehnte Jahrhundert und die geschichtliche Welt," (first published in 1901), *Gesammelte Schriften*, III (1927), 209-268. Friedrich Meinecke supports and refines Dilthey's thesis in *Die Entstehung des Historismus*, 2 vols. (1936); and Cassirer restates it in a fine chapter on "The Conquest of the Historical World," in *The Philosophy of the Enlightenment*. J. B. Black, *The Art of History* (1926) devotes one searching chapter to Voltaire; E. Bourgeois has a helpful introduction to his edition of Voltaire's *Siècle de Louis XIV* (1890). J. H. Brumfitt, *Voltaire Historian* (1958) is a reliable survey of Voltaire's predecessors, his major and minor historical writings, and his method and philosophy of history. It has a useful bibliography on Voltaire as historian. G. P. Gooch, "Voltaire as Historian," in *Catherine the Great and Other Studies* (1954), 199-274, properly connects Voltaire's histories to French and European politics.

As I have suggested in the text, Voltaire scholars have long agreed that Voltaire was not an optimist. Of the considerable literature, I mention only George R. Havens, "Voltaire's pessimistic revision of the conclusion of his *Poème sur le désastre de Lisbonne*," *Modern Language Notes*, XLIV (1929), 489-492; "The Conclusion of Voltaire's *Poème sur le désastre de Lisbonne*," *ibid.*, LVI (1941), 422-426; Rita Falke, "Eldorado: le meilleur des mondes possibles," *Studies on Voltaire and the Eighteenth Century*, II (1956), 25-41. See also Mina Waterman, *Voltaire, Pascal and Human Destiny* (1942), which should be read in conjunction with J.-R. Carré's book on the same subject. On Leibniz's influence on Voltaire there is an intelligent recent study, W. H. Barber, *Leibniz in France from Arnauld to Voltaire* (1955). I found Theodore Besterman, "Voltaire et le désastre de Lisbonne: ou, la mort de l'optimisme," *Studies on Voltaire and the Eighteenth Century*, II (1956), 7-24, interesting but unconvincing: Voltaire's mood changed far more gradually than this article implies. On that mood, Ernst Cassirer's *aperçus* in *The Question of Jean-Jacques Rousseau* (English tr. 1954) are profound.

No one is better aware than I that my discussion in the text of the relation of German historians to the Enlightenment is no more than a sketch. In thinking about this topic, I found illuminating suggestions not only in Nietzsche, whom I quote, but also in Pieter Geyl, "Ranke in the Light of the Catastrophe," *Debates with Historians* (1955), 1-18; and in Ludwig Dehio, "Gedanken über die deutsche Sendung, 1900-1918," *Historische Zeitschrift*, CLXXIV (1952), 479-502; as well as in the same author's moving "Um den deutschen Militarismus," *ibid.*, CLXXX (1955), 43-64.

On Voltaire's empiricism and his "philosophic modesty," Cassirer's *The Philosophy of the Enlightenment* is basic. His predecessors in skepticism and empiricism are well discussed in Henri Peyre, "The Influence of Eighteenth Century Ideas on the French Revolution," *Journal of the History of Ideas*, x (1949), 63-87. There is some helpful material in Howard Robinson, *Bayle, the Skeptic* (1931); and in M. Dréano, *La renommée de Montaigne en France au* XVIIIe *siècle* (1952). Karl Bornhausen, "Das religiöse Problem während der französischen Vorrevolution bei Bayle, Voltaire, Rousseau," *Historische Zeitschrift*, CV (1910), 496-514, is thin despite its promising title; Henry E. Haxo, "Pierre Bayle et Voltaire avant les *Lettres philosophiques*," PMLA, XLVI (1931), 461-497, is a detailed and informative study of Bayle's influence. René Pintard, *Le libertinage érudit dans la première moitié du* XVIIe *siècle*, 2 vols. (1943), is erudite and illuminating. Still, there remains room for a good study of the impact of Montaigne, Naudé, Saint-Evremond, Bayle on Voltaire.

There is nothing satisfactory on Voltaire and natural law. Francis J. Crowley's critical edition of *Voltaire's "Poème sur La Loi naturelle"* (1938) is scholarly, but fails to deal with the relation of empiricism and sensationalism to natural law theories. For a good discussion of Locke's view of natural law, see

J. W. Gough, *John Locke's Political Philosophy* (1950), which takes account of Locke's early essays on natural law, since edited by W. von Leyden (1954). Eighteenth-century natural lawyers like Vattel are brilliantly dissected in Robert Derathé, *Jean-Jacques Rousseau et la science politique de son temps* (1950). As any student of political theory knows, the literature on natural law is large but unsatisfactory. Perhaps the most illuminating essay is Ernst Troeltsch, "Das stoisch-christliche Naturrecht und das moderne profane Naturrecht," *Gesammelte Schriften*, IV (1925), 156-191.

The classic modern statement of the rule of law is in A. V. Dicey, *Introduction to the Study of the Law of the Constitution*. It should be read in the 9th edition (1939), which includes a lengthy critical introduction by E. C. S. Wade, bringing Dicey up to date. Franz Neumann has two brilliant essays on the subject from a democratic Marxist viewpoint: "The Change in the Function of Law in Modern Society," *The Democratic and the Authoritarian State* (1957), 22-68; and "Types of Natural Law," *ibid.*, 69-95.

CHAPTER I
ENGLAND: A NATION OF PHILOSOPHERS

For Voltaire's early years, Gustave Desnoiresterres, *La jeunesse de Voltaire* is still of value. All essential information about his family is gathered in Guy Chardonchamp, *La famille de Voltaire, les Arouet* (1911), an uninspired but indispensable monograph. It may be supplemented with Augustin Gazier, "Le frère de Voltaire," *Revue des deux mondes* (1906), 615-646, informative but with little psychological penetration. Voltaire's education is treated in Henri Beaune, *Voltaire au collège* (1867), a collection of letters (now superseded) with a lengthy introduction that exaggerates Voltaire's early radicalism. See also Alexis Pierron, *Voltaire et ses maîtres* (1866), which has useful material on Voltaire's Jesuit teachers and their program of study; and a recent article by René Pomeau, "Voltaire au collège,"

Revue d'histoire littéraire de la France, LII (January-March 1952), 1-10. On the still unsolved question of the change of name from Arouet to Voltaire, consult Ira O. Wade, "Voltaire's Name," PMLA, XLIV (June 1929), 560-564. Earlier biographers (encouraged by John Morley) exaggerated the playfulness of the young Voltaire. This bias has now been corrected in Lanson's *Voltaire,* and elsewhere. Fernand Baldensperger, "Voltaire Anglophile avant son séjour d'Angleterre," *Revue de littérature comparée,* IX (1929), 25-61, is a revealing article. Cleveland B. Chase, *The Young Voltaire* (1926) gives a pleasantly written and fairminded summary of the scholarship.

The society frequented by the successful young author of *Oedipe* is depicted in the illuminating study by Roger Picard, *Les salons littéraires et la société française* (1943). I am deeply indebted to Maurice Pellisson, *Les hommes de lettres au XVIIIe siècle* (1911), a brilliant and judicious survey of the philosophes' legal, social, and literary situation. Henri Carré, *La noblesse de France et l'opinion publique au XVIIIe siècle* (1920) is justly considered the standard work. Informed, but sometimes maddeningly superficial, is the widely praised survey by Philippe Sagnac, *La formation de la société française moderne,* 2 vols. (1945-1946). Part I of the second volume has much useful social history on the Regency. Voltaire's quarrel with Rohan is of course described in detail in all the biographies. The most reliable analysis of the confused affair is by Lucien Foulet, "La querelle de Voltaire avec Rohan-Chabot," *Correspondance de Voltaire* (1726-1729), (1913), 211-232.

Voltaire's visit to England remains one of the most puzzling periods of his life. Unfortunately, many of his letters are lost, and the real Voltaire disappears behind a curtain of literary gossip. J. Churton Collins made a beginning in the 1880's, and later published *Voltaire, Montesquieu and Rousseau in England* (1908). Archibald Ballantyne added little to Collins' researches in *Voltaire's Visit to England, 1726-1729* (1893), but his book, filled with long excerpts from correspondence, remains readable. Fernand Baldensperger, "La chronologie du séjour de Voltaire en Angleterre et les *Lettres philosophiques*," *Archiv für das Studium der neueren Sprachen und Literaturen*, cxx (1913), 137-153, is scholarly and informative. Voltaire continued to correspond with Englishmen after his return; later he received scores of English visitors at Ferney. Ballantyne gives an account of these relations, but his work has now been made obsolete by Sir Gavin de Beer's fascinating collection of reports, "Voltaire's British visitors," *Studies on Voltaire and the Eighteenth Century*, iv (1957), 7-136. Lucien Foulet's edition of Voltaire's English correspondence is invaluable, not for the letters which can now be read in Besterman's definitive edition, but for the scholarly appendices, which clear up numerous vexed questions, and prove the inauthenticity of many rumors concerning Voltaire. Lytton Strachey, "Voltaire and England," *Books and Characters* (1922), 107-135, is a perceptive and imaginative essay.

For Voltaire's England, see Basil Williams, *The Whig Supremacy, 1714-1760* (1939), reliable but old-fashioned, and W. E. H. Lecky, *History of England in the Eighteenth Century*, 8 vols. (ed. 1891), even more old-fashioned but marvelously rich in its picture of English society. Both works are now obsolete on political history since Sir Lewis Namier has demonstrated that it is unhistorical to speak of a two-party system in the eighteenth century. Namier's writings cover the period after 1760, but he has an impressive general essay that splendidly reveals his point of view, "Monarchy and the Party System," *Personalities and Powers* (1955), 13-38. J. H. Plumb's excellent summary of English society and politics in the first quarter of the eighteenth century is in *Sir Robert Walpole*, i (1956), 3-78. An example of Namier's school in action, following the master's lead but lacking his grace, is Robert Walcott, *English Politics in the Early Eighteenth Century* (1956), a painstaking analysis of party politics under Queen Anne. E. T. Williams, "The Cabinet in the Eighteenth Century," *History*, xxii (1937), 240-252, is a scholarly examination of a controversial subject, with immensely useful bibliographical footnotes. For parliamentary politics, A. S. Turberville, *The House of Lords in the Eighteenth Century* (1927); and Edward Porritt, *The Unreformed House of Commons*, 2 vols. (1903), remain useful, especially read in conjunction with Namier's writings. Norman Sykes, *Church and State in Eighteenth Century England* (1934) is definitive—a superb study.

English social and literary life is portrayed briefly and a little superficially in G. M. Trevelyan, *Illustrated English Social History*, III, *The Eighteenth Century* (1951). More searching are Dorothy George's *England in Transition* (1931); and *London Life in the* XVIIIth *Century* (2d ed., 1930). Leslie Stephen, *English Literature and Society in the Eighteenth Century* (1907) is a valuable essay.

The lot of English men of letters—their finances, their patrons, their publishers, their sales (all of decisive importance to Voltaire)—is analyzed with care and verve in Alexandre Beljame, *Men of Letters and the English Public in the Eighteenth Century* (tr. 1948). First published in 1881 and revised in 1897, the book remains immensely rich and informative. It can be supplemented with A. S. Collins, *Authorship in the Days of Johnson* (1927); R. W. Chapman, "Authors and Booksellers," *Johnson's England*, ed. A. S. Turberville, 2 vols. (1933), II, 310-330; and Leo Lowenthal and Marjorie Fiske, "The Debate over Art and Popular Culture in Eighteenth Century England," *Common Frontiers of the Social Sciences*, ed. Mirra Komarowsky (1957), 33-112. All three studies are full of revealing material. James L. Clifford's fine *Young Sam Johnson* (1955), throws much light on the early eighteenth century in England.

These studies, excellent as they are, of course do not supersede the writings of eighteenth-century authors themselves. Samuel Johnson's *Lives of the English Poets* is justly a classic and filled with information about English literary life. However, the reader must be warned that not all its anecdotes are accurate. Another delightful work, beautifully written and extremely revealing of English politics at the time of Voltaire's visit is John, Lord Hervey, *Some Materials Towards Memoirs of the Reign of King George II*, ed. Romney Sedgwick, 3 vols. (1931). See also Oliver Goldsmith, *An Enquiry into the Present State of Polite Learning in Europe* (1759), which is an ambitious comparative study.

On the legal right to speak and write, see in addition to Collins, Laurence Hanson, *Government and the Press, 1695-1763* (1936); and William H. Wickwar, *The Struggle for the Freedom of the Press* (1928), both important studies which rather date the earlier Douglas M. Ford, "The Growth of the Freedom of the Press," *English Historical Review*, IV (1889), 1-12; and F. Knight Hunt, *The Fourth Estate*, 2 vols. (1850). See also William T. Laprade, *Public Opinion and Politics in Eighteenth Century England to the Fall of Walpole* (1936).

The most important result of Voltaire's visit to England was, of course, his *Lettres philosophiques*. In addition to Lanson's classic edition, already cited, there are other good editions, particularly F. A. Taylor, *Lettres philosophiques* (1954), with excellent notes and an introduction that is informative on Voltaire's predecessors in Anglomania and on his own stay. Albert Lantoine, *Les Lettres philosophiques de Voltaire* (1931) is a competent analysis of the book, its origins, its publication, and its reception. C. Luporini, *Voltaire e le "Lettres philosophiques"* (1955) is an ambitious and interesting interpretation from a radical point of view. French opinions of England are authoritatively and exhaustively studied in Gabriel Bonno, *La culture et la civilisation britannique devant l'opinion française de la paix d'Utrecht aux Lettres philosophiques (1713-1734)*, *Transactions of the American Philosophical Society*, New Series, XXXVIII, Part 1 (June 1948). The same author's *La constitution britannique devant l'opinion française de Montesquieu à Bonaparte* (1931) has some good comments on Voltaire's persistent Anglomania which are much more to the point than Joseph

Dedieu's speculations in *Montesquieu et la tradition politique anglaise en France* (1909).

I want to make special mention of Erich Auerbach, *Mimesis* (English tr. 1953), which has a brilliant analysis of Voltaire's stock-exchange metaphor. I have learned much from these pages (401-413) and from the book as a whole, and my paragraph on this subject leans heavily on Auerbach. His technique of linguistic analysis, extremely fruitful in the hands of a skilled practitioner, is in the tradition of Leo Spitzer, whose remarkable essay, "Einige Voltaire-Interpretationen," *Romanische Stil- und Literaturstudien*, 2 vols. (1930), II, 211-243, had considerable impact on me.

It is necessary to compare some of Voltaire's assertions in his book on England with the facts. Much of this has already been done in the critical editions. To them should be added: on the Quakers, Edith Philips, *The Good Quaker in French Legend* (1932); on taxation, Stephen Dowell, *A History of Taxation and Taxes in England*, 2 vols. (2d ed., 1888), II, book 2; on the aristocracy, H. J. Habakkuk, "England," *The European Nobility in the Eighteenth Century*, ed. A. Goodwin (1953), 1-21; on the British Constitution, Sir David Lindsay Keir, *Constitutional History of Modern Britain, 1485-1951* (ed. 1955); on toleration, the volume by Norman Sykes cited above.

The English deists, whom Voltaire cautiously fails to mention in the *Lettres philosophiques* but exploits later, are examined in Norman Torrey's important *Voltaire and the English Deists* (1930). It adopts the distinction of critical deists and constructive deists first made in Leslie Stephen, *History of English Thought in the Eighteenth Century*, 2 vols. (3d ed., 1902), a magnificent warhorse, full of idiosyncratic judgments. Bolingbroke is the subject of a special study by Torrey, "Bolingbroke and Voltaire, a fictitious influence," PMLA, XLII (1927), 788-797, which is illuminating but overargued. Thomas R. Lounsbury, *Shakespeare and Voltaire* (1902) greatly oversimplifies Voltaire's complicated feelings for the playwright whose plays, he said, reminded him of dunghills studded with diamonds. Lounsbury's thesis is corrected in F. C. Green's stimulating *Minuet* (1935). Edouard Sonet, *Voltaire et l'influence anglaise* (1926) is fair and comprehensive, but offers little that is new.

CHAPTER II
FRANCE: THE KING'S PARTY

Until Ira O. Wade's authoritative studies compelled a revision, Voltaire's Cirey years were largely treated as an amorous episode. See Desnoiresterres, *Voltaire à Cirey* and most later biographies. But in Wade's *Voltaire and Madame du Châtelet* (1941); *Studies on Voltaire, with Some Unpublished Papers of Madame du Châtelet* (1947); and his fine critical edition, *Voltaire's "Micromégas"* (1950), Cirey appears as a place of serious study and intellectual preparation. Nancy Mitford's witty *Voltaire in Love* takes account of his new view but her very choice of subject has compelled her to stress the erotic over the intellectual side of Cirey life. There are several books on madame du Châtelet; in addition to Mitford, see Frank Hamel, *An Eighteenth Century Marquise* (1910). In 1938, G. F. Aubry published some startling love letters of Voltaire to his niece, *Lettres d'Alsace à Madame Denis*. As Theodore Besterman has pointed out in "Voltaire's Love-Letters," *Times Literary Supplement* (30 August 1957), 524, these and similar love letters are unquestionably authentic and throw much new and unexpected light on the canny Voltaire.

How much the philosophes suffered from the censors in eighteenth-century France remains a matter of controversy: estimations range from an extreme defense of the old regime to extreme condemnations. A superb analysis, which I have already cited, is Pellisson, *Les hommes de lettres au* xviiie *siècle*. J.-P. Belin, *Le commerce des livres prohibés à Paris de 1750 à 1789* (1913) has much useful information; as does Albert Bachman, *Censorship in France from 1715 to 1750: Voltaire's Opposition* (1934), which I used extensively for information about police espionage, tacit permissions, and the role of Malesherbes. It prints as an appendix a list of books prohibited in the first half of the century. Joseph Le Gras, *Diderot et l'Encyclopédie* (1942) is good on Diderot's embroilments with the authorities; it has been largely superseded by Arthur M. Wilson, *Diderot, The Testing Years, 1713-1759* (1957), a scholarly and judicious account of Diderot's life until the prohibition of his *Encyclopédie*, which contains all necessary information concerning Diderot's imprisonment. For a demonstration of how the fearful printer tampered with the *Encyclopédie*, see Douglas H. Gordon and Norman L. Torrey's startling *The Censoring of Diderot's Encyclopédie and the Re-established Text* (1947). Gabriel Peignot, *Essai historique sur la liberté d'écrire* (1832) prints excerpts from the many decrees under which the censors worked; Paul Dupont, *Histoire de l'imprimérie*, 2 vols. (1854), is excellent on the book trade; the second volume has an appendix with the principal laws and regulations. It can be supplemented by Paul Mellottée, *Les transformations économiques de l'imprimérie sous l'ancien régime* (1905). On the illegal distribution of books and manuscripts see Ira O. Wade, *The Clandestine Organization and Diffusion of Philosophic Ideas in France between 1715 and 1750* (1938). Eugène Vaillé has an interesting description of the government's opening of letters, which so annoyed Voltaire, in *Le cabinet noir* (1950). Malesherbes, who did more than anyone else to weaken censorship, still needs his biographer. The best available studies are by Henri Robert (1927) and J. M. S. Allison (1938). Censorship began of course with the invention of printing; Lucien Febvre, *Le problème de l'incroyance au xvie siècle; La religion de Rabelais* (1947), has much interesting material on sixteenth-century interferences with free expression. Two articles by David T. Pottinger, "Censorship in France during the Ancien Regime," *Boston Public Library Quarterly*, vi (1954), 23-42, 84-101, are reliable summaries. After Tocqueville, whose opinion I cite in the text, the most impressive apologist for the old regime is Frantz Funck-

Brentano, *The Old Regime in France* (English tr. 1929). There is controversy, too, over how much the philosophes suffered in jail. Once again Pellisson is indispensable. Joseph Delort, *Histoire de la détention des philosophes et des gens de lettres à la Bastille et à Vincennes,* 3 vols. (1829), is informative but not always reliable. S. N. H. Linguet, *Mémoires sur la Bastille* (1783) is a good antidote for those who think of the Bastille as a kind of Guggenheim fellowship.

What part, if any, did the philosophes play in fomenting the French Revolution? Conservatives have usually argued either that the philosophes were wholly responsible for this calamity, or were powerless to affect the course of events. Best known for this controversy are Charles Aubertin, *L'esprit publique au* xviiie *siècle* (1873) and Felix Rocquain, *L'esprit révolutionnaire avant la Révolution* (1878) who argue that the Revolution was caused by the struggle between the crown and the parlements, a claim for the insignificance of the philosophes greeted with applause by Faguet and other opponents of the spirit of 1789. Marius Roustan, in his familiar study *Les philosophes et la société français au* xviiie *siècle* (1906) argues against both Aubertin and Rocquain that the radical *littérateurs* were a powerful force in the eighteenth century. The impact of this sensible correction of earlier work can be observed above all in Kingsley Martin's book on eighteenth-century France. Lucien Brunel, *Les philosophes et l'académie française au dix-huitième siècle* (1884) is an informative analysis of the philosophes' reputation through the century. A significant and influential recent study is Daniel Mornet, *Les origines intellectuelles de la révolution française* (1947), which traces the triumph of philosophic ideas by painstaking research into hundreds of libraries. It is an important survey but rather pedestrian in the realm of ideas.

R. R. Palmer's vigorous *Catholics and Unbelievers in Eighteenth Century France* (1939) is a welcome corrective to the professional liberal view that the philosophes were all-virtuous and the defenders of the old order all-vicious. In its reaction to the unhistorical praise of the philosophes it is a little harsh, but its case remains just, and the book replaces the earlier A. Monod, *De Pascal à Chateaubriand* (1916). A dissertation by John N. Pappas, *The journal de Trévoux and the philosophes, Studies on Voltaire and the Eighteenth Century,* III (1957) confirms Palmer's analysis.

No student of eighteenth-century France can afford to neglect Taine's *The Ancient Regime* (English tr. 1876) and Tocqueville's classic *Old Regime and the French Revolution,* of which there is an excellent version by Stuart Gilbert (1955). Both books have been immensely influential, but their interpretations have been undermined by recent scholarship. For a general history of the period, see Henri Carré, *Louis XV* (ed. 1911), Vol. VIII, Part 2 of Lavisse's great *Histoire de France;* Pierre Gaxotte, *Le siècle de Louis XV* (1933) strongly royalist in its bias and unreliable on foreign policy but valuable on domestic affairs; Alfred Cobban, *A History of Modern France,* I, *Old Regime and Revolution,* 1715-1799, (1957), a marvel of economy, good judgment, and helpful organization. No better short history of the century seems possible. Marcel Marion, *Dictionnaire des institutions de la France aux* XVII *et* XVIII *siècles* (1923) is an invaluable reference work. The same author's monographs on taxation are most helpful, especially *Les impôts directs sous l'ancien régime* (1910); and the first two volumes of *Histoire financière de la France depuis 1715,* 6 vols. (1914-1931). Marion's *Machault d'Arnouville* (1891) is an authoritative examination of Louis XV's daring finance minister, on which I have relied heavily. Much important work has been done in the field of economic history by C. E. Labrousse. I mention only his encyclopedic *Esquisse du mouvement des prix et des revenus en France au* XVIII *siècle* (1934). George T. Matthews unravels the complicated story of tax farming in the Old Regime in *The Royal General Farms in Eighteenth Century France* (1958), an important monograph.

The best recent histories of the French Revolution have had

much to say on the structure of the Old Regime. See A. Aulard, *Histoire politique de la révolution française* (1913), which has some interesting observations on the republicanism of Voltaire and his political allies; A. Mathiez, *La révolution française*, I, *La chute de la royauté* (1922); and Georges Lefebvre's superb *Coming of the French Revolution*, first published in 1939 on the Bicentenary of the Revolution (English tr. 1947). These three books have been instrumental in calling attention to the aristocratic counterrevolution after 1715 as a major cause of the events of 1789.

Political controversies in eighteenth-century France were also religious controversies. Of the many monographs, most valuable are L. Cahen, *Les querelles religieuses et parlementaires sous Louis XV* (1913); P. de Crousaz-Crétet, *L'Eglise et l'état, ou les deux puissances au* xviiie *siècle* (1893); and E. Préclin's important *Les Jansenistes du* xviiie *siècle et la Constitution civile du clergé* (1928).

Eighteenth-century Frenchmen were much addicted to keeping diaries—witness the voluminous, brilliant, and spiteful jottings of the duc de Saint-Simon. Of the memoirs I used for this book, most interesting but splenetic and unreliable is the *Journal et mémoires du marquis d'Argenson*, ed. E. J. B. Rathéry, 9 vols. (1859-1867). Two educated and articulate lawyers also left revealing diaries: E.-J.-F. Barbier, *Journal historique et anecdotique du règne de Louis XV, 1718-1763*, ed. A. de la Villegille, 4 vols. (1847-1856); and Mathieu Marais, *Journal et mémoires sur la régence et le règne de Louis XV*, ed. M. de Lescure, 4 vols. (1863-1868). The *Correspondance littéraire, philosophique et critique de Grimm, Diderot etc.*, ed. Maurice Tourneux, 16 vols. (1877-1882), is a fascinating collection of literary reviews, political news, and gossip. Charles Pinot-Duclos, *Considérations sur les moeurs de ce siècle* (1750) is a penetrating survey of manners and ambitions by a brilliant man of letters. All these memoirs, and others, are used in Louis Ducros' social history of the period, *La société française au* xviiie *siècle* (1922).

Among the significant monographs on society and politics under the old regime, special mention should be made of Roland Mousnier, *La vénalité des offices sous Henri IV et Louis XIII* (1945), which traces the sale of offices during an important period; Martin Göhring, *Die Ämterkäuflichkeit im Ancien Regime* (1938), a pioneering study that did much to clarify the legal, social, financial, and political significance of venality; Franklin L. Ford, *Robe and Sword, the Regrouping of the French Aristocracy after Louis XIV* (1953), an important social and political analysis that traces the rise of the courts and the social structure of the robe nobility down to 1748; Hedwig Hintze, *Staatseinheit und Föderalismus im alten Frankreich und in der Revolution* (1928), which examines the conflict between centripetal and centrifugal political forces in eighteenth-century France. Martin Göhring, *Weg und Sieg der modernen Staatsidee in Frankreich* (1947) is a popular summary that uses this scholarship.

Voltaire was, of course, not the first French reformer. For French political ideas in the sixteenth century, see J. W. Allen, *A History of Political Thought in the Sixteenth Century* (3d ed., 1951), Part III, a useful summary. The seventeenth century is surveyed in Henri Sée, *Les idées politiques en France au* xviie *siècle* (1923), which makes the inevitable distinction between absolutist and antiabsolutist theorists. Rudolf von Albertini, *Das politische Denken in Frankreich zur Zeit Richelieus* (1951) is a good monograph; it should be supplemented with some brilliant chapters on Richelieu and other Frenchmen in Friedrich Meinecke, *Die Idee der Staatsräson in der neueren Geschichte* (1924), perhaps Meinecke's most impressive work; and Wilhelm Mommsen, "Richelieu als Staatsmann," *Historische Zeitschrift*, cxxvii (1923), 210-242. Louis André has an important edition of Richelieu's *Testament politique* (1947) with a revealing section on Voltaire's claim that the testament was inauthentic.

André comes to the conclusion (wholly unacceptable to me) that Voltaire's doubts were based on his opposition to French absolutism—a complete misreading of Voltaire's political writings. See J. H. Brumfitt, *Voltaire Historian*, 147-160 on this issue. Fénelon has been well treated in the brief book by Elie Carcassonne, *Fénelon, l'homme et l'oeuvre* (1946); and the detailed study by Albert Chérel, *Fénelon au xviiie siècle en France* (1715-1820), (1917). The great specialist on Boulainvilliers is Renée Simon. See especially her *Henri de Boulainviller, historien, politique, philosophe, astrologue* (1942); and her "Boulainviller et Voltaire," *xviie siècle*, No. 11 (1951), 103-114; there is also a recent article by Vincent Buranelli, "The Historical and Political Thought of Boulainvilliers," *Journal of the History of Ideas*, xviii (October 1957), 475-494. Marshal Vauban's treatise, *Projet d'une dixme royale* has been well edited by E. Coornaert (1933).

A. Lombard has written an extremely informative biography of *L'Abbé Du Bos* (1913), which unfortunately slights the political implications of DuBos' history as well as the similarities of his views to Voltaire's. On Hénault, see Henri Lion, *Un magistrat homme de lettres au dix-huitième siècle. Le président Hénault 1685-1770* (1903). A good book still needs to be written on the marquis d'Argenson. Jean Lamson, *Les idées politiques du marquis d'Argenson* (1943) tries to identify him with enlightened despotism. Far better is Sée's brief chapter in his *Evolution de la pensée politique en France au xviiie siècle*. In her *Staatseinheit und Föderalismus*, Hedwig Hintze has an important appendix discussing the various editions of d'Argenson's posthumously published *Considérations*.

On Montesquieu's role in French politics, see above all Franz Neumann's admirable introduction to Montesquieu's *Spirit of the Laws*, reprinted under the title "Montesquieu" in *The Democratic and the Authoritarian State*, 96-148. It was this essay that introduced me almost ten years ago to the distinction between the *thèse royale* and the *thèse nobiliaire*. Joseph Dedieu,

Montesquieu, l'homme et l'oeuvre (1943) is a short biography, rather weak on politics. Göhring and Hintze deal with Montesquieu in some detail, and Ford has a stimulating reassessment in his *Robe and Sword*, chapter 12. To these works should be added the all too famous controversy between Carcassonne and Mathiez. In his *Montesquieu et le problème de la constitution française au* xviiie *siècle* (1926) Elie Carcassonne tries to make Montesquieu into a liberal, while Albert Mathiez paints Montesquieu as a reactionary in his powerful but ill-tempered replies, first in a review of Carcassonne's book, *Annales de la révolution française,* iv (1927), 509-513, and in a more comprehensive statement, "La place de Montesquieu dans l'histoire des doctrines politiques du xviiie siècle," *ibid.,* vii (1930), 97-112. Voltaire's relations with Montesquieu deserve fuller treatment than they have so far received. See E. H. Price, "The Opinions of Voltaire concerning Montesquieu's Theories of Roman Greatness," *Philological Quarterly,* xvi (1937), 287-295; and his "Voltaire and Montesquieu's Three Principles of Government," pmla, lvii (December 1942), 1046-1052. Too much has been made of Voltaire's criticisms of Montesquieu, not enough of his admiration.

For Voltaire at court, see his correspondence (particularly his recently discovered letters to his niece). Desnoiresterres, *Voltaire à la cour* is excellent on Voltaire's literary and courtly experiences during these years, but the unpolitical orientation of the book (and of the whole series of Desnoiresterres' biographies) is strikingly revealed by its failure to analyze or even discuss Voltaire's intense political activities in 1750. Nancy Mitford, *Madame Pompadour* (1954) is an intelligent biography of Louis XV's most philosophic mistress.

CHAPTER III
PRUSSIA: SPARTA IN A COLD CLIMATE

It is almost impossible to obtain a balanced view of Voltaire's relations with Frederick of Prussia: Germans are all too anxious to attribute low motives to Voltaire, Frenchmen all too anxious to attribute them to Frederick. One exception is Bellessort's *Essai sur Voltaire*, which has some severe but generally just comments on Voltaire, pp. 163-164, 190-196. Even the editors of their correspondence differ on how to interpret these men; it is instructive to read Theodore Besterman's editorial comments side by side with the comments by Reinhold Koser and Hans Droysen, *Briefwechsel Friedrichs des Grossen mit Voltaire*, 3 vols. (1908-1911). Besterman is icily objective; Koser and Droysen are passionately pro-Frederick. Desnoiresterres' account in *Voltaire et Frédéric* may be supplemented by Emile Henriot, *Voltaire et Frédéric II* (1927); and the illuminating article by Fernand Baldensperger, "Les prémices d'une douteuse amitié: Voltaire et Frédéric II de 1740 à 1742," *Revue de littérature comparée*, x (1930), 230-261. Lytton Strachey has a good essay on "Voltaire and Frederick the Great," *Books and Characters*, 159-189. The German view of the friendship is well represented by Reinhold Koser, *Geschichte Friedrichs des Grossen*, 4 vols. (4th and 5th eds., 1913). Like Koser, Werner Langer, *Friedrich der Grosse und die geistige Welt Frankreichs* (1932) is convinced that the Prussian was morally superior to the Frenchman, but despite this bias his book is an informative review of Frederick's dependence on (and occasional rebellion against) French civilization. This dependence is illuminated in Max Posner's edition of "Die Montesquieu-Noten Friedrichs II," *Historische Zeitschrift*, xxxxvii (1882), 193-288. A somewhat different story emerges from the rather hostile biography by Pierre Gaxotte, *Frederick the Great* (English tr. 1941), an excellent study with a full bibliographical essay. Very revealing is Theodore Besterman's edition of "Voltaire's Commentary on Frederick's *l'Art de la guerre*," *Studies on Voltaire and the Eighteenth Century*, II (1956), 61-206, which demonstrates that Voltaire was by no means always the cringing courtier.

There are all too many books on Frederick. Good guides are Gaxotte's bibliography, as well as the older but much fuller bibliographical notes in Volume 4 of Koser's biography. The most important studies for my chapter were Arnold Berney, *Friedrich der Grosse, Entwicklungsgeschichte eines Staatsmannes* (1934), a remarkably objective examination of the development of Frederick as a thinker and statesman; Otto Hintze, *Die Hohenzollern und ihr Werk* (ed. 1916), a great history of Prussia's growth; and Wilhelm Dilthey's suggestive essay on "Friedrich der Grosse und die deutsche Aufklärung," *Gesammelte Schriften*, III, 81-205. Friedrich Meinecke's long chapter in *Die Idee der Staatsräson* is a profound examination of Frederick's prolonged inner conflict between Enlightenment philosophy and *raison d'état*. Frederick's state is dissected in a series of important articles by Walter L. Dorn, "The Prussian Bureaucracy in the Eighteenth Century," *Political Science Quarterly*, XLVI (1931), 403-423; XLVII (1932), 75-94, 259-273. For Frederick as reformer see, in addition to Koser, Gaxotte, and Dilthey, M. Springer, *Die Coccejische Justizreform* (1914). Kurt Mehring, *Inwieweit ist praktischer Einfluss Montesquieus und Voltaires auf die strafrechtliche Tätigkeit Friedrichs des Grossen anzunehmen bezw. nachzuweisen?* (1927) is a fatuous attempt to show that Frederick was in no way dependent on the philosophes for his reform ideas; it is of interest only to the pathologist of patriotism. For Frederick's revealing political testaments, see especially G. B. Volz, "Zur Entstehung der Politischen Testamente Friedrichs des Grossen von 1752 und 1768," *Forschungen zur Brandenburgischen und Preussischen Geschichte*, XXXII (1919), 369-384. Volz has a handy edition of the testaments in a German translation by Friedrich von Oppeln-Bronikowski: Friedrich der Grosse, *Die Politischen Testamente* (1922), from which I have cited.

Voltaire's friendship with Frederick inevitably brings up the vexed question of "enlightened despotism." I have suggested in the text that the term does not adequately describe more than a small segment of Voltaire's thinking, and indeed of anyone else's thinking. Still, most interpreters of the eighteenth century insist on affixing this label on him—every reader can supply his own examples. I have quoted Gershoy in the text; to add only a few examples, see Cassirer, *Question of Jean-Jacques Rousseau*; Alfred Cobban, *Rousseau and the Modern State* (1934); Per Fuglum, *Edward Gibbon* (1953). There are many others. At the other extreme, Constance Rowe treats Voltaire as practically a democrat in *Voltaire and the State*; as does Julien Benda in his fine introduction to the *Dictionnaire philosophique*. Sée, however, classifies him among the liberals. The confusion about Voltaire's politics is exemplified in Sakmann's *Voltaire's Geistesart und Gedankenwelt*: on p. 328 he calls Voltaire an instinctive monarchist; on p. 338 he calls him a conservative liberal; and on p. 365 he expresses surprise that Voltaire should have been so favorable to democracy. The evolution of Gustave Lanson's ideas is also illuminating. In the first edition of his *Histoire de la littérature française* (1894) he flatly calls Voltaire a supporter of the *despote bienfaisant*. But as his history went through edition after edition, and Lanson read Voltaire with care, he changed his mind and finally suggested in a long note to the 11th edition that the *despote bienfaisant* was no more than an expedient in Voltaire's mind, and that he was really a democrat at heart. I suspect that if Lanson had ever written the book on Voltaire's politics that he promised to write, the present volume would have been a redundancy.

The prevailing confusion over Voltaire's politics reflects a confusion about the subject of "enlightened despotism" in general. In 1889, Reinhold Koser published a pioneering article in the *Historische Zeitschrift*, LXI, 246-287, entitled "Die Epochen der absoluten Monarchie in der neueren Geschichte," in which he sought to establish a sequence of types of monarchies. His views were thoroughly criticized by Fritz Hartung in an article with the same title, *Historische Zeitschrift*, CXXXXV (1931), 46-52. In the 1930's, an international group of historians began to examine *despotisme éclairé* country by country, reporting their findings in the *Bulletin of the International Commit-*

tee of Historical Sciences. See especially Volumes I, II, V, and IX.
The most representative sample of their thinking is Michel
Lhéritier, "Rapport général: le despotisme éclairé, de Frédéric II
à la Révolution française," *Bulletin,* No. 35, IX (1937), 181-225,
Lhéritier, incidentally, adopts the characterization of Voltaire by
R. Mayr as "the theoretician of enlightened kingdoms." Doubtless, this group of historians has done much valuable work, but
most of them assume as given the very thing that needs to be
proved—the existence of a particular kind of monarchy that
can be categorized with the single phrase "enlightened despotism." It is, I think, not an accident that Leo Gershoy's interesting volume, *From Despotism to Revolution* (1944), which
makes excellent use of all this material, never clearly defines the
concept. Geoffrey Bruun, *The Enlightened Despots* (1929) is
a brief, elementary survey, no clearer than Gershoy. To my mind
the most original contributions to this discussion are the articles
by Heinz Holldack, subtly aware of the ambiguities of eighteenth-century statecraft. I have borrowed from him the three-
fold division of authoritarian centralism, aristocratic conservatism, and administrative decentralization. See his "Die Bedeu-
tung des aufgeklärten Despotismus für die Entwicklung des
Liberalismus," *Bulletin,* V (1933), 773-779; "Der Physiokratismus und die Absolute Monarchie," *Historische Zeitschrift,* CVL
(1932), 517-549; and "Die Neutralitätspolitik Leopolds von
Toskana," *Historische Vierteljahrsschrift,* XXX (1935-6), 732-
756. See also Fritz Hartung, "Der aufgeklärte Absolutismus,"
Historische Zeitschrift, CLXXX (1955), 15-42.

Leonard Krieger's *The German Idea of Freedom* (1957),
wholly free from such ambiguities as plagued the Lhéritier
group, is an immensely stimulating addition to the history of
the German mind. I found its first section (pp. 3-80) an invaluable analysis of eighteenth-century Prussian absolutism. Hajo
Holborn, "Der deutsche Idealismus in sozialgeschichtlicher
Beleuchtung," *Historische Zeitschrift,* CLXXIV (1952), 359-384,
is an important study of the gulf between German intellectuals

and practical politics. I learned much from its comparison between the German and French situations. Another valuable study is Albert Köster, *Die deutsche Literatur der Aufklärungszeit* (1925), a brilliant essay.

Finally, Voltaire's relations to Frederick raise the question of Voltaire's pacifism. For a view somewhat different from mine, see Julien Benda's introduction to Voltaire's *Dictionnaire philosophique.*

Recent scholarship has done much to undermine earlier views of Catherine the Great. It is fully taken into account in Gershoy's excellent pages in *From Despotism to Revolution.* A Catherine neither liberal nor conservative but in quest of security appears in A. Kizevetter, "Catherine II (1762-1796)," *Histoire de Russie,* eds. Paul Milioukov *et al.* (1932), II. The most important recent student of Catherine's reign was Georg Sacke. See his "Zur Charakteristik der gesetzgebenden Kommission Katharinas II. von Russland," *Archiv für Kulturgeschichte,* XXI (1931) 166-191; "Katharina II. im Kampf um Thron und Selbstherrschaft," *ibid.,* XXII (1932), 191-216; "Adel und Bürgertum in der gesetzgebenden Kommission Katharinas II. von Russland," *Jahrbücher für Geschichte Osteuropas,* III (1938), 408-417; "Die gesetzgebende Kommission Katharinas II." *ibid.,* Beiheft 2 (1940). See also the brilliant study by G. T. Robinson, *Rural Russia under the Old Regime* (1949), which discusses the peasant question in chapter 2.

In his general articles, Sacke demonstrates that Catherine was trying to cooperate with the progressive, commercial aristocracy and small but energetic Russian bourgeoisie. In some special articles, he has thrown much light on Voltaire's relation to Catherine. See, "Entstehung des Briefwechsels zwischen der Kaiserin Katharina II. von Russland und Voltaire," *Zeitschrift für französische Sprache und Literatur,* LXI (1938), 273-282; "Die Kaiserin Katharina II., Voltaire und die 'Gazette de Berne,'" *Zeitschrift für schweizerische Geschichte,* XVIII (1938),

305-314; "Die Pressepolitik Katharinas II. von Russland," *Zeitungswissenschaft*, XIII, No. 9 (1 September 1938), 570-579. His findings have been confirmed in Louis-Edouard Roulet, *Voltaire et les Bernois* (1950).

Since Catherine took care to be in the good graces of other philosophes besides Voltaire, there has been room for a few general studies. Dimitri S. von Mohrenschildt, *Russia in the Intellectual Life of Eighteenth-Century France* (1936) is sound but not nearly so exciting as Albert Lortholary's acidulous but carefully documented *Les "philosophes" du* XVIIIe *siècle et la Russie* (1951). Lortholary's book is a brilliant indictment which slights the social pressures under which the philosophes had to work. Still, I have learned much from it. W. F. Reddaway, in his edition of *Documents of Catherine the Great: The Correspondence with Voltaire and the Instruction of 1767 in the English Text of 1768* (1931), is much kinder without being naïve. See also G. P. Gooch, "Catherine the Great," *Catherine the Great and Other Studies* (1954); and Jean Fabre's sharply critical (but charitable) study of the relations of the philosophes to the amiable dethroned king of Poland, *Stanislas-Auguste Poniatowski et l'Europe des lumières* (1952). On the murder of Catherine's husband, Voltaire said some foolish and callous things, but I think that Cobban infers too much from them in his *Rousseau and the Modern State*, 50-51n.

CHAPTER IV

GENEVA: CALVIN'S THREE CITIES

Voltaire's later years, filled with his quarrel with Rousseau, *écrasez l'infâme*, and the Calas case have generated lively interest and first-rate research. Desnoiresterres' volumes for this period are particularly rich on Voltaire's literary career and his relations with Rousseau; see *Voltaire aux Délices*; *Voltaire et J.-J. Rousseau*; and *Voltaire et Genève*. These volumes must be supplemented by the important collection of Voltaire's correspondence with Cramer and the Tronchins, already cited.

L. Perey and G. Maugras, *La vie intime de Voltaire aux Délices et à Ferney* (1754-1778), (1885), adds much to Desnoiresterres. Jean-Pierre Gaberel, *Voltaire et les Genevois* (1856) has now been superseded by Paul Chaponnière, *Voltaire chez les Calvinistes* (2d ed., 1936), a fair, fully documented, and finely written study from which I have borrowed freely. It is during these years that Voltaire corresponded with Diderot; his collaboration with the *Encyclopédie* is minutely examined by Raymond Naves, *Voltaire et l'Encyclopédie* (1938). Voltaire's politics are incidentally illuminated by studies of Diderot. See above all Jean Oestreicher, *La pensée politique et économique de Diderot* (1936), interesting but imposing too much system on an unsystematic mind; Jean Thomas, *L'humanisme de Diderot* (2d ed., 1938), crisp and suggestive; and Wilson's biography. Jacques Barzun and Ralph H. Bowen's translations of some of the major writings, *Rameau's Nephew and Other Works* (1956) are so good that I could do no better than borrow from them.

Every biographer of Voltaire (and of Rousseau) has naturally something to say on their quarrel. Chaponnière is excellent on this subject as on all others, but he tells the story from the side of Voltaire. Rousseau's side is brilliantly represented in an important book by Gaspard Vallette, *Jean-Jacques Rousseau Genevois* (2d ed., 1911), which places Rousseau in his Genevan environment. Vallette is a little harsh on Voltaire, but his book should be required reading for Voltaire enthusiasts, many of whom are unfortunately unable to extend sympathy, let alone admiration, to Rousseau. M. Fuchs has a good critical edition of J.-J. Rousseau, *Lettre à Mr. d'Alembert sur les spectacles* (1948), which illuminates the quarrel over the theatre. John Stephenson Spink, *Jean-Jacques Rousseau et Genève* (1934) is a revealing scholarly study, untangling Genevan politics during the great controversies of the 1760's. Of the many Rousseau biographies, Charles W. Hendel, *Jean-Jacques Rousseau Moralist*, 2 vols. (1934), is one of the few that has anything useful to say on the Genevan situation. F. C. Green's recent biography, *Jean-Jacques Rousseau* (1955) is better on literature than on politics. Much light on Rousseau is shed by René Hubert, *Rousseau et l'Encyclopédie* (n.d.); and Robert Derathé's brilliant *Le rationalisme de J.-J. Rousseau* (1948). But this is not the place for a bibliography on Rousseau; the reader will find a survey of the literature in my introduction to Ernst Cassirer, *The Question of Jean-Jacques Rousseau.*

Voltaire's complicated real-estate, financial, and industrial operations are thoroughly examined in Fernand Caussy's important *Voltaire, seigneur de village* (1912). P. Calmettes, *Choiseul et Voltaire* (1902) has a good discussion of Voltaire's relations to the powerful minister. A recent study by Jane Ceitac, *Voltaire et l'affaire des Natifs* (1956) considerably expands our information concerning Voltaire's championship of the Genevan "proletariat." It is somewhat too admiring of Voltaire, but very useful. On the same matter, see Bernard Gagnebin, "Le médiateur d'une petite querelle genevoise," *Travaux sur Voltaire et le dix-huitième siècle*, I (1955), 115-123. Fernand Caussy's edition of Voltaire's proposals to settle the Genevan quarrel, "Voltaire, pacificateur de Genève," *Revue Bleue*, ve série, IX (4 January 1908), 9-15, is of decisive importance. F. Baldensperger gives a useful survey of Voltaire's meddling, with citations from diplomatic correspondence, "Voltaire et la diplomatie française dans les 'affaires de Genève,'" *Revue de littérature comparée*, XI (1931), 581-606. The same author has an account of Voltaire's panicky proposal to move the philosophes out of France, "Un projet Voltairien d'évasion des clercs," *Revue de Paris* (1 April 1937), 656-699. The Covelle affair is treated in Desnoiresterres and Chaponnière.

Chaponnière's penetrating study has much to say on Voltaire's relations with the Genevan pastorate. See also André Delattre, "Voltaire and the Ministers of Geneva," *Church History*, XIII (December 1944), 243-254, which sees Voltaire as pro-Protestant; and H. Tronchin, *Le conseiller François Tronchin et ses amis, Voltaire, Diderot, Grimm* (1895).

There is a remarkable shortage of good social history of Geneva. The constant civil conflicts were at least in part class conflicts, but it is almost impossible to find out from the literature what were Geneva's social structure and social development. It is thus not surprising that even a leading Voltaire expert like Norman Torrey confuses the various classes of citizens in his *Spirit of Voltaire*, 115-116. On these classes, the best observations are in Chaponnière, and in Caussy, "Voltaire, pacificateur de Genève." The recent collective *Histoire de Genève des origines à 1798*, ed. Alexandre Jullien (1951) is pedestrian but informed; Henri Fazy, *Les constitutions de la république de Genève* (1890) prints excerpts from the various edicts that served Geneva as a constitution; Georges Goyau, *Une ville-église, Genève* (1919), I, gives an account of the prolonged political controversies. Pierre Bertrand tells the important story of the influx of Huguenots after 1685 in *Genève et la révocation de l'édit de Nantes* (1935). Probably the most revealing political history of Geneva in the eighteenth century is the emotional, partisan account of a participant, Francis d'Ivernois, *An Historical and Political View of the Constitution and Revolutions of Geneva* (English tr. 1784), despite its passion (or perhaps because of it) an informative book. André-E. Sayous, "La haute bourgeoisie de Genève entre le début du XVIIe et le milieu du XIXe siècle," *Revue historique*, CLXXX (July-September 1937), 30-57; and Louis Dufour, "Industrie et état social de Genève au dix-huitième siècle d'après les minutes des notaires," *Mémoires et documents publiés par la société d'histoire et d'archéologie de Genève*, XX (1879-1888), 229-308, are very different, but they have this in common: both articles keep less than their titles promise. The first is a superficial survey, the second a pedestrian catalogue. Far more helpful is André Corbaz's biography of the leader of the 1707 troubles, *Pierre Fatio* (n.d.).

Whether Voltaire's arrest in Frankfurt was legal has been debated in several of the books I have cited in chapter III. Theodore Besterman, "Voltaire's arrest in international law," Appendix 67, *Voltaire's Correspondence*, XXII, 295, argues that it was illegal. His position seems to me amply sustained by the documents he prints in the volume.

The vexed question of Voltaire and the *canaille*, which I try to solve in the text, also has caused much debate. I found welcome support of my position in Pellissier, *Voltaire philosophe*; Rowe, *Voltaire and the State*; and in the careful analysis of an important Voltaire letter in Roustan, *Les philosophes et la société française*.

CHAPTER V
FERNEY: THE POISONOUS TREE

Voltaire, the man of *écrasez l'infâme*, has long occcupied the commentators. It is not necessary for me to print here a full survey of the various positions that have been argued—that has been done in René Pomeau, *La religion de Voltaire*. A few prominent representatives will be sufficient. The view that Voltaire was a good Catholic is closely associated with Alfred Noyes, *Voltaire* (1936), a witty plea in the guise of a biography. His gallant crusade, worthy of a less chimerical cause, got him in trouble with the Holy Office which, apparently, would rather condemn Voltaire than embrace him. (See Cabeen's *Critical Bibliography of French Literature*, IV, 190). Noyes quotes Saintsbury in support: "L'infâme is not God; it is not Christ; it is not Christianity; it is not even Catholicism. Its briefest equivalent may be given as 'persecuting and privileged orthodoxy'. . . ." This is not the only time that Saintsbury was wrong about Voltaire. Constance Rowe is in the same camp: "Voltaire had never wished to eradicate Catholicism or any religion. By l'infâme, the 'Infamous Thing,' he meant neither Christianity nor Catholicism, but the brutalizing power of superstition." *Voltaire and the State*, 67.

389

That Voltaire was anti-Catholic but really on the side of Protestant Christianity has not unnaturally been maintained in Protestant countries. See the biographies of John Morley; H. N. Brailsford; and S. G. Tallentyre. I am in full sympathy with the strictures on the indecisiveness of this group of interpreters leveled by Ben Ray Redman, "Editor's Introduction," *The Portable Voltaire* (1949), 24-27.

For Voltaire as atheist, see Mitford, *Voltaire in Love*, 110; and Daniel Mornet, *Origines intellectuelles de la révolution française*, 86: "Au fond de lui-même Voltaire, à l'ordinaire, est sans doute athée."

The position defended by most Voltaire scholars is that Voltaire was a deist, although the question can never be wholly closed. Norman Torrey's *Spirit of Voltaire* has an important chapter which suggests that Voltaire's deism was tinged by both humanism and mysticism. René Pomeau's exhaustive analysis, *La religion de Voltaire*, which has used all possible texts, is an excellent work, but its conclusions are not startling: Voltaire was indeed a deist. I read M. Pomeau's book after I had written my chapter on Voltaire's religion, but I was happy to be able to borrow some illustrations from it. It is a fine piece of scholarship. Ira O. Wade's careful edition of Voltaire's *Epitre à Uranie*, PMLA, XLVII (1932), 1066-1112, provocatively keeps the debate open.

There are some special studies that deserve mention: Norman Torrey, *Voltaire and the English Deists*, is an important survey of an important influence on Voltaire. See also A. R. Morehouse, *Voltaire and Jean Meslier* (1936). Eugène Ritter has shown that Voltaire's notorious *Sermon des cinquante*, published in 1762, had been written at Potsdam ten years earlier, "Le sermon des cinquante," *Revue d'histoire littéraire de la France*, VII (1900), 315.

For the development of anti-enthusiasm in England, see the excellent studies by R. F. Jones, "The Background of the Attack on Science in the Age of Pope," *Pope and His Con-*

temporaries, eds. James L. Clifford and Louis A. Landa (1949), 96-113; James L. Clifford, "Swift's *Mechanical Operation of the Spirit*," ibid., 135-146; Clarence M. Webster, "Swift and Some Earlier Satirists of Puritan Enthusiasm," PMLA, XXXXVIII (1933), 1141-1153; Ernst Cassirer, *The Platonic Renaissance in England* (English tr. 1953); and Louis I. Bredvold, *The Intellectual Milieu of John Dryden* (ed. 1956).

Two studies of seventeenth-century France have strongly influenced me: Paul Bénichou's remarkable survey of the social significance of Corneille, Pascal, Racine, and Molière, *Morales du grand siècle* (1948); and E. B. O. Borgerhoff, *The Freedom of French Classicism* (1950) which argues, as its title implies, that the great neoclassic playwrights and essayists were far from being stiff, formal, unemotional thinking-machines.

Arthur O. Lovejoy's essay, "The Parallel of Deism and Classicism," *Essays in the History of Ideas*, 78-98, is suggestive. One final point: Voltaire's Sinophilia is significant in his rejection of Christianity. See W. Engemann, *Voltaire und China* (1933); Virgile Pinot, *La Chine et la formation de l'esprit philosophique en France* (1932); and Arnold H. Rowbotham, "Voltaire Sinophile," PMLA, XLVII (December 1939), 1050-1065. An interesting counterpart of these studies is Durand Echeverria, *Mirage in the West, A History of the French Image of American Society to 1815* (1957), which can be read in conjunction with Gilbert Chinard, *L'Amérique et le rêve exotique dans la littérature au* XVIIe *et* XVIIIe *siècle* (1913); and H. N. Fairchild, *The Noble Savage* (1928).

CHAPTER VI
FERNEY: THE MAN OF CALAS

Marcello T. Maestro, *Voltaire and Beccaria as Reformers of Criminal Law* (1942) is a good monograph, pedestrian but reliable, that traces the growth of Voltaire's legal thinking from his early days to his reading of Beccaria and beyond; it has a full bibliography. Eduard Hertz, *Voltaire und die französische*

Strafrechtspflege im achtzehnten Jahrhundert (1887) is by no means dated: it treats in detail all the major legal cases that engaged Voltaire's attention and gives much accurate information about eighteenth-century legal practices in France.

There is an enormous literature on the Calas case. The most important books are by Athanase Coquerel fils, *Jean Calas et sa famille* (2d ed., 1867), passionately certain of Calas' innocence, still valuable for its painstaking review of the evidence. F. H. Maugham, *The Case of Jean Calas* (1928) makes a persuasive case for Calas' innocence, without rhetoric and with a lawyer's thoroughness. On the other side, the most respectable study is Leopold Labat, *Le drame de la rue des Filatiers (1761)* (1910), definitely worth the attention of the student who wants to make up his own mind, but not convincing to me. On the Sirven case, Camille Rabaud, *Sirven, étude historique sur l'avènement de la tolérance* (1891) and Elie Galland, *L'affaire Sirven* (n.d.), give the essential facts. On the La Barre case, see Marc Chassaigne, *Le procès du chevalier de La Barre* (1920).

Of the many histories of French legal procedure, the most authoritative is A. Esmein, *Histoire de la procédure criminelle en France* (1882), which has a long, informative section on the Criminal Ordinance of 1670. It may be supplemented by Albert Du Boys, *Histoire du droit criminel de la France depuis le xvie siècle jusqu'au xixe siècle*, 2 vols. (1874), which has comparative material on the law of Italy, Germany, and England.

Voltaire's aid to Huguenots remains somewhat mysterious, and will continue so until we find all the letters. Information can be pieced together from Charles Dardier, "Voltaire agissant en faveur des protestants en 1754," *Bulletin de la société de l'histoire de protestantisme française*, XXXII (1883), 528-529; Edouard Champendal, *Voltaire et les protestants de France* (1919); Joseph Dedieu, *Histoire politique des protestants français*, 2 vols. (1925); and Edmond Hugues, *Histoire de la restauration du protestantisme en France au xviiie siècle*, 2 vols. (1872).

There is much room for a study of the growth of humanitarianism in the seventeenth and eighteenth centuries from a sociological and psychological point of view. Georg Rusche and Otto Kirchheimer, *Punishment and Social Structure* (1939) is a pioneering and suggestive analysis, but because of its Marxism a little mechanical and not enough interested in psychological questions. Finally, the famous case of Elizabeth Canning, which Voltaire used with such effect, is described with verve in the fascinating account by Lillian de la Torre, *Elizabeth is Missing* (1945), exciting on the case, but somewhat mistaken on Voltaire's reporting of it.

Incidentally, the reader who feels that this chapter relies too heavily on the testimony of the critics of French procedure should peruse Robert Anchel, *Crimes et châtiments au* xviiie *siècle* (2d ed., 1933), a sobering survey.

CHAPTER VII
FRANCE: CONSTITUTIONAL ABSOLUTISM

Desnoiresterres fully describes Voltaire's last years in *Retour et mort de Voltaire*. The political controversies of the 1760's and 1770's continue earlier controversies, and the books by Cobban, Lefebvre, Mathiez, Carré, Gaxotte, listed in chapter ii, also apply here. Add Bernard de Lascombes, *La résistance janseniste et parlementaire au temps de Louis* XV (1948). Jules Flammermont, *Le chancelier Maupeou et les parlements* (1895) is a masterly treatment of the resurgence of the "sovereign companies" after 1750; its only flaw—and a serious one—is its strong partisanship in behalf of the magistrates. J. de Maupeou, *Le chancelier Maupeou* (1942) is a brief monograph. Diderot's ideas on the controversial chancellor are collected in Maurice Tourneux, ed., *Diderot et Catherine II* (1899). The remonstrances of the most powerful parlement and some of the royal replies have been edited by Jules Flammermont and Maurice Tourneux, *Remontrances du parlement de Paris au* xviiie *siècle*, 3 vols. (1895). Elinor G. Barber, *The Bourgeoisie in*

18th Century France (1955) is an interesting sociological study of middle-class values and aspirations; it incidentally throws much light on Voltaire's radicalism by stressing the conservatism of French bourgeois. C.-E. Labrousse's important and controversial thesis of a decline in the French economy under Louis XVI can be found in his *Crise de l'économie française à la fin de l'ancien régime et au début de la Révolution* (1943). See Georges Lefebvre's searching review of this book in *Revue historique*, cxciv (1944), 168-172.

The leading economic theorists of the period were, of course, the physiocrats, whom Voltaire cruelly lampooned in *L'homme aux quarante écus*. The volumes by G. Weulersse are standard, *Le mouvement physiocratique en France de 1756 à 1770*, 2 vols. (1910), summarized in *Les physiocrates* (1931); and *La physiocratie sous les ministères de Turgot et de Necker, 1774-1781* (1950). Turgot, who was only half a physiocrat, has been fortunate in the hands of Douglas Dakin. His *Turgot and the ancien régime in France* (1939) is far more than an informative biography; it is an illuminating survey of French politics after mid-century, on which I have relied heavily. It supersedes the earlier studies listed in his bibliography.

Voltaire's economic views could use further exploration. Roger Charbonnaud, *Les idées économiques de Voltaire* (1907) is a competent survey; Marguerite Goubard, *Voltaire et l'impôt* (1931), equally competent, confines itself to Voltaire's attitude toward taxation. But an imaginative analysis, relating Voltaire's economic opinions to his social philosophy, is still needed. My remarks in the text are no more than a sketch. In this connection, A. Morize, *L'apologie du luxe au xviiie siècle, "Le Mondain" et ses sources* (1909) helps to put into perspective Voltaire's playful ideas concerning luxury as expressed in his lively poem *Le mondain* and elsewhere. It may be supplemented with Maurice Gaffiot, "La théorie du luxe dans l'oeuvre de Voltaire," *Revue d'histoire économique et sociale*, xiv (1926), 320-343.

The struggles between king and parlements were, of course, struggles for power, but they were expressed in legal and constitutional language. André Lemaire, *Les lois fondamentales de la monarchie française d'après les théoriciens de l'ancien régime* (1907) traces the conception of the unwritten French constitution through the centuries; it is far more original than Léon Ameline, *L'idée de la souveraineté d'après les écrivains français du xviiie siècle* (1904), which handles the texts with little imagination. Robert Bickart, *Les parlements et la notion de souveraineté nationale au xviiie siècle* (1932) helpfully summarizes the parlementary position. Göhring, *Weg und Sieg der modernen Staatsidee in Frankreich*, already cited, can also be consulted with profit.

For Voltaire on natural law, see the Prologue. As for Voltaire's anti-Semitism, consult Georg Brandes' biography, the only one to deal with the subject. See also Hanna Emmrich, *Das Judentum bei Voltaire* (1930), a relentlessly detailed study especially useful on Voltaire's attitude toward the Biblical Jews. Voltaire's complicated and unpleasant suit against Hirschel can be followed in Besterman's edition of the *Correspondence*, Vols. xviii and xix, and in Wilhelm Mangold, *Voltaires Rechtsstreit mit dem königlichen Schutzjuden Hirschel, 1751* (1905). See also Besterman's brief appendix No. 56, "Voltaire and Abraham Hirschel," in *Correspondence*, xviii, 263. Voltaire's relations with English Jews are briefly discussed in Pomeau, *La religion de Voltaire*, 130. It will be evident to the reader that I do not accept R. R. Palmer's interpretation of Voltaire's general intolerance, offered in *Catholics and Unbelievers in 18th Century France*, 7.

INDEX

Voltaire's ideas and activities are entered in section A of this index under "Voltaire" as well as under scattered entries; e.g., Voltaire's admiration of the English constitution may be found under "England, *Voltaire.*" His writings, whether quoted, cited, or mentioned, are entered alphabetically in section B; his letters are entered in section C by correspondent. Letters to Voltaire follow the word *"from."*

A. GENERAL

397

INDEX

Barber, Elinor, 265
Barbier, 71, 102, 122n, 123, 127n, 131, 132, 132n, 133, 291
Bargeton, *Lettres (Ne repugnate bono vestro)*, 132, 134, 134n, 138n
Barnave, 312n
Barraud, 228
Bastille, 77, 78n, 146; Voltaire in, 36, 38, 78
Bavaria, 168n
Bayle, 257, 260, 263, 286, 303; Voltaire and, 24, 146, 353
Beaudrigue, 274-75, 284. See also Calas case
Beaumont, archbishop, 139
Beauteville, 229
Beccaria, 177n, 286, 287, 292; *Trattato dei delitti e della pene*, 287; Voltaire and, 287, 292
Bellessort, 335
Benedict XIV, 117
Bengesco, 347, 348
Bentham, 286
Berger, on Voltaire's *Lettres philosophiques*, 5n
Berlin, 151n; Voltaire on, 149, 153. See also Frederick the Great
Berne, 194, 219
Bernis, cardinal de, *Mémoires*, 243
Berryer, 129n
Berkeley, Voltaire meets, 41
Beuchot, 142n, 239n, 347, 348
Bible, *Chronicles*, 247; *Kings*, 247; *Proverbs*, 353; *Song of Songs*, 353-54
la Bigarrure, 142
billets de confession, see France, parlement of Paris
blasphemy, 286, 291. See also Voltaire, *ideas*
Bodin, 315; *Six livres de la république*, 92
Bolingbroke, Lord, 41, 59n, 80n Voltaire: friend of, 10, 40; follows historical maxim of, 182; speaks in name of, 270
Bonnet, 229
Bossuet, bishop, 93, 318, 353
Boswell, visits Voltaire, 47, 258,

270; Théodore Tronchin talks about Voltaire to, 203n
Boulainvilliers, comte de, 50, 93, 94, 106, 313-14; Voltaire criticizes, 103, 105, 105n
Boulanger, 80n
Boyle, 51n; Voltaire on, 26
Breteuil, 174
Brittany, parlement of, 312-13, 319-20. See also d'Aiguillon, France
Browne, *Pseudodoxia Epidemica*, 256
Burckhardt, 8
Burgundy, duc de, 70
Burke, 27
Burlamaqui, 195
Burton, 256, 257, 260; *Anatomy of Melancholy*, 23, 255, 255n
Butler, Voltaire reads *Hudibras* of, 256
Byng, admiral, 296
Byron, 322; *Childe Harold's Pilgrimage*, 6

Calas case, 84n, 210, 278, 282, 287, 297, 298, 299n, 306, 308, 315n; Catherine the Great interested in, 175; *canaille* in, 274, 284; dramatizes failings of French code, 274, 274n, 275, 275n, 276, 284, 296; conviction overturned in, 281, 284
  Voltaire: obsessed by, 175; active in, 204, 244, 244n, 262, 273, 281; educated by, 275-76, 284; meddles in, 276-77; as "Man of Calas," 281, 307, 339. See also Voltaire, *ideas*; *Traité sur la tolérance*
Calas, Jean, 275, 289, 301, 303, 304, 307, 315. See also Calas case
Calvin, 190, 191, 196, 252. See also Geneva
canaille, see Calas case; Voltaire, *ideas*
Canning case, 299-301, 306. See also *Histoire d'Elizabeth Canning*
capitation tax, 55, 55n
Carlyle, 181; on Voltaire, 5-6
Carré, 249

398

Nicole, 130
Nietzsche, 30, 138, 251, 283n; defends Enlightenment, 12; admires Voltaire, 353
Nobility of the robe, see France
Nobility of the sword, see France
Nouvelles ecclésiastiques, 137n
Numa, 167

Oldfield, mlle, 43, 63

Palatinate, 49, 113
Palissot, Les philosophes, 78n
Palmer, R. R., 55n, 254
Pan, Mallet du, 262-63
parlement of Burgundy, 339. See also Lally case
parlement of Paris, 67, 73, 74, 74n, 94, 95, 104, 126; François Arouet in, 36; and clergy, 139, 310-11; condemns books, 199, 205, 234; cruelty in law cases, 279, 280n, 291, 307; and Louis XV, 312n, 313, 321, 322, 322-23n; ideology of, 314n, 320n; tries duc d'Aiguillon, 320; supplanted, 325-26, 328 Voltaire: on, 111, 111n, 315-16, 317-19. See also France, La Barre case, Louis XV, Maupeou, Voltaire
parlement of Rouen, 314n
parlement of Toulouse, see Calas case, Sirven case
parlements, 73, 74, 98, 126, 131, 140; described, 94-95; ban books, 76; under Louis XIV, 90-91, 328; under Regency, 96; against Jesuits, 311n; enemies of reform, 312, 338; under Louis XV, 312n, 313-16; and thèse nobiliaire, 313; ideology, 313-14; against Maupeou, 314n, 316; popularity, 315, 323, 325; strength, 316; Jansenism, 318; Diderot on, 323n; Tocqueville praises, 325; against Turgot, 332; exploit hunger, 338-39
Voltaire: against, 111, 140, 309-10, 312-13, 315-16, 318-19, 326-28, 330-31. See also France, parlement of Paris, Voltaire

Pascal, 130, 131; Voltaire on, 22, 66, 249-50; Lettres provinciales, 310
Paul, prince of Russia, 172
Pellissier, 327n
Penn, William, 61n
permission tacite, 75, 76
Peter the Great, 173, 174, 182, 182n; Voltaire and, 101, 181, 182
Peter III, czar, 172-74, 182; Voltaire on murder of, 175-76, 176n
Philip the Fair, 319
philosophes, 75, 311n; called Utopians, 7-8; as historians, 11; oppose esprit de système, 28; criticize Newton, 29; political ideas of, 30, 32n, 136, 244n, 323n, 335; powerful after 1750, 34, 138, 310; denounced as conspirators, 76; harassed by government, 79, 83; Voltaire on, 81, 270; touchy and humorless, 83, 167; secularists, 88, 137, 254, 254n; philosophers of action, 89; and enlightened rulers, 164, 167; need for audience, 168; generally undoctrinaire, 168; and Catherine the Great, 171-72, 184; on legislator, 180-81; on defensive after 1757, 207; on canaille, 223; unable to compromise, 254; on respect for law, 293; Maupeou against, 316-17. See also Enlightenment, France, Voltaire
physiocrats, 168-69; Voltaire ridicules, 234
Pictet, colonel Charles, 200, 214n; and Voltaire, 200n
Pictet, François-Pierre, 174-75
Pinto, 352, 353
Pitt, Andrew, Voltaire argues with, 41
Plato, 167, 259; Voltaire on, 28, 29
Poland, 168n, 178, 179; Voltaire on, 101, 218n
politiques, see France
Pöllnitz, baron, 160n
Pomeau, René, 37n, 244n, 269-70n
Pompadour, madame de, 74, 75, 79-80, 117, 122, 136, 138, 321; Voltaire and, 75, 119
Pompignan, 254

B. VOLTAIRE'S WRITINGS

C. VOLTAIRE'S LETTERS

DATE DUE

MAY 12 2001			

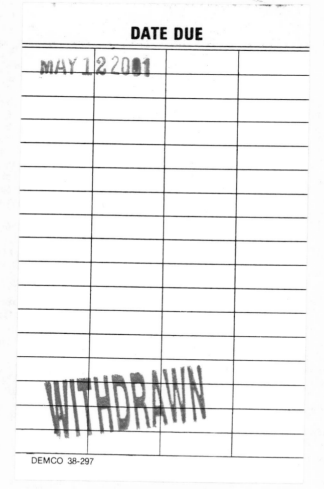